Poetics of the Hive

T0346053

Poetics of the Hive

The Insect Metaphor in Literature

CRISTOPHER HOLLINGSWORTH

UNIVERSITY OF IOWA PRESS ⑂ Iowa City

University of Iowa Press, Iowa City 52242

Printed in the United States of America

Design by Richard Hendel

http://www.uiowa.edu/~uipress

The publication of this book was generously
supported by the University of Iowa Foundation and the
David L. Kalstone Memorial Fund of the English
Department of Rutgers University.

Printed on acid-free paper

Library of Congress
Cataloging-in-Publication Data
Hollingsworth, Cristopher, 1961–
Poetics of the hive: the insect metaphor in literature / by
Cristopher Hollingsworth.
p.   cm.
Includes bibliographical references and index.
ISBN 0-87745-786-7 (cloth)
1. Insects in literature.   2. Insects—Symbolic
aspects.   3. Bees in literature.   I. Title.
PN56.163 H65   2001
809′.9336257—dc21
                                    2001034730

01 02 03 04 05 C 5 4 3 2 1

For my mother, Sonya V. Hollingsworth

CONTENTS

PREFACE

It is an ancient observation, ancient already at the time of Aesop (who must have known a lot about animals), that all extremes are found in animals. There are enormous and tiny animals, extremely strong and extremely weak, bold and skittish, fast and slow, cunning and foolish, splendid and horrendous: the writer has only to choose, he does not have to take into account the truths of the scientist, it is enough for him to scoop up with both hands examples from this universe of metaphors. Precisely by coming out of the human island he will find every human quality multiplied a hundredfold, a vast thicket of prefabricated hyperbole.

    Primo Levi, *"Novels Dictated by Crickets"*

To be preoccupied with the building blocks is not to be indifferent to the architecture; indeed, the architecture is often the expanded expression of the constituent blocks; they determine the ultimate shape, which grows like a crystal, like a cool reef, like Emerson's "Limestone of the Continent."

    Justice George Lawler, Celestial Pantomime

A quotation is not an excerpt . . . [it] is a cicada. It is part of its nature never to quiet down.

    Osip Mandelstam, "Talking about Dante"

This book investigates one member of the universe of animal metaphors, a building block of the imagination that for the sake of convenience I will call the Hive.

Although I will often be concerned with the description of a city as a beehive, I mean the word "Hive" more abstractly, to signify a mental structure that informs any representation that, implicitly or explicitly, defines the individual and the social order in relation to each other. For example, one common version of the Hive frequently appears when a character is positioned above and surveys a crowd or a city. Usually the feelings and concepts that arise from this view-from-above are expressed through an insect metaphor, which gives substance and focus to the intuition that the observed collective is a social organism and is therefore distinct from the individual. For example, Honoré de Balzac closes *Père Goriot* with Rastignac surveying Paris from a hill and seeing it as a *ruche bourdonnante*, a buzzing or murmuring beehive.[1] Paris is Rastignac's antithesis, his enemy, a collective organism from which he, the heroic individual, will seize the social honey of success.

But while the Hive is strongly associated with insect metaphors, since it is a mental structure, a habit of seeing and thinking, we should not confuse it with any particular language of description, image, or metaphor. In the 1928 film *The Crowd*, for example, director King Vidor uses a crane shot to give us a view-from-above of a precisely organized and busy office. Because we see these people from above and at a distance, they are difficult to individualize and are unified by what from our position appears to be their common industry. Through the power of the Hive's visual structure, Vidor makes a symbol of this office: it represents modernity as an insect-like condition that diminishes and hence threatens the individual. In order to accomplish his intentions, Vidor does not need to explicitly figure these clerks as insects. He lets the shot — and through it the Hive that we possess in common — do the work.

Nor is the Hive useful only for making pictures of collectives. Its structure commonly informs representations of the alienated individual. A familiar example is Franz Kafka's Gregor Samsa. Here the physical distance implied by the Hive's requisite view-from-above is partially translated into cultural and emotional terms. Because Kafka wants us to precisely gauge the tension between the social order and the individual and — more importantly — to witness this tension's human consequences, rather than surveying the collective from a distance, we are, so to speak, positioned within it.

The Hive, then, subtends a variety of representational situations and metaphors — and it may do so because it is rooted in a particular, everyday, visual experience, one that helps to structure our thoughts and feelings. The distinct sights of a busy street viewed from above, a line of ants crossing a sidewalk or raising a hill between its slabs, a moth frantically bouncing against a window screen, a cockroach struggling to scale bathtub walls — all are similarly informed by the reasoning that accompanies a specific instance of seeing. The physicist Arthur Zajonc has this to say about the relationship between cognition and seeing, which is crucial to our understanding of the Hive: "Vison requires far more than a functioning physical organ. Without an inner light, without formative visual imagination, we are blind."[2] I argue that the Hive is a creature of Zajonc's "inner light." More precisely, I contend that the Hive is an imitation of a particular visual experience, one whose spatial grammar and dramatic potential have been structurally coded and constellated into the "visual imagination." The Hive is more than a poetic convention — it is an experience in its own right that mediates between the imagination and the phenomenal world and thus shapes both how we think and how we see. If we think of the Hive as a "visual machine" that similarly informs actual and imaginative vision and recognize the insect as its most appropriate object, then careful attention to how we see insects in real life will shed light on how artists, ancient and modern, use a variety of entomological figures and what they mean by them.

In literature the Hive usually appears as a special instance of metaphor: a poetic picture. It is therefore appropriate that while we trace the Hive's literary evolution we also explore the eye's use of artistic images, for part of our visual response to the insect is to clothe it from our collective storehouse of images. Upon these small beings and their mysterious life, we project the fashions of the past; the difference between us and the insects elicits antique principles and inherited feelings, which we then easily confuse with ourselves and our social circumstances. Writing in the first half of the eighteenth century, Giambattista Vico warns us about this danger of metaphor: "when [man] does not understand he makes things out of himself and becomes them by transforming himself into them."[3]

Perception is both fashion and fashioning. Proper to but never content with the surface of things, the eye is charmed most by the hidden prospect. Clinging to the back of its orb, sealed from and yet continually bathed in the outer world's luminescence, lies the retina. And because the retina lives by light, in contrast to the moth it tends toward shadow, especially that cast by old things. If we extrapolate from Vico — and through the prism of his thought let pass Zajonc's metaphor of inner and outer light — we may say that our eyes recognize and read by two sorts of illumination: the lamp of understanding and the moon of story. It is by the second that we prefer to know the Hive.

The heavens illustrate the proposition that what we have received from our elders (one sort of habit) is vital to seeing. With the exception of the Milky Way, no more than glowing congestion, the night sky lacks obvious pattern. Over time and with patience we may indeed discern a celestial regularity, such as the cycling of the fixed stars, but this order of knowledge is irrelevant to that night sky that for us brims with shapes and names. Significantly, these must be studied into existence. Once we see a picture in the stars, learn its name and story, we are unlikely to conceive, much less seek out, an alternative. And certainly once it is discerned, we cannot remove such a shape from our minds.

Like the stars, the insect — the insect society in particular — invites a name and a story. Unlike the stars, however, a beehive or anthill confronts us with obvious, even excessive, order. The insect society is a miniature world whose motives are written in the hieroglyphs of an alien biology. To the eye it is a walled orchard, an island lit by moonlight. Although the life and behavior of a bee has strikingly little in common with human existence, and a beehive is similarly distinct from a human city, since Homer Western poets, philosophers, and scientists have been subject to what Jules Michelet describes as a "force" that "compels" one to "descend below the earth, and embark . . . on the great sea of metamorphosis. A world of mysteries and gloom."[4] This subterranean sea, this dark world, belongs to the insects. Once there, the human observer tends to ardently court resemblances. He returns to our human island bearing marvelous analogies, fabulous tales. In these stories, we overhear the voices of the dead — among them Homer, Aesop, Aristotle, Pliny, Virgil. Far more troubling than the stars, the insect society is a locus of what Levi might call "prefabricated hyperbole."

Like no other object in nature that can be translated into a portable verbal image, the insect society enables a picture of ourselves as a jewel of feeling distinct from and yet embedded in hierarchy. For over two thousand years such images have accumulated in dialogue with each other and under the eye's sovereignty. Once disseminated the past's most sublime expressions are to the imagination mere vernacular loam. The new almost always turns out to be the fruition of or response to an earlier design. One example that we will spend much time with is Milton's reversal of the old model of the divine beehive. From Virgil until Shakespeare, a summer of seventeen centuries, bees expressed the sacred Order. And if one needed a negative image of cooperation, then like Virgil one looked to the ants. In the fourth book of the *Aeneid*, he uses them to describe the Trojans' rapacious provisioning as they are preparing to leave Carthage.

Although where and how an insect actually lives has always informed its artistic uses, the weight of imaginative habit is such that we tend to see the bee, the ant, and their kin through the lens of the past — but this past, and hence our seeing, is by no means simple. Like the ancients, our core response to the insect is metaphorical, to see and hence to represent these as living emblems of the human social order and our place within it. However, notions of society and its contents are ideologically charged abstractions, things of the mind that lend themselves to division and reversal. Nor is the idea of Nature stable. Owing to cultural changes that have been noted and debated by generations of scholars — shifts in thought and feeling that Michel Foucault has recently described as "immense reorganization[s]" of knowledge[5] — the West has several times altered its picture of Nature, events that always involve the modification of both natural symbols and humanity's definition of itself. The combination of the Hive's rhetorical instability, its shifting context, and the preservation of its meanings through art, means that our sense of the insect is complex, both old and new, the product of change within a continuity.

My argument therefore meshes traditional and contemporary methods of understanding the past and its contribution to how we think, feel, and see. I find indispensable Foucault's thesis that knowledge systems and their special languages, and hence the ground(s) of Being, have changed and shall continue to do so. Indeed, only profound shifts in worldview can account for the vigorous extremity of some of the Hive's reformulations. For example, Milton's Pandemonium, a creation of the late Renaissance, is the antithesis of medieval Dante's Celestial Rose. Dante — a Catholic who saw creation as complete and perfect and the beehive as an ideal for human society — embraced, elaborated, and placed in Heaven the picture of righteous souls as bees that appears in book 6 of Virgil's *Aeneid*. In contrast, Puritan Milton knew this world to be Satan's and thought the bee's lack of free will made the beehive a poor model for human government. Milton's bees are fallen angels, and he warns us against confusing ourselves with insects.

The cultural differences between Dante and Milton do not mean, however, that the latter found his model's bees unintelligible. Nor do these differences determine that Milton's dark formulation extinguishes the light of Dante's swarm. To the contrary, Dante's heavenly bees and Milton's infernal swarm issue from and are aspects of the same mental structure. During the reign of the golden, classical Hive that Dante brought to fruition, the demonic Hive, powerful but potential, slumbered beside its luminescent brother. Its presence was felt but not fully explored and articulated until the emergence of a new theory of creation and a more modern — which is to say, a protoexistentialist — definition of humankind. Furthermore, because he was working within the epic genre, Milton approached his predecessors' versions of the Hive according to ancient rules of reworking, principles that oblige a poet to honor his models even while prosecuting their conquest. For these and other reasons that I will explain in more detail in the body of this argument, Milton's infernal swarm confirms its predecessor, joins with it to form a larger whole that is close to how we know the Hive today: a bipolar fixture of the mind, whose opposite but complementary potentials I call the angelic and the demonic.

Because the Hive has evolved through a process of complication that to an extent depends upon specific acts by individuals, the Hive and forms like it cannot be adequately explained by any theory of cultural change that emphasizes discontinuity at the expense of continuity and categorically denies individual Being and, hence, agency. And since I have matured during an intellectual moment in which literary studies is dominated by such theories, part of the writing of this book has been a search for and the selection of more useful theoretical tools. Hence, this book has been a personal education in literature and history and a testing ground for method. After much reflection I have reached the following conclusions about the current obligation to see history as necessarily and radically discontinuous. First, this obligation is itself badly in need of historicization. Second, this obligation carries with it assumptions that often obscure more than they illuminate.

It is on similar grounds that I cannot accept the current denial that the individual exists and has a role in shaping his or her mind and local aspect of the world. I recognize that ideology and other social codes profoundly influence our minds and actions. However, a person is much more complicated — and certainly more active — than the "subject" who is "constructed" through a confluence of historical factors, ideologies, and knowledge systems. That each of us is a person, that we are unique and possessed of an independent and active consciousness, and that we act within and upon a world that is both of and distinct from us, are but a few of the foundational intuitions that are ours long before we have the language to express their presence and to systematically explore their functions and implications. I am convinced that, in order to understand how the Hive works and why it has endured and evolved over the centuries, we must intelligently make the individual part of our inquiry's circle. We shall, therefore, have need of the science of individual Being, phenomenology, for which Foucault reserves a special attack. According to him, phenomenology is wrong because it "gives *absolute* priority to the observing subject, which attributes a constituent role to an act, which places its own point of view at the origin of *all* historicity — which, in short, leads to a transcendental consciousness" (xiv). In this passage I have emphasized "absolute" and "all," words that Foucault has chosen in order to picture his opponent unflatteringly. While Gaston Bachelard — who I would have represent my approach to phenomenology — indeed gives "priority" to the observing subject, his subject's observations are frequently provisional and always in dialogue with the phenomenal world, much of which is presented as a cultural product. The observing subject of Maurice Merleau-Ponty, another phenomenologist from whom I have learned much, is even more responsive to cultural factors. As you will see, a particular kind of phenomenology is proper to the study of rhetorical forms like the Hive, and therefore should play a key role in what Foucault calls the historical analysis of discourse.

Foucault titles his project an "archaeology of knowledge," a metaphor that informs his view of the cultural "soil" as "silent and apparently immobile" (xxiv). This soil is important to me also, but the Hive is neither buried nor a fossil. The Hive is a viable and still evolving artistic form and feature of the literate mind. I have, therefore, profited from Ernst Robert Curtius's *European Literature and the Latin Middle Ages* (hereafter *ELLMA*), which its author calls a demonstration of "literary biology" (83). Rather than pursue "archaeology," I will practice "evolutionary biology" — a metaphor whose naturalizing implications are appropriate for this investigation, because, as I shall argue and illustrate, the Hive's essential structure and function, as well as its basic evolutionary logic, are natural for our species. Here is how Max Delbrück, as quoted by Ernst Mayr, describes the problem of biology for the material positivist, in this instance, a "mature physicist": he "is puzzled by the circumstances that there are no 'absolute phenomena' in biology. Everything is time-bound and space-bound. The animal or plant or micro-organism he is working with is but a link in an evolutionary chain of changing forms, none of which has permanent validity." Clarifying and extending Del-brück, Mayr writes: "There is hardly any structure or function in any organism that can be fully understood unless it is studied against this historical background. To find the causes for the existing characteristics, and particular adaptations, of organisms is the main preoccupation of the evolutionary biologist. He wants to know the reasons for this diversity as well as the pathways by which it has been achieved. He studies the forces that bring about changes in faunas and floras (as in part documented by paleontology), and he studies the steps by which the miraculous adaptations so characteristic of every aspect of the organic world have evolved."[6]

What Delbrück's physicist notices about the natural world, we may accept of the artistic realm: "everything is time-bound and space-bound." Each version of the Hive that we will be "working with is but a link in an evolutionary chain of changing forms, none of which has permanent validity." And since, as Mayr has it, "there is hardly any structure or function in any organism [i.e., artistic form] that can be fully understood unless it is studied against this historical background," we shall keep at the ready the history of culture and ideas. Similar to Mayr's biologist of the natural world, it is my "main preoccupation . . . to find the causes for the existing characteristics [of the Hive], and [to explicate how it has been] adapt[ed]." I will document the Hive's diversity and provide "reasons for this diversity as well as the pathways by which it has been achieved." As part of this investigation of diversity through adaptation, by using rhetorical theory obtained from Aristotle, Cicero, Quintilian, Kenneth Burke, and other thinkers and artists who are interested in the formal basis of invention, I will illuminate the practices "that bring about changes in [rhetorical] faunas and floras." And I have structured this book chronologically, according to "the steps by which the miraculous adaptations so characteristic of every aspect of the . . . [rhetorical] world have evolved." The task seems daunting but is made easier because written texts preserve both original formulations and their adaptations, versions of a phenomenologically stable template that we may compare with one another and with the structure of our actual experience.

Almost every text I open and many of the films I see contain interesting and sometimes significant uses of the Hive. I sense that I have touched but am not yet able to clearly view a region of the imagination whose contents are property common to us all and that link our psychology with our forebears'. This means that the Hive and forms like it follow rules of transmission and expression that may be unfamiliar to some and troubling to others, especially those more historically exacting readers. Even though literary invention has always emerged from imitation (the artistic equivalent of organic adaptation through mutation), once a certain metaphor and its implications become widely disseminated and thus part of a civilization's way of thinking, we need not and indeed *cannot* account for its influence entirely through what we traditionally think of as direct allusion. For instance, Shakespeare need not have known Dante's *Paradiso* when he was crafting the bee simile that appears in the first act of *Henry V*. Indeed, we have no historical evidence of Dante's influence; the obvious source for these bees is Virgil. Yet the simile's context of music and a hierarchy that converges into unity suggests Dante's picture of heaven. Another example: Much of Aristotle was unavailable to Augustine, but in him there is much of Aristotle — and some improvement of Aristotle. I am arguing that a particular system of ideas or an artistic structure can have nearly as powerful an influence at a remove as through direct contact. There is nothing occult about either the psychological import of mental forms or their sometimes anonymous modes of transmission. Consider an idea that you once prized because original but whose essence (and sometimes full execution) turned out to belong to another. Consider the synonymy of styles and works across a range of mediums and cultures that unify what we call cubism. Does a painter have to study a Picasso in order to intuit from a derivative painting — or even a parody — some essence of the original's intentions, possibilities, and techniques — and through this essence some echo of Picasso's mind? In these pages, whenever possible, I note and argue from allusions that have been established through scholarship. However, because I also seek to recover less obvious but nonetheless powerful influences, I choose to highlight the mark of original patterns. If I sense, for instance, that a writer is contending with Dante's paradigm, even in the absence of definitive evidence of influence I will speak of Dante. I will be as clear as I am able so that the reader may decide what is gained by this approach.

Within a specific genre such as the epic, one writer consciously studies and seeks to best, and thereby to honor, another. Under these conditions, visible reworking is required. We are able to trace influence with confidence. Such is generally the case with the Hive until the nineteenth century. However, owing to the rise of modern print culture, the number and variety of texts explode. Rhetorical relations become increasingly complicated, threatening a new confusion of tongues, which is to a degree exacerbated by new codes of realism: physical, psychological, and stylistic. As literature becomes more democratic and classical learning based on imitation declines, especially in the twentieth century it is no longer customary for a writer to confess — obviously — an image's pedigree. As Harold Bloom points out in *The Anxiety of Influence*, under such conditions open allusion is repressed. We must therefore be prepared to think of influence as an effect of precedent, as a system of potentials that exist in the shared imagination. Of course writers are palpably aware of these potentials, but they are not always nor equally conscious of all that an evocation of an ancient metaphor brings to their art. It shall be part of my task to study these linked roots of invention. Hence I may at times be seen to range widely and to speculate — but always on the trail of a useful paradigm.

When conceived as a mental shape borne of experience, the Hive transcends time and cultural boundaries. A visual tableau, it gets translated as such. Its sense, or substance — which Martin Heidegger might call "the language of the matter itself"[7] — is not easily blunted by its movement from one language to another. Most times translation means new beauty, invites a new way of seeing. Further, because the Hive's sense derives from how we actually see, it is not bound to any particular sort of discourse or representational art. Again, I claim the liberty to explore connections across boundaries. However (recalling our earlier image of ants crossing a sidewalk), it should be said that, because it imitates the experience of looking down upon an insect or an insect community, the Hive is most clearly delineated in representations where we are observing persons and objects from without. The Hive favors the grand prospect; it flourishes in the epic, the romance, and the realist novel. It holds up well, too, in drama and philosophy. Even in narratives that subdue metaphor so that a particular internal life may be better heard, we find it camouflaged, reduced in size, functioning as a sign or emblem. Interestingly, despite the lyric's supposed opposition to the epic, the Hive is significant to a number of important lyricists, such as Dickinson and Plath. And then there is the moving image, a fascinating ground for investigation that because of the limits of space I cannot explore in these pages. With the exception of a few brief references to films and television shows that appear in the body of this argument, the shot from Vidor's *The Crowd* that I have discussed above will have to represent cinema's phenomenological riches. I would also have it suggest that, at the level of visual metaphor, what applies to literature illuminates film.

The following seven exploratory principles together anticipate what the subsequent pages will unpack, illustrate, test, and refine:

1. The aesthetic presence of the past subtends newer forms and, therefore, frequently appears as part of a hybrid. Even so, the older form is no less generative in its hybridized rather than pure form.

2. If they are coherent and resonant with experience, imaginative structures may be successfully transmitted through either direct or indirect contact. In some instances a transmitting model need not be either entirely explicit or complete for its essence to be grasped and then clarified, completed, and elaborated.

3. Though in itself the insect does not signify, its image is to us a powerful symbol that resonates with and associates personal experience and structurally or affectively similar artistic formulations and their containing narratives.

4. The Hive tends to appear in a context that is concerned with the individual's relationship with the collective and is usually expressed through the insect metaphor. Hence, the insect metaphor is often used to make power relations visible and to establish or refine an ethical principle.

5. The insect metaphor is almost always a vehicle for analogy — hence, its operation combines picturing and reasoning (i.e., it stimulates and coordinates the imaginative and the rational — the visual and the dialectical — faculties).

6. Because the Hive is an imitation — a re-presentation — of a motivated act of seeing in a context, the Hive's structure replicates the act of seeing and its situation as a unit that is inherently dramatic. It follows, then, that the Hive's attendant metaphors and their analogies imply and therefore may evoke the original dramatic unit. This means that any instance of either the insect metaphor or analogy should be studied as part of its generating scene: a unit that includes but is not limited to the observer, the act, the

motive, and the intentions of figuration or analogizing, and the process of observation.

7. Since the Hive imitates and represents a contextually embedded and motivated visual act, we should think of this structure's representation as a tableau: a design that gives form and expressive power to spatial relationships, proximity, relative size, and other elements of actual experience. Accordingly, this tableau overlaps and is energized by, on the one hand, the biology of seeing and, on the other, by the sometimes conflicting meshing of artistic precedent and old psychologies with new forms and psychologies. And because the Hive is constituted by the intersection of the body and the symbol, it must be dealt with as a habit of the imagination that is at once universal and eternal, culturally specific and mutable.

Here is an overview of this book's organization and topics: The introduction explains how the Hive works and lays down the argument's foundation in cognitive, phenomenological, and rhetorical theory. Since I am arguing that the Hive — and hence the way that we see the insect, understand its metaphors, and use them to picture the individual in relation to society — evolves and grows more complicated over time, the book's primary organization is chronological.

Accordingly, in addition to extending and complicating the introduction's theoretical aspects, chapter 1 considers the Hive's origin in Homer and its clarification by Virgil. I show how Virgil reworks the wild bees of the *Iliad*, book 2, through a series of engagements that are informed by the *Georgics*'s theme of domestication.

Chapter 2's subject is Dante's Christianization of Virgil's bees, their purification and elevation to the *Commedia*'s Paradise, and their inversion by Milton. This chapter prepares the ground for a discussion of the West's shift from the collective metaphorics of the Christian synthesis to the individually focused modern system that is developed in chapter 3.

In the third chapter, I examine the role of the fable in Bernard Mandeville's *Fable of the Bees* and Jonathan Swift's *Battle of the Books*. I argue that Swift, in particular, prepares the ground for the insect metaphor's later use as a vehicle for the existentialist condition and subject. As a way of summarizing the Romantics' use of the Hive, I examine John Keats's response to Swift's *Battle*, interpreting it as a struggle over the psychological significance of inherited forms and over which metaphor should be used to represent modern consciousness.

The remaining three chapters form a unit that treats the Hive's amazing evolution during the twentieth century. Chapter 4 describes how the Hive is used to picture the Other. Through instances taken from Joseph Conrad, H. G. Wells, and others, I diagnose the impact of colonialism on the European imagination. Chapter 5 in turn shows how the Hive is used to conceive of the modern existential self. Here I explore Jean-Paul Sartre's use of the Hive to articulate his theory of consciousness and society and measure the response of postcolonial writers through their insect metaphors.

Chapter 6 — a foundation for further cross-cultural work — proposes that Sartre's version of the Hive and its associated unitary subject are both selectively adopted by postmodern writers. I argue that through its adaptation of Sartre's Orestes and his way of seeing, Kobo Abe's *Woman in the Dunes* anticipates elements that A. S. Byatt further explores in her novella *Morpho Eugenia*. Working according to their culture but in dialogue with defining inherited models, Abe and Byatt similarly construct an "affective" formulation of the Hive that serves as an armature for "local" subject formation and aesthetics to counter Sartre's scientific outlook and instrumental poetic, thereby enabling the Orestean type's integration into society.

No single volume may accomplish what I attempt here. But I will not excuse my deficiencies with the statement that I mean to be "suggestive." My argument is as complete and useful as I now can make it. Its subject is great enough to survive the peculiarities and limits of my execution, for which I take sole responsibility. Beyond any service this book may render the scholarly community, I have for it three ambitions. First, that it will interest a wider readership in the history, identification, and psychological significance of artistic forms like the Hive. Second, that it will sensitize the layperson to the finer connections between times, texts, and cultures — thereby increasing his or her appreciation of literature's humanistic value in the largest sense: embracing and granting value to artifacts from all times, places, and peoples. Third, I hope that its style both pleases the reader and complements the work of reason.

ACKNOWLEDGMENTS

Because of this argument's ambition, which became clear to me only after the work was well under way, my debts are considerable. I owe two people in particular. The first is my wife, Debra Roy, whom I profusely thank for her kindness and graceful endurance, for making available her remarkable grasp of literature, for listening to me talk about bees and ants and flies and moths and cockroaches for six years, and for thoroughly and intelligently editing each of this argument's many drafts. In the absence of her encouragement and genuine good nature, this book would not have been completed. Ronald Christ, my mentor and friend, also has my deepest appreciation. At every stage of this project his role was active: no question was too trivial or problem too large for his attention. A rare combination of stylist, editor, advocate, and teacher, Ronald guided me through what I now know was my apprenticeship as a thinker and writer. Upon occasion it was only his unwavering belief in this project and my ability to do it that kept me hunched over my keyboard.

Another sign that the fates have smiled on me is A. S. Byatt's genuine interest in these pages. Not only did she read them in dissertation form, she has since taken the time to ensure their growth and maturation. I have discovered few texts, however esoteric, that she does not know well — and from her singular understanding of metaphor, I have learned much.

Because this argument began as a dissertation, I wish to thank Michael McKeon for approving what must have seemed an unusual — if not an impossible — proposal. My thanks also to John Belton and T. Michael Peters (an entomologist who wisely suggested that I write about insect metaphors) for serving on my dissertation committee. Thomas R. Edwards, who was also on this committee, has my special thanks. With grace and honesty he closely edited three drafts of the manuscript, thus helping me to discover my own voice and through it my own mind.

For reading the near-final manuscript, and for their insightful criticism and their encouragement, I wish to thank Dore Ashton, Charles G. Bell, and Paul West.

Thus far I have acknowledged immediate intellectual family and patrons. But this book's making was a community effort — one whose final stages were professionally and humanely overseen by Holly Carver,

Prasenjit Gupta, and Charlotte Wright of the University of Iowa Press. I am honored and gratified by their gift of stylistic freedom.

What follows is as complete a list as I am able to prepare at this time of persons whom I have not yet recognized and who have contributed instances of the insect metaphor or have otherwise lent me their expertise, advice, protection, and time — including help with translations and last-minute editing and proofreading. If I have forgotten anyone, my sincerest apologies, for without such friends and colleagues this scale of comparative work would be impossible: Robert Abboud, Robert Barton, Robert Bee, Claire Berardini, Fred Booth, Patricia Cain, Jan Carew, Joy Carew, Patrick Cesarini, Robert Coleman, Tina Crafton, Kathleen Crown, Rosanne Currarino, Edward Denault, Dennis Dollens, John Donovan, Sarah Ellenzweig, David Evans, T. M. and F. M. Face, Donald Fallon, Rita Finstein, Kathleen Formosa, Donald B. Gibson, Darcy Gioia, Stephanie Girard, Agnieszska Zylowska Goeller, Michael Goeller, Mr. and Mrs. Theodore P. Green, Amy Nelson Hahn, Margaret Hall, Nancy M. Hollingsworth, Joshua Jacobs, Judy Karwowski, Ann Kiernan, Raymond Klimek, Linda Kozusko, Elise Lemire, Anthony Lioi, Antonio López, Susan Mayer, Rosalind McInerney, Nancy Miller, Richard E. Miller, Samuel C. Morse, Barry O'Connell, Stephen M. Parker, Christopher Peters, Harold Pettersen, Ellen Pratofiorito, Richard Quaintance, Barry V. Qualls, Heather Reusch, Jon Roberts, Annette Saddik, Patricia Saunders-Evans, Carol Smith, Jay Stevenson, Andre Stipanovic, Ty Tempel, Alison Unger, Thomas Van Laan, William Vesterman, Stephanie Volmer, Christopher Warley, Richard Wasson (who is sorely missed), Andrew Welsh, Harriet Whitlock, William Wolff, Jonathan Worley, and Ruth Yeselson.

Finally, I wish to acknowledge my mother's singular contribution to this effort's foundations and execution. From her I learned to love the English language, to observe nonhuman creatures, and to prize intellectual freedom. Before I had any ambition that did not involve remortgaging the farm, her actions taught me what quality above all others is necessary if one wishes to create: courage. But not courage in the abstract — rather, the courage to endure the daily, a fatalism given strength through stubbornness and sweetened with wordplay.

Poetics of the Hive

INTRODUCTION   The Alphabet of the Bees

*The teacher who expounds what he understands in the scriptures
expounds it to his listeners, like the reader of a text articulating
the letters which he recognizes; whereas the teacher who teaches to
understand the scripture is like the teacher of the alphabet, one who
teaches how to read. So the person who knows how to read, on finding a
book, does not require another reader to explain what is written in it;
and in the same way the person who has assimilated the rules that I
am trying to teach, when he finds a difficulty in the text, will not need
another interpreter to reveal what is obscure, because he comprehends
certain rules (the equivalent of this analogy).*
    Augustine, On Christian Teaching

*We knowers are unknown to ourselves, and for good reason: how can we
ever hope to find what we have never looked for? There is a sound adage
which runs: "Where a man's treasure lies, there lies his heart." Our
treasure lies in the beehives of our knowledge. We are perpetually on our
way thither, being by nature winged insects and honey gatherers of the
mind. The only thing that lies close to our hearts is the desire to bring
something home to the hive.*
    Friedrich Nietzsche, The Genealogy of Morals

*My approach [is] unique, [in that] . . . my thinking is not separate
from objects; that the elements of objects, the perceptions of the object,
flow into my thinking and are fully permeated by it; that my
perception itself is a thinking, and my thinking a perception.*
    *Johann Wolfgang von Goethe, "Significant Help Given by an
    Ingenious Turn of Phrase"*

The variety of insect metaphors issues from a dramatic tableau, one that defines the individual and society in relation to each other.[1] This tableau imitates a particular visual experience, as when we observe a creature or creatures from a distance, usually from above. Even an object so large and complex as a city is by such a perspective miniaturized and simplified. While there are recent versions of the Hive that explore the collective from within, its traditional forms picture it from the outside. Therefore it is from such instances that we will extract our first principles.

Below are two examples. The first is a modern formulation taken from the essay "Social Talk" by the biologist and science writer, Lewis Thomas. The second is a picture of the city of Carthage as it appears in H. R. Fairclough's translation of Virgil's *Aeneid*.

Here is Thomas: "Nobody wants to think that the rapidly expanding mass of mankind, spreading out over the surface of the earth, blackening the ground, bears any meaningful resemblance to the life of an anthill or a hive."[2]

And Virgil:

> now they [Aeneas and Achates] were climbing the hill that looms large over the city and looks down on the confronting towers. Aeneas marvels at the massive buildings, mere huts once; marvels at the gates, the din and high-paved roads. Eagerly the Tyrians press on, some to build walls, to rear the citadel, and roll up stones by hand; some to choose the site for a dwelling and enclose it with a furrow. Laws and magistrates they ordain, and a holy senate. Here some are digging harbours, here others lay the deep foundations of their theater and hew out of the cliffs vast columns, lofty adornments for the stage to be! Even as bees in early summer, amid flowery fields, ply their task in sunshine, when they lead forth the full grown young of their race, or pack the fluid honey and strain their cells to bursting with sweet nectar, or receive the burdens of incomers, or in martial array drive from their folds the drones, a lazy herd; all aglow is the work and the fragrant honey is sweet with thyme.[3]

In order to better appreciate their similarities, let us first examine the apparent and considerable differences between these passages. The first is late twentieth century in origin. Its mode is prose and its genre the essay. The second was written in the first century B.C. Although cited in prose translation, its mode is poetry, its genre the epic. Furthermore, each passage represents a different magnitude of human collectivity by means of a different metaphoric vehicle, and each views its collective according to a distinct perspective. The first has us viewing the whole of humanity from orbit and favors its comparison with an anthill (suggested by the phrases "spreading out" and "blackening the ground"), whereas the second positions its observers on a hill above a preindustrial city, which is explicitly figured as a beehive.

Despite their differences, however, both metaphors employ the same pattern of spatial positioning and subject/object relations. In both, a seeing subject is placed above an observed, collective object so as to apprehend it as a whole. The subject's distance from the object encourages a particular sort of abstraction. As a consequence of the subject's placement, the observed entities and their actions (which from a different and closer position would appear individual and discrete) are unified.

Because of their visual emphasis (each enables us to "see" a human collective as an insect society), these passages are verbal pictures. However, this sort of picture is produced by more than the ordinary language of description, for here seeing is of a piece with obvious figuration. Furthermore, this act of figuration is conceptual as well as poetic. Now, by "conceptual" I mean that our view from above enables us, first, to take in a given collective as a whole and, second, to conceive of this whole as being philosophically different from ourselves. In Thomas's passage, for example, not only does his language enable us to think of human action on a global scale, it also asks us to suppose that all actions in our visual field, observed as well as implicit, are aspects of a single organization whose philosophical essence is a natural and therefore *unconscious* "expansion." Although by way of extension we are implicitly part of the "rapidly expanding mass of mankind, spreading out over the surface of the earth, [that is] blackening the ground," not only are we physically separate from this picturing of the action, we are also aware of this action's inexorable and probably self-destructive nature. Our individual (self-)consciousness — our sovereign capacity to see, to know, and thus to judge the whole as philosophically distinct — sets us apart from the mass below.

This rational, classificatory apprehension is a product of the Hive tableau's structure, which arises from the way that the observing consciousness (with which the reader is consubstantial) is positioned vis-à-vis the observed collective. We are distant enough from the collective to see it as a thing in itself, and yet close enough to infer from its elements' apparent similitude an essential action — its mode of Being.

Yet, while the Hive tableau's general conceptual limits are imposed by the biology of seeing, the exact sense of each instance derives from how these limits are imitated. In the Thomas passage, because we are to apprehend all of humanity as a mass and are therefore positioned so as to observe the entire planet, we cannot make out individual actors, only the signs of their collective life. If we were seeing the Earth from any farther away, the details necessary for our apprehension would be denied us, and the figure's sense would fail. This passage generally represents the Hive's farthest visio-conceptual extreme, and by the same logic the Virgil passage marks the opposite. Here the observing subject sees the whole as composed of independent and clearly human elements, which are nevertheless perceived as unified. If a spectator were to draw any closer to the city (as when Aeneas enters its gates), the Hive's structure, and hence its sense, would be lost along with the city's figuration as an organic unit.

When we are shown many actors who occupy the same space, and are denied by distance the information we need to meaningfully differentiate one from the other, the mind generalizes. We easily perceive similarity, and from this we intuit organic unity. But without form, without a structure that concretizes and amplifies this intuition, one that makes this moment's psychological process visible, any such categorical understanding of what we see must remain transitory, and thus on the margins of expression.

Our tableau is more than an image, an object that we see in our mind's eye. Rather, the Hive is a unit composed of an image and an observing subject in precise relation to each other. Hence, the Hive does more than merely suggest a special state of cooperation. A drama in potential, it uses the grammar of seeing to evoke and strategically charge a heterogeneous space, one that makes the social order visible and provides us with both an observational seat and the terms of spectatorship. It is proper, then, to more fully distinguish our object from its emblematic, suggestive uses: versions of the image that do not involve any particular and complex imitation of space and position.

For instance, the image of the dome-shaped skep, a traditional European bee house, appears on the original seal of the Massachusetts Historical Society, which was founded in 1791.[4] The skep also graces the *Deseret Alphabet, 2nd Reader*.[5] On the cover of this book printed in 1868, one of a handful written in the phonetic Mormon alphabet, the bee house is positioned top center. The summit of a phallic design and hovering above a drawing of a six-spired Mormon temple, this skep resembles a bullet on its way to heaven. A more modern interpretation of the skep serves as the logo for Fatbeehive, a London-based Web design company.[6] A boxtop from La Colmena cookie shop in Barcelona features a skep that resembles a solitary domed skyscraper towering in a field. In the background is the outline of an urban skyline that the foregrounded skyscraper-skep dominates, serving as the city's entrance, and emblem, and as a mediator between nature and culture.[7] The beehive's associations with industry, efficiency, cooperation, and order may be communicated even more abstractly. Beehive Technologies aligns itself with the bee's natural command of geometry by using a triad of hexagons for its emblem.[8] In fact, the beehive's emblematic meanings are so conventional that they may be expressed by a single element: a representation of a solitary worker bee, an instance of visual synecdoche.[9] Even the word itself is frequently sufficient to evoke the Hive's positive associations,[10] a synecdochic mode that also informs the compound nouns "spelling bee" and "quilting bee."

In written language the hive and the bee are many times put to the same emblematic work. In such instances, entomologically derived symbols function as a verbal shorthand, furthering economy, clarity, and elegance of expression. There are two types of written emblems, the *philosophical* and the *descriptive*. I call the first "philosophical" because the entomological word or image expresses a concept obviously and with precision. Some random but representative examples: Like so many before him, Ralph Waldo Emerson sees the universe's "great Order" in the beehive's design.[11] To Karl Marx, the insect society — specifically, the bond between the bee and its hive — epitomizes the nature of cooperation "at the dawn of human development."[12] In her first extant poem, written in 1850, Emily Dickinson echoes the English Romantics by using the bee to represent nature's creative principle, the male and ardent "high" and "great" that seeks the "lowly" and "small" flower: "The high do seek the lowly, the great do seek the small, / None cannot find who seeketh, on this terrestrial ball; / The bee doth court the flower, the flower his suit receives, / And they do make merry wedding, whose guests are hundred leaves."[13]

More common than a philosophical emblem, but harder to see, is the *descriptive.* Though less precise than the former, these mild and nearly unnoticeable analogies also embody concepts. But there is more to them than that. We employ a descriptive emblem when through comparison we color or intensify a person, thing, or action with words belonging to the social insects: "He's as busy as a bee." "On the day before Christmas, the mall is a hive of activity."

Etymologically related to this descriptive use of the beehive as a locus of frenetic activity is the verb "to swarm," which descends from the Old Norse *svarmr*, "tumult." It is habitual to combine some form of the verb "to swarm" with a crowd or army: "The mob swarmed into the bank." Of course, the philosophical emblem is also analogical, and its use does indeed involve some metaphorical blending. However, to refer to an example, the tight philosophical analogy between Dickinson's bee and a descending, creative principle is distinct from the more general and prosaic association between crowding shoppers with swarming bees. Relatedly, the metaphorical affect of Dickinson's bee is firmly subordinate to those elements that further the explicit dialogue of ideas. Not so with the homey descriptive emblem. Of the two types of emblems, the descriptive most clearly reports the close relationship between visual and spoken metaphor. While their apparent structure is grammatical, nonetheless such descriptive locutions suggest exactly the design that is essential to the Hive tableau. For when one figures a full mall as a hive, does one not subtly evoke the same sort of subject-object relations that the Hive tableau more fully pictures? Doesn't this analogy suggest that its speaker stands at a distance and observes a collective that the speaker senses is distinct from her- or himself? The greater point I wish to make is that, unlike its sophisticated complement, the descriptive emblem more equally combines philosophical process and pictorial capacity. This does not need to mean much now, but later I will show that this same medial characteristic allows the Hive tableau complexity as well as its remarkable flexibility, a combination of qualities that ensures its longevity.

Regardless, because they are signs and therefore cannot explicitly imitate structured experience, philosophical and descriptive emblems lack the capacity to fully evoke, much less orchestrate, our aesthetic faculties. To attribute communal being precisely and powerfully requires not only the imitation of how we actually see insect communities (hence, the structural consonance between the Thomas and Virgil passages), but also the construction of a particular sort of space, one that clarifies and amplifies the opposition between the individual observing consciousness and the observed collective.

The space that constitutes the Hive tableau is bipolar, arranged along a visual axis that relates subject and object. Within it, the abstractions of singular observer and regarded community are simultaneously fleshed out through contrast. One cannot exist without the other; each constructs the other. The image of a collective organism is no more fabulous than its opposite, a singular observing consciousness that, like Emerson's transparent eyeball, takes in the design of things from above. The arts of language have long anticipated and experimented with our moment's technological extensions of vision.

While we do not ordinarily think of metaphors as optical machines, it is instructive to do so. We do not look through the Hive as if it were a window. It is more accurate to compare it with a stereoscope, an optical toy still to be found in antique shops. This device produces an illusion of depth by presenting to each eye separately a nearly identical photograph, most usually of a notable landscape feature or building. The brain overlaps these photographic images; it resolves the problem of dissonance by telling itself a minor three-dimensional lie. In a manner of speaking, our tableau functions similarly. Two concepts, two modes of being, each embodied in an image — one of the insect community and the other of a human collective — are meshed. During this operation, the mind ignores differences, seeking a shared pattern. Not only does one image color the other, but their blending gives a greater product, the equivalent to the stereoscope's illusion of depth. By resolving conceptual difference in favor of resemblance, we get the concept and picture of the collective organism. Truly, if the Hive is such an optical device, then its lenses have been ground by the imagination. And to be observable through it, every specimen must be stained by poetry and illuminated by the riddle of cooperation.

Any creature viewed from the Hive's sovereign position is part of an animate whole, a context that gives the isolated ant or bee special significance. One such lone creature provokes questions loaded with feeling and full of dramatic potential: Where are the rest of them? Why is this one by itself? From this insignificant part, this living synecdoche, we infer the whole. In order to conceive the collective organism, we need not see all its elements together. A few ants, or even one, tell us all we need to know about the hidden many. When from a high building we gaze down upon a busy street, a similar calculus applies. Because we cannot make out details, it does not matter what these people below are actually doing. And we do not need to see the whole city thus in order to extrapolate.

Even though we know that each tiny form is a human being, from our position they are reduced to parts of a unified, homogeneous whole. If we are close enough and kind, we might speak of this unity as a crowd. If farther away and we want to make a point like Thomas's, we use words usually reserved for the social insects: these figures *swarm*, they are a *hive* of activity. If it is 8:50 in the morning, this crowd or swarm is going to work. Eight hours later this mass is on its way back to its *nest* — a word that our view from above makes insect specific. It seems, then, that the meanings of insect-related words are influenced by the laws of physical proximity. Perhaps this is why it is acceptable to speak of a crowd as a swarm or a city as a hive, but an insult to call another person an insect to his or her face.

The word "insect" implies distance, reduced or negligible importance, absolute difference. Three examples: Gulliver overhears the Prince of the Brobdingnagians remarking to his first minister "how contemptible a thing was human grandeur, which could be mimicked by such diminutive insects as I [Gulliver]."[14] When confronting his creation for the first time, Dr. Frankenstein calls him a "vile insect" and a "devil."[15] To symbolize the extremity of Gregor Samsa's alienation, Kafka figures him as a beetle-like "monstrous vermin."[16]

One may similarly define and reduce an entire race or culture. By inverting the classical notion of the divine beehive, the authors of an early twentieth-century pamphlet titled "Meat vs. Rice" dramatize the threat to America by Chinese immigration: "To begin with, they have a hive of 450,000,000 Chinese to draw from with only one ocean to cross, and behind them an impulsive force of hunger unknown to any European people."[17]

We are so familiar with the Hive's peculiar space, its operation and the attributions it allows us to make, that it seems natural. And indeed it is. Even at its most ornamental, the Hive is a visual tool, a process of reasoning that, to borrow from George Lakoff's and Mark Johnson's *Philosophy in the Flesh*, signifies at both the conscious, "phenomenological" level of language and concepts and the semiconscious "neurocomputational" level. Current thinking about the mind has it that neurocomputational objects mediate between the hidden, automatic neurobiological processes and those we are aware of and over which we exercise volition. According to this theory, which confirms our analysis thus far, a medial object such as the Hive evidences (imitates) its undergirding neurobiology. In turn, this imitated pattern shapes words and ideas.[18] Thus, by studying a medial object's structure and function, we may infer much about the relationship between mind and body that illuminates the arts of language.

It must be said that the Hive is only one of a great many cognitive blueprints. But it is also part of a select group that enables us to translate visual experience into language. As I conceive it, language is an artistic medium, a substance that gives solidity to the immaterial percept, thought, or feeling. But like any other medium, language is far from passive. It reacts back upon the blueprint and the mind that wields it. Once palpable, phenomenologically significant, our tableau may be shaped: amplified, ornamented, inverted, even camouflaged as a sign. Because my purposes are to discover and identify the Hive wherever and however it appears, to search out the meaning and origin of its instances in their considerable variety, I must discuss these actions and the processes they imply. But the Hive, captured alive from its original text, shall remain my focus — one that these pages and the theory I present must serve.

In order to clarify both the Hive's essential structure (and thus the relations between actors and objects within its bipolar space), as well as the structural similarities between my models, I have diagrammed both the Thomas and the Virgil passages. Because the latter is older and more substantial, initially I will devote most of my explication to it (see figures 1 and 2).

From the hill, Aeneas the "subject" (S) looks down upon the "object," Carthage (O). His visual field (F), which is enabled by his sovereign position, encloses the city, thereby allowing him to apprehend the myriad persons and their actions below as a single unified entity — in this instance as a symbol of peace and cooperative growth. Furthermore, and significantly, relative to Carthage's wholeness and its supernatural alignment, this unified entity is alien and antithetical to Aeneas. (Juno, Aeneas's divine adversary, claims Carthage as her own; it represents a feminine principle that must be transcended so that Rome may rise.)

Figure 2 emphasizes the division of this scene into two different and opposed spaces, each congruent with the person or thing contained. Because to see is to know, and to know is to have power, the elevated and

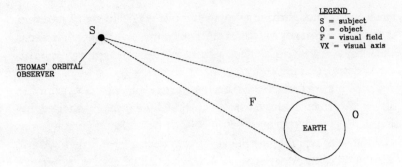

1. Thomas's orbital view of the earth.

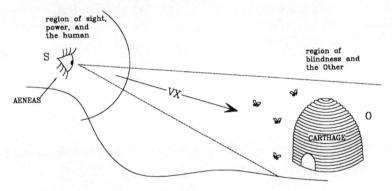

2. Aeneas's local view of Carthage.

therefore sovereign subject, Aeneas, defines his space — and this space is ours as well. We are proximate to Aeneas. He is our object of identification, and, within the compass of the Hive, it is only in his space, the sovereign space, that we may be fully human. Thus, the form gratifies us, makes an elemental, emotional appeal: we are attracted to the implications of the superior position and repelled by those of its opposite.

Hence, spatially and philosophically, as well as emotionally, Carthage is "outside." It is the locus of Otherness: it symbolizes what we are not, and thus may function as a stable abstraction against which we may measure ourselves. This is why, like Aeneas, when we look down upon Carthage with longing and desire, we see and "feel" it only in the image's terms that are evoked and directed by the Hive's structure. These terms have their own agency, which in the latter part of the simile render the scene golden and Carthage a utopia. It is by the Hive's agency, its dream of order that, paradoxically, we are joined to this city. We are drawn to it along the visual axis (VX), an azimuth aligned with the narrative's goal, the Trojans' fate: the future city of Rome.

Entrances are privileged. Frequently they define the essence of the players as well as the play. Perhaps this is why Aeneas enters Carthage "veiled in a [divine] cloud." Even though he no longer occupies the position from which he can know without being known, this cloud of invisibility extends his moment of visual sovereignty. Its purpose is to restore to us the essential differences between levels and spaces that the bee simile has constructed and then overwhelmed with desire. The cloud's function, what it tells us about the space that we have just left, may be inferred from the veiled Aeneas's destination. His first stop in Carthage is the basement of Juno's temple, on whose walls "he sees [pictured] the battles of Ilium," the story of his people's suffering. Apparently Virgil recognizes as seductive the ideal community that the Hive allows us to imagine. Indeed, the affect of his simile's amplification threatens to erode the sovereign observer's isolation and, hence, his power. Thus, here we have an example of the tension and dialectic between the Hive's utopian space and one particular narrative world, a system of motives and expectations that our object works within and yet resists.

The Hive is a structure that courts antithesis, but it is also a process — one that tends toward its own resolution, namely, the incorporation of the individual into the whole. Therefore, as much as the Hive's rules may broadly complement those of any narrative that would contain it, by its very nature the Hive cannot be entirely subject to its container's purposes. So distinct is the Hive's charged space that a mere transcription of what we see when we look at an anthill or a beehive is not entirely sufficient for its office.

The Hive's view from above seems congruent with — even identical to — actual experience. However, because this tableau is an imitation, a purposeful selection of aspects of the visual process and their adaptation to the demands of the verbal medium, as I have already mentioned, its figurative and philosophical work derives as much from the eye's limitations as from its powers. The effect of distance, which ordinarily confounds understanding because it denies the viewer individuating particulars, is often exploited by the writer while reworking the Hive.

In real life, the content of our sovereign spectator's visual field would initially present itself as a simultaneous and probably overwhelming experience, one that naturally engages the mind's ability to abstract. Because of the linear nature of verbal language, however, this sort of affective simultaneity cannot be represented as such. Therefore, because Virgil needs to evoke this abstracting response so as to allow his Hive its office, the first part of his tableau is a catalog of details, not all of which are naturally possible for Aeneas to see. For example, Virgil tells us that from his hill Aeneas sees "laws and magistrates . . . ordain[ed]." From his position outside the city walls, the ordination of laws would be difficult to make out — unless this activity were already known to the observer as a necessary element of the picture. Virgil includes such percepts because his purposes require more than merely accurate description for their realization. Rather, he is using the weight of accumulating details, many of which are heavily symbolic, to prepare us for the imaging of utopia: the living allegory of the beehive, Carthage.

Since the Hive is an unfolding and progressive structure experienced over time, its operation may be understood according to the gestalt "principle of psychophysical isomorphism," which, when applied to the arts of language, holds that the structure or manner of figuration must be congruent with how the mind uses the visual process to think.[19] This is to say that, just as the Hive must convincingly imitate the facts of actual seeing by arranging subject and object within an imagined space according to the logic of these facts, so, too, must its poetic arrangement — the order and manner of elements on the page — imitate the way that we would process the actual visual experience of looking down upon a collective from an appropriate height.

While our seat above the collective does indeed establish a frame for quick, holistic classification, this frame becomes experientially apparent only as it is progressively filled with details, which, when represented in written language, accumulate in a perceptible rising action. For example, in Thomas's passage, we begin our "think[ing]" with the abstract, compound substantive "rapidly expanding mass of mankind," which suggests, at the very least, our philosophical position as one of standing apart from and in judgment of "mankind." In the sentence's next division, Thomas confirms our position as orbital, because we are observing the initial substantive, the sentence's subject and our object of figuration, "spreading out over the surface of the earth." This element of the sentence thereby establishes the Hive's essential spatial structure. This structure is now more than a mere preface for metaphor: it is an evolving container whose value we actively shape by filling it with actions in a particular order — in this instance with the gerunds "expanding," "spreading," and "blackening." Notice that it is not until we reach the tricolonic and descriptive peak of this accumulative unit that we are ready for the analogical proposition.

The same progressive structure characterizes the first division of Virgil's extended simile. We begin with an abstract container, with the visual facts and limits enabled and imposed by our seat above the city. This container is then filled with and thereby further realized by a progressive order of actions. Cartographically, Virgil begins his catalog of actions at Carthage's walls and works inward. Historically and sociologically, he begins with an evocation of the city's rustic past (it was once "mere huts"), and then proceeds up the cultural scale until he reaches the idea of theater, whose penultimate social import he signifies with the simile's most monumental action, that of "hew[ing] out of the cliffs vast columns, lofty adornments for the stage to be." This city is not complete, but the Hive's structure enables Aeneas to imagine it in its future wholeness, a projection that elicits and shapes his emotions. What Aeneas sees moves him to a longing that we may share.

Though it is useful to speak of the Hive as a structure and I hope illuminating to compare it with an "optical device," as I have done above, how and what our tableau signifies considerably exceeds the explanatory powers of these or conceivably any investigative metaphors. Meaning is an action of the human mind, what Dante would call a movement of the spirit. And we are no closer to understanding this movement than he. If how the mind makes meaning is mysterious, then artistic forms such as the Hive complicate this mystery with paradox. On the one hand, because the Hive derives from our visual experience of the world, it preexists what we normally — and, I think, properly — classify as art. Yet, on the other, its fullness as a visual experience comes into being only when realized in writing, which is to say during the act of reading. Perhaps part of the pleasure we take in the poetic Hive issues from an intuition that through its imitation we are discovering and perfecting something in ourselves. Virgil understood this paradox of the poetic Hive as an artistic resource. He knew the Hive need not be complete in order to powerfully signify, that the reader's mind may be depended upon to run ahead of and to "finish" it eagerly and in a predictable manner. If artists know the mind as well as they know their craft, like Virgil they make room in their art for the unfolding of the eye's natural artistry.

It is my theory that when we perceive the Hive in nature we do so according to the dispassionate laws of space, the stern logic of similarity and difference, and the emotional rules of affinity and proximity. Our seeing is thus founded upon complex operations: we grasp a collective's organic unity and use this percept to attribute the whole's difference from our singular selves. In an instant the eye defines and opposes actors, divides the universe — thereby creating meaning, the seed of drama. However, the drama of seeing is implicit; the poet who uses the Hive must create at a double remove — but not without compensation. Because the natural sight of the Hive builds upon philosophical difference and spatial separation, its artistic representations tend to assume exile and evoke longing. In exchange for the original speed and subtle mystery of the eye's operation, from the poetic Hive the reader gets simplicity and power, feelings solid enough to remember and talk about.

When in real life we are observing a collective from a distance, our psychophysiological processes are so quick and efficient that we do not ordinarily think of them as they are: a balletic series of interwoven responses, a minor but miraculous process of creation. Because it is an imitation of seeing, the poetic Hive simplifies and slows down what may be translated from its model. Our verbal tableau shapes, focuses, and augments the subtle affect of sight; it is an enhanced sketch of how the mind makes patterns and then charges these patterns with feeling. In the case of Aeneas's view of Carthage, what we may assume is the eye's pleasure (namely, discovering a patterned wholeness in the manifold activities laid out before it) is translated into an active and positive emotional response. Carthage's incompleteness, its *becoming*, invites us to imagine its future and to join it. Aeneas accomplishes the first and attempts the second but is thwarted by powers that serve an even greater city-to-come, Rome. And if you examine the second epigraph that heads this introduction, you will see that, although Nietzsche's subject is a belonging distinct from Virgil's, he begins *The Genealogy of Morals* with an invitation to join the collective. Tellingly, he uses the Hive to make this appeal. More forcefully than in Virgil's picture of Carthage, Nietzsche assumes that we are by nature citizens of the Hive: "We knowers are unknown to ourselves, and for good reason: how can we ever hope to find what we have never looked for? There is a sound adage which runs: 'Where a man's treasure lies, there lies his heart.' Our treasure lies in the beehives of our knowledge. We are perpetually on our way thither, being by nature winged insects and honey gatherers of the mind. The only thing that lies close to our hearts is the desire to bring something home to the hive" (149).

The Hive's pictorial space is bipolar; its emotional associations follow suit. Community attracts, but it also repels. To know a social order as a whole is an act of simplification that extends to all of its elements. Yes, to see the whole, the city, the future from afar is to long for it, to wish, as it were, to join the masons raising its walls. However, to see in this way is also to stand apart and above, to be superior. To see a human group thus is to be privileged with the big picture, to be beyond and thereby relieved of the problems of cooperative becoming, of history, of a shared present and a future complicated by others. I suspect this is why the Hive is so popular a psychological instrument for radical social engineers and thinkers. For instance, when squaring the human dimension of "vertical" Manhattan's many windows with the antithetical proportion of its skyscrapers, Le Corbusier invokes the Hive to naturalize and eulogize his vision of the total city: [20]

Thus punctuating the blue sky in a very simple, regular, and automatic way — yes, a fatal and indisputable way — there are now in the sky hundreds and thousands of windows, perhaps millions. It is very moving. Mediocre and retrograde poets who write about sunsets falling on old stones, you deny that many a good-natured man, with two feet, a head, and a heart — is an ant or a bee subject to the necessity of living in a box, a case, behind a window; you ask for a complete freedom, a complete fantasy, in accordance with which everyone would act in his own fashion. . . . Well, here is the proof that a man holds fast to the box which is his room; and a window open on the outside world. It is a law of human biology; the square case, the *room* is a useful creation, proper to human beings. The window behind which a man stands is a poem of intimacy, of the free consideration of things. A million windows in the blue sky. The fairylike atmosphere begins with them. [21]

Le Corbusier is exquisitely sensitive to the emotions aroused through the Hive's capacity to unify through vision: he finds "very moving" the image of "a million windows in the blue sky," "behind [each of] which a [metropolitan] man stands." For Le Corbusier each apartment window is a synecdoche for civilization and an instrument through which the individual gaze travels to join with its manifold equivalents, thereby generating the paradoxical source of the metropolitan's happiness: the intimacy of the crowd.

Another aspect of the Hive's emotional import has to do with a poet's choice of entomological symbol — for instance whether a collective is described as an anthill or a beehive. As evidenced by my model passages, the Hive's essential calculus is visual. Perceptions of similitude and proximity undergird acts of classification and division. At this level any collective natural symbol is identical to another. But such a pure structure does not account for how a metaphor actually gets written and is experienced. In practice, it matters a great deal exactly how a crowd or a city is figured. And at the moment when the image takes hold of the imagination, nothing is of greater consequence.

Nonhuman creatures embody principles. Some lend themselves to descriptions of individual character and others to imaging a social whole. There are different sorts of people, so in literature we find a variety of animals used to flesh out types. And since feelings and ideas about order and hierarchy also differ, writers have discovered in nature animal societies capable of symbolizing a range of psychological and organizational states. Even though I will return to this subject again and from a slightly different angle when I discuss Homer in chapter 1, it is useful to think about it now in some detail. The animal symbols we use for the group may be ordered along a continuum from herd to beehive, from the least and most primitive to the highly organized and most civilized. But where an animal lives is no less important than how. So let me map this scale of organization onto creation, which I here imagine traditionally: Heaven — the realm of spirit, harmony, and light — is above and distinct from the earth — the place of brute matter, conflict, and darkness.

At the bottom is the herd, one of Nietzsche's prized metaphors, and to which, however ironically, he opposes his Superman. Many of us tell ourselves that we are above the herd, that we would rather be lonely than surrender our individuality to a collective "animal" will. As much a natural force as collective flesh, the herd's human analog is the crowd or purposeless mob. While there is strength in numbers, and a herd animal may indeed be strong, this group, along with its members, tends to be stupid and subject to predation. All of us are familiar with one or more comparisons between unprepared soldiers and domestic animals. Men go to war "like lambs to the slaughter"; once there "they are slaughtered like cattle." To emphasize their vulnerability and inconsequence, in a nod to Homer we say that they "drop like flies" or are "cannon fodder." While the herd can be violent, premeditation and strategy is not its forte. As demonstrated by Jesus when casting out the demon, Legion, evil is a superior organizing power that enters the herd from without.

Some birds live in herds — flocks — but even though most are far duller than their mammalian counterparts, because heaven is superior to the earth, in general, any winged creature is nobler than the animal that lives in or on the ground. Hence — if for a moment we exclude Christian symbolism — a flock of birds or even a swarm of flies is superior to a flock of sheep. The variety of names used to distinguish one type of animal group from another tends to confirm this hierarchy of value: the lion, traditionally the noblest of animals, lives in a "pride." But though apparently good for lions, elsewhere "pride" has negative connotations. Compare the lion with the hummingbird, quintessence of avian excellence: when hovering with its kind over blossoms, magical and luminescent, the hummingbird does so in "charms." The lion may leap, but he cannot fly; rarely does a hummingbird touch the earth. The big cat is built to kill, eats flesh; the hummingbird has been fashioned to sip the living wine of flowers. The same logic informs how we think and speak of the crow, who in some sense completes the lion's work: though winged, a flock of crows is called a "murder."

Give a small herd teeth, intelligence, and mobility and you have the pack. However, while a pack may be said to swarm, it cannot make much of one. Small in membership, its quality of organization cannot exceed a rough, face-to-face hierarchy. The pack is ruled by and seeks the satisfaction of basic needs. Its human equivalents are the gang, the bourgeois picture of the lower-class family, and the clan. Its members are bound to each other by emotion and the blood tie, a local coherence too weak for the true swarm.

While some blending of herd and swarm is allowed when one is talking about human beings (thus the horde, the mob's most dangerous form), a herd that swarms violates the rules. Organize and motivate a herd of cows or a flock of birds as a swarm and you can pitch a horror movie. Although more purposeful than the herd, the swarm's organization is simpler than the hive's. While the swarm may indeed hold within it a potential city, since it is less civilized than the hive, the swarm's action tends to be direct. Impatient and peripatetic, if it must labor, it does so in order that it may sustain or resume travel. To live, the swarm must gather what it needs but cannot produce. It may build, but what it makes cannot be permanent. It has been known to enslave or kill any who would interfere.

Of the many insects that exhibit swarming behavior, the most poetically significant are flies, hornets and wasps, locusts, ants, and honeybees. Because in nature each behaves uniquely, together their images form a palette of colors enough for painting almost any desired or undesirable cooperative state. And unlike real insects these images may be blended. For instance, *Paradise Lost*, lines 766–68: Before the gates of Pandemonium the fallen angels "Thick swarm'd, both on the ground and in the air, / Brusht with the hiss of rustling wings. As Bees / In spring time." [22] This moment introduces one of Milton's most admired similes, wherein Satan's host is figured "as Bees in spring time." Subtly but effectively, the poet gives these bees an unwholesome aspect by lending them the behavior and sound of locusts. Bees may swarm in the air or around a branch, but rarely are they seen to swarm so thickly "both on the ground and in the air." Moreover, instead of producing that buzzing which Virgil and Dante both thought musical, these bees' wings "hiss" and "rustle." Milton's diction is important. By itself neither the word "buzz" nor its gerund may express the two distinct threats communicated by "hiss" and "rustle." And these ominous words are onomatopoeic: Milton means them to evoke sounds that are at once higher and lower than those made by bees. For the moment these devils may look like bees, but by their sound we are reminded that their purpose is darker.

Of the swarming insects, the least organized are the flies. Not social, they gather more than swarm. Except for the biting variety, they have no natural defenses and so may be easily killed. In Medieval Christian art the fly is sometimes used as a symbol for the soul. But writers have long prized these creatures as a sign of vulnerability, death, and uncleanliness. In the Hebraic tradition, alone of all the insects the flies have their particular demon, Beelzebub. As in so many things, Homer provides the model. He tells us that the Trojans stripping the armor from Sarpedon's corpse "kept forever swarming over his dead body, as flies / through a sheepfold thunder about the pails overspilling / milk, in the season of spring when the milk splashes in the buckets. / So they swarmed over the dead man."[23] Sarpedon's blood, his young life that has poured out into the dust, is sanctified by its comparison with fresh milk. The picture of flies feeding on such purity energizes the image, makes it visceral. We are newly sensitized to what men do in war. Shakespeare, also sensing that the fly uniquely expresses a creaturely fragility before the higher powers of existence, has Gloucester make the following analogy: "As flies are to wanton boys are we to the' gods, / They kill us for their sport."[24] It appears that the epic frame dignifies the least of us.

Satirists, however, emphasize the fly's more prosaic behavior. And since it is their business to examine things closely, they exploit the Hive tableau's instrumental potential: the Hive's structure allows them to extend the powers of vision, to magnify and miniaturize. For instance, Swift's vivid picture of bird-sized flies "leav[ing] their loathsome excrement or spawn" on food served before the queen of Brobdingnag emphasizes the low democracy of the flesh. Another example: Gulliver's miniature, magnifying eyes penetrate social distinctions and shrink giants. However, Twain is after even bigger game. He uses the fly, the lowest of God's visible creations, to question the idea of a just cosmos and to blast what Satan, the speaker of *Letters from the Earth*, calls "the disastrous Moral Sense, the parent of all the immoralities" (27).

Letters relates the observations of Satan, who "on account of his too flexible tongue" has been banished by God into the void. Satan decides to "hunt up the earth and see how the Human-Race experiment [is] coming along" (14). Carefully observing the travails of Noah and his family, in his third private letter to St. Michael and St. Gabriel, Satan relates that on the third day of the ark's journey it was discovered that a fly had been left behind. The ark must return to fetch it. In several of what are perhaps the most blasphemous passages in American literature, Twain pictures the disease-carrying fly as God's "sacred bird," His "special pets . . . his darlings" (35). Here is Twain at his most Swiftian, and doubly armed with germ theory: "The fly harries the sick man in his home, in the hospital, even on his deathbed at his last gasp. Pesters him at his meals; previously hunts up patients suffering from loathsome and deadly diseases; wades in their sores, gaums its legs with a million death-dealing germs; then comes to that healthy man's table and wipes these things off on the butter and discharges a bowel-load of typhoid germs and excrement on his batter cakes. The housefly wrecks more human constitutions and destroys more human lives than all God's multitude of misery-messengers and death agents put together" (35).

If we imagine Gulliver as looking through a hand lens, then Twain's Satan peers through a morally charged compound microscope. What in Swift's time were invisible creatures, mere rumors of the Great Chain of Being, were by Twain's a visible and formidable adversary of mankind. Just as the power of Twain's magnifying vision exceeds Swift's, so does his ire's intensity and ambition. Swift has his fly's visitation signify that all persons live in the same filth, inhabit the same world. By dirtying us all, he strikes against social pretension and its consequent abuses. To him these are substantial but mundane and entirely human failings. In contrast, Twain's fly is an instrument that carries him heavenward, bearing in its stomach evidence to tumble down the very idea of God.

Twain's argument recalls Swift's "A Modest Proposal" but is more extreme: Since filth harbors microbes and microbes cause sickness, which causes death, then filth equals death. And because God made disease as well as the fly that delivers it, then this insect proves that God is a murderer and His cosmos perverse. Paradoxically, it is Twain's magnified view of the fly that gives him a place to stand above and in judgment of the Almighty. Finally, we should note that these two satiric instances confirm what we already know about the Hive tableau. Namely, it is a unique tool of the imagination, a space within which relations among entities and their relative proportions may be used to image and debate the great moral issues.

The ancients would have recognized the skeptical and irascible character represented by Twain at his most savage. They knew that sometimes a short-tempered and excitable person may also show courage and a readiness for action. Their animal types for this personality were the hornet and the wasp. Homer uses the latter to show how in one instance the Greeks defended their ships:

> The Myrmidons came streaming out like wasps at the wayside
> when little boys have got into the habit of making them angry
> by always teasing them as they live in their house by the roadside;
> silly boys, they do something that hurts many people;
> and if some man who travels on the road happens to pass them
> and stirs them unintentionally, they in heart of fury

come swarming out each one from his place to fight for their
   children.
In heart and fury like these the Myrmidons streaming
came out from their ships, with a tireless clamour arising.
(16.259–67)

Aristophanes reverses Homer's analogy, thereby demonstrating the
Hive's capacity for inversion: he sums up the temper of Athenian society
by titling a satire *The Wasps*. But in *Gulliver's Travels*, even though Swift
inverts it, the Homeric model's primacy is confirmed. Instead of defending ships against heroes, Gulliver defends a sweet cake against insects. A
swarm of wasps lets him show his mettle: "I remember one morning
when Glumdalclitch had set me in my box upon a window . . . to give
me air . . . after I had lifted up one of my sashes, and sat down at my
table to eat a piece of sweet cake for my breakfast; above twenty wasps,
allured by the smell, came flying into the room, humming louder than
the drones of as many bagpipes. Some of them seized my cake, and carried it piecemeal away; others flew about my head and face, confounding
me with the noise, and putting me in the utmost terror of their stings.
However I had the courage to rise and draw my hanger, and attack them
in the air. I dispatched four of them" (115).

Unlike some flies, locusts do not bite flesh. Nor do they have what to
us is a painful, and would have been to miniature Gulliver a deadly, sting.
While they travel together and share a common purpose, locusts are not
highly organized. What we fear is their numbers: they can blacken the
skies and devastate our crops. But they are also the fuel of visions, eaten
with honey by holy men. Plague sent of God, ravenous horde, John the
Baptist's simple meat — our seemingly irreconcilable images of the locust resolve into a single principle of hunger.

Remaining, then, are the ants and the bees. These insects are biological and poetic relatives. Both are highly social, build nests, protect their
young, express caste differences behaviorally and morphologically, and
swarm — albeit differently from each other. And to the poets some
swarms matter more than others. As for the ants, one might say that
swarming is their way of life. Their swarming over food is very much
like their swarming to defend their nest or to attack another. If one
wishes to imitate what the unaided eye sees in nature, finer distinctions
are difficult to make. Archaic Homer never figured his heroes as ants, but

Romantic Thoreau's picture of "a war between two races of ants, the red always pitted against the black," makes each insect an Achilles and every woodyard an *Iliad*.[25]

Because it makes frequent war on its own kind (an observation that did not threaten the world before Romanticism), for us the ant, and sometimes the termite, is the living image of the pitiless and ravaging army and the oppressive antihuman organization. In *War and Peace*, Tolstoy describes both the French and Russian armies as ants: "The French swarming around their guns seemed to be ants" (242); and "Several battalions of [Russian] soldiers, in shirt sleeves despite the cold wind, were digging like a swarm of white ants [termites] in these earthworks" (219).

Writing in 1905, nearly half a century after *War and Peace*, and clearly inspired by Conrad's *Heart of Darkness*, H. G. Wells uses evolutionary ideas to extend the ants' poetic threat. Wells's short story "The Empire of the Ants" pictures a newly evolved race of sentient, tool-using ants that from their origin deep in the Amazon basin are spreading outward and northward. The story's unnamed narrator reports the predictions of Holroyd, an English entomologist who was the first European to actually witness "these . . . intelligent ants" in action:

> So far their action has been a steady progressive settlement, involving the flight or slaughter of every human being in the new areas they invade. They are increasing rapidly in numbers, and Holroyd at least is firmly convinced that they will finally dispossess man over the whole of tropical South America.
>
> And why should they stop at tropical South America?
>
> Well, there they are, anyhow. By 1911 or thereabouts, if they go on as they are going, they ought to strike the Capuarana Extension Railway, and force themselves upon the attention of the European capitalist.
>
> By 1920 they will be halfway down the Amazon. I fix 1950 or '60 at the latest for the discovery of Europe. (285)

Wells's ants do indeed discover and conquer European civilization — or at least its imagination: witness the more recent flurry of aesthetic activity surrounding the advance of South American "killer bees."

Most ants native to the northern hemisphere's temperate zone generally do not fly. Nor do they have a sting or bite that matters to humans — a fact exploited by Wells (his Amazonian super ants manufacture their venom). The bee, however, is a strong flyer and has a formidable defense. And though admirably cooperative and industrious, the ants do not exhibit the same degree of order and obvious hierarchy as the bees; their hidden architecture is far from geometric. The ant is also frequently a pest, and it may be destructive. Nor do we value their labor. One suspects that if it were not for Aesop and the Psalmist, the ants would be much less admired than they are. Because of where it lives, the ant is easily aligned with dark purposes. And color matters as well. Ants are black like the earth or red like blood; the honeybee is banded gold.

In contrast to the ants, and to borrow Swift's noble expression, the bee embodies sweetness and light. Gathering nectar, making honey, living in harmony, and taking no slaves, the bee is the beehive's smallest element and thus a synecdoche for social perfection. Of all nature's societies, the bee's home, the beehive, singularly embodies the Western fantasy of a just and happy order. Even an empty hive signifies this ideal. Here is part of Tolstoy's picture of Moscow abandoned in the face of Napoleon's armies:

> Meanwhile Moscow was empty. There were still people there, perhaps a fiftieth part of the population had remained, but it was empty: empty as a queenless, dying hive is empty.
>
> In a queenless hive there is no longer any life, though to a superficial glance it seems as much alive as other hives.
>
> The bees hover about a queenless hive in the heat of the midday sun as buoyantly as they do over living hives; they fly in and out of it in the same way, and from a distance it smells of honey. But one has only to examine it carefully to realize that there is no life in the hive. . . .
>
> The beekeeper opens the upper compartment and examines the top of the hive. Instead of serried rows of bees sealing up every gap in the combs and keeping the brood warm, he sees the artful, complex structure of the combs, but no longer in their pristine state. All is neglected and befouled. . . .
>
> So was Moscow empty when Napoleon, weary, uneasy, and morose, paced back and forth by the Kamerkollezhshky Rampart.
>
> (1048–49)

No other insect has been as acutely observed as the bee. Nearly every aspect of its life has been explored by the poets. For instance, literature distinguishes between four types of bee swarms, which may be arranged from least to most organizationally intense: (1) the loose and methodical swarm that collects nectar; (2) the bees that issue from the hive in defense; (3) the cloud of males who accompany the queen on her nuptial flight; and (4) the swarming that announces a new hive's founding. All but the third type of swarm were understood by the ancients and became conventional. For the image of the queen pursued and mobbed by drones, it is not until Michelet's poetic exegesis that she truly receives her due. In poetry, as far as I know, only the speaker of Sylvia Plath's bee poems dares ascend as a new queen: "Now she is flying / More terrible than she ever was, red / Scar in the sky, red comet / Over the engine that killed her — / The mausoleum, the wax house."[26]

Sometimes the anthill and the beehive are interchangeable, but as a rule they are opposed images: the heap and the hive. Nowhere is this antithesis more finely expressed than in the *Aeneid*.[27] We have already studied its picture of Carthage as a beehive, that supreme object of Aeneas's longing. Virgil emphasizes both the power of the city's image and his hero's desire for it by making a single line of the following: at the sight of Carthage's walls, wandering Aeneas cries, *o fortunati, quorim iam moenia surgunt*, "Happy they whose walls already rise" (1.437). In book 4, Virgil shows us the beehive's antithesis, Trojan ants preparing to leave this once happy city, aggressively provisioning themselves with its spoils:

> Then, indeed, the Teucrians fall to and all along the shore launch their tall ships. The keels, well-pitched, are set afloat; the sailors, eager for flight, bring from the woods leafy boughs for oars and logs unhewn. One could see them moving away and streaming forth from all the city. Even as when ants, mindful of winter, plunder a huge heap of corn and store it in their home; over the plain moves a black column, and through the grass they carry the spoil on a narrow track; some strain with their shoulders and heave on the huge grains, some close up the ranks and rebuke delay; all the path is aglow with work. What feelings were thine, Dido, at such a sight! Or what sighs didst thou utter, viewing from the top of the fortress the beach aglow far and near, and seeing before thy eyes the whole main astir with loud cries! (423)

The image of Carthage as a beehive belongs to both the poet and to Aeneas. We take in the city from a stationary position and through a single pair of eyes. Like a honeybee, this simile is focused on the hive, its energy is centripetal. Spatially, we move inward from Carthage's walls; historically, we imagine its development from a past of "mere huts" to its promise as a capitol of arts and laws. This visual frame is lit by the light of "early summer"; the manifold actions it contains are unified. These meanings derive from, contribute to, and move toward Carthage and its civilized future. As far as is possible in language, Virgil mimics his natural model.

His ant simile, however, is entirely the speaker's. We are not given a particular place to stand; we do not look through Dido's eyes; for the moment, her perceptions and feelings are to be surmised. Freed from the restrictions imposed by a single perspective, Virgil answers our focused experience of the city-as-beehive with its opposite. This picture imitates the action of swarming, gathering ants as they flee a dissolving center.

Nonetheless, this image of Trojan ants is a version of the Hive tableau, and it functions accordingly. Within an axial and bipolar space, details are accumulated in preparation for metaphor. But while the beehive simile works in toward the city, this one moves out toward the Trojan ships. In the place of bees "lead[ing] forth the full-grown young of their race" and "strain[ing] their cells to bursting with sweet nectar," Virgil shows us swarming ants, "mindful of winter," who bear the future away from the city. There is little variety to the Trojans' labor; "eager for flight," their goals are immediate. Virgil paints them as "a black column . . . carry[ing] the spoil on a narrow track."

This picture of the Trojans as ants is the public analog to Aeneas's private betrayal of Dido; we are supposed to judge the Trojans' actions and find them immoral. Whatever the cultural heights their descendants may reach, at this moment and as compared with the Carthaginians, these people "bringing from the woods leafy boughs for oars and logs unhewn," hurriedly loading their ships, are opportunistic, inhospitable, barbaric.

To this day ants are frequently used to signify these negative qualities, serving writers as a locus for ethical judgment. For example, when Elizabeth Becker, author of *When the War Was Over: Cambodia's Revolution and the Voices of Its People*, needs to depict the Khmer Rouge's unconscionably brutal policies, she chooses the image of ants. Significantly, she does not have to invent this verbal picture, nor must she recover it from either nature or poetry — all three procedures and sources might weaken her historical argument. She finds what she needs in a description of Jayavarman VII by the distinguished historian, George Coedès. According to him, Jayavarman VII was a "megalomaniac whose foolish prodigality was one of the causes of the decadence of his country. One must visualize the armies of carriers, slaving on the slopes, of porters dragging those enormous blocks of sandstone, of masons fitting the stones together, of the sculptors and decorators, these human ants, not inspired by a collective faith . . . but recruited by conscription to erect mausoleums for the glory of their princes."[28]

Dissatisfied with the theory that Cambodia's modern suffering resulted from imported Marxism, Becker wants a more complicated and, if possible, a native origin for Pol Pot and his bloody revolution. In this regard Coedès is her guide, her Virgil. She sees his ant simile for what it is, a way of seeing that is both a tool for reasoning and an instrument that can evoke a specific moral response. She properly names it a *vivant tableau*, deploying it as a historical and stylistic precedent. This is to say that she wields this version of the Hive as both argument and ornament, and in such a way as to demonstrate what rhetors call *retractatio*, the purposeful and visible reworking of an inherited form: "Seven centuries later the Khmer Rouge would recreate the same *tableau vivant*, working the people like ants under the direction of Angka to build modern monuments to their rule of Cambodia. Under the Khmer Rouge, laborers would once again be housed in 'work camps' and given meager food rations. They would be forced to build an ill-conceived irrigation system meant to propel Cambodia into a rich future by copying the methods of the past" (201). Like Virgil, Coedès and Becker sense that the ant heap — or in this instance, and more accurately, the anthill — uniquely signifies a dark and inhuman cooperative. But our picture of the city is more complicated than Rome's. In contrast to Virgil's ants, who under divine orders take from one city so that they may found their own — one so great that any action is justified — these Cambodian "ants" labor to raise bad cities for bad men. However ambivalent Virgil may be about Aeneas, his people, and their conduct, their future is as admirable as it is inevitable. They will lay the cornerstone of Rome, the eternal city and epicenter of civilization.

In no respect may either Coedès's or Becker's laboring heap be construed as happy. These civilizations and their capitols are the produce of bad actions — they do not belong to, much less compensate, the people who suffer to raise them. History and the imagination are littered with the ruins of such designs, which we may speak of as *negative* cities: dystopias.

Though the dystopia as I conceive it has one beginning in Virgil's Tartarus, the underworld prison that holds the titans, it is more deeply and obviously rooted in the Christian view of this world as the opposite of the soon-to-come Heavenly Jerusalem. It is not until the Renaissance, however, that we see the golden hive so clearly inverted. Furthermore, Coedès's and Becker's pictures have a different focus from their classical forebears. By this I mean that in no uncertain terms are we to identify with these "human ants." Furthermore, because they work against their will and for ends that will only consume them, we are to separate these ants from their heap. Another instance from Becker will help to clarify this.

When expressing the alienation and suffering of a single Cambodian woman named Hout Bophana, Becker employs a version of the Hive tableau whose logic we have studied in Lewis Thomas. The following analogy complements and completes the moral conclusions suggested by Becker's earlier insect simile. Separated from her husband and exiled to a "cooperative" (i.e., a labor camp), Bophana "became one of the stooped antlike figures dotting the landscape that dry season, one of the women picking up stones and carrying them in baskets to the damsite or shoveling earth and balancing baskets of dirt across her shoulders" (231). Beyond echoing passages from Thomas Hardy's *Tess*, this view of one Cambodian woman, a victim of the Khmer Rouge, reduced to "one of the stooped antlike figures dotting the landscape," is a detail from Becker's original picture. As such, this image of a human being as one "antlike figure" clarifies my earlier point that in some modern versions of the Hive tableau it is the individual who is the object of vivid figuration and not the collective. However, this is not to say that the collective, the hive or swarm, is not vitally present in this sort of tableau. Indeed, though we do not see it, we nonetheless sense the Khmer Rouge as a force, an abstract system that regards and hence treats human beings as insignificant units, insects. And as will become clear, as we follow the Hive tableau through time and approach our own moment, the picture of the individual as a solitary insect beset by the ideological force of the collective becomes more and more common.

Much of the latter part of this book will explain how the classical picture of the just, orderly, and stable society is inverted and then adapted for imaging the alienated human being. This means that, although its structure and general sense derives from the biological facts of seeing, the Hive is not immutable. Its visual core is a flexible armature around which a range of shapes may be formed. As I shall argue starting in chapter 1, the largest part of which treats Homer's use of the swarm and Virgil's domestication of it, for all of its long history the Hive has been the object of vigorous reinterpretation. Each age tends to favor a particular idea of the Hive, but any such emphasis does not negate nor undo earlier and often contradictory formulations. Accordingly, I shall approach the Hive as a habitual symbolic complex: an accumulation of mutually defining, interrelated models that determines how we understand and use the image of the beehive as well as the field of possibilities that constitute the insect analogy. Hence, although I have and shall continue to speak of it as a "form," I do not regard the Hive as such in the conventional sense. Because it is grounded in everyday seeing, and is therefore in one way or another intuited by each person during his or her discovery of the world, we cannot properly say that the Hive was ever invented. Nor may we hold it to be the product of any one historical moment, civilization, or literature, because it has been made and remade by so many. There is even evidence that higher primates grasp elements of the logic that we have been discussing.[29] The Hive is shared aesthetic and cognitive property, an analogy whose evolution suggests that its meanings — and indeed some aspects of visual processing — are cumulative, inflected, and defined by the past.

Because the Hive develops over time and, until recently, entirely in the light cast by a conversation of exemplary models (Homer, Virgil, Dante, Milton), I shall approach this convention as a structure of related possibilities so pervasive that to some extent a writer's compositional process and intentions may be reconstructed through his or her particular formulation of it. It is in this sense that this argument is a study of allusion. But as I approach our moment, I shall need to be increasingly flexible about what I mean by allusion, for the democratization of education and the decline of classicism and the rhetorical tradition change the nature and hence the rules of literary reworking.

Especially in the twentieth century, we need not concern ourselves overmuch with marking out any particular writer's or paradigm's influence, unless it is signaled explicitly, because together our object's recent, gradual, but increasing dissociation from literary models and its literalization through scientific analogies make the Hive at once more pervasive, habitual, and evasive of formal analysis than is the case with earlier versions. Nevertheless, and as I have already mentioned in the preface, for the sake of clarity I will tend to speak of contemporary writers as directly engaging with one or more canonical writers and their paradigms. For whether or not a writer is consciously aware that he or she is reworking an inherited form is not the issue. Nor, as I have established above, is it essential that the reworked image be of a particular type of insect or insect collective. My object of scrutiny is, rather, the insect analogy as it involves and has been shaped by a tradition of verbal picturing. Accordingly, upon occasion I will read a modern formulation through the patterns of the past, even when a classical structure is camouflaged or pointedly avoided. My motive in such cases is to test one of this study's fundamental propositions: namely, that the presence of the past subtends and thus may help us to account for artistic choices and ways of thinking that would otherwise remain mysterious.

I

Hiving the Dark Swarm

Let us begin at the beginning, — and that, as everybody knows, is Homer. He is, indeed, so much at the beginning for that very reason (if even there were no other) he is, and will be, supremely interesting.
    Thomas De Quincey, "A Brief Appraisal of the Greek Literature"

The true hero, the true subject, the center of the Iliad is force. Force employed by man, force that enslaves man, force before which man's flesh shrinks away.
    Simone Weil, The Iliad, or The Poem of Force

The transplanted insect could not be expected to furnish its biographer with other than fragmentary evidence, very weak in those biological details which form the principal charm of entomology. To study the habits of insects one must observe them long and closely on their native heath, so to speak, in the place where their instincts have full and natural play.
    J. Henri Fabre, The Life of the Caterpillar

The Hive's Lost Dimension

If we forget what modern science has taught us, we may assume that Virgil saw the insect societies much as we do — specifically, that the beehive is brighter and better organized than the ant heap. Indeed, what could be more commonsensical and aesthetically necessary than his division of human cooperation into the images of the golden hive and the dark swarm? Given Rome's long history of contact with alien peoples and Virgil's considerable influence, we should expect Western literature to be filled with contending images of beehives and ant heaps, utopian and dystopian cities. But this is not the case.

With no significant exceptions, from Virgil through the Renaissance the beehive is used to picture the city. Hence, even when details suggest dissonance between the actual and the ideal, a poem's present and an inherited picture, we are supposed to see the beehive city as good. We are to note and to value the antique theory of social organization that the Hive uniquely embodies. This is to say that, in order to understand instances of the classical and classically influenced Hive, we must recover an older sense of allegory. Prior to the sweeping and uncompromising metaphors of modern science (powers of the imagination birthed by a new set of mental and material instruments), the insect analogy served poets and thinkers richly and well. Even Milton, who is close enough to us to imagine the universe as if through a telescope, complicates instead of rejects the ancients' ideal model, its satisfaction with philosophical process, and its poetic theory of nature.

In the days before Jan Swammerdam — the sixteenth-century student of the microscopic realm whom Michelet titles the "martyr of patience"[1] — the symbolic relationship between human beings and nature was such that any comparison between city and hive, human being and insect, was made and received without the suggestion of biological synonymy, much less the sociological identity that is now generally accepted as truth. But we will never entirely outgrow our forebears' thoughts, the ever-accumulating presence of the past. Kenneth Burke likens one's experience of the history of ideas to joining a dinner party long after it has begun, a gathering that we have no choice but to leave early. Similarly, in the first sentence of *The Sleepwalkers*, Arthur Koestler sums up what he has learned from his survey of Western cosmology: "We can add to our knowledge, but we cannot subtract from it." Indeed, so weighty are the old ways of seeing and thinking that it is not until the nineteenth century that the picture of the anthill (or, as in the instance below, a picture of a termite nest) begins to express a new definition of nature and humanity's position within it, one that flows from the hybridization of old and new ideas of the world. In a tableau of St. Ogg's, George Eliot mixes the antique and the new, the Hive's poetic inheritance and its scientific possibilities:

> In order to see Mr and Mrs Glegg at home, we must enter the town of St Ogg's—that venerable town with the red-fluted roofs and the broad warehouse gables, where the black ships unlade themselves of their burthens from the far north, and carry away, in exchange, the precious inland products, the well-crushed cheese and the soft fleeces, which my refined readers have doubtless become acquainted with through the medium of the best classic pastorals.
>
> It is one of those old, old towns, which impress one as a continuation and outgrowth of nature as much as the nests of the bower birds or the winding galleries of the white ants: a town which carries the traces of its long growth and history, like a millennial tree, and has sprung up and developed in the same spot between the river and the low hill from the time when the Roman legions turned their back on it from the camp on the hill-side, and the long-haired sea-kings came up the river and looked with fierce eager eyes at the fatness of the land.[2]

This passage illustrates the modern double-mindedness about natural symbols in general and the Hive in particular. In the first paragraph, because she speaks of "classic pastorals," we know that Eliot has in mind the old conventions. Because her readers are "refined" (i.e., familiar with the classics), Eliot assumes that they know this bucolic region's "precious inland products." Of course, she means her "cheese" and "fleeces" literally. (In Eliot's time, cheese and wool — and *lenses* — were among Holland's primary exports: an allusion highly appropriate for this picture of a town's miniaturization.) But these objects also signify the ancient models, among which is numbered the image of the city as a beehive.

Eliot knows the classical Hive, but she also wields a new sense of the insect analogy: one that naturalizes — or, more accurately, *biologizes* — human cooperation. I think this is why she reserves "the winding galleries of the white ants" for her second, chronologically later, paragraph.

Here she leaves behind the literary "inland" and its poetic obligations; she turns outward, to nonpoetic nature, the nature of modern science. Rather than occupy her white ants with their traditional office of poetic allusion, she uses them to introduce the natural history of St. Ogg's. Here the insect analogy, which for so long had been understood and treated by poets as a grand and elevating ornament, is subdued, deployed as one of several metaphors that together merge the human and animal realms. History is thereby rooted in familiar soil. By orienting her Hive toward nature instead of poetry, Eliot is able to mesh the traditional view from above with the modern insights of science. Eliot's metaphor asks us to consider human and insect as equivalent, each a "continuation and outgrowth of nature."

We are now entirely used to this sort of analogy, one that accepts a prescientific form as a habit, uses it as an armature for invention. By this I mean that the scientific metaphor tends to repress its poetic origins and thus redirects poetic invention. The inherited, original form is treated abstractly: even though we see through it, we do not ordinarily think of it as a designed structure. Thomas's orbital view of human expansion is an excellent example. In this instance, the Hive's poetic structure subtends and furthers the evocation of new feelings and of a seemingly objective insight into biological process. Because it stands closer to the origin of the modern scientific outlook, Eliot's metaphor is less extreme (i.e., biologically presumptive) than Thomas's. Nonetheless, both metaphors use the past similarly and assert the same sort of truth: both assume that without science the visual analogy between insects and man is superficial and misleading, that science pierces the surface of creation to reveal the verity of hidden connections.

In *The Insect*, Jules Michelet pursues these connections, clarifies what the relationship between surface and depth means to the scientifically empowered, modern outlook. His mechanism for piercing the surface is the microscope:

> The most attractive forms are living forms. Take a drop of blood, and submit it to the microscope. This drop, as it spreads, rewards you with a delightful arborescence, — with the delicacy and lightness of certain winter trees, when revealed in their actual figure, and no longer encumbered with leaves.

> Thus, Nature's infinite potency of beauty is not limited to the sur-

face, as antiquity supposed. It does not trouble itself about human eyesight, but labours for its own behoof, and on its own work. From the surface to the interior, it frequently increases in beauty as in depth. It invests with surpassing loveliness things which are absolutely hidden, and which death alone can unveil. Sometimes, as if to contradict and confound our ideas, it clothes in ravishing forms the organs which, from our point of view, accomplish the vilest functions. I am thinking of the exquisite beauty and delicate tenderness of that coral-tree which incessantly pours out the chyle of our intestines. (203–4)

Like Thomas and Eliot, Michelet intends to be scandalous. Because nature's beauties and purposes are her own, we must be shaken from the slumber of obvious resemblances and conventional seeing: in the body's hidden depths, for instance, Michelet discovers a digestive organ that has the appearance of "coral-tree." More significant to us is how he speaks of the surface. Through the microscope's agency, humanity's traditional sense of order and definitions of beauty are shown to be superficial, outmoded, inaccurate. This passage suggests that a poetry adequate to the reality of nature, one that is sensitive to the "surpassing loveliness [of] things which are absolutely hidden," must eschew the temptations of the surface, free itself from the dominion of inherited forms and their conventional ways of seeing.

Michelet's poetic style obscures, if not denies, his scientific program and its new definition of the natural symbol. This program and definition are clearer in Eliot's passage. Here, compared with its poetic ancestor, Eliot's scientific metaphor is leaner, more dependent upon and highly inflected by context. Unlike entirely literary insects, her termites do not strongly assert figural integrity — which is to say that Eliot subordinates artifice to ideas. And to any such shift in emphasis there are cost and compensation: intellectually potent though it may be, the scientific metaphor is rarely as beautiful and in no way as aesthetically generative as what it presumes to replace. In compensation, however, the new metaphor confirms a novel world picture, one that makes humans a part of nature and offers us what seems to be the power to view things directly. Once cut off from the ocean of expressive language and the obligations of the past, many old poetic resemblances and their ornaments simply pass away. But some — if they are necessary and strong like the Hive — survive their translation.

One should not then too energetically adhere to the commonplace that modern science and its outlook (its contentious mix of Cartesian psychology and Romantic assumptions) are poetry's negation and cure. For instance, is Darwinism truly the enemy of the neoplatonic metaphor for the universe, the Great Chain of Being? Or is Darwinism this metaphor's restorer, its preserver? The same point from a slightly different angle: When stated extremely, the scientific outlook holds that nature and art are distinct and that the latter is inferior to the former. Hence, nature cannot be improved by art, and aesthetic excellence is proportional to its fidelity to nature. How Platonic these principles seem if for "nature" we substitute the "world of forms." When he chides artists for not going straight to nature — specifically, to the insects — for inspiration, Michelet epitomizes the Romantic idea that nature is the supreme artist: "Frankly, is there aught approaching such a degree of excellence in our human arts? How great the necessity that, in their apparently fatigued and languid condition, that they should gain life and strength from these living sources! In general, instead of going straight to Nature, to the inexhaustible fountain of beauty and invention, they have solicited help from the erudition, the history, and the antiquity of man" (203). Michelet believes that any artist who *without the aid of science* "solicit[s] help from the erudition, the history, and the antiquity of man" is no artist at all — but blind to beauty, a mere copyist: "We have copied ancient jewels; sometimes those of barbarous peoples which first procured them from our own merchants. We have copied the old robes and the stuffs of our ancestors. We have copied, especially, the painted-glass windows of Gothic architecture, whose colours and forms have been selected haphazard, and transported to objects utterly discordant and unsuitable, — as, for instance, to shawls" (205). In order to regard properly even the modest beauties of human art, Michelet would have us study nature. His example merges Gothic stained glass and the iridescence of beetles. Again, his instrument is the microscope:

If we were desirous of comprehending and rehabilitating these ancient windows, we might have taken a lesson from the enamels of certain scarabaei. Seen beneath the microscope, they present very analogous effects, simply because they possess the same elements of beauty. The thirteenth century glass-windows (you may see them at Bourges, and especially in the museum of that city) were double. The light therefore remained in them, did not pass through them, gave them the magical effects of precious stones. And of a similar character are those insect wings composed of numerous leaves, between which you may detect, with the microscope, a network of mysterious hieroglyphics. (205)

Michelet's "mysterious hieroglyphics" are inspired by his nation's and era's fascination with Egypt, but the idea of a natural language alludes to a commonplace far older than Rousseau: nature is a book. And it is from this book's chapter on the insects that we are to "take a lesson." However, it seems that the Book of Nature's letters, like those in the more recent, affordable editions of the Oxford English Dictionary, have become miniaturized.

What I am saying is not new, but it is important enough for me to struggle with its restatement through an example. When Virgil wrote about bees, the book of nature could be read with the unaided eye. Virgil had little science as we now know it. He made do with the surface of things and thought his forebears wiser than he. Nowhere in the antique world could be found Blake's "dark satanic mills." In no way was Virgil anxious about the implications of mechanical reproduction; he was, therefore, comfortable with and happy to oblige exactly what Michelet opposes and would have modern science replace: the insect as a human creation. This is to say that, in addition to seeing bees as creatures in themselves and sensing their symbolic possibilities, Virgil recognized them as an *artifact* — a specific and palpable formal achievement — that before all others belonged to Homer. And it is the insect's antique, prescientific dimension that we must, to use Michelet's word, "rehabilitate" and keep always in our thoughts if we are to understand why, in order to have his own bees for his own uses, Virgil must so vigorously contend with Homer. Virgil's task is daunting. And his first challenge is that Homer's bees are wild: they cannot simply be lifted from the *Iliad* to signify the city, which to a Roman audience *is* civilization. Virgil discovers his Hive gradually, a process that begins with the swarm and its domestication.

That Homer and Virgil were keen observers of nature should not be disputed. But we need to remind ourselves that until Romanticism nature (our nature, anyway) was neither the primary object of artistic imitation nor the highest source of inspiration. During the rule of rhetoric, one did not either approach nature unaided or wish to see her un-adorned. The precedent served as guide and was itself an object of ven-eration. In a manner of speaking, under the old system a worthy model *was* nature. The flowers of one's poetry had to be won from the soil of earlier verse.

To explicate the Hive's evolution during its first two thousand years, I must, therefore, approach it rhetorically, as an imitation of nature that was itself imitated and complicated over time. Thus, in this chapter and the next I will present the inherited model as a template for invention and closely examine the technology of allusion proper to it. But I must also allow for and be equally sensitive to visible as well as immanent structure, for sometimes it is only when reworked by a later poet that an original form's implications become clear. And finally I will attempt to show how much may be gained by seriously considering the novelty that naturally accompanies the committed and explicit reworking of lit-erary form.

Domesticating the Swarm

Our story begins where it should: not only with Homer but also with the *Iliad*'s first extended simile.[3] In book 2, as translated by Richmond Lattimore, Nestor has just spoken to the council of Greek royalty, and they are now resolved to marshal the Achaian armies:

So he spoke and led the way departing from the council,
and the rest rose to their feet, the sceptred kings, obeying
the shepherd of the people, and the army thronged behind them.
Like the swarms of clustering bees that issue forever
in fresh bursts from the hollow stone, and hang like
bunched grapes as they hover beneath the flowers in springtime
fluttering in swarms together this way and that way,
so the many nations of men from the ships and the shelters
along the front of the deep sea beach marched in order
by companies to the assembly, and Rumour walked blazing among
    them,
Zeus' messenger to hasten them along. Thus they were assembled
and the place of their assembly was shaken, and the earth groaned
as the people took their positions and there was tumult.
(84–96)

I must first address Homer's decision to figure the Greeks as bees rather than ants, a discussion that will introduce the related and even more significant topic of why he chooses the swarm rather than the hive. Homer never pictures an individual as an insect. The simile just quoted represents Homer's practice. In his poetry insects are exclusively used to figure groups and collective action; these insects are always winged, and it is winged things that evoke the fugitive soul.

Homer was not sentimental about war. He regarded it as natural to our kind, a contest that brought out the best in a man. In his poems the only life that matters is this one; after death the soul languishes forever in darkness. And it is death's finality that lends terrible beauty to Homer's many descriptions of slaughter. Trojan and Achaian alike, hundreds and perhaps thousands of them, many young and beautiful, many with wives and children, are "unstrung," struck down in battle. Imagine the action thus: Gods armed and descending into the dust of our world, the sound of bronze on bronze and flesh, the cries of captains and dying men. With the body's last breath each smitten man's soul flies from his body and the sun. No wonder, then, Homer's affection for the winged swarm.

To my way of thinking, the ants' dark coloring, their warlike nature, and their proximity to the earth fit an army better than this gentle image of "clustering bees . . . hang[ing] like bunched grapes as they hover beneath the flowers in springtime." But to Homer these warriors are heroes; their lives and their deaths are proportionally great. Illuminated by a sun younger than ours, even Paris, vain and weak, is superior to us who live in this age of iron. Homer's universe is uncompromisingly hierarchical — by our reckoning, primitive. To him there is no ambiguity that light is better than darkness, that the past exceeds the present, that the higher is superior to the lower. It would not do, then, for Homer to speak of heroes, his listeners' ancestors, as scrambling creatures whose nature it is to live beneath the earth.

I now turn to the choice of swarm by comparing Homer's and Virgil's insect metaphors. Reserving for the moment what we have already established, there are, I think, three reasons why Homer chose to figure his Greeks as "fluttering in swarms" instead of as Virgil describes his Carthaginians, in concert joyfully raising their walls and young. First, these Greeks have no city — they are living on a rocky beach and sleeping in and around their rotting ships. They are Troy's antithesis, a force bent on its destruction.[4]

Second, in comparison with Virgil's Carthage, whose cultural diversity is bounded by a cosmopolitan ideal of the city, Homer's Achaian host is a horde, a contentious assemblage of clans. These warriors hail from disparate parts of what cannot in any way be described as either a nation or an empire. And even though we may say that they are joined here to sack Troy, I would argue that the Greeks enjoy no single goal. These men are kings and followers of princes; their actions are consonant with a hierarchy based upon obligations to a hereditary chief.

Third, Homer's Greeks do not fight like Romans. For instance, as Homer means it, *stratoi* (armies) have little or nothing to do with a well-disciplined force for which patriotism is the highest motive. Homer's prized subject is neither the action of groups nor the affirmation of grand causes realized collectively; his focus, the contest of individual actors. Thus, like his heroes' style of war, his symbols for the collective preserve and communicate an ancient and even primitive psychology.

The military historian John Keegan classifies Homeric warfare as tribal.[5] According to his research, it was not until the sixth century B.C. that the Greek city-states (a new political organization that marks the emergence of an equally novel subjectivity) began to practice a "new form of warfare" — one based upon the phalanx and which anticipates fundamental aspects of the Roman art of war. In contrast to tribal, or "traditional," warfare, which was characterized by "tentativeness, preference for fights at a distance, reliance on missiles and reluctance to close to arm's length until victory looked assured," phalanx warfare was brief, localized, and "turned on the function of battle as a decisive act . . . and dedicated to securing victory . . . in a single test of [massed] skill and courage." Keegan observes that "phalanx warfare was won not by encouragement by example [as in the *Iliad*] but by the united courage of equals in a terrifying, short-lived clash of bodies and weapons at the closest range." In sum, the disciplined military unit — the phalanx, legion, and modern infantry unit — more strongly recalls the behavior and appearance of ants than bees.

Just as Homer's representations of warfare are primitive, tribal, so too are his other symbols for social organization. For instance, there is no evidence in his poetry that he understood the city as a *polis*, as the center and defining principle of what it was to be human. There are several cities in the *Iliad*: the Olympian home of the gods; the two allegorical human cities that Hephaistos makes part of Achilles's shield; those occasionally named by the longing, homeless Greeks; and Troy. Of these, Troy is the one that matters. Yet Homer figures it with only simple epithets such as "strong-walled" or "well-founded." Even when he alludes to it as a locus of social order, he describes it as "Priam's city." In Homer's universe, political power and the hierarchy that sustains it are organized around a person, not an abstraction embodied through masonry. Accordingly, I think that the city's (by Homeric standards) minimal figuration in the *Iliad* suggests that the Hive as we now understand it — the proper natural symbol for the city — was simply not available to Homer.

Nonetheless, Homer's bee simile is marvelously realized: it treats the crowd as *the* natural unit of human cooperation and uses the view-from-above to decisively link the human social order with the image of the social insect. This means that if Virgil is to make Homer's bees his own, he cannot simply ignore his model's archaic psychology. Such an act would violate the custom of *retractatio*, the rhetorical procedure of reworking a model so as to venerate and surpass it.[6] And also, at a more practical level, since Homer had already worked out three of the four ways to figure the human collective, ignoring him would restrict Virgil's poetic options.

Until the invention and dissemination of technological systems (whose attendant verbal forms are not yet entirely separable from their prescientific analogs) poets have had available four classes of symbols for groups, each of which represents a different degree or intensity of social organization. Here they are arranged according to the old and omnipresent logic (from the least to the most organized, from the level of matter to that of intelligence): the natural force (fire, flood, storm), the herd, the swarm, and the hive. Tellingly, Homer figures human sociality and action with metaphors from the first three classes, but to speak of a group or city as an insect *society* does not occur to him. Nowhere in the Homeric corpus is a city pictured as an anthill or a beehive. In fact, it is not until around the time of Plato's *Republic* that we begin to see the peculiar admiration for the insect society that marks Western philosophy and poetry to this day. Thus, because Virgil must have both the crowd *and* Homer, his act of invention must preserve and yet modify so as to extend the psychology and the sense of his master's simile. The result: the Hive's visual structure is clarified and complicated, its poetic value increased.

To clarify the monumentality of Virgil's task, as well as how he goes about it, I will return to Homer's swarm and discuss how it works. More than just a pretty picture, it bridges two distinct oral episodes. This simile moves us precisely from a mode of oral to visual imitation, from one scale and degree of social organization to another. It foreshadows what the Great Council will accomplish and communicates a sense of *progressive* social organization — a quality that agrees with Virgil.

Like the story in which it appears, Homer's simile begins *in media res*; it is an instrument that defines and places us vis-à-vis the action. We begin by "rising" from an intimate position appropriate for overhearing the council proceedings to one that allows us to see the army "throng[ing]" behind their leaders. We then conceive their collective action as one of transformation from "fluttering . . . swarms" into "many nations of men . . . march[ing] in order by companies." In this narrow compass we have moved from a stage, and a style, fit for the drama of the spoken word to one that more fully engages the visual imagination. The language of the king's council is worldly, political, necessarily oratorical, created to delight the ear. The language of line 87 announces a mode appropriate for a more purely visual imitation.

Lines 87–93 do not mention smells, sounds, or textures — a restriction of sensory data that reinforces our spatial separation from the Greek host. And by examining a translation other than Lattimore's, we may quickly confirm that this passage's structure (its elements' particular order and spatial relationships) and, hence, its functions (moving us from oral to visual imitation and the enforcement of physical separation) are not Lattimore's invention. Here is A. T. Murray's prose rendering: "He spake and led the way forth from the council, and the other sceptred kings rose up thereat and obeyed the shepherd of the host; and the people the while were hastening on. Even as the tribes of thronging bees go forth from some hollow rock, ever coming on afresh, and in cluster over the flowers of spring fly in throngs, some here, some there; even so from the ships and huts before the low sea-beach marched forth in companies their many tribes to the place of gathering. And in their midst blazed forth Rumour, messenger of Zeus, urging them to go; and they were gathered" (vol. 1, 57).[7] As in Lattimore, the Murray translation moves us from speech to seeing, from the ground upward to a seat that enables us to see the Greek host as a whole. While this picture gives us a conventional perspective on war, that we actively construct it suggests that it is much more than an emblem.

This tableau's sense derives as much from the eye's limitations as from its powers. Our view of the gathering armies is restricted but not static. This is not an image of the world as a whole, as is the case with the Shield of Achilles. Rather we see a particular army gathering on a particular beach. Like the men they figure, these bees are fleeting, mortal, passing from one state to another. For only a moment do these swarms enjoy peace and plenty. And the gentle near-whimsicality of their description graphically contrasts with the next image, that of the Achaians marching to the Great Council, a crucial move forward to greater slaughter.

What makes this contrast, contest, and marriage between the image of bees working the flowers of spring and that of men going to their doom even more chilling is the sudden appearance of Rumor. This deity simultaneously signifies divine will and fate, as well as externalizing a shared psychology of apprehension and curiosity among the heroes. Furthermore, because it restores to us a sense of the Greeks' humanity, Rumor's appearance indicates that the simile's visual center has peaked. Thus, our elevated position vis-à-vis the action begins to shift downward in preparation for the next oratorical situation.

Like human cooperation, this simile is at tension with itself. Homer has nobly formulated a way of picturing human cooperation that fore-grounds its either/or, life/death polarities. He has also given the audience a crucial role in the poetic process. By this I mean that even here, where for the first time in our tradition we see human beings as insects, we are actively engaged in their figuration as such. Because this simile imitates, builds upon, and intensifies a natural visio-conceptual experience, it is we, not the gods, who gain knowledge and power by dehumanizing our own kind. Even at the moment of its poetic conception, the Hive tableau is the locus of an ethical dilemma, one that no later formulation is able to entirely resolve. This structure gives us a taste of godlike vision, but the price is the individual's supreme diminishment. Because of its creator's identity and the quality of its execution, this shape establishes a tradition of seeing and thinking about people as insects. In opposition to his poem's model of heroic action, Homer's own bee simile authorizes an appetite for the human subject's submission to the collective principle.

Like its symbols for the collective, the epic frame remains true to its primitive origins. Its spirit is incompatible with peace and a progressive view of both history and cooperation. But to Virgil the future-oriented plan is everything; submission to authority is the foundation of peace and plenty. Perhaps this is why Virgil's domestication of the Homeric swarm begins down on the farm, the locus of planned and practical becoming and the seat of Roman virtue, and not before the walls of a besieged city. He approaches the city-as-hive by way of its poetic opposite, the hive-as-city. In *Georgic* 4 the insect collective appears not once but in four distinct versions.

This series' first three elements communicate how Virgil wrests the Hive from Homer but cannot resolve the problem of peace. Virgil offers the peaceful hive as the third term in a progressive dialectic from wild nature to peaceful culture. However, the universe of the *Georgics* is agricultural. All things and all creatures on a farm share a purpose, and their being leads them toward harvest. And harvest assumes dominance and hierarchy. To complicate matters, in some respects Virgil intends the poem as an allegory of Roman history and, most importantly, an exploration and justification of "official" Roman psychology. In other words, the poem's deeper purpose is to reconcile the motives and practices of Imperium with those proper to the rustic life, thereby naturalizing and sanctifying Roman rule. This means that Virgil's allegory itself overrules the idea that the peaceful hive may serve as a terminus for human social evolution. In an attempt to resolve the paradox of agricultural (Imperial) peace, Virgil concludes the poem with two pictures of *bugonia*, the process by which bees are spontaneously generated from the rotten flesh of sacrificial animals. The first, a secular attempt, produces a swarm that is lost. The second, through the influence of the gods, is successful and closes the story of the bees with an allusion to Homer and a visual assertion that this new race of Roman bees is superior.

I will treat the *Georgics* as preparation for the *Aeneid*. Because its frame is agricultural, we may say that its purpose is to rework and domesticate inherited models. Virgil, who possesses a sense of historical and political progress that his Greek models lack, must therefore deal with Hesiod's model of decline. Hesiod, whom Virgil himself draws upon in *Georgic* 1, expressed his retrograde historiography through the myth that human beings, who had once lived in a golden age of harmony and plenty, and having passed through the increasingly lower stages of silver and bronze, now struggle in an age of iron, a time of sin and strife.[8] Homer and Hesiod had no place in their poetry for and probably could not have imagined the psychology expressed in the following passage, which its translator L. P. Wilkinson describes as "the climax" of *Georgic* 1: "Gods of our fathers, Heroes of our land / And Romulus, and mother Vesta, guardian / Of Tuscan Tiber and Roman Palatine, / Do not prevent at least this youthful prince [Caesar] / From saving a world in ruins."[9] Here Virgil makes plain that Imperium equals peace. This is a cosmopolitan ideology that, much like Plato's ideal Republic, cannot accommodate the uncertainties of the crowd or of what a certain sort of poetry represents: undisciplined, irrationally generative energy.

Despite what I sense is some antipathy between Virgil's worldview and his master's, in Homer's swarm Virgil found inspiration and an essential poetic shape that he would make his favorite. Obviously he recognized Homer's greatness, but he also found his master's figures to be wild, uncivilized. His reworking of Homer's bees, then, would have to be substantial, beginning with clarification and culminating in a reorganization that would domesticate them for Roman use.

Virgil perceives that Homer's simile implies three distinct and separable cooperative modes. The first is natural (congruent with our observations of actual bees), and the last two are human, artificial: our war and our peace. Each of these states Virgil isolates, amplifies, and subjects to order. Significantly, he chooses to do so within the context of agriculture, the justification for which provides us with his definition of poetic invention. The following passage is from Fairclough's translation of *Georgic* 1: "Much service, too, does he who turns his plow and breaks crosswise through the ridges which he raised when he first cut the plain, ever at his post to discipline the ground, and give his orders to the fields" (87). Through the metaphor of replowing roughly broken soil, Virgil makes physical the classical world's sovereign method of poetic invention, *retractatio*, which means "to handle again, take in hand again, undertake anew." In this light Homer is both the "ground" and the "first [to] cut the plain." Virgil, then, is the second farmer, whose effort of "break[ing] crosswise through the ridges" renders the "service" of "disciplin[ing] the ground" and "giv[ing] his orders to the fields."

Georgic 4 begins in the natural mode of cooperation. Virgil's speaker shares with us advice about feeding bees and the best location for their hives. But when these bees are humanized, the poem takes a sudden turn. With battle imminent, the speaker's elegant, instructional voice shifts to a muscular style capable of replowing, one that is fit for controlling epic amplification. This region of the poem is Virgil's second mode, our first simile, a picture of warring bees:

But, if haply for battle they have gone forth — for oft-times strife with terrible turmoil hath fallen on two kings; and straight away you may presage from afar the fury of the crowd, and how their hearts thrill with war; for the warlike ring of the hoarse clarion stirs the loiterers, and a sound is heard that is like unto broken trumpet blasts. Then, all afire, they flock together: their wings flash, they whet their stings on their beaks and make ready their arms. Round their king, and even by his royal tent, they swarm in throngs, and with loud cries challenge the foe. Therefore they have found a clear spring day and open field, they sally forth from the gates. There is a clash; in high air arises a din; they are mangled and massed in one great ball, then tumble headlong: no thicker is hail from the sky, not so dense is the rain of acorns from the shaken oak. In the midst of the ranks the chiefs themselves, with resplendent wings, have mighty souls beating in tiny breasts, ever steadfast not to yield, until the victor's heavy hand has driven these or those to turn their backs in flight. These storms of passion, these conflicts so fierce, by the tossing of a little dust are quelled and laid to rest. (201, 203)

Because Virgil is a provincial whose region and patrimony have been newly Romanized, in contrast to the older pastoral condition evoked by allusion to Hesiod ("the rain of acorns from the shaken oak"), his nature is a scene of struggle and mastery — but not of the Homeric variety.

In this space even the bees think of the State. There is no question that the natural order (and by way of extension all regionally distinct peoples) is to be tamed and situated within one greater and more abstract. This simile's energy is as primitive as Virgil gets. It is focused on "the fury of the crowd," a cooperative mode that has no place in his ideal State. Clearly Virgil would have us see these bees as archaic warriors, who "round their king, and even by his royal tent [a temporary and rustic dwelling], they swarm in throngs."

I think it highly significant that Virgil has these miniature warriors bloodily engage "in high air." Notice that, although we are watching bees, we do not, as is our usual experience of how Virgil handles them, find prepared for us our familiar sovereign seat. We are placed *below* this crowd, a position that, however naturalistically plausible, functions as a means of distancing us from its "fury." Instead of describing these martial bees' deeds of valor in the detailed manner that he soon applies to his apicultural third term, the peaceful hive, Virgil presents them as a visually (and thus conceptually) mysterious whole. We see them in "high air . . . mingled and massed in one great ball," which "tumbles headlong." Especially since Virgil was a member of a society that regarded objects in the sky as portents and that feared the crowd's political force, it is telling that at this moment Virgil backs away from his efforts to psychologize. At work here is not so much a repression of Homer's example as a retreat from describing a subjectivity that Virgil does not wish to present as either natural or heroic. This is to say that, while he desires, needs, and after modification uses the structure and some of the themes of Homer's bee simile, Virgil does not find its psychology either agreeable with his cosmopolitan alignment or adequate to his poetic ambitions.

In theme and structure Virgil displays his fundamental belief that Imperium and progress are complementary. To him they are the necessary foundation for peace and the social perfection of humanity. Virgil's next and third picture of bees evidences this belief, represents both Virgil's ideal republic and a fully domesticated Homeric swarm:

> Come now, the qualities which Jove himself has given bees, I will unfold — even the reward, for which they followed the tuneful sounds and clashing bronzes of the Curetes, and fed the king of Heaven within the cave of Dicte. They alone have children in common, hold the dwellings of their city jointly, and pass their life under the majesty of law. They alone know a fatherland and fixed home, and in summer, mindful of the winter to come, spend toilsome days and garner their gains into a common store. For some watch over the gathering of food, and under fixed covenant labour in the fields; some within the confines of their homes, lay down the narcissus' tears and gluey gum from tree-bark as the first foundation of the comb, then hang aloft clinging wax; others lead out the full-grown young, the nation's hope; others pack purest honey and swell the cells with liquid nectar. To some it has fallen by lot to be sentries at the gates, and in turn they watch the rains and clouds of heaven, or take the loads of incomers, or in martial array drive the drones, a lazy herd, from the folds. All aglow is the work, and the fragrant honey is sweet with thyme.
> (207, 209)

Here Virgil definitively reverses Hesiod's model of decline, renames and recovers for his own uses the Grecian past that persists in his "Attic bees."

When viewed as a series, the poem's first three pictures of the bee image progress from nature to culture, from bloody past to Caesar's peace. Virgil's metropolitan bees do as they should: eject from their city the uncivilized (Homeric) swarm of lazy drones. And in keeping with his progressive historiography, Virgil would have us accept this considered and disciplinary action as an expression of natural law.

In a sense, then, this simile merges a post-Homeric fantasy of Troy with elements of the Achaian Great Council. Like its model, this picture of the hive-as-city is a moment of social integration, a space where subordination to a common goal is the only permissible action. Homer's Great Council is temporary and a setting for individual oratorical performance. And its goal of ending the war is frustrated. In contrast, Virgil's Hive of peace is permanent. In itself this self-sustaining hierarchy is a goal already realized, and its picture images a different, and to us, a more acceptable idea of perfection. Virgil highlights this idea by inverting a key element of Homer's story. Instead of seeking noble Achilles's return, Virgil's peaceful council of bees formalizes his exile, thereby making a public virtue of a social necessity.

Unlike the uncivilized, unproductive "herd" who must be ejected from the hive, Virgil's Romanized bees "alone know a fatherland and a fixed home." But, again, Virgil does not describe this home architecturally. These details belong to the sections that treat the natural hive. Instead of a blueprint, something that an actual farmer might use, Virgil's image of the peaceful hive is a social plan. As such, its psychology is newer than its epic armature and ornaments. Virgil is free to append to his Hive a particularly complex fusion of myth and psychological description:

> And as, when the Cyclopes in haste forge bolts from tough ore, some with ox-hide bellows make the blasts come and go, others dip the hissing brass in the lake, while Aetna groans under the anvils laid upon her; they, with mighty force, now one, now another, raise their arms in measured cadence, and turn the iron with gripping tongs — even so, if we may compare small things with great, an inborn love of gain spurs on the Attic bees, each after its own office. The aged have charge of the towns, the building of the hives, the fashioning of the cunningly built houses. But the young betake them home in weariness, late at night, their thighs freighted with thyme. (209)

There is much more like this that I could quote, as Virgil continues to weave his anthropomorphic conceit. However, a comparison of this passage with the earlier description of contending bees is sufficient to illuminate several important things. First of all, while earlier Virgil distances us from the battling swarms, here he does the opposite. Upon these laboring cosmopolitan bees he lavishes a superior order of description that evokes intense identification. By doing so Virgil is not betraying an inability to fully imagine and poetically evoke his warrior bees' archaic sensibility. I think, rather, that he would have us see his earlier bees as simpler, incomplete, not as human as his peaceful bees. The poem shows us miniature Greeks evolving into miniature Romans.

Second, whereas the details particular to the warrior bees and their mythologization together form a seamless tissue, when talking about his peaceful Hive Virgil is careful to more precisely and obviously relate bee and myth. The passage above hinges upon the locution *si parva componere magnis*, "if we may compare small things with great" (209). A pointed exposure of the analogical process, it joins the old mythic image and the new anthropomorphic ideal — and also separates them. Virgil may thus mythologize his bees without polluting them with the Cyclopes' rebellious nature.

Why does Virgil construct his peaceful Hive through such a complicated process? A partial answer: he wants his peaceful Hive to be natural, original, a perfect social order sanctioned by Zeus — but he would test its fitness as the final term in a dialectic of historical progress. You may verify this interpretation by examining a contradiction that Virgil builds into the above passage. As part of his psychologization, Virgil employs a mini simile that figures his bees as Cyclopes, Titans, laboring at their forges beneath Mount Aetna. This figuring-of-a-figure echoes Homer's technique of multiple, layered metaphor making, as when he recasts his Achaian bees "hanging like bunched grapes." But Virgil's purpose here is not his master's. His Titan bees affirm an entirely un-Homeric notion of heroic action: these bees labor and do so together.

This comparison of bees with Titans is a version of the trope *gianto-machia*,[10] a common Homeric device for elevating and dramatizing a conflict, as when in the *Iliad* Ares is "unstrung . . . spread out over seven acres in his fall" by Athena, who has struck him in the neck with an impossibly huge stone (21.403–7). Consistent with his (comparatively) modern cosmopolitan motives, instead of applying this figure in true

Homeric fashion to individual combat, Virgil uses it to elevate and dramatize the life of labor.

Virgil's bold usurpation of one of Homer's signature tropes serves as an excellent example of how the compositional method of *retractatio* operates when practiced by a master. It lays bare the mechanism by which Virgil changes the cultural orientation, the organization, and hence the signification of poetic bees. While I insist upon calling Virgil's bees "Roman," he calls them "Attic" — which is to say, "Greek." And for a Roman, to be Greek is to be at once admired and conquered; it is to be, simultaneously, a giant cultural presence and a subject province.

Along with meaning and beauty, the Hive gathers paradox from every iteration; once quickened, paradox lays hands on the poet. In a manner of speaking, then, the Hive is not finished with Virgil, a Mantuan, whose native and beloved land has only just been absorbed by Rome. Domestication implies harvest: the hive will be robbed of its honey. The third term of Virgil's progressive dialectic, the Hive of peace, must be reimagined. How should peace and, indeed, the cosmos, be defined so as to allow for the collective's inevitable disruption? The chaotic energy that Virgil has exiled from the Hive returns from without. Virgil confronts this darkness, turns his poem toward death and its undoing. He chooses a transcendence singularly Roman in character, one that elevates the whole at the expense of the individual. The *Georgics'* agricultural frame guides Virgil toward images of sacrifice and collective rebirth.

Building upon his earlier dramatization of labor, Virgil boldly redefines his "Attic" bees' love of gain. In preparation for the Hive's death and renewal — in part, I sense, so as to begin solving the ethical dilemma of imperialism — Virgil purifies his bees of what Homer shows us to be the root of war, sexual passion and the obligations of blood relation: "they indulge not in conjugal embraces, nor idly unnerve their bodies in love, or bring forth young with travail, but of themselves gather their children in their mouths from leaves and sweet herbs, of themselves provide a new monarch and tiny burghers, and remodel their places and waxen realms" (211). There is no place in this natural city for the foreigner or tyrant: "of themselves" these citizens "provide a new monarch and tiny burghers." Through their own arts and with their own bodies, these marvelous creatures "remodel their palaces and waxen realms." While it is true that in their marvelous chastity these bees no longer signify the human, so great is Virgil that a new and finer sympathy accompanies this act of dehumanization. The picture of them collectively "gather[ing] their children in their mouths from leaves and sweet herbs" overwhelms us with a novel combination of tenderness and strangeness. These bees are insects and human, and yet more than either. The contentious and penurious "Attic" bee has been thoroughly redefined: "Often, too, as they wander among ragged rocks they bruise their wings, and freely yield their lives under their load — so deep is their love of flowers and their glory in begetting honey."

Having reimagined his players, Virgil proceeds to rewrite the play and its implications of domestication. His argument: "Therefore, though the limit of a narrow span awaits the bees themselves — for never stretches it beyond the seventh summer — yet the race abides immortal, for many a year stands firm the fortune of the house, and grandsires' grandsires are numbered on the roll." This race is immortal and yet the "fortune of [any particular] house" is not. The allegory thus swings back toward the human, but at such a level that the individual as such is of no concern. Virgil provides us with a theory of the soul and the universe — a solution to, and absolution for, the suffering that comes of domestication: "some have taught that the bees have received a share of the divine intelligence, and a draught of heavenly ether; for God, they say, pervades all things, earth and sea's expanse and heaven's depth; from Him the flocks and herds, men and beasts of every sort draw, each at birth, the slender stream of life; yea, unto Him all beings thereafter return, and, when unmade, are restored; no place is there for death, but, still quick, they fly unto the ranks of the stars, and mount to the heavens aloft" (211, 213).

This prayer fortifies us for our next and double role as bees and beekeepers. We are thus, simultaneously, Romans and provincials, complex beings sent to "break into the [bees'/our] stately dwelling." Their/our honey is taken but not without ceremony: "first with a draught of water sprinkle and rinse your mouth." Or without art: "and in your hand hold forth searching smoke." Or without admirable mortal sacrifice, death: "their rage is beyond measure; when hurt, they breathe poison into their bites, and fastening on the veins leave there their unseen stings and lay down their lives in the wound" (213).

While the narrator's powers of observation are undiminished, his cosmic perspective requires a stance and voice distinct from that which enabled the feelings of tenderness and strangeness evoked by the images of bees "gather[ing] their children in their mouths from leaves and sweet herbs." The Roman view of bees, of all creatures including humans, is practical, satisfied with appearances. While we know that these bees "rage," this emotion "is beyond measure." At this moment the poetry favors clinical description. Uninterested even in our own discomfort, we observe only how the bees use their weapons and that they "lay down their lives in the wound." Violence and sacrifice are thus accepted as the warp and woof of *de rerum natura*, the nature of things.

I do not think that Virgil is entirely sure how to end his bee poem. The movement from line 227, which closes with the sublimity of creatures "mount[ing] to the heavens," to line 228, which begins the hive's breaking, is abrupt. While I understand and have explained how the vision of creaturely connection prepares for what follows, the juxtaposition of cosmic unity and renewal with the facts of farming destabilizes the rest of the poem. Virgil cannot square his Epicurean idea of peace with the implications of either domestication or Imperium. Thus, Virgil chooses to leave us with his final and fourth picture of the Hive, an image of the swarm's renewal through the flesh's putrefaction, *bugonia*.

As if he finds it as fantastic and incongruous as we do, Virgil awards *bugonia* a double certification. First, he establishes it as wisdom obtained from older peoples (Eygptians, Persians, Ethiopians). Then he pictures it again, this time sanctified by a complicated interweaving of various Greek myths (Aristaeus, Proteus, Orpheus and Eurydice). Below is his first image of the method, one that subordinates sympathy for the sacrifice to clinical detail and procedure. Of the three actions already identified as proper to the getting of honey — ceremony, art, sacrifice — the latter two are emphasized at the expense of the first:

First is chosen a place, small and straitened for this very purpose. This they confine with a narrow roof of tiles and close walls, and towards the four winds add four windows with slanting light. Then a bullock is sought, one just arching his horns on a brow of two summers' growth. Spite of all his struggles, both his nostrils are stopped up, and the breath of his mouth; then he is beaten to death, and his flesh is pounded to a pulp through the unbroken hide. As thus he lies, they leave him in his prison, and strew beneath his sides broken boughs, thyme, and fresh cassia. This is done when the zephyrs begin to stir the waves, ere the meadows blush with their fresh hues, ere the chattering swallow hangs her nest from the rafters. Meantime the moisture, warming in the softened bones, ferments, and creatures of won-

drous wise to view, footless at first, soon with buzzing wings as well.
(217, 219)

The Hive is *reborn*, not renewed. The old barbarian art has produced wild insects that "swarm together, and more and more essay the light air." Virgil first compares them with "a shower pouring from summer clouds." Then, returning to the register of images proper to his warring bees, Virgil describes these elemental beings as arrows springing from Parthian bowstrings (217–19).

According to the Loeb edition's notes, Servius tells us that, originally, the poem concluded with a eulogy on C. Cornelius Gallus, who by Octavian was made prefect of Egypt and later in disgrace committed suicide. This eulogy, now lost, was replaced with a complex and somewhat puzzling frame and quest narrative of how humans acquired knowledge of *bugonia*, an appropriate terminus for the poem whose themes and images have immense significance for the Hive's subsequent evolution.

The bees belonging to Aristaeus, son of the divine Cyrene, have died. The shepherd movingly prays to his mother for an explanation; she hears his cries and admits him to her cave beneath the river. Aristaeus's descent into an underworld space to learn how to renew his bees (the secret of life) and the poet's attention to topological wonders together anticipate both the story of Orpheus, which is retold a few lines later, and Aeneas's journey to the underworld in *Aeneid* 6. Once underground Aristaeus "marvel[s] at his mother's home, a realm of waters [and] lakes locked in caverns." He is "daze[d] by the mighty rush of waters [as he gazes] on all the rivers, as, each in his own place, they glide under the great earth" (221, 223). Welcomed by his mother in her grotto, he is told that he must bind and question Proteus, who knows everything. Fortified with ambrosia, Aristaeus ambushes and restrains this god, who tells him of unhappy Orpheus, how he lost Eurydice twice and was torn to bits by worshipers of Bacchus. Cyrene tells her son that to the Nymphs with whom Eurydice once danced he must offer a special sacrifice: "Pick out four choice bulls, of surpassing form . . . and as many heifers of unyoked neck. For these set us four alters by the stately shrines of the goddesses, and drain the sacrificial blood from their throats, but leave the bodies of the steers within the leafy grove" (235). Following these and the rest of his mother's instructions, after nine days Aristaeus returns to this sacred place to make two more sacrifices: to Orpheus he is to offer a black ewe and to Eurydice a calf. Once there, he sees "a portent, sudden and wondrous to tell — throughout the paunch, amid the molten flesh of the oxen, bees buzzing and swarming forth from the ruptured sides, then trailing in vast crowds, till at last on a tree-top they stream together, and hang in clusters from the bending boughs."

In contrast to his first and "barbarian" picture of *bugonia*, which happens in a small building with four windows open to the winds (a portent of scattering), both the scene of this second picture and its living produce are sanctified and bound by the power and proximity of four altars. In the first instance of *bugonia*, art and sacrifice created bees, but these animals were wild and therefore lost to the shepherd. The bees of the second instance, however, have been made with all three elements of honey gathering. While they still must be hived, they are not associated either with a sudden rain or images of war. Instead of disappearing like a shower or taking off like Parthian arrows, these religiously made bees eventually "stream together, and hang in clusters from the bending boughs" of a tree that is within Aristaeus's sight. And, significantly, he is standing near the shrine.

We shall never know whether this second instance of *bugonia* was written of a piece with the rest of the poem or in fact made to replace Gallus's eulogy. Certainly it should not escape us that the frame tale of Aristaeus and Cyrene, which contains the first's struggle with Proteus and the puzzling retelling of the Orpheus myth, feels different from what it concludes. Nonetheless, this complex ending brings the poem full circle. Now that his bees are renewed, Aristaeus must begin as the poem does, by "seek[ing for them] a settled home." And where Virgil leaves his renewed bees "hang[ing] in clusters from the bending boughs," this is also a return that sweeps back to the start of it all, Homer's *Iliad* 2 bee simile:

> the sceptred kings, obeying
> the shepherd of the people, and the army thronged behind them.
> Like the swarms of clustering bees that issue forever
> in fresh bursts from the hollow stone, and hang like
> bunched grapes as they hover beneath the flowers in springtime
> fluttering in swarms together this way and that way,
> so the many nations of men . . .

In light of the ancient practice of *retractatio*, we should feel confident that we indeed do hear an echo of Homer's wild martial bees in these half-tame clusters that, bending a tree bough, await their enhivement.

But *retractatio* is an allusive practice that asks a poet to remake all of a model's aspects. Virgil's conclusion to his *Georgics* attempts no less; it is no mere nod to Homer. The Roman wishes to surpass his master on his own ground, which in the case of the Hive includes both the space it creates and organizes and the degree of organization this space makes possible. In a word, the Hive is a *topos*, not a metaphor — a distinction that I shall presently explicate. Homer pictures his bees, the many nations of Achaians who are soon to die, as "hover[ing] beneath flowers in springtime / fluttering in swarms together this way and that way." In general, within the Hive's charged space, what is higher and better organized is superior to the lower and less social. Virgil has indeed returned to Homer's simile but has placed his more highly organized and immortal bees in a tree, at a superior height.

Although my expression of Virgil's motives falls short of their poetic execution, I am convinced that this moment of reimagining Homer's bees is crucial for what happens both in the *Aeneid* and later in the epic tradition. And the epic is the ground for all subsequent versions of the Hive. In sum, *Georgic* 4 is the origin of and model for a series of even more daring reversals and renamings. In this putatively agricultural and didactic poem, Virgil shows his inheritors how to read and to analyze one of Homer's most suggestive metaphors. Moreover, Virgil has adapted its terms to a progressive ideology in a way that introduces the following elements, later exploited by Christian poets. First, as more fully worked out in book 4 of the *Aeneid*, the beehive and its verbal imitation are henceforth and together associated with both the idea of ultranatural generation and a sacred space that contains and thus domesticates the ancient energies of the swarm. Second, the Hive is now a primary vehicle for expressing an ideal and abstract order, be it purely divine, purely human, or a mixture of both. And, finally, because of its new status as a sociological model, philosophically and aesthetically the Hive authorizes ideological cleansing, the community definition and physical ejection of unwanted elements. Henceforth, exile, longing, and the Divine shall together occupy the Hive.

The Hive as Topos

As is by now apparent, because the Hive does more than assert identity between two different things, it is not really a metaphor. Moreover

I have shown that this tableau is a discrete and portable convention grand enough to contain lesser figures (such as metaphor) and subordinate them to its purposes. I have also explained that the Hive is not easily more than a narrative element. Though it is certainly dramatic, the picture of a crowd or city as an insect collective is not a drama. No doubt this limitation results from the Hive's visual core, which is an imitation of a particular visual experience.

In order to distinguish this species of intermediate figure from those lesser and greater, rhetoricians have designated the topos, or "place" (Gk. pl. *topoi*; L. *locus, loci*; Eng. topic, topics). The category of topos is divided into two distinct orders, which Walter Ong labels the "analytic" and the "prefabricated."[11] The first are the Aristotelian special and general topics. They are argumentative, in the service of logic.[12] The second are set-pieces that because they involve artistic language may be generally (but not altogether accurately) described as "irrational." Because the Hive as I conceive it combines the offices of the logical and the poetic topoi, it is instructive to spend a little time establishing the conventional way of thinking about the topos so that we may then adapt it to our investigation.

The first type of analytic topoi are the "special," those modes of argument that we would now call "discourse specific," meaning that each discipline, occupation, or discourse has its own "special" ways of conducting argument. For example, a forensic entomologist may make arguments about the approximate time of a person's death based upon knowledge of how a certain species of fly develops and how this development is affected by temperature, relative humidity, and other such factors. Such knowledge is "special," particular to the discourse of entomology, and has no place in or bearing upon, for instance, the equivalently specialized arguments that an engineer is empowered to make regarding forces and the varied characteristics of materials.

The second type of analytic topos is called "general," because these modes of argument are available to all discourses and disciplines, a flexibility that, according to Edward P. J. Corbett, springs from the mind's essential capacities. Below is a passage about the general topics from Corbett's *Classical Rhetoric for the Modern Student*, which I have quoted because it suggests an intimate connection between certain types of verbal patterns and the way the mind works. The Hive topos, although literary rather than analytic, seems to evidence and to work according to an essential human affinity for hierarchy and its symbols:

the (general) topics were the general heads under which were grouped
arguments for a particular subject or occasion. They were the "regions," the "haunts," the "places" where certain categories of arguments resided. . . . The human mind, of course, does think about
particular things, but its constant tendency is to rise above the particulars and to abstract, to generalize, to classify, to analyze, and to
synthesize. The topics represented the system that the classical rhetoricians built upon this tendency of the human mind.

The rhetoricians saw, for instance, that one of the tendencies of
the human mind is to seek out the nature of things. So they set
up the topic of Definition. Another tendency of the human mind is
to compare things, and when things are compared, one discovers
similarities or differences — and the differences will be in kind or in
degree. (95)

As Corbett suggests, one example of a general topic, a mode of argument that is common to all discourses and specialties, is that of comparison, which he divides into three subtopics: "similarity," "difference,"
and "degree." If we apply this general topic to two very different regions of human experience — let us say to the legal process (as in the
case below, an invented but I hope illustrative situation) and to the science of archaeology (an actual incident) — we may readily understand
that comparison is indeed a common, analytic, and, as Richard Lanham
observes, a "formal" rather than "material" way of understanding and
expression.[13]

If in an effort to establish the location of a witness — Mr. Smith —
at a particular time, an attorney *compares* Mr. Smith's phone records with
his sworn statement and those of other witnesses, the attorney may argue one of three conclusions: (1) if Smith's phone records confirm (are
highly *similar* to) his testimony, then he is truthful; (2) if Smith's phone
records contradict (are markedly *different* from) his testimony, then he is
lying; or, (3) if Smith's phone records only approximate (are similar only
to a *degree* with) his testimony, then he is confused and, consequently,
unreliable.

Similarly, when making arguments about Heinrich Schliemann's archaeological veracity — or more specifically about the genuineness of
the unique gold burial mask, known as the Mask of Agamemnon,
which Schliemann (allegedly) found in grave 4 at the "site of Troy" —
David A. Traill uses the general topos of comparison. In a review of

Traill's book *Schliemann of Troy: Treasure and Deceit*, Richard Jenkyns
sums up Traill's arguments, which I have clarified with the insertion of
italics and brackets:

> In the case of . . . the Mask of Agamemnon — Traill can point to
> some disconcerting oddities. It is strange that this mask alone should
> be bearded. He also notes the curiously nineteenth-century flavor of
> the "imperial," or tuft, under the mouth and the "handlebars" at the
> end of the moustache, not found elsewhere in Mycenaean art. He
> states firmly that the handlebars were an afterthought and that "the
> addition was rather crudely affected" (either in the 1870s or in the
> middle of the second millennium BC). He indicates *three possibilities*:
> that the mask is genuine [*similarity*], that it is fake [*difference*], and
> that it is ancient but altered after discovery [*degree*]. (15, 18)

To reiterate, in both the fictitious but characteristic legal instance of
Mr. Smith's phone records and the archaeological debate about the Mask
of Agamemnon, exactly the same sort of argumentative options emerge
when one compares the unknown with the known.

Cognitively indispensable and formally discrete, a general analytic
topos is portable. It is a building block of expression, not a complete
argument, and so may be used in a range of linguistic situations. Unlike,
for instance, the special topic of radiocarbon dating, the topos of comparison may be used as happily by an archaeologist as by a poet. Indeed,
as Shakespeare's Sonnet 18 demonstrates, the analytic topic of comparison and its subtopics are quite at home in the poetic realm. In the
sonnet's first eight or nine lines (before it takes a committed turn to the
literary topos of "immortality via poetic art") Shakespeare uses comparison to generate a rich tissue of similarities and differences and an
overall argument by degree.

Shall I compare thee to a summer's day?
Thou art more lovely and more temperate:
Rough winds do shake the darling buds of May,
And summer's lease hath all too short a date;
Sometime too hot the eye of heaven shines,
And often is his gold complexion dimmed;
And every fair from fair sometime declines,
By chance or nature's changing course untrimmed:
But thy eternal summer shall not fade.

I have not yet discovered exactly when the literary, or "prefabricated," topos — what rhetoricians call a "commonplace" (*locus communis*) — becomes terminologically linked with the analytic. Perhaps, however, that the analytic topos's cognitive and formal discreteness are sufficiently analogous to how the commonplace functions helps to explain why, at least by Quintilian's time, both species are housed under the same term.[14] Thus, although the distinction between analytic and prefabricated topoi has long since been systematized and, hence, accepted as a principle, these two forms tend always to merge into each other.

Ernst Robert Curtius recognized as much, and so, in his singular catalog and analysis of commonplaces, *European Literature and the Latin Middle Ages*, he treats the prefabricated topoi as the "daily bread of the mind," the staple from which the banquet of literature is made.[15] In comparison with the standard division of the topoi into what amounts to two antithetical categories — the "analytic," a rational form good for invention, and the "prefabricated," irrational and suggestive — his definition is refreshingly flexible. Curtius understands the commonplaces to be more than mere conventions, empty formulas. Instead, he believes that the commonplaces are psycho-historical indicators, "templates" for invention (82).

Although he does not explicitly say so, Curtius makes the literary topos's office complementary to that of Aristotle's common topics, an exceedingly useful refinement in rhetorical understanding. He does not rest here, however, for his project hinges upon an equally significant principle: unlike the more abstract and cognitively essential analytic topoi, the literary sort are born of specific historical conditions and therefore are subject to decay. They may, and indeed do, pass away. And since such forms are preserved and disseminated textually, their generation and development may be located, traced, and interpreted. Thus, Curtius thinks of his project as one of "literary biology," as "the basis for a historical topic" (83).

The Literary Topos as an Intermediate, Combinatory Form

Aristotle thinks of the general topics as a set of places in the mind where all orators go to hunt for arguments. This analogy presupposes both that the topoi are common property and that there is a connection between verbal form and space — which I take as permission to situate my object and its relatives spatially, as a "scale of forms." Accordingly,

I conceive of the literary topos as a unit of cognition and expression whose power to organize thought and language falls between the levels of grammar and arrangement. As a consequence, the literary topos's office combines aspects of the forms above and those below. If we position all verbal forms on a scale according to their organizational magnitude, a topos tends to be "larger," to "contain more" than a trope, such as metonymy or synecdoche, but less than strategies of arrangement,[16] such as argumentative divisions, dramatic acts, or narrative chapters.

Quintilian treats metaphor as a "figure of thought," which he calls a *trope* and defines as "the artistic alteration of a word or phrase from its proper meaning to another."[17] His definition's key concept is "alteration" (*mutatio*) of "proper meaning" (*propria significatione*). He means that a trope (from the Greek verb *terpo*, meaning "to turn") transfers the usual signification of one word to another, thereby creating from two terms a new meaning, a new conceptual entity.

For example, the statement "my love is a rose" merges the beloved with the flower. Within the compass of a very few words and without deviating from either normal syntax or grammar, this metaphor works by causing the former object to take on some of the latter's characteristics (and to a degree vice versa). In comparison with the Hive's complex way of picturing, the image produced by the metaphor "my love is a rose" is suggestive rather than clear, as it does not spring from any sort of structured and specific imitation. At its purest, the verbal metaphor, or trope, produces an image that operates similarly to what I have already called the emblem. But so that we may better contrast this sort of image with the Hive's, we need more descriptive terms. Let us then call the pure trope's image *iconic* and that produced by our topos and its kin *architectural*.

To better establish what I mean by the iconic image, let us consider the Psalmist's metaphor, "the Lord is my shepherd." Here the usual and general signification of the word "Lord" is altered, focused by its combination with the meaning of the phrase "my shepherd." This act defines the Godhead as protector and casts the speaker as a sheep in need of divine care. As is the case with our first metaphor, "my love is a rose," the transfer of meaning between objects is economical, occurs within a single unit of sense. Nor does this transfer and sharing of qualities require a change in the usual sequence of words. This image is simple and overwhelmingly immediate. As Gaston Bachelard points out in *The Po-*

etics of Space, such a verbal product refers to itself and not to the larger world (xi–xiv).

I will now compare the iconic image's appeal with that made by the argumentative example. Imagine that we are prosecuting a capital murder case. Now argue as we might before a jury that a certain sort of wound was produced by a double-edged knife of particular dimensions, our forensic reports and reasoning are unpersuasive in comparison with the physical existence of a knife meeting our specifications. Such a knife does not have to be the murder weapon. The appeal of such an object is its *presence* — and this presence is immediate, overwhelming, an irrational and therefore incontrovertible proof. Such an object, much like the iconic image, exerts what, in *The Psychoanalysis of Fire*, Bachelard calls the "fascination [of] the object" (5). And we do not need to have passed the bar to know that such an object is neither easy to deny nor to alter.

The challenge presented the defense attorney by the object under these circumstances is not far from the poet's experience. Since the counsel for the defense cannot deny this object's existence, which would contradict the jury's immediate experience, he or she must call into question its context. If we think of our forensic object as the rhetorical equivalent to a pure trope, such is the power of its (irrational) presence that the defensive strategy is clear: the knife must be contained if not entirely written out of the poem of disputation. A correct and novel context very well might alter the argumentative alignment of any physical evidence. To reiterate: if wise, our defending counsel will not argue against the knife's existence. Instead, because this object makes an irrational appeal, functions in much the same way as a pure trope, a successful act of legal *retractatio* would need to be directed at what is beyond the knife, what it cannot evoke: the scene in which it appears.

Although the metaphor "the Lord is my shepherd" produces a visual image in our minds, its metaphoric process neither requires nor expressly evokes the categories of time and space, which would lend itself to naturalistic mimesis. Consequently, for our purposes we may say that the iconic image occurs nowhere and is instantaneous. In psychophysiological terms, the pure trope's simplicity determines its efficiency and, consequently, its irrationality. From this we may then infer that in order to be engaged, the mind's higher functions require that order be unfolded over time and within a stabilizing context — the very characteristics displayed by the literary topos and that distinguish it from the tropes.

Returning once more to the Psalmist's metaphor: However one has been trained to visualize the image Lord-is-my-shepherd, as perhaps holding a shepherd's crook or even a sheep, this picture is independent of and even opposed to any temporally or structurally necessary imitation of space. Like the double-edged knife I just discussed, the image Lord-is-my-shepherd cannot evoke its context because the details required for natu-ralistic mimesis are not part of what we may call its tropological core. I wish to emphasize that this particular image's simplicity is not the exclu-sive product of its transcendent subject. Rather, because this trope fulfills its office with minimal data, it favors the intuitive experience of presence over the rational process of construction. Thus, since a literary topos like the Hive presents us with a *structured* image, as I have already suggested, it may be said to combine the trope's associational/imagistic office with rational/structural aspects that are more proper to the schemes.

Like their close relatives the tropes, the schemes are economical and tend to occur most powerfully at the level of the sentence. However, unlike tropes, they (1) work by altering, purposefully organizing the usual grammatical and syntactical order of discourse, and (2) do not nec-essarily lose their clarity when used to organize larger linguistic units. In contrast to a pure trope's imagistic immediacy, because a scheme's mode of figuration necessarily involves organization, a principle that rhetori-cians call "arrangement," its expressiveness tends to appeal to the rational faculty. For example, if we want to draw special (i.e., logical) attention to one item in a group or to emphasize a progression, rather than mak-ing a metaphor or listing the elements as they come to mind, we would do well to arrange them in a series of ascending value. This scheme, *cli-max*, Lanham defines as "mounting by degrees through linked words or phrases, usually of increasing weight and in parallel construction" (36).

A contemporary instance of this scheme combined with another, a tripartite structure known as *tricolon*, is the following sentence, uttered by George Wald as part of a speech delivered at the Massachusetts Insti-tute of Technology, 4 March 1969: "I think we've reached a point of great decision, not just for our nation, not only for all humanity, but for life upon the earth."[18] Even though we may not know exactly what de-cision Wald is speaking about with such urgency, we see and feel the shape of his thoughts as they move upward categorically and in intensity from the level of the nation to that of all "life upon the earth," the locution's third term. Beyond the value of repetition, this scheme works because it draws attention to its madeness. An expression of control, this scheme economically delivers a structurally dependent message whose appeal to reason is beyond a trope's capacity. Part of this scheme's rational appeal is due to its accumulative, tripartite structure, which parallels the deliberate, categorical movement of the syllogism. Although Wald's scheme does not engender a rational inference, it does suggest a process, a "logic" that makes us feel as if we go through several stages of increasing transcendence until we reach the last and motivationally proper level: an elevated and global position from which our decisions appear to be of the highest consequence.

Though we usually think of figures of speech as being proper to the level of the sentence, the three ascending levels of Wald's tricolonic climax may be equally used to either introduce or to sum up a much larger system. This capacity for organizing large as well as small verbal systems suggests that, in contrast to the tropes, the schemes possess greater organizational efficacy. Unlike metaphor, certain schemes, such as climax, embody structural principles that may be used easily and obviously to order larger units of discourse. Although it is arguable that the metaphoric function may be expanded into a conceit or even into an allegory, both of these words signify modes of expression that are distinct from metaphor. When a metaphor is taxed with the duties of arrangement, as in a sonnet or an epic simile, it loses its purity, its power as a singular cognitive event. In Lanham's words, when one "amplifies," which is to say enlarges, a metaphor, one is actually "introducing a *seeming* synonymy by dividing and particularizing an assertion" (9). As I have indicated with italics, the key qualification here is that this synonymy is "seeming" rather than actual. Lanham's use of the word "seeming" alerts us to what is obvious about enlarging a metaphor: when we do so we change it fundamentally.

In contrast, one may effectively and obviously structure an entire drama according to the principles of climax — and might be well advised to do so. In sum, a scheme such as climax is *structurally* potent whereas a trope, such as metaphor, is *visually* so. And because the hive topos combines the structural and rational potency of a scheme with the visual and intuitive powers of a metaphor, it exceeds our conventional way of thinking about verbal figures.

The Hive as Type and Its Connection with the *Nekuia*

Though it may sometimes be difficult to speak assuredly about the unity of Western culture, when it comes to its verbal arts we may make one such claim with confidence. From Hellenic Greece to nearly the present, rhetoric singularly defined Western civilization. It was the theory and practice of education, aesthetics, psychology, and communication. And because this system established and was the soul of expression written and spoken, for two millennia its improvement occupied the very best minds. But, like rhetoric, these minds were divided.

Aristotle's most quoted definition of rhetoric is practical: "So let Rhetoric be defined as the faculty of discovering in the particular case what are the available means of persuasion" (7). But this is his second definition. The first part of the *Rhetoric*'s first sentence identifies rhetoric as "the counterpart of dialectic" (1). By this Aristotle means that rhetoric is logic's more versatile and indispensable complement. From its origin, then, rhetoric presents a double image. It is a "faculty," an instrumental power of discovery and influence that adheres in and may be wielded by the individual. But rhetoric is also a system, a science that describes how and why human beings communicate. It is the author of literature and the father of psychology.

Then as now rhetoric's critics occupied themselves with the image and ethics of the orator. For instance, it did not sit well with the aristocratic Plato that any free citizen could, potentially, acquire power through practical instruction in how to speak. Once rooted in Greek soil, however, the system of rhetoric prospered. Alexander's brief empire merely matured it. The Hellenistic schoolmasters founded libraries, mastered style, and made Homer the god of letters. The Romans came conquering and were in turn conquered by rhetoric. And so, over their roads and the centuries the Romans sent victorious legions and tax collectors, engineers and all the apparatus of forcible peace — rhetoric and the rhetorical imagination.

While in many respects our imagination is still rhetorical, new powers and assumptions screen the past from us: we think with science and through Romanticism. What distinguishes the rhetorical imagination is that it is typological. Thus, to know this imagination and continue our recovery of the Hive's lost dimension, we need to define and discuss the *type*, a convention that assumes pervasive social conservatism, flourishes in an environment where memory is trained, and mediates between the written text and the spoken word. In school and adulthood, educated Greeks and Romans memorized, publicly recited, and understood their lives through the words of very few writers — most notably Homer. As my reading of Virgil's fourth *Georgic* suggests, to know and to use Homer was to be obliged to struggle with him for mastery, to best him with his own forms. A poet of the classical age — especially an epic poet — would therefore need to know his Homer very well indeed. And to command several texts as complex, distinct, and yet mutually resonant as the *Iliad* and the *Odyssey* is to have built them up in one's mind as a complex tissue of associations. This means that any rhetorically trained poet — Virgil or Shakespeare, Hardy or Joyce — understood and used received figures as constellations of related images, not as rigid, perfect instances to be cited or copied.

In other words, as a precondition to engaging with Homer on his own ground, any poet so disposed would need to have internalized his work to the extent that related forms, symbols, and incidents would combine into what A. O. Lovejoy might describe as "symbol complexes." The emphasis of such an understanding would then be the system, its perpetuation and refinement, and not the particular work and its maker. An artist thus trained sees his predecessors as positions and potentials within and elements of an unfolding design. To the rhetorically trained poet, in addition to being Homer's, a particular Homeric incident would be understood as a *unified locus of associated patterns*. The art produced through engaging with such loci is therefore learned, densely allusive. But rarely does this art obscure — much less deny — its generating armature, for by its very existence the typological imagination confirms the value of and its debt to the past.

The rhetorical imagination is conservative, inherently elitist; its idea of progress is making the immanent visible; its procedures are quasi-religious, and its morality is derived from precedent. We may recover a sense of this imagination in the way some devout Christians study and know the Bible, filtering their lives through emblems, incidents, and stories already ancient when first written down. In Biblical interpretation, a type may be defined as a first, and therefore defining, incident whose meaning and symbolism is subsequently incarnated in an unfolding series of similar moments. A type is not a single object. It is, rather, a connective tissue of allusion that makes a whole from a text's disparate parts. The elements of such a tissue are not copies of an original; instead, each is felt to resonate with its model, to explore and extend its terms, thereby perfecting a greater design.

To the epic poets the Hive was this sort of design — one that they understood and approached as Virgil did Homer's swarm: perfect and yet perfectible, both a specific "place" in a particular text and a shared fixture of the mind. This notion of our topos illuminates what to Dante and Milton is perhaps Virgil's most important version of the Hive, its appearance at the very center of the *Aeneid*, in an instance of the under-world space known as the *nekuia*. This is a space that we have already met in two different versions near the end of *Georgic* 4. Apparently, to Virgil, bees and the underworld are related. Let me then explore what is here an all-important imagistic and thematic rhyme.

As I am using it, *nekuia* means any otherworldly or supernatural space that is sufficiently imagined for a character or characters to enter. According-ing to Liddell and Scott, *nekuia* signifies "a magical rite by which ghosts were called up and questioned about the future." Thus, we see why Homer's Hellenistic editors came to refer to *Odyssey* 11, which contains the scene in which Odysseus evokes and speaks with the dead, as "the" *nekuia*. However much they believed in their anonymity, by recasting a word for an archaic ceremony as a descriptive and generic literary cate-gory, in effect Homer's first and greatest commentators announced, if not created, both a new poetic form and instructions for its use. Their titular act officially located the underworld in a particular text and thereby made poetic law of this text's images and rules. And since this text is a singularly impressive moment in the Homeric corpus — a body of work that formed the very ground of education in the classical world and for centuries to come — the swarm became a required part of all subsequent representations of the underworld, especially within the epic frame.

In book 6 of the *Aeneid*, no doubt having in mind the version of the story of Aristaeus and Orpheus that appears in his fourth *Georgic*, Virgil has Aeneas enter the underworld to learn his fortune and his people's future. Aeneas gets the full tour, discovering that this space is divided into a region of dark and light, and that at the center of each region is what I shall treat as a swarm. Once ferried by Charon across the Styx — and depending upon their status and conduct when alive or the nature of their death — souls go either to Tartarus or Elysium, to a place of eternal punishment or to the fields of rebirth. Interestingly, and including the righteous dead's "peaceful homes" along the banks of Lethe, the Castle of Tartarus is the only structure in his underworld that Virgil chooses to describe in spatial terms: "Suddenly Aeneas looks back, and under a cliff on the left sees a broad castle, girt with triple wall and encircled with a rushing flood of torrent flames — Tartarean Phlegethon, that rolls along thundering rocks. In front stands the huge gate, and pillars of solid adamant, that no might of man, nay, not even the sons of heaven, may uproot in war; there stands the iron tower, soaring high, and Tisiphone, sitting girt with bloody pall, keeps sleepless watch o'er the portal day and night" (545). From inside this structure Aeneas hears "groans and the sound of the savage lash; withal, the clank of iron and dragging of chains." He asks the Sibyl to explain, and while she is speaking the "infernal gates open," giving Aeneas a view into the castle. But Aeneas cannot see past Tisiphone, and thus he continues to depend upon his guide, who tells him that within these walls, "Tartarus itself yawns sheer down, stretching into the gloom twice as far as is yon sky's upward view to heavenly Olympus. Here the ancient sons of Earth, the Titans' brood, hurled down by the thunderbolt, writhe in the lowest abyss" (547). Because the interior of Castle Tartarus is cosmic in scale as well as vertically organized (it counters this underworld's, and indeed the epic's, horizontality), it makes sense that Aeneas must be told, rather than witness for himself, its contents. He cannot see past Tartarus's mythological guardian.

To Virgil this space is prearchaic, prior to and thus qualitatively distinct from the *Georgics*' setting, the middle world of nature and living men. What is fantastic in Virgil's agricultural poems is subject to the laws of nature and is moderated by reason — which helps explain the poem's dialectical structure. Although Virgil approaches his ideal city through images that ascend from and never cease to refer to the state of nature, these images' sequence echoes and is steadied by rational process. The *nekuia*'s rules, however, are different from the farm's. In this region of shadow, which until Virgil was dimly imagined and poorly mapped, nature and reason have no purchase; any natural symbol or human art here contained becomes abstract and plastic. Virgil, who is not finished with Homer's swarm, has descended to reprise and to perfect the swarm's domestication — but on the grandest of scales. It is Virgil's ambition to bring the *nekuia* to heel, to suborn the laws of life and death to his ideology of progress and rebirth. He must and will have a righteous swarm, a model of cooperation fit for an ideal Rome. Thus, once and for all, collective evil, the crowd's dark energy of rebellion, must be cast out and sealed from the cosmos. To accomplish this, via the powers of the *nekuia*'s supernatural space, Virgil will forge a new human psychology. His most powerful move against Homer's swarm must then be an act of creation, an instance of reworking that directly engages with the most potent elements of his civilization's typology.

Virgil accomplishes his act of cosmic domestication in three ways. The first is a matter of surveying: he does to the *nekuia* what he did to Homer's bees — he makes it Roman. The second involves architecture and eliminates barbarism from his calculus: Virgil represents rebellion as the Titans, whom he confines within an inescapable prison. The third concerns itself with individual psychology and remedies the dangers of personal attachments: as a precondition of rebirth, his righteous dead must forget their lives and themselves by drinking Lethe's water. Virgil does not imagine shades without memory; their purification depends upon it. Because recollection is the seat of individuality, it has no place in the new and cosmopolitan Golden Age.

In this underworld there are two points through which a universal axis passes, and each is the center of its own particular sort of city. The Romans called such a locus an *umbilicus*, and each of their towns and cities was organized around one. In *Flesh and Stone*, Richard Sennett writes about the connection between the *umbilicus* and the cosmic axis:

> To start a city, or refound an existing city wrecked in the process of conquest, the Romans tried to establish the point that they called the umbilicus, a center of the city approximating the navel of the body; from this urban belly button the planners drew all measurements for spaces in the city. . . . The planners also pinpointed the umbilicus of a city by studying the sky. . . . To found a town, one sought on the ground a spot that reflected directly below where the four parts of the sky met, as if the sky were mirrored on the earth. . . . The umbilicus had immense religious value. Below this point, the Romans thought that the city was connected to the gods interred in the earth; above it, to the gods of light in the sky — the deities who controlled human affairs. (106–9)

Virgil's underworld is thus quite Roman. The affairs of the higher world, the plane of living persons and of history, is "mirrored" by the lower's preoccupations, by its sky-oriented organization.

Given Virgil's attention to the Roman urban model, it is revealing that his *nekuia* sports a double *umbilicus*: two axes of vertical organization, one static and one dynamic. The first is Tartarus. This spatial locus is less a prison for the dead than a container for the poetic past, the antisocial energies suggested by the Homeric swarm. Castle Tartarus is a synthesis of monumental architectural forms and the abyss. It is a structure that surrounds and defines a void. At its bottom lies the primal half of the original *giantomachia*. As you may recall, this word signifies a particular heroic trope. But it also refers to the primordial battle fought between generations of immortals. Virgil's relationship with Homer is agonistic; his reliance upon the living prison of domestication, which he expresses variously in both form and content, expresses a peculiar and very Roman need for and idea of control. One very well wonders whether among Tartarus's titanic inmates, beside Homer's Rumor, there is chained one human being, a blind but deathless singer.

The second axis, antithetical to the Tartarean, occupies the center of Elysium and thus defines this region's purpose. On the banks of the river Lethe, having by a thousand years of "school[ing] with penalties" become "pure flame[s] of spirit," here "in vast throng" the righteous dead come to forget so that they may "conceive desire to return again to the body." In contrast to the stony Tartarean axis, which of cosmic, poetic, and social necessity must hold still and forever, the Elysian is alive with the unfolding plan of becoming. Hence, Virgil represents the scene as natural: trees, grass, running water, and rustic shelters. But this is a theme park, a rest area on the way to empire. The only law here is Virgil's desire for Rome: there is no love, no death, no passion — above all no war. Elysium requires only the signs of nature. And since in Elysium there is no nature, and thus no striving or war, there is no need for durable or monumental structures. As Anchises's lecture on "life-seeds" and flesh suggests (6.557–59), Virgil believes that the natural order is both pure and progressive — and now, finally, so too is his swarm.

The irony of this picture of a pure and progressive crowd is that it omits the reason for its existence, the very object that Virgil would have the cosmos serve: the human city. Homer is silent on this subject that is so dear to Virgil; Virgil is on his own when it comes to squaring the human condition with the bees' ideal sociality, a problem that in *Georgic 4* he could not resolve. And if we look upward to the world of the living that is mirrored by the land of the dead, the fate of Carthage anticipates this Elysian irony. Subject to only its own, local history, Carthage is happy before the Trojans' arrival. But the Queen lacks a mate. This lack attracts

Aeneas, who flees and so bears with him a past of intercultural violence that moves toward a troubling solution: conquest and Imperium. This force and this institution are antithetical and deadly to the natural and benevolent commonwealth.

Dido's suffering is her own; the story of the Trojans is known by all. Carthage is feminine, static; the Trojans are masculine, peripatetic. The Queen cannot live without Aeneas; her city cannot accommodate his warrior race. Betrayed, Dido takes her life; peaceful Carthage is raided for its honey. How mighty and implacable is Rome to Virgil. How he must love its image, too, for happiness to be so fugitive, so violently deferred. The message here is that the Roman may be contained only by those walls he builds himself. But is it not also suggested that the materials for these walls are to be appropriated from other cities? That Rome is a vision pursued through sword and subjugation? As in his earlier poem, Virgil is acutely sensitive to the contradiction of Roman peace. We have already seen this ambivalence in Virgil's picture of Trojan ants, wherein he attempts to join the languages of darkness and light. We see it again in the best-lit and happiest region of his *nekuia* — more specifically, by how Virgil uses the metaphor of the swarm.

Joined with the soul of his father, Anchises, Aeneas overlooks the scene of rebirth, the bucolic, amnesiac source of a cosmopolitan order yet to be:

> in a retired vale, Aeneas sees a sequestered grove and rustling forest thickets, and the river Lethe drifting past those peaceful homes. About it hovered peoples and tribes unnumbered; even as when, in the meadows, in cloudless summertime, bees light on many-hued blossoms and stream round lustrous lilies and all the fields murmur with humming. Aeneas is thrilled by the sudden sight and, knowing not, asks the cause — what is that river yonder, and who are the men thronging the banks in such a host? Then father Anchises: "Spirits they are, to whom second bodies are owed by Fate, and at the water of Lethe's stream they drink the soothing draught and long forgetfulness." (555)

These souls awaiting rebirth have gathered so that they may migrate upward into bodies and a higher state of organization. As in Homer's *Iliad*, book 2 bee simile, this swarm gives flesh to the entwined abstractions of a communal being and purpose and promises the emergence of a greater order. The swarm is also appropriate to the bucolic setting, a locus of naturalness, purity, and the past. As in the *Georgics*, however, though much more intensely, here nature (however extraordinary) is subject to order; like the disciplinary farmer and the fields he commands, this swarm exists to serve.

Virgil's chthonic swarm serves — which is to say, reflects — the world of the living. But the metaphor is more active than this. First, because it contains these spirits, the swarm may be regarded as an agent essential to their rebirth (a stunning inversion of Homer's swarming Achaians gathering and then marching toward their deaths). Second, the metaphor naturalizes the machinery of resurrection. Even though these souls have been purified of war, and the types for rebellion have been walled up in Tartarus, as if to make triply sure that no soul resists, the river ensures forgetting (a figure that Dante, in turn, will reverse). Aeneas's hesitant response to this scene confirms what I have pointed out elsewhere in Virgil, a pervasive ambivalence toward hierarchy and empire. Despite the knowledge that these shades' second lives will be Roman, Aeneas asks his father: "What means, alas! this their mad longing for the light?" (557).

If we think of Virgil's underworld as an imitation of actual space that must also serve as an imitation of Homer, then we find that Virgil has enclosed his master's swarm, thereby subordinating its sense and form to new purposes. This Virgil does by treating his model as an image: he harnesses its "fascination" by placing it in a new context. We are in a vast cavern at whose center trembles an image of heroic souls drinking forgetfulness and then rising into the future. This aspect of Virgil's *nekuia* is a pastoral mechanism for translating Homer's mythic figure into a more progressive idiom. Earlier I discussed how and why Virgil usurps the Homeric trope of *giantomachia* in *Georgic* 4; thus, it should be clear that he comes to *Aeneid* 6 armed with a singularly complicated means of reworking: inversion combined with a shift in scale. While creating his *nekuia*, Virgil uses this same technique to enhive the Greek epic's naturalism and grand scale, thereby miniaturizing it.

Yet, even though he has previously engaged with Homer's bees and enters to the fray well armed, *Aeneid* 6 is a new territory inhabited by a different sort of bee. Virgil must build a container for his swarm of rebirth, but it is to be entirely imaginary. As I have suggested, he cannot draw from nature. Thus, he studies the entirety of Homer's verse typologically, and thereby discovers the elements he requires for his own work. When composing the fourth *Georgic*, Virgil amplified and adapted the progressive movement that he sensed in Homer's *Iliad* 2 bee simile. Now, elsewhere in Homer, Virgil discovers an equally vital type, the division of the swarm into light and dark categories.

I have already located and named these swarms: Tartarus and Elysium. I have also spoken of their duality as an extension of Roman beliefs about the *umbilicus*, the urban locus through which the cosmic axis passes and around which the city is organized. Next I will consider the Homeric foundations of this double-axis model because to the rhetorical imagination *retractatio*, the vigorous reworking of an inherited model, is the only acceptable process of discovery, novelty's truest source.

For Homer the doorway to "the house of Hades and dread Persephone" is Circe's island, itself a place of transformation.[19] Here Odysseus's crew are by magic transformed into their animal equivalents — the first step in a symbolic movement down the scale of being from members of a human social unit to the swarming shades of *Odyssey* 11. Indeed, now that we are sensitive to Virgil's habits, when read typologically *Odyssey* 10 and 11 may be seen to assert a three-part descent from the order of social existence into the disorder of nonexistence. Because this scheme of organizational decay is consistent with archaic historiography, it is antithetical to Virgil's poetry of progress. It is a pattern ripe for inversion.

In *Odyssey* 11, after having dug, according to Circe's careful instructions, the votive pit and then making threefold libations "to all the dead," Odysseus fills it with sheep's blood, the stuff of life for which the shades hunger. Immediately, "there gathered from Erebus the spirits of those who are dead, brides and unwedded youths, and toil-worn old men, and tender maidens with hearts yet new to sorrow, and many, too, that had been wounded with bronze-tipped spears, men slain fighting, wearing their blood-stained armour. These came thronging in crowds about the pit from every side, with wondrous cry; and pale fear seized me [Odysseus]. . . . And I drew my sharp sword from beside my thigh and sat there, and would not suffer the powerless heads of the dead to draw near to the blood until I had enquired of Teiresias" (389). Set beyond the world and nature, this scene is barren of naturalistic language. This container is equal to its contents: darkness, strangeness, death. Odysseus eschews the language of flowers and bees, the metaphors of life. Here such figures would be obvious illusions, trivial and trivializing. Here all symbols recall the skeleton.

One's overall impression of the scene is the image of Odysseus surrounded by an amorphous mass of spirits recoiling from the light and hungry for blood. Indeed, because they are disembodied and drawn from Hades to this strange place, Homer does not wish to picture the dead as having volition, purpose, or organization. Homer's language emphasizes the dead's strangeness to the living. The shades are simply *ethnoi nekros*, the tribes of the dead. The ties to other human beings that make life bearable and even sweet no longer bind. And because these spirits have been removed from their proper place and the sovereignty of Hades, they are strange even to themselves. Death and displacement negate all organization. The dead do not, for instance, present themselves to Odysseus in martial array. Even the symbols of force are beyond them. Odysseus senses as much; what he fears is their difference from life, from himself. The *ethnoi nekros* are the dark swarm freed from flesh but not its memory; they are the dark swarm unencumbered by metaphor.

The land of the dead, the locus of Homer's dark swarm, lies literally and imaginatively off the map. When giving Odysseus directions, Circe tells him that to reach this land he must journey so far to the north that he will cross "the stream of Oceanus." As the paradigmatic topos and map of the world — the "Shield of Achilles" — suggests, the "Ocean River" is the limit of order and of knowledge: "He [Hephaistos] made on it the great strength of the Ocean River / which ran around the uttermost rim of the shield's strong structure."[20] According to the Shield's allegory, within the world's ocean boundary Zeus's balance of peace and war reigns. Beyond it lies a region of danger and uncertainty into which Odysseus must venture if he is to speak with Teiresias. Neither Homer nor Odysseus imagined their dead as contained and controlled by some cosmic analog to the bureaucratic State. Their dead know only sorrow. And they are hungry. They envy us even our brief struggle in the light. I think we understand why Homer places this dark swarm nowhere and behind the ocean wall.

In *Odyssey* 10 and 11, Homer associates bees and the *nekuia*, thereby suggesting the type that Virgil later recovers and articulates. This association is established in the following three ways. First, Homer confirms the crowd's dangerous alterity through the macabre scene of shades gathering to feed on blood. Second, he creates an otherworldly place to contain this crowd, this swarm of disembodied souls. Finally, in the intelligence of this swarm (Teiresias) he plants the seeds of the future. Odysseus needs Teiresias's words so that he may find Ithaca and live, so that his line, in the person of his son, Telemachus, will not die. In *Aeneid* 6, upon the dead's wisdom as well as their forgetting hinges the future of Empire.

It is accurate to say that Virgil's underworld was influenced by *Odyssey* 10 and 11. However, it is the structure and its concomitant drama — the type — suggested by Homer's association of bees and the otherworldly space that Virgil imitates and perfects through its reconciliation with Roman beliefs. The Homeric dead inhabit an ambiguous and dismal space; Virgil's underworld, divided into regions of darkness and of light, is topographically and architecturally exact. In keeping with its *nekuia*'s geographical eccentricity, the dyad of books 10 and 11 is not the *Odyssey*'s physical center. Not so Virgil's underworld. It is the subject of the sixth book of twelve.

Thus far I have focused on the poetic, and to a lesser degree a linguistic, connection between Homer's land of the dead and Virgil's underworld. Now I will strengthen this bond of image and language by returning to Roman custom. Earlier I used the idea of the *umbilicus* to illuminate the motivational and structural relationship between the realm of the living and Virgil's *nekuia*. The same pages of Richard Sennett's *Flesh and Stone* that describe how the Romans organized their cities also explain that near the umbilicus was dug a hole called the *mundus*, "a chamber, or *two* such chambers, one above the other . . . consecrated to infernal gods below the earth's crust" (108; my italics).[21] The *umbilicus* and the *mundus* are themselves a dyad — a design doubly echoed by the *mundus*'s two-chambered shape. Arguably, then, there is a tissue of Roman custom that resonates with the structure, theme, and incidents particular to the Odyssean dyad. It is therefore permissible to speculate that such rituals prepared the ground for and indeed guided some of Virgil's most important choices and most memorable images.

Sennett helps frame this powerfully suggestive resonance between Roman custom, Virgil's typological art, and Homeric tradition, pointing out that "the imposition of 'Rome' [upon the Greeks from whom 'so much of Roman high culture derived'] was more like the overlaying of a memory of 'home' in order to legitimate rule" (110). The *Aeneid* is an artificial epic, a national "memory" of a home city's founding written after the fact and justifying Roman conquest. When viewed as a "legitimat[ing]" memory, Virgil's great poem "overlay[s]" the Homeric corpus but does not obscure it — indeed, we may compare the *Aeneid* to an elaborate transparency that assumes but modifies for new purposes a map of familiar terrain.

Virgil possessed Homer as a whole and typologically. The Roman understood the swarm as a complex but coherent system of images centered around the *Iliad* 2 bee simile, the poem's first and perhaps most important moment of dense figuration. This means that even when broken down into its cooperative modes, as in *Georgic* 4, and then purified of war in *Aeneid* 6, the swarm retained its intimate linkages to the crowd's dark force, that disturbing essence witnessed by Odysseus. And it is this essence — its implications and related images — that helps explain Virgil's *nekuia* and presages the Hive's evolution. This space, this grand structural act of hiving, is the honey of Homer's bees. It is the richly suggestive and challenging form that centuries later Dante will transform into the space of paradise.

2

FROM DANTE TO MILTON

The Hive Translated, Then Damned

In the reception histories of metaphors, the more sharply defined and differentiated the imaginative stock becomes, the sooner the point is reached where there seems to be an extreme inducement to veer around, with the existing model, in the most decisive way and to try out the unsurpassable procedure of reversing it.

Hans Blumenberg, Shipwreck with Spectator

Virgil "sharply defined" the Hive, clarifying its structure and mapping its extremes. He showed us the insect society's two faces, gave us two indispensable pictures of society: the beehive's golden hierarchy and the ant heap's dark swarm. Thus the post-Virgilian "reception history" of the Hive is a series of "decisive" attempts "to veer around . . . [Virgil's double] model . . . and to try out the unsurpassable procedure of reversing it." To the classically trained poet, Virgil's presence was second only to Homer's. But when it came to imaging the city and the feelings of those who served it, the Roman overshadowed his master. This means that Virgil's imitators had to be as bold as he was, their reworkings as inventive as his and, if need be, as extreme.

I have already discussed the cultural power that authorized and indeed required such a treatment of inherited forms. For most of its textual life the Hive has been subject to rhetoric, a system that equated invention with, and hailed as a virtue, a model's vigorous, controlled revision. We may then imagine the Hive's evolution as a curve. Its point of origin is Homer's natural swarm, whose domestication Virgil begins in his fourth *Georgic*. The Hive then descends into Virgil's underworld and is divided. But this three-part movement is a unity, only the first of four such efforts to claim and reform the Hive. In this chapter I will treat the second stone of this arch for which every piece is a keystone. I will examine how and why Dante raises Virgil's bees to heaven, makes them angelic, part of the Celestial Rose. Then I will investigate Milton's amazing response. He sends the Hive back underground, this time to Hell — he uses our topos to image an alien, demonic order: Pandemonium.

The Dantean Translation: The Hive and Divine Cosmos

Magnifying Virgil's point on this curve makes it clear that several paths converge to form his underworld. As I have shown, Virgil merged the dark swarm implied by the dyad of *Odyssey* 10 and 11 with the Hive of peace in *Georgic* 4. This mixing of categories and their symbols (the natural and the supernatural, order and chaos, good and evil) amplified and made palpable traditional contradictions that, of consequence, required control. This Virgil accomplished through dividing his underworld into two antithetical regions, Tartarus and Elysium. Dante builds upon this division. His Christian cosmography empowers him to separate good and evil to a degree that his pagan master could not. Working in the vernacular, he translates the Latin Hive to Catholic Paradise:

> So, in the shape of that white Rose, the holy
> legion was shown to me — the host that Christ,
> with His own blood, had taken as His bride.
> The other host, which, flying, sees and sings
> the glory of the One who draws its love,
> and that goodness which granted it such glory,
> just like a swarm of bees that, at one moment,
> enters the flowers and, at another, turns
> back to that labor which yields such sweet savor,
> descended into that vast flower graced
> with many petals, then again rose up
> to the eternal dwelling of its love.[1]

Because Virgil is Roman, when dealing with natural symbols he chooses the poetic strategy of domestication, which suggests that nature's patterns are discrete powers that must be worked with on their own terms. And because he is pagan, the uncertainty of Virgil's universe is only heightened through the presence of many gods, Olympian and local, most of whom are proud, inconstant, and needy. For instance, Venus, Aeneas's mother, helps her son as she may, but she cannot entirely counter Juno's hatred for Trojans. The classical mixture of divine and human substance is passionate and political, as worldly and unsympathetic as human Imperium.

Dante, however, is Christian. For him God is One, absolute in His rule, His justice, and His love. Thus, Dante suffers a longing distinct from Aeneas's: Dante's is defined by the anxiety of sublime courtship and the procedures of Augustinian interpretation. He knows nature to be a reflection of a higher design. His sense of creation is suffused with the conviction that its forms and processes express the Creator's abstract, and therefore perfect, order. Hence, the symbols nature inspires and their placement function like scriptural language, as signs through which we may and must come to know God: "come natural lo suo corso prende / dal divino 'ntelleotto e do sua arte"; "how nature follows — as she takes her course — / the Divine Intellect and Divine Art" (*Inf.*, 11.99–100). Needless to say, this idea of nature is quite different from Homer's. His nature has no plan outside itself. And even Zeus is subject to a fate whose workings are never clear. In Homer's archaic universe, even though the ruler of the gods may command the elements, he is not their creator.

This uncertain relationship between a limited divinity and an amorphous and mysterious nature has its poetic consequences: neither Homer nor Virgil could conceptualize and hence imaginatively orchestrate natural symbols as systematically or — in my opinion — as grandly as Dante.

The key to Dante's natural symbols is his belief that natural patterns reflect a perfect and unfolding order that transcends earthly designs. Since to him nature symbolized a greater and truer reality, I believe that he felt free to rework and renew his models even more ambitiously than Virgil. And to Dante's sense of poetic license we should also add that he had the advantage of Virgil's example. When representing the cooperative perfection of "both of Heaven's courts" — which together form Paradise, the peak of creation — Dante did not first have to choose, domesticate, construct, and purify a fitting poetic form. Virgil handed it to him ripe for reworking.

What Dante does with the Hive is stunning and complex, but this action and its poetic consequences are nonetheless structurally comprehensible. In the main, Virgil's otherworld is a horizontal field divided into the separate and opposed regions of Tartarus and Elysium, each organized around a distinct vertical axis. The center of Tartarus is a monumental castle (a prison, really) containing a vertical space at whose top rises Olympus and at whose bottom lie chained the Titans, the Ur-forces of rebellion. Like its opposite, this axis bisects and thus unifies the three levels of Virgil's cosmos, but, unlike the Elysian axis (the scene of purified souls moving upward into new bodies and the future), the Tartarean is static.

Although he restricts his palette, Virgil paints Elysium with naturalistic, organic images. For Tartarus he uses a language of stone and confinement. This locus is a sculpture, not a garden. It speaks of a divine hierarchy founded upon oppressive order, a decidedly un-Christian formulation with which Dante could only disagree. Because the Virgilian underworld's bipolarity asserts a disjunction between divine will and organic process, and also because Virgil's Tartarus suggests that this will is oppressive, perhaps unjust, and in some sense mutable (it is founded upon patricide and rebellion), I am convinced that together these poetic elements both challenged and sparked Dante's Christian sense of order. We may imagine him reading these elements as contradictions that flow from pagan blindness. Dante understands Virgil's underworld to be an anticipation and imperfect expression of a perfect form.

So exactly how does Dante reveal the form he believes lies unexpressed in Virgil? How does Dante "convert" Virgil's Roman bees to a Christian worldview? At the most obvious level, we know that Dante places Virgil's chthonic bees in Paradise, a promotion that in itself tells us how seriously he regarded the cooperative order expressed by the natural hive. But in contrast to his master's bees, Dante's are not human souls. Rather, they are the "other host," the angels who mediate between God above and the "holy legion" seated in the Rose. This redefinition perfects Virgil's Hive, completes its author's struggle to domesticate and purify Homer's bees. Dante, who did not know Homer directly, would not have understood his poesis in this way. However, with the advantage of historical hindsight and access to a good bit of the Homeric corpus, we are privileged to see in Dante's poetry the emergence of what I call the angelic hive.

In itself, the Celestial Rose is a fascinating object: part organic, part Roman coliseum, part city. But more than a fusion of pagan and Christian, humanmade and natural elements, the Rose is a feminine sphere bathed in the living light of God. It is thus a difficult form to imagine. And Dante would have it so. We are in a sublime region, one where the resources of human sight and language (generally one and the same for Dante) are by nature inadequate. Indeed, when faced with the Ultimate, like his earthly vision, Dante's poetry lags behind what it would represent. In the *Paradiso*'s final cantos seeing and poetry are at odds: Dante's poetry sets up but cannot realize what the "sublime vision" of the inner eye enjoys.

In a journey that as it spirals upward plays more and more to the *nerbo del viso* (the optic nerve, which in *Inferno* 9.73–74 Virgil speaks of as a distinct object and faculty), it is highly significant that by the time Dante reaches *Paradiso* 30, the *Commedia*'s language of light has become an unbearable force. Dante's first sight of Paradise is blindness: "Like sudden lightning scattering the spirits / of sight so that the eye is then too weak / to act on other things it would perceive, / such was the living light encircling me, / leaving me so enveloped by its veil / of radiance that I could see no thing" (46–51). Although more satisfying than paralysis, the speaker's second experience of Paradise (below), which he describes as the product of a "new vision," is still poetic — his vision is not yet purely conceptual and thus not yet in accord with the Divine. Although he sees "living sparks, / settl[ing] on the flowers" like bees, Dante cannot

yet inwardly discern their divine structure, the ideal state that their mode
of cooperation imitates:

> I saw light that took a river's form —
> light flashing, reddish gold, between two banks
> painted with wonderful spring flowerings.
>   Out of that stream there issued living sparks,
> which settled on the flowers on all sides,
> like rubies set in gold; and then, as if
>   intoxicated with the odors, they
> again plunged into the amazing flood:
> as one spark sank, another spark emerged.
> (61–69)

I read this moment of "second sight" as a comment on Virgil's Elysian
axis and its pagan model of resurrection. The river here is the "form" of
Lethe. And in accord with Anchises's theory of life's fiery essence, these
living sparks symbolize the souls of the righteous dead whose "intoxi-
cat[ion]" in this instance appears to draw them back down. And since to
Dante seeing and poesis are one, in order to rework the Hive, Dante's
visual imagination must be strengthened and purified.

Beatrice, knowing his mind and need, his "mighty thirst" for a third
and higher sort of vision, which she calls *superbe* (sublime), tells him to
drink from the river, about which she says (as a comment on mortal as
well as poetic vision): "The river and the gems / of topaz entering and
leaving, and / the grasses' laughter — these are shadowy / prefaces of
their truth; not that these things / are lacking in themselves; the defect
lies / in you, whose sight is not yet that sublime" (76–81). And so Dante
bathes his face in the paradisiacal water,

> to make still finer mirrors of my eyes,
> I bent down toward the waters which flow there
> that we, in them, may find our betterment.
>   But as my eyelids' eaves drank of that wave
> it seemed to me that it had changed its shape:
> no longer straight, that flow now formed a round.
>   Then, just as maskers, when they set aside
> the borrowed likeness in which they hide,
> seem to be other than they were before,

> so were the flowers and the sparks transformed,
> changing to such festivity before me
> that I saw — clearly — both of Heaven's courts.
> (85–96)

This passage is Dante's Christian and spiritual answer to Virgil's narcotic and bodily model of resurrection. Virgil's model suggests that new life depends upon the end of knowledge, which is effected through a form of ingestion (drinking). Dante's entirely transcends the flesh, showing us that rebirth is of the spirit. Dantean resurrection hinges on knowledge gained, not lost. The significance and power of water is also reversed. In place of the medicinal draught: Baptism, a symbolic cleansing, the soul's entry into the new life of *viste superbe*, the ability to correctly perceive divine patterns.

Once baptized, Dante's eyes report that *the shapes of things have changed*. The river, which up to this point has been flowing "straight" in proper sublunar fashion, now assumes the impossible and perfect shape of a circle. And the flowers and sparks as well reveal their divine shapes, their most perfect forms. There is an order to this process of discerning pattern, a scale of efficacy along which Dante would have us position the several degrees of seeing.

Since the manner in which one enters a sacred space tends to define that space, it is significant that Dante's approach to the paradisiacal Hive is a tripartite, progressive structure that strongly recalls how Virgil domesticates Homer's bees in *Georgic* 4. Dante takes the visual apprehension of natural forms through its paces. In canto 30, lines 46–50, our earthly and untutored eyes are blinded by the "living light," which Dante describes naturalistically as "lightning." Then, our "new vision" of "both of Heaven's courts" as a river, flowers, and sparks is revealed as defective, insufficiently sublime. In that he mixes natural and fabulous images (for instance, flowers and gems), Dante means us to know this second way of seeing as both generally poetic (a comment on his own art) and specifically Virgilian, which is suggested by its allusion to Anchises's Lucretian theory of generation.[2] As I have already mentioned, this process's third term is baptism, which allows for the transcendence of natural and pagan ways of knowing. Dante is telling us that what we will now see is neither natural to nor representable in the ancient tongue, and certainly not in everyday language.

Before Dante is the Celestial Rose, an unfathomably huge circular structure rising in a "thousand tiers" and lit from above by the light of God, which streams from the *Primum Mobile*. Beatrice calls this Rose a "great . . . council of white robes . . . our city" (129–30). One would think that this image's scale and import would make poetry impossible and silence the human speaker. Yet not only does the poem continue, much of its final Canto is devoted to the premise that *"mio veder fu maggio / che 'l parlar nostro"* (my vision was greater than our speech) (33.55–56).

The poem continues because, although it seems that even purified sight cannot take in anything beyond the general form, Dante believes that his *vision* at this moment (not the bodily fact of perception but rather the conceptual structure of the Hive topos) is "greater / than speech can show." As I understand his purpose here, Dante hopes that his audience will be able to make the leap to God by way of what to him is the topos's highest office: its conceptual, philosophical aspects. In chapter 1, I spent some time defining the Hive as a "combinatory form." This is to say that I defined the Hive topos in three ways: first, as a phenomenological event; second, poetically — as a metaphor; and third, conceptually — as a topos. The Hive thus participates in and unites the three levels of human understanding. Because Dante senses something in how the Hive topos structures space — an energy, a possibility, that not only outstrips language, but exceeds the poetic imagination and thereby reaches out to the Divine — he uses this form to bring us to the point that we may intuit *"la forma universal"* (33.91).

In *Paradiso*'s final canto, the *forma universal* that Dante approaches through extending the Hive's conceptual shape is not simply the visual and symbolic unity of the "three circles" (33.115–20): "As the geometer intently seeks / to square the circle, but he cannot reach, / through thought on thought, the principle he needs, / so I searched that strange sight: I wished to see / the way in which our human effigy / suited the circle and found a place in it" (133–38). Dante "searches" the universal shape for how humans fit in a cosmos sublimely and absolutely organized. He seeks our place in an order that is, quite literally, the creation of a single and complete *act* of Divine imagination. I sense that Dante crowns his work with a monumental version of the Hive because this topos's visual structure and its attendant conceptual process come closest to how, in his mind, the paradox of a complete and hierarchical, and yet "continuous," creation must be organized.

I am suggesting nothing less than that Dante conceives of Creation as a transcendent version of the Hive. As I have come to understand it, the Hive is an unfolding visual and conceptual experience that yokes together a human observer with his opposite, a collective organism that enjoys and signifies a different order of being. My theory is that when the observer (in this case, Dante) looks along a visual axis and perceives at its terminus a social organism, not only does he thereby comprehend his simplicity and his powerlessness, he also — paradoxically — experiences the godlike power of his sovereign position. Such an apprehension of power makes sense in our everyday contact with actual insect communities, but how do we square it with Dante's experience? In Dante's case, far from being dwarfed into mortal insignificance and silenced by the Celestial Rose, the Hive's essential logic of empowerment (the same design that attracted Dante to Virgil's bees, and Virgil to Homer's) allows him to share something of the knowledge and command of pattern that belongs to God. Because the apprehension of ourselves as godlike is basic to the Hive's structure, the form enables Dante to imagine and thus to seek consubstantiality with the Divine.

Dante's Paradise pushes to its farthest extreme a basic experience that the Hive makes possible, one that links his poetry-beyond-poetry with a commonplace of everyday perception. In most instances of the Hive, in order to conceptually grasp a mass of distinct entities as a whole, the observing consciousness must assume a seat that accords with the logic and *process* of seeing. This means that the reader's experience of the Hive necessarily features the sensation and implications of elevation. This is a movement that makes otherwise invisible spatial categories palpable, expressive; it also engenders a process of classification and division that culminates in the attribution of essences. Now because *Paradiso* seeks to reveal the Divine Order, the intellectual essence of forms, it makes sense that we find the Hive exactly where this concern most powerfully asserts itself. Such an intersection of motive and structure is not, then, fortuitous in the least. I therefore think it insufficient to hold that Dante chose to modify and elevate Virgil's bees simply because they were Virgil's. Rather, I suggest that we view his choice and treatment of the Hive as a clear statement that, like his *autore*, Dante sensed that the Hive holds within it a blueprint for the refinement and conversion of an everyday experience into the shape of purposeful becoming. The Hive allows Dante to knit together his hierarchal, visual universal order with his love of the city and his belief that Nature reflects the Mind of God.

Now is a good time to recall again that however much of Virgil's and Dante's bees we may see in Homer's original simile, the Hive is a visio-conceptual form that has been developed and refined over time. Virgil does not find in Homer the Hive delineated as a coherent topos. In fact, the crucial and clearly articulated link between the city (the immortal and transcendent human organism) and the natural hive (the locus of Divine order) is not fully available until there are cities that know themselves to be the center of Imperium. But even Virgil was not able to completely realize the Hive's possibilities, for our object's positive formulation did not achieve maturity until Dante reconceived it within a Christian frame. And it was the Christian idea of God that allowed Dante to visualize a natural hierarchy that was as transcendent as it was absolutely good.

The Hive's evolution has not been either smooth or gradual. Each step in its development evidences revolution and confirms the discontinuous nature of history. Not surprisingly, in Milton's hands the Hive is developed further via another muscular reversal. I have shown how Dante breaks with Virgil while yet continuing his project of domesticating and purifying the swarm; next I will discuss how Milton completes the Hive by developing its infernal possibilities. In a manner of speaking, he accomplishes this by repaganizing the Hive, by undoing Dante so as to get at the dark swarm. He returns to the scene of Virgil's original contest with Homer and recapitulates the Hive's division into its three basic cooperative modes: the natural Hive, the Hive of war, and the Hive of peace.

The Magic and Philosophy of Damnation

Thus far I have discussed the Hive's development as a process of perfection, elevation, and formal integration. Dante's Celestial Rose paradigmizes — and pictures — an attitude toward order which holds that Divine hierarchy and Nature are at root one and the same; together they form a circle in which human beings must discover the place that has been prepared for them. This circle and the terms and forms that it once so harmoniously contained weakened during the Baroque Age. By Milton's time this Medieval worldview was broken: revolution and reason had made an anachronism of the old Christian vision of wholeness.[3] For my purposes, in the English tradition, Milton's *Paradise Lost* testifies not only to this circle's disintegration, but also to its reintegration into new patterns that speak to and help construct the modern situation and its anxious subject.

What I am after, then, is a reading of Milton's bees that amounts to what Kenneth Burke might call a "*diagnosis* (simplification) of our partially conscious, partially unconscious situation."[4] Indeed, by comparing the structure and "situation" (i.e., spatial positioning) of Dante's Hive with Milton's, it is possible to begin to construct a simplified and therefore interpretable chart of how Milton (and after him the Western world) felt himself (itself) to be "situated" vis-à-vis what the Hive uniquely evokes and articulates: namely, our "partially conscious, partially unconscious" notions of and relationship to social and political existence. And since Dante's and Milton's opposed versions of the Hive together define the ground for all further reworking, it is appropriate to note that both poets, albeit each in his own way, are concerned with *appearance* and *position*, key elements of the Hive's grammar that gain significance as we approach our moment.

Dante places his Hive in Paradise. The Celestial Rose is a vast structure that harmoniously merges organic and architectural elements, pagan and Christian imagery. His bees are a host of white angels who in perfect accord mediate between the souls of the blessed and the living light of God. In stark contrast, Milton places his Hive in Hell. Like the Rose, Pandemonium is monumental in scale, but it is made from dead matter and according to the genius of Mammon. It rises on the foundations of Virgil's Castle Tartarus. And it is exactly because Pandemonium's inhabitants are devils — fallen and contentious, simultaneously divided and ruled by fear — that Milton figures them as bees. In their numbers and unified by Satan's unspeakable motive, they suggest the appearance of social life. Obviously, then, between Dante and Milton the beehive's signification has changed. But this change implies a greater shift: Milton understands nature and hence natural symbols differently than Dante.

One might argue that Milton placed his Hive in Hell so as to "answer" Dante's Catholicism and leave it at that. Such a position would profit by Rebecca W. Smith's article "The Source of Milton's Pandemonium," to which Merritt Y. Hughes refers in his notes to lines 755–68 of *Paradise Lost*: "Smith points out in her architectural comparison of *Pandemonium* with St. Peter's in Rome . . . that the bee was the emblem of the Barberini Pope Urban VIII, who dedicated the basilica in 1636, and that 'his followers were often referred to as bees.'"⁵ But this sort of explanation takes us only so far. For Pandemonium's papal associations are really only a small part of the accretive movement of images and contexts that combine to form this instance of the Hive.

First, because we are dealing with a form that is at once exceedingly flexible and yet organized around a visio-conceptual process, lines 768–75 of *Paradise Lost* do not serve as either a complete topos or its center, but as an epic commonplace. As Milton himself suggests, the distinction between commonplace and topos is one of limits. The commonplace is bookish, expressing an unexamined relationship with inherited symbols. In comparison with the topos's communicative range and aesthetic utility, the commonplace is a minor form:

> As bees
> In spring time, when the Sun with Taurus rides,
> Pour forth thir populous youth about the Hive
> In clusters; they among fresh dews and flowers
> Fly to and fro, or on the smoothed Plank,
> The suburb of thir Straw-built Citadel,
> New rubb'd with Balm, expiate and confer
> Thir State affairs.
> (768–75)

Hughes's exceedingly helpful note to these lines tells us that this "simile opens vistas on comparisons of throngs of people to bees." In this regard, he cites the simile's obvious and essential connections with Homer (*Iliad*, 2.87–90) and Virgil (*Aeneid*, 1.430–36, and *Georgics*, 4.149–22). But he also directs us to a section of *Defensio Prima* (First Defense) in which Milton uses the Bible and dialectic to refute the then common position that Virgil, as the spokesman for both the wisdom of antiquity and the natural order's political truth, authorizes us to see in the natural hive a situation of and divine authorization for absolute monarchy.

Here Milton reminds his opponent, Salmasius, that, unlike human monarchs, the king bees do not harm their subjects. He thereby maintains the classical notion that the natural hive's organization is superior to ours, but he breaks with the ancients by focusing on the differences between bees and men. He rejects the idea that the natural hive's organization is comparable to human absolutism and contends that by definition any such human society would be barbarous and tyrannical: the

bees's kings are nothing more (but no less) than bees. Nor does he believe that Virgil's bees condone such a government. Virgil tells us that
the bees "pass their lives under mighty laws." These are Zeus's laws, and
because Milton thinks of Zeus as a code for the Christian God, Zeus's
laws are just.

A reader of *Defensio Prima* quickly discovers that in neither nature,
antiquity, nor the Bible does Milton find evidence that humans or beasts
should live "under kings that are loosed from all law."[6] To the contrary,
he finds only arguments against such evil. From this position of threefold authority, he goes on to attack Salmasius's position. Milton claims
that Salmasius's use of the beehive to justify absolutism is derivative,
taken from "some divines of the Council of Trent." And hence is the
"put[ting] on of a borrowed mask." Beyond its obvious function as part
of an ad hominem argument that titles Salmasius a "knave," this language of masking suggests that Milton thinks of the *commonplace* of the
hive — how it has come to naturalize the evil of political tyranny — as a
problem of, rather than a tool for, interpretation.

Milton would have us see Salmasius's commonplace and "unexercised" reading of the Hive as a fool's mask that one wears without knowing its full implications.[7] Furthermore, according to Milton, the argument for a natural absolutism aligns one with unnatural powers that, in
the face of Biblical truth and the powers of reason, presume to cloak
themselves in the forms of everyday life. But this argument raises poetic
difficulties for one who so commands the classics and who possesses
a rhetorically trained imagination of the highest order. Milton is convinced that the idea of absolute tyranny is unnatural and evil. Yet it is to
Virgil — the pagan apologist for Roman tyranny — and to the natural
hive — a society indigenous to the world over which Satan was given
dominion — that he looks for patents of artistic origin and authority. If
Milton is to use the epic to achieve a new vision of order, one that is true
to both rhetoric and an "exercised" Christianity, he must make unmasking his business.

In his own way Dante is also concerned with masks, the problem
of appearances. But in contrast to Milton's, Dante's cosmos is secure:
through its many levels and forms shines the unifying Divine Intellect.
Despite both his reference to Italy's hope for a redeemer (*Inf.*, 1.101–6)
and his beloved Florence's agonistic political life (6.61), Dante's focus is
not the place of worldly institutions in the battle between good and evil.

Even more than union with Beatrice, he wants to "see / the way in which our human effigy / suit[s] the circle [of God's order] and f[inds its] place in it" (*Par.*, 33.136–38). And because God has prepared for each of us a place within His circle, we are doubly sure that the *Commedia* explicates an order that is as good as it is absolute. What unmasking goes on seems to be part of the tour, and is not, as in Milton's thought, explicitly linked to our day-to-day conduct. For Dante, unmasking is revelation, a purification and strengthening of the mortal faculties so that we comprehend the pattern of things as they are: complete and inclined by Divine Love to elevate the "thirsty" soul. And because God is rather distant throughout Dante's vision, so is Satan. They are at opposite ends of the cosmic axis. The former basks in the light and mystery of His threeness while the latter, like Virgil's Titans, is forever chained below.

As even a cursory reading of *Paradise Lost* shows, Milton's Satan is much more active and present than Dante's. Milton's evil is seductive, and if we are not careful, admirable. The many levels and variously and exactly punished sinners of the *Inferno* suggest that for Dante the sins (and thus the technology of their avoidance) are well mapped. In contrast, even Milton's Heaven is not free from the artillery of rebellious angels. Milton's strenuous definition of free will — the most Protestant of his several obsessions and his touchstone for truth — does not occur to Dante.

When compared with the *Commedia*, how different seems the intensity, manner, and value of masks and unmasking in *Paradise Lost*. Dante knows good by its light, evil by light's absence — and part of his security is that all symbols have their proper interpretation. In *Paradise Lost*, like that "darkness visible" that is Satan, symbols may be used as camouflage and to lie. Milton's Satan, who once was Lucifer, the angel of light, may fool all but God. Clearly, then, the distinction between good and evil for Milton is not made apparent by light alone. It is, rather, earned by often bitter experience. In the *Commedia* the degree of evil may be plotted exactly according to its proximity to God; in *Paradise Lost* evil incarnate walks the earth, enraged and vigilant, eager to strike at God through humankind. We are all fallen because of Adam's conscious choice, and Satan in his various guises and instruments, as in *Job*, has his part to play in God's plan. Although no less interested than Dante in the ultimate fate of individuals, Milton does not believe that the key to salvation is discovering our place in the circle of living light, which is a state rather than a struggle, one in which the power to choose is secondary to an acceptance of God's Love. To Milton, if we would be saved, moment by moment we must read energetically and correctly God's plan and then act accordingly, so that we may play our role as a "true warfaring Christian" in an ongoing drama of testing and purification. Thus Milton's urgent and even strident concern with masks and his ambivalence regarding accepted symbols like the Hive.

In the *Commedia* we know good and evil in themselves, both by sight and by position in the cosmic hierarchy. If we are at a loss, near us always is an informed and protective companion: first Virgil, then Beatrice, and finally St. Bernard. Even the devils play their role by briefly and colorfully showing the way. Conversely, Milton believes that because of our fallen state we cannot distinguish good from evil in themselves. Because they exist together, like "two twins," we cannot without labor, "dust and heat," come to know them — and even then we may know the one only by the presence of the other. In a much-quoted passage of *Areopagitica*, Milton lays out his model of discovery:

> Good and evil we know in the field of this world grow up together almost inseparably; and the knowledge of good is so involved and interwoven with the knowledge of evil and in so many cunning resemblances hardly to be discerned, that those confused seeds which were imposed on Psyche as an incessant labor to cull out and sort asunder, were not more intermixed. It was from out of the rind of one apple tasted, that the knowledge of good and evil, as two twins cleaving together, leaped forth into the world. And perhaps this is the doom which Adam fell into of knowing good and evil, that is to say, of knowing good by evil.
>
> As therefore the state of man now is, what wisdom can there be to choose, what continence to forbear without the knowledge of evil? He that can apprehend and consider vice with all her baits and seeming pleasures, and yet abstain, and yet distinguish, and yet prefer that which is truly better, he is the true warfaring Christian. I cannot praise a fugitive and cloistered virtue, unexercised and unbreathed, that never sallies out and sees her adversary, but slinks out of the race where that immortal garland is to be run for, not without dust and heat. (728–29)

The interpretive principles here are juxtaposition and contrast, which are to be deployed within a frame of labor and conflict. In "this [fallen] world," not only are good and evil "involved and interwoven," but evil has the power to take on "so many cunning resemblances" that its nature is "hardly to be discerned." He compares our process of distinguishing good from evil with the plight of Apuleius's Psyche, who by Venus (the antagonistic mother of Psyche's lover, Cupid) is tasked with "sort[ing] the various kinds of grain out of a vast, mixed pile." Not only is this task "an incessant labor," but without the help of some friendly ants it would never have been accomplished. This myth's presence at the heart of Milton's summation of man's interpretative problem suggests that, in the struggle for knowledge, when hard-pressed for aid we may call upon and be answered by the social insect. Milton's thought here directs us to attend to his social insects elsewhere, his bees.

We should expect the poetry engendered by such a contentious model of discovery to follow suit in both form and content — and so it is in *Paradise Lost*. As to its feel, Milton's *nekuia*, his underworld, is closer to Virgil's than to Dante's, for both the Roman and the English poet choose to conduct their symbolic conversation about cooperation in proximity to evil. No doubt this choice has something to do with biographical similarity. Both Virgil's Italy and Milton's England are recovering from civil conflicts that profoundly altered each nation and its people's sense of themselves and their future. Thus, each poet's Hive emphasizes violence and physical change.

Behind adamantine walls and at the bottom of the abyss, Virgil chains rebellion, the crowd's dark power. But Milton's dissolution is deeper than his progenitor's, for as C. M. Bowra observes, *Paradise Lost* "was written after a great crisis in Milton's life. He, who had believed that the Commonwealth would establish the Rule of the Saints on earth, and had looked forward to 'a universal and mild monarchy' in England, had seen all his hope founder. He turned from the stricken political scene to his poem and hoped to create in it the order which he had failed to find in the common world. . . . In style, as in subject, Milton withdrew from active life in the hope of finding something more durable and more satisfying."[8] As Bowra has it, the unabated power of evil, its ability to corrupt political designs at every turn, causes Milton to choose another and higher subject for his genius, that of "assert[ing] Eternal Providence, / And justify[ing] the ways of God to men" (*PL*, 1.25–26). Through this lens Milton may view and express what to him is the primary skill required for salvation, how to know "good *by* evil," and show us how to act so as to save ourselves.

To Milton, because evil may take on virtually any appearance, and good and evil exist together in the "rind" of any symbol, the making of his Hive must also be an unmaking. Necessarily, then, his Hive's success will be measured by contrast rather than spatial separation and structural balance, which is Virgil's and even more so Dante's strategy. Because our topos holds within it the potential for several and antithetical types of cooperation, if he is to write an epic, Milton must have the Hive, rework it boldly and yet according to tradition. But, again, Virgil's particular strategy of *retractatio*, his division of light and dark energies and the former's absolute containment, simply cannot work for Milton the Puritan.

Milton's solution to the problem of the Hive is as radical as Dante's but dissimilar as to method and goal. The former continues and indeed perfects Virgil's process of division, spatial separation, and purification. Milton, however, goes against the Hive's evolutionary current by returning to the Homeric symbol complex. Around a reworked version of Rumor, he reorganizes the Hive's original three modes of cooperation, thereby shifting the imagistic center of Homer's simile. Milton's strategy is more philosophical than poetic: by unearthing the Hive's origins, Milton is able to dissociate the signifier from the signified, which the accumulative work of Virgil and Dante had cemented together.

Let us return to the *Iliad* 2 bee simile. I have explained how Rumor signifies both the divine force (fate, Zeus's will) and the warriors' psychology. To these powers we should now add two more. First, in that Rumor disrupts the ease and order of the naturalistically rendered peaceful swarm and thereby moves the Greeks toward death, it is a locus of alterity. By this I mean that Rumor is antithetical to the human. It is an agent of what Simone Weil identifies as the *Iliad*'s "true subject": "force," which is "that x that turns anybody who is subjected to it into a *thing*."[9] Clearly Homer's image of bees hanging beneath flowers signifies a natural and happy condition and is the simile's visual summit. Albeit briefly in the epic scheme of things, the *Iliad* lingers over this picture of life, treating it as a qualitatively distinct space and experience, against which Homer asks us to measure what immediately follows: the gathering of the Greek armies. I propose that the process by which the Greeks organize — are by Rumor transformed from bees into a martial array — may be read as a departure from what is natural, a movement away from life that Milton interprets as unchristian and thus unadmirable.

The *Iliad* 2 bee simile expresses a powerful contradiction that Milton notices: in addition to conflating the natural swarm and the human army, the simile opposes them. The swarm is active but does not participate in any order greater than itself. Until Rumor's appearance, Homer's bees, his Greeks sleeping and gaming between their ships, have no *telos* beyond what is natural to them. I would suggest, therefore, that the swarm's members are happy precisely because their motives are intrinsic to themselves. Their homelessness certifies that they are free of even that hierarchy which is natural to their species, for at this moment any suggestion of kingship and order would raise the poetic specter of extrinsic, alien purposes. Indeed, the flowers, the sun, and physical need are this swarm's entire ground of motivation. Of consequence we may say that these "bees" enjoy an unconscious state of Being.

The assembling army's nature, however, is to perfect itself, to strive toward an ideal order, one distinguished by hierarchy and predicated upon the individual's submission to a higher and external authority. In abstract terms, the Achaians' transformation is a movement from a comfortable disorder to its opposite. Seen poetically, this movement suggests a *telos* from swarm to hive, from the natural to the unnatural, from good to evil. To Milton war is evidence of human beings' fallen state and is opposed to our original Godlike nature. I think, then, that through the contrastive relationship between Homer's drowsy swarm and the Achaian army, Milton discerned an opinion about human cooperation with which he was deeply congenial: this world's hierarchy and the thoughts, habits, social processes, and institutions that work toward its formation and justification are all equally the enemy of free will. To Milton, logically, any such hierarchy is a bar to salvation, and thus its instruments, social and ideological, are agents of damnation. A corollary that applies only to the sublunar realm: the more hierarchical a group, the less human (i.e., farther from God) its members may be.

Furthermore, I think that to Milton this simile confirmed an idea that he championed and that in the eighteenth century would have reasonable currency before being enveloped and silenced by Romanticism: insect and human societies are different in kind and are therefore comparable only poetically. Milton, I am convinced, wishes to denaturalize the act of war by showing us that its evil is grounded in *personal* choice. Since Homer's Rumor acts to eliminate the individual's will, Milton reads it as evil. Hence, it is the principle behind this entity (the cause) and not the swarm (the effect) that is Milton's real focus of reworking.

It is my argument that the following lines from *Paradise Lost*, which

above all express a concern for the proper interpretation of poetic transformation, are the true center of and guide to Milton's Hive. Pandemonium is complete, and within its walls Satan assembles his host:

> the Signal giv'n,
> Behold a wonder! they but now who seem'd
> In bigness to surpass Earth's Giant Sons
> Now less than smallest Dwarfs, in narrow room
> Throng numberless, like that Pigmean Race
> Beyond the Indian Mount, of Faery Elves,
> Whose midnight Revels, by a forest side
> Or fountain some belated Peasant sees,
> Or dreams he sees, while over-head the Moon
> Sits Arbitress, and nearer to the Earth
> Wheels her pale course; they on their mirth and dance
> Intent, with jocund Music charm his ear;
> At once with joy and fear his heart rebounds.
> Thus incorporeal Spirits to smallest forms
> Reduc'd thir shapes immense, and were at large,
> Though without number still amidst the Hall
> Of that infernal Court. But far within
> And in thir own dimensions like themselves
> The great Seraphic Lords and Cherubim
> In close recess and secret conclave sat
> A thousand Demi-Gods on golden seats,
> Frequent and full.
> (1.776–97)

The preface to this scene is lines 768–75, which I have already identified
as a commonplace rather than a topos and now requote:

> As bees
> In spring time, when the Sun with Taurus rides,
> Pour forth thir populous youth about the Hive
> In clusters; they among fresh dews and flowers
> Fly to and fro, or on the smoothed Plank,
> The suburb of thir Straw-built Citadel,
> New rubb'd with Balm, expiate and confer
> Thir State affairs.

These lines strongly recall Virgil's peaceful Hive in *Georgic* 4, and thus sharply contrast with Milton's image of Pandemonium and its inhabitants. In accordance with his belief that in all human efforts good and evil are to be tasted in the same figural "rind," Milton intends for these versions of the Hive to contend. Despite our wish that these images should, like Dante's Celestial Rose, form some greater shape of accord, their contentiousness blocks any such synthesis.

Milton uses the tension between the Virgilian Hive of peace and the dark Hive of Pandemonium to focus our attention on the problem of interpretation. In this light, the "wonder" of the devils' physical transformation stands in for the seductions of the symbol — especially those that bear the *ethos* of antiquity. Significantly, Milton redefines wonder as illusion. In lines 777–78 he tells us that the fallen angels only "seem" to "surpass [in size] Earth's Giant Sons." This "seem[ing]" is a clue that their monumental stature and their power are similarly produced by our (and also perhaps their) imagination. The credulous reader is then cast as "some belated Peasant [who] sees / Or dreams he sees" this miracle by moonlight (783–85). Like some *personal* Rumor, this section of the poem would with "mirth and dance" and "jocund music charm [our] ear" and our eye, so that "with joy and fear [our] heart rebounds" (786–88) from the Adversary's threat. Such a feeling is an error, the product of "unexercised" interpretation. And we may infer that Milton believes "unexercised" interpretation to be common, for he gives its refutation a key role in his preparation for the devil's "great consult" — which is a return to the themes and method that we noticed when, in *Defensio Prima*, Milton exposed Salmasius as a borrower of masks.

Here Milton's philosophical rigor is doubly apparent: it is related to and enriches his focus on the individual psyche — the *reader's* psychology — and its singular importance to his salvation. This focus, while not entirely new to the epic, exceeds even Dante's. But Milton is no theoretical psychologist. His model of meaning is determined by consequences of the highest order. In chapter 2 of *The Christian Doctrine*, Milton tells us that out of a desire that He shall be truly perceived, God "has lowered himself to our level, lest in our flights above the reach of human understanding, and beyond the written word of scripture, we should be tempted to indulge in vague cogitations and subtleties. . . . It is better therefore to contemplate the Deity, and to conceive of him, not with human passions, that is, after the manner of men, who are never weary of forming subtle imaginations respecting him" (905–6). What this passage communicates in the language of reason, Milton's Hive expresses spatially. Both show us the error of those conceptions of the Divine (about His Person as well as His Ways) made "with human passions" and "subtle imaginations." Milton's Hive may be read as an attack on the poetic imagination. Not because this imagination is evil, but because its "charms" of both sound and movement arouse in human minds experiences that are "passionate" and "bodily." These sorts of experiences have become habits of thought whose aesthetic and social power obscure the intellectual labor required for true perception. Thus, Milton would have us know that only in degree does the language of the "belated" peasant's "dreams" (myths, stories of Eastern wonders, magical transformations) differ from the devils' lying and manipulative rhetoric.

Dante corrects Virgil's bees; Milton would have his correct us. Milton's pedagogical Hive tells us that we cannot any longer *naively* picture, much less discuss, the problem of cooperation, human or divine, in either natural or poetic forms. Milton brands Virgil's natural commonwealth as dangerous fantasy: he would thereby unseat the natural hive from its venerable position as *the* model for human collective life. And the rest of his poem follows suit. Neither does Milton degrade his Creator by later describing Him or His Order in insect terms, nor does he wish us to take seriously that the society of fallen angels can be either so reduced or associated with a state of true concord. As indicated in the section of his *Defensio Prima* that I have discussed above, and as far as I have been able to discover elsewhere, Milton never argues with the ancients' notion that the natural hive is a superlatively organized and therefore admirable state. But to him, bees are bees and men are men, and to confuse them is to indulge in fantasy. Milton would not have humanity's most miraculous gift, the power to choose, overshadowed by any dream of order that assumes that the individual and the individual conscience are less than central to this mortal life, which is our single opportunity for salvation and eternal union with Christ.

How do we then square Milton's rejection of metaphor — specifically, his desire to "kill" the traditional Hive topos — with his clarification of the demonic Hive, a symbol for an oppressive and alien sociality that is firmly seated in our imagination as the (evil) twin to Dante's angelic formulation? Simply put, just because Milton gives us good reason to reject the Hive as an unequivocal standard for human government does not mean that we are inclined to do so. Nor, even, was he the first thinker of his Age to make such an argument. For instance, although Hobbes's careful refutation of the Hive's efficacy as a political model preceded Milton's poetic attempt by two decades,[10] sixty-nine years before the publication of *Leviathan* Virgil (and through him, nature) was already seamlessly partnered with a very modern notion of the State as an economic organism.

In Richard Hakluyt's preface to *Divers Voyages*, the rooted, classical model of the Hive — behind which, for a thousand years, had glowed the ideal of singular Rome and its imperial peace — is merged with a sense of the nation as a naturally expansive organism, as one "hive" among many in an environment of stark competition. The dark swarm emerges in this era as a necessary symbol.[11] When speaking of the English nation and its need to "possess . . . of those landes, which of equitie and right appertain unto us" (175), Hakluyt uses the dark swarm to naturalize and justify imperial expansion: "We reade that the Bees, when they grow to be too many in thir own hive at home, are wont to be led out by their Captaines to swarm abroad, and seeke them selves a new dwelling place. If the examples of the Grecians and Carthaginians of olde time, and the practice of our age may not move us, let us learn wisdom of these smal weake and unreasonable creatures" (176). Although antiquity provides us with some talk of swarming in the apicultural sense, the ease with which Hakluyt understands in classical terms an England that by nature is expansive and warring suggests that the carefully delineated class and occupational relations fundamental to Virgil's allegorical hive no longer apply. If he has Virgil in mind then it is the pro-Caesar, bring-on-the-empire Virgil.

Hakluyt is, as he claims, a "reader" of the classics, but he is a selective reader. In the preceding paragraph Hakluyt gives us a picture of England that is so far from the order proper to the Hive that he attempts no allegory:

> Yea, if we woulde beholde with the eye of pitie how al our prisons are pestered and filled with able men to serve their Countrie, which for small robberies are dayly hanged up in great numbers, som twentie at a clapp out of one jayle (as was seene at the last assises at Rochester) wee would hasten and further every man to his power the deducting of some Colonies of our superfluous people into those

temperate and fertile partes of America, which being within sixe
weekes sayling of England are yet unpossessed by any Christians: and
seems to offer themselves unto us, stretching neerer unto her Majes-
ties Dominions, then to any other part of Europe. (175–76)

Instead of treating the men who "pester" and "fill" English prisons in
Virgilian fashion, as "drones" to be forcibly ejected, Hakluyt figures
these criminals as little hives of their own, as "Colonies of our superflu-
ous people" who may yet serve England by populating "those temperate and fertile partes of America." Clearly the rootedness, together with
the cooperative virtue of the Virgilian bee and its admirable collective,
have been reimagined. To Hakluyt, any population may be described as
a hive, even those that, according to the old rules, would be excised from
the body politic. This abstraction of the Hive from its original ground
of concord and virtuous cooperation, as well as its presence in a document that is neither philosophical nor poetic, suggests that several generations before Milton the symbol complex of the Hive was already
available for a new range of figural possibilities.

Hakluyt's language signals not only that the circle of medieval Chris-
tendom is dissolving, but also that its center is filled with a new spirit,
one that is also evident in *Microcosmography*, a pamphlet written by John
Earle, which enjoyed considerable popularity after its publication in 1628:

Paul's Walk [the center of London's merchant district] is the land's
epitome, or you may call it the lesser isle of Great Britain. It is more
than this, the whole world's map, which you may here discern in its
perfectest motion, justling and turning. It is a heap of stones and
men, with a vast confusion of languages; and were the steeple not
sanctified, nothing liker Babel. The noise in it is like that of Bees, a
strange humming or buzz mixed of walking tongues and feet: it is a
kind of still roar or loud whisper. It is the great exchange of all discourse, and no business whatsoever but is here stirring and afoot. It
is the synod of all pates politic, jointed and laid together in most serious posture, and they are not half so busy as Parliament. . . . It is the
general mint of all famous lies, which are here like the legends of Pop-
ery, first coined and stamped in the Church. All inventions are emp-
tied here, and not a few pockets. The best sign of a temple in it is, that
is the thieves' sanctuary, which rob more safely in the crowd than a
wilderness, whilst every searcher is a bush to hide them. . . . It is the
ears' brothel, and satisfies their lust and itch.[12]

Earle's use of the hive follows quite nicely from Hakluyt's and anticipates some of the central images of Milton's Pandemonium. Milton himself wrote pamphlets and no doubt knew the genre's terrain. Little wonder, then, Milton's infernal bees.

Having now in hand the rudiments of a psychosociological explanation for why, especially after Milton's unforgettable Pandemonium, it became possible to speak of both good and evil hives, it is appropriate that we add to our ideological frame the notion that it was during this period that together the modern subject and the State emerged as conceptual — and possibly warring — entities. Certainly, the content of Shakespeare's plays and the quality of his characterization indicate as much. In such an environment, the nature of the social order and one's relation and obligations to it became, and remain to this day, a primary subject of figural attention. Thus, the Hive, in its three major formulations, endures as a singularly expressive "diagnosis" of our complicated idea of order.

Despite his best attempts to destroy the Hive (Earle's "Paul's Walk"?) as a model for human cooperation, as far as the West's imagination is concerned, Milton completed what lay for two thousand years undeveloped in Homer's original symbol complex. Although Milton was answering what was already in the air, his version of the Hive is an argumentatively convenient and artistically influential marker. After Milton, the Hive acquires a wider currency as both a poetic figure and as a unit of ideology, what Fredric Jameson calls an "ideologeme."[13]

As an illustration of both the Hive's habitual status and its bipolarity, below are two passages taken from arguments about the same subject, the Internet. In each, the observed collective is figured as either an angelic hive or its opposite, the demonic. First the angelic: "Just as a beehive functions as if it were a single sentient organism, so does an electronic hive, made up of millions of buzzing, dim-witted personal computers, behave like a single organism. Out of reworked parts — whether of insects, neurons, or chips — come learning, evolution, and life. Out of a planet-wide swarm of silicon calculators comes an emergent self-governing intelligence: the Net" (21). And now the demonic:

In our technological obsession we may be forgetting that circuited interconnectedness and individualism are, at a primary level, inimical notions, warring terms. . . . We sacrifice the potential life of the solitary self by enlisting ourselves in the collective. . . . Whether this sounds dire or not depends upon your assumptions about the human condition — assumptions, that is, in the largest sense. For those who ask, with Gauguin, "Who are we? Why are we here? Where are we going?" — and who feel that the answering of those questions is the grand mission of the species — the prospect of a collective life in an electronic hive is bound to seem terrifying. (18–19)

These passages' context is a staged "exchange" that the editors of *Harper's* call "The Electronic Hive: Two Views." The first passage, Kevin Kelly's, is procomputer, prohive. He would have us imagine the Internet as a whole infinitely greater than the sum of its "reworked parts." His World Wide Web is alive, evolving, generative, an "emergent self-governing intelligence" that is at once a utopian place and a truly democratic future. Kelly would have us think of our on-line experience as the Rapture-via-modem, a visa to utopia. If his language is religious, it recalls the Catholic High Mass. And if we look beyond this passage's anti-hierarchical guarantee and focus instead on its recipe for human perfection via community, its affect moves us into the orbit of Dante's vision of the ultimate order, the Celestial Rose.

In contrast, Sven Birkerts paints the electronic hive as an illusion. Or even worse, if you share his assumption that the genuine human condition is the individual's pursuit of great questions, then the hive's philosophical essence of "interconnectedness" is the end of humanity. Like Milton's greater drama, Birkerts's smaller one depends upon a powerful adversary, one who threatens to steal the show, if not our souls. This Internet is negative. Its associations and dramatic alignment are demonic. To get on-line is to "sacrifice the potential life of the solitary self by *enlisting ourselves in the collective*" (my emphasis). This is the language of coercion, war, sin. At stake is nothing less than each human being's "potential life." These extremes and their ultimate frame are Protestant. But even as this argument echoes Milton's attack on the apicultural metaphor, its figural pattern merges with and affirms what Milton never intended Pandemonium to be: a model for human society.

That these two writers disagree about the implications of a technological device whose social import is, as yet, impossible to gauge is neither surprising nor properly our interest. What I would point out, however, is that despite their ideological differences both writers choose the same topos to figure their object, the "electronic hive." In both arguments the Hive is used to represent an abstract but philosophically stable state of cooperation against which we, the audience, are to measure not only the quality of our social existence but also the degree of our humanity.

Both writers would not have us see their metaphors as such: each is embedded in argumentation to a degree that is not possible for Hakluyt, who understood forms typologically (as being public and artistic, artificial, rhetorical) rather than ideological (self-evident, natural, antirhetorical). In contrast to Hakluyt, our modern essayists deploy their metaphors in what Kenneth Burke might call a "partially conscious, partially unconscious" manner.[14] By this I mean that for us moderns, the Hive topos's appeal tends to be more ideological than rhetorical. I am arguing that, in general, our relationship with persuasive form is inferior to, more limited than, our forebears' — a position that contradicts the way we prefer to imagine ourselves in relation to the past.

I am strongly impressed that, in the main, pre-twentieth-century writers knew the Hive as an artistic and therefore *artificial* analogy, a construct with a specific history and clearly delineated meanings and limits. I do not, however, get the same sense of self-consciousness and, thus, rhetorical control about many contemporary uses of the Hive. I have not yet settled this issue to my satisfaction, but I speculate that the loss of a rhetorical understanding of figured language permits us to adapt and deploy verbal forms without public — and frequently without conscious — recognition of either their history or their philosophical limits. For instance, in the two Internet passages, each technologically engendered "future" and its implications are created according to the terms of a preindustrial variation of the Hive topos: Kelly's angelic Internet shares the structure and motives of Dante's Celestial Rose and Birkerts's infernal version similarly merges with those of Milton's Pandemonium.

Kelly and Birkerts are in the business of persuasion — they evoke and then ask us to choose between contrary visions of our on-line future. We may only speculate as to what degree each writer is conscious of his strategic use of inherited forms, but Kenneth Burke gives us a way to think about how and, more important, why such a strategy works. You will recall from my discussion in the preface that Burke argues that "form is the psychology of the audience" (30–31). By this he means that the consciousness and to a degree the physiology of, for example, a reader of *Macbeth* merges with the psychological states and processes — the attitudes and perspectives — encoded within the drama's elements and their organization. Burke implies that a text is more than a simple dispenser of meaning and that reading is more than merely understanding the meaning of words and the elements of a plot. Burke theorizes that the enjoyment of art is its resurrection as a coherent imitation. Through its direction we transcend form and join with a virtual world that knits together the artist's intentions and aspects of the artist's mental life with ours. One does not need to have read De Quincey's "On the Knocking at the Gate in Macbeth" to be startled by the knocking at Macbeth's door. And one experiences this same thrill with every reading of the play. Our reaction, designed by Shakespeare and preserved in the form of *Macbeth*, is an effect and an aspect of the sum of the play's words, sentences, and characters and their actions in the context of a specific tragic structure. When we hear this knocking and respond, De Quincey's, ours, and the play's "psychology" are congruent, consisting of the same experiential substance. And much the same occurs when we are engaged with the powerful instances of the Hive that Kelly and Birkerts deploy.

Moreover, because our unconscious "knowledge" of the Hive is a constellation of inherited forms (psychologies), while we may not have read Dante or Milton, their formulations are available to us as antithetical states of cooperation, each of which inclines toward a distinct cooperative state and implies its opposite. We may equally understand and be similarly persuaded by Kelly and Birkerts because the structural logic of each essayist's version of the Hive is already part of us. And when this tacit knowledge is engaged and amplified by contact with the details of a seminal formulation — even if it is evoked at a distance — our already receptive psychology becomes attuned to and to an extent synonymous with the attitudes and motives encoded in the original form. To reiterate: I am arguing that in Kelly's passage there is some of Dante's mind and that in Birkerts's there is some of Milton's — and that in each instance it is this mind, a formally coded and psychologically potent core belonging to the past — that enables us to intuit and assent to these modern essayists' ultimate and futuristic claims.

Of course, there are limits to this or any theory of experiential synonymy. Michel Foucault notes "two great discontinuities in the *episteme* of Western culture" — the first he locates in the midseventeenth century and the second at the close of the eighteenth. As I discussed in the preface, these discontinuities are moments when "the mode of being of things, and of the order that divided them up before presenting them to the understanding, was profoundly altered" (*OT*, xxii). But one does not need to subscribe to the extremity of Foucault's argument in order to find him useful. Foucault's thought — from a rhetorical perspective — is valuable here because it suggests a relationship between epistemic change and poetic invention. Judging from the instances of the Hive that I have thus far compared, I would speculate that the vigor with which inherited forms are reworked is to an extent modulated by the "distance" between the inherited model's and the ambitious poet's *episteme*. The more alien a poet finds a text's or a figure's epistemic context (whose essentials are recoverable through artistic form) the greater the license required and allowed for a poet to effect a successful translation. That Kelly's and Birkerts's futuristic visions involve us — cognitively and affectively — in past psychologies rather than speak to conditions we have yet to experience suggests that some elements of past epistemic contexts remain actively part of our own.

I find the presence of the past in Kelly's and Birkerts's "futures" intriguing. But their manner of figuration, the way that each writer presents his version of the Hive, troubles me. Birkerts, in particular, tries to be literary, but under this gloss is a brute philosophical impulse, a will to power shared by his opponent. As in virtually every instance of the Hive topos, these passages display a familiar perspectival logic: a singular observer surveys a human collective and "sees" it as an insect society. Furthermore, this imitation of an actual experience is organized along a visual axis that constructs a knowing subject against an unknowing object. Again, in the Kelly and Birkerts passages, this object is not so much the Net as it is a model of contemporary society that is presented as our future collective life. The entity who looks down is privileged with sight, a capacity that in the West has long been equivalent to knowledge. Thus, what is presented as a self-evident transcript of visual experience is actually an organized mode of description, one whose form enables the narrating eye/voice to actively inscribe the world. Therefore, far from being an unmediated glimpse of the Real, this seeing is an act of making, an exercise of intellectual sovereignty. It is in this sense that I believe Kelly and Birkerts intend their figures philosophically and are using them to picture and thus to control a future that is actually what they fear about the present.

The same motive and technique are at work below in a passage from "Foes in Angola Still at Odds over Diamonds," a story written by Suz-

anne Daley for the *New York Times*. Analyzing this passage will further
clarify the connection between the philosophical uses of the Hive and
the anxieties about controlling perception and social relations that mark
almost all contemporary uses of this topos. This discussion will be all
the more revealing because its subject appears in a newspaper (the most
popular of any publication quoted in this book) and is presented in the
style of factual reporting. While reporting the politics and abuses of Angola's diamond industry, Suzanne Daley uses the Hive philosophically
(rather than artistically) to master her impressions of the mines along
the Luachimo river: "The mines now are unbelievably primitive, square
holes in the ground so close together that, from a distance, the riverbank
looks like a huge honeycomb. The mine workers live in shallower holes
covered in straw. Occasionally mine walls collapse, burying someone"
(A10). Like Kelly's and Birkerts's speakers, Daley's is privileged with the
big picture. Above the suffering, benighted miners, she occupies a sovereign seat. In a way that I trust is by now familiar, this view from above
is axially organized: it deploys the terms of vision to simplify and to
divide the world into two antithetical regions. These acts of simplification and division, which occur simultaneously, charge this space, beg the
illumination of contrast. The speaker is empowered to attribute essential
differences.

When used as an ideological rather than an artistic figure, more than
either "making our ideas clear" or creating a picture in our minds,[15] this
use of the Hive functions as a semiconscious instrument, a means to
power and its protections that we are not meant to see as such. However,
whether we are conscious of it and its history or not, the Hive brings
with it the flavor of its Homeric origin. Please compare Daley's picture
of the miners with the following passage from *Stalingrad Fights On*, by
Konstatin M. Simonov, a Soviet journalist whose account of the Battle
of Stalingrad brought him fame in his country and abroad. Simonov
describes the conditions of the besieged citizens just before the Nazi advance in September 1942: "We crossed a bridge over one of the gullies
intersecting the city. I shall never forget the scene that opened out before
me. This gully, which stretched to my left and right, swarmed with life,
just like an anthill dotted with caves. Entire streets had been excavated
on either side. The mouths of the caves were covered with charred
boards and rags. The women had utilized everything that could be of
service."[16] Although Daley and Simonov use different insect vehicles,

both verbal pictures are similarly interested in the protections of visual sovereignty and display the same axial structure. Furthermore, I sense that both journalists use the Hive to add an epic perspective and flavor to their narration. While Daley is probably less conscious of her picture's history and implications than Simonov is of his, these journalists' strikingly similar analogies suggest that to use the Hive thus is to link a text and its audience with other such descriptions of mass suffering. And when this linkage is examined through Burke's theory of form, the complexity of its powers is revealed. Because figural connection involves imitation, our response is psychophysiological: it is an experience, an aspect of the Real that communicates across the centuries. In the eternal present of deep allusion, we are through the pleasures and powers of form married to an encoded intelligence. And if this intelligence's maker was as great as Dante or Milton and its preserving form as rich as the Hive, through attention to our experience we may overhear the memory of older minds still. But such intelligences and forms may also be used to reason and as a vehicle for reason's context and true antithesis — ideology.

Philosopher's Hive: Philosopher's Stone

Having broached the subject of the Hive's ideological function — usually that of measuring the quality of our social condition — it is appropriate now to turn to Jean-Jacques Rousseau, one of modernity's supreme architects. Specifically, I have in mind what he calls *des notions justes,* a term which I translate as "true ideas." In the preface to his *Discourse on the Origin of Inequality,* in order to speak about the effect of culture on human beings, Rousseau creates an idealized, original human condition. Of his method, he writes: "For it is no small matter to distinguish what is original from what is artificial in the present nature of man, and to have a clear understanding of a state which no longer exists, which has, perhaps, never existed, and about which it is necessary to have accurate notions [*des notions juste*] in order to judge our present state properly."[17] As is the case with all substantive, public acts of the imagination, neither the idea of the noble savage and his natural state nor this construct's philosophical office originated with Rousseau. Like all complex thinkers, Rousseau drew upon past models, adapted them to his audience and purposes. The ultimate source for this manner of philosophical picturing is, of course, Plato, whose equivalent to the literary topos I will presently discuss.

In order to make his true idea of man's original state, Rousseau embraces and intensifies the oppositions between country and city, past and future, superstition and reason implied by Plato's philosophical image of the ideal city. Rousseau needs Plato's method, the power of his dialectical idealism. But Rousseau is not an Athenian noble dedicated to preserving a way of life already lost. Rousseau is a late-Enlightenment radical awakening Europe to Romanticism, a novel aesthetic that defines human beings as natural (and yet independent of nature) and starkly opposes pure nature to corrupt society. Interestingly, Rousseau does not, however, classify philosophy as unnatural. He believes that *logos* is an efficacious path to human liberation, but both his opinion of civilization and his argument's aim are distinct from Plato's. Rousseau's invention proceeds through a clever but disturbingly contradictory and, therefore, unstable synthesis: he merges the ideological foundations of Plato's *philosophical* image with aspects of a *literary*, mythological picture: namely, the ancient idea of the Golden Age.

The pre-Socratic idea of the Golden Age presupposes identity between humans and nature, which is a state of abundance and peace. Within this frame there is no need for the arts and technics of civilization. And if the first is practiced by the people of the Golden Age, they are enjoyed unconsciously and without effort. These natural humans lack nothing; they do not need either politics or the city (one and the same for Plato) or theories of socialization and visions of righteous hierarchy (also synonymous for Plato).

We are used to and in this argument need not bother with the broad contradictions of Romantic utopianism: the planned economy that presupposes an unregulated market and its "natural" forces, and the preservation or even creation of "nature" through human law. Let me instead tighten my focus on Rousseau's technique of using a hybridized image as a rational benchmark. His practice suggests (but ultimately does not show) that the contradictions produced by the mixing of forms may be eliminated by fixing an unstable image in a philosophical argument, that a poetic form may thus be made rational and, of consequence, "true."

The Golden Age is a myth, a poetic convention that Rousseau uses as an argumentative fact. When viewed as exclusive to Rousseau's argument, the original state of human beings functions as a proposition, giving no hint of instability or historical association. Complementary to its argumentative truth is the Golden Age's intellectual pedigree. Poets and thinkers such as Hesiod, Plato, Virgil, and Dante have engaged with it and have contributed to its authority. They have prepared the ground for Rousseau. Nearly all of his force, the truth of his ideas, is borrowed. The myth's psychological truth has been prepared as well, in that the Golden Age resonates with, confirms, the common and deep-seated perception that life in the past was more natural, more genuine, than it is now. The sources of this perception are private as well as public. Its truth is felt personally, by way of the family and its narratives. And it is felt socially — publicly, historically — as well. In comparison to the flux and uncertainty of the present, a condition that does not require a notion of progress to cause anxiety, both one's childhood and the days of one's predecessors were times when social relations were known, families were closer, identity was clearer, people were more polite to each other, the air and water purer. It is easy, then, to understand how this feeling, along with its comparative terms, may be projected upon a regional, a national, or even upon a global chronology.

When used as a true idea, the Hive's veracity is similarly resistant to any argument that would fix it and hold it rationally accountable. The Hive, too, is an imaginative benchmark against which we may measure the quality of our social existence. Much like Rousseau's Golden Age, but on a smaller scale, the Hive is a conceptual system of similarities and differences that enables a thinker or an artist and his or her audience first to define and then to measure one philosophical essence against another. Furthermore, just as the true idea of the Golden Age has no basis in nature, so, too, is there no necessary correspondence between insect and human society. Referring again to Daley's representative formulation: her verbal picture assumes just such a synonymy between human mine shaft holes in a riverbank and the instinctual architecture of *Apis melli-fera*. What, then, does the true idea's naive way of picture-making tell us?

To be fair, Rousseau is clear that the true idea, epitomized by his Golden Age, is artificial, a philosophical construct. Nonetheless, the true idea of the Hive — a philosophical verbal picture — asserts that the image is the world. To put it another way, while the true idea may claim truth because it appears to be a faithful transcript of what the eye sees, its veracity is actually the product of an artistic structure and its implicit drama. Indeed, as either a poetic or a philosophical form, the Hive works only and exactly because we receive its imitation as self-evident, as real. Such is the power of structural abstractions when visually coded. As a result of this coding, it is unnecessary to explain the Hive. No one need teach us how to "see" through it, to think with it, and therefore to feel according to its terms. Hence, its attraction to the philosopher.

When used for thinking, the Hive's ideological potential comes to the fore. Within its charged tableau, spatial categories have a degree of agency that can derive only from simplification. The speaker's position at one terminus of the visual axis evokes the illusion of distance that in turn establishes size and detail within the visual frame. For example, when through the Hive's structure the awareness of Daley's speaker is focused on the many, closely situated "square holes in the ground" beneath her, in Milton's words: "Behold a wonder!" The riverbank is perceived as a "huge honeycomb."

Because the meaning of the Hive springs from a metaphorical comparison, its philosophical formulations follow the same rules as its poetic: observed collectives tend to be either angelic or demonic. Daley's version falls under the latter category. From above, all the distinct persons and their manifold actions on and in the ground are made available to the observer's mind as a discrete entity of squalor and suffering. In Daley's text, the singular observer stands apart from the collective in a godlike position. Below her are human figures who appear to be much smaller than normal. Hence, of visual and therefore rational necessity, any perception of their individual qualities is difficult, if not impossible. Because seeing is believing to the visual imagination, and as pictures of family groups drawn by children powerfully demonstrate, the relative size and position of persons and objects in a visual frame determine value and, most importantly, define relationship.

When the visual imagination seeks to understand (which is as much as to say that it "makes a picture"), relative size and position suddenly become present, hungry for meaning. The logic of mental picture-making demands that appearances be organized, simplified so as to domesticate, if not to deny, the complexity and uncertainty of the actual visual experience. In literature such a denial reveals something about the subject and the act of observation and is therefore featured. But when philosophizing among the moderns, owing to our ignorance of rhetoric and our consequent distrust of visible and therefore accountable strategies of persuasion, we are truly satisfied only if structure is presented as natural. Similar to our attitude toward the convention of single-point perspective in painting, to us the truest Hive is the one that most strongly organizes the visual field around a singular and therefore sovereign subject, thereby naturalizing the philosophical process and, more important, its conclusions.

While writers indeed make vivid pictures, when compared with the plastic and visual mediums the discursive is a disadvantage. If a written imitation of seeing is to be effective and portable, its maker must be precise and simple. The Hive meets these requirements by ascribing to an aesthetic code, which runs something like this: *What is my size and proximate to me is like me; therefore, what is different from me in size and distant from me is unlike me*. Accordingly, we can understand why when Daley "sees" the hive she necessarily knows it to be a locus of difference and also, most importantly, why she chooses this figure to communicate her insight.

But what exactly is Daley's speaker seeing? What, exactly, is being imitated here? Is she, from her position above the river, looking at an object through the nothingness, the absolute passivity of Newtonian space? Or, as I have been arguing, because she sees in these "square holes in the ground" a form, a hive, would it not be more accurate to hold that instead of seeing something "out there" she is seeing something that is already inside her?

Rainer Maria Rilke tells us how to speak of this "inside" space and how through it we discover patterns "in" the world. He refers to this space that invents and intensifies form as *vetraute Raum*, which may be translated as the "space of intimacy." In his poem "What birds plunge through is not the intimate space," Rilke explains that this space "reaches from us and construes the world," thereby allowing us to know. For Rilke, knowledge is a power that is synonymous with human existence, which is the very same equivalence asserted by the Hive's required sovereign observer. If, for example, "we want to know a tree, in its true element, / throw inner space around it, from that / pure abundance in you. Surround it with restraint. // It has no limits. Not until it is held / in your renouncing is it truly there" (6–10). Notice that, unlike Newtonian space, which is simply a "nothing" between bodies, Rilke's *vetraute Raum* is itself "something." If not a body, then it is a presence, and he speaks of it as such. The *vetraute Raum* is a force of "restraint," of "limits" — qualities that Rousseau's true idea exploits even while it denies them.

Rilke teaches us that, beyond its function of *informing*, a metaphor is the sign of a mind seeking to understand. So when we measure Daley's Hive against its context's plain style, it emerges as a shaped structure of a different and higher order, one that expresses a distinctly philosophical motive. More than to see, Daley wishes to understand. And if we follow Rilke's suggestions, then Daley's purpose requires her to "renounce" the mutable complexity of her actual experience. We may then say that, much like Kelly and Birkerts, Daley is "throw[ing] inner space around" those miners and their holes, around that river and the economic and political relations that otherwise "ha[ve] no limits." When Daley uses the Hive to make an ordered whole of what is not actually so, she "surround[s] with restraint," intellectually domesticates, experience.

Even though the Hive's structure presupposes our spatial separation from the whole, and hence requires our difference and exclusion from its unity, perhaps it is because this form allows us to picture social perfection that it strikes us as self-evident, familiar. It is in this sense that I think of it — and by extension all true ideas — as being intimate. Especially when presented as reality, the true idea engenders systematized fantasy, a poetic understanding that has the force and social clout of reason. Gaston Bachelard, who has intensely studied the poetic image from a phenomenological perspective, has this to say about the "space of intimacy": "Space that has been seized upon by the imagination cannot remain indifferent space subject to the measures and estimates of the surveyor. It has been lived in . . . [and] . . . it nearly always exercises an attraction. For it concentrates being within limits that protect."[18] Bachelard reminds us of what we abundantly know from our experience of the home, of a familiar geography, and of art: space that has been created and ordered by the imagination is not simply the lack of something. Quite the opposite is true. *In itself* this sort of space is expressive, symbolically potent. Thus, because the Hive's axially organized space is designed, motivated, its space is expressive, architectural rather than Newtonian. Because this space "has been lived in" — which is to say pervaded with the associations, the emotional residue of both personal and artistic experiences — it exerts what Bachelard calls "an attraction." According to this way of thinking, Daley chooses the Hive because "it concentrates being within limits that protect." The hive "attracts" Daley because it allows her to know, to visually organize a complex social and political situation, one in which she is positioned as a disinterested spectator: the position of a philosopher.

Whatever is visible from her sovereign position confirms a familiar and gratifying pattern: within her picture she alone is gifted with sight, thus knowledge and its (alienating) power are also hers alone. Only she and her audience are fully human. Within the figure's frame, words are a form of action, and the knowledge that comes from rehearsing a pattern is sufficient, equivalent to Being. Together writer and reader are "protect[ed]" from the world. When human suffering and society are imaged via the ideological Hive, we are distanced from the Real, freed from its demands and free to deny complicity and finitude. Thus, a verbal experience that should stir the conscience gratifies us by transmuting appearance into philosophical substance, one that confirms our superiority. For this substance cannot exceed, much less question, the adequacy of seeing what we already know and knowing only what we see. The twentieth century has been a period of suffering on an unprecedented scale, and the twenty-first gives no indication of unfolding differently. Like no earlier age, we are confronted with evidence of this misery, broadly understand its causes, and so may at least imagine remedies. No wonder that the true idea of the Hive is so common. Because the sort of picture modeled by Daley is philosophical but embedded in a context that cannot accommodate reason and is expressed through a style that is inadequate to dialectic, her version of the Hive does not either admit the past or confront the problem of mimesis: the mystery and self-consciousness of interpretation and the arts of language. Like all true ideas, her Hive orients us toward the putative certainties of the visual experience, thereby offering us the illusion that knowledge and seeing are one and the same. Perhaps this explains better why Plato, who claims that poets are liars, uses so many metaphors and without qualm. Like the Hive, his most celebrated figures are more architectural and frankly ideological than iconic and poetic. And similar to Daley's and Simonov's, the figures by which we know Plato best are meant to illustrate "actual" experience, to turn the body of language toward what to him is a higher office.[19] He is the grandfather of the true idea, the source of the Hive's ideological capacity.

Let me illuminate my position with the "allegory of the cave" (henceforth, the Cave), a philosophical "form-that-pictures." It will serve as the paradigm for a mode of figure-making that informs Rousseau's philosophy and hence many recent instances of the Hive. First, similar to how the Hive works, the Cave issues from a careful arrangement and orchestration of copious visual description. Below, from Allan Bloom's translation of *The Republic*, Plato's Socrates addresses Glaucon:

Next, then . . . make an image of our nature in its education and
want of education, likening it to a condition of the following kind.
See human beings as though they were in an underground cave-like
dwelling with its entrance, a long one, open to the light across the
whole width of the cave. They are in it from childhood with their legs
and necks in bonds so that they are fixed, seeing only in front of them,
unable because of the bond to turn their heads all the way around.
Their light is from a fire burning far above and behind them. Between
the fire and the prisoners there is a road above, along which see a wall,
built like the partitions puppet-handlers set in front of the human
beings and over which they show the puppets.

I see, he [Glaucon] said.

Then also see along this wall human beings carrying all sorts of
artifacts, which project above the wall, and statues of men and other
animals wrought from stone, wood, and every kind of material; as
is to be expected, some of the carriers utter sound while others are
silent.

It's a strange image . . . [Glaucon] . . . said, and strange prisoners
you're telling of. (7.514 a–c)

When compared with the Hive topos's relatively simple structure and direct cognitive work, Plato's complex visual device (complete with movement and sound) may seem to be quite another species of image. However, exactly because Plato's philosophical project was framed in Homer's
shadow, we should not read this "allegory" as an act whose only concern
is philosophical process — in other words, "truth."

In Plato's day, philosophy was suffused and indeed contended with
poetry for cultural authority, a relationship that Bachelard suggests continues to inform the modern psyche.[20] However, because he is a philosopher, Plato cannot rework Homer as a singer might. Consequently, in
order to make philosophically available the poetic topos's unique capacities (to evoke an image whose logical structure is dramatically suggestive
and yet naturalistic in its affect), Plato must create a "counter-poetry."
This is a discourse that will subdue, if not negate, the irrationality of
figured language, and thereby turn its appeal toward reason. I cannot
say, therefore, that Plato's method of composition entirely falls under the
aegis of *retractatio* as I have thus far spoken of it. Since there is no known
model for the Cave, Plato is not reworking in the poetic sense. Rather, I
think that Plato is answering Homer's naturalistic, mytho-poetic style

with one that helps intensify the architectural faculty's capacity for abstraction. If the true idea is the poetic topos's philosophical analog, then, like its complement, it is an action that communicates purpose. Plato wishes to elevate and to purify form, but not poetically. From poetry, rhetoric, and the mob, he would wrest the natural linkage between visual imitation and reason.

As Daley and others who share her motives and audience will do more than two millennia after him, Plato creates for us a singular, sovereign position from which we see "strange prisoners" who are qualitatively different from ourselves. Yes, Socrates ostensibly places us all in the cave, but we who hear him can neither logically nor spatially be numbered among the prisoners because, unlike them, we are free to move and to see. Unlike these prisoners — and also unlike the equivalent sufferers who are figured entomologically by Daley and Simonov — we have the knowledge that comes from perspective. We are aware that the cave has an entrance and that it is "a long one." It is their bodies, not ours, that are "in bonds so that they are fixed, seeing only in front." We are witnesses to a drama that, however much it is intended to sum up the human condition, is largely devoid of that sort of creaturely identification that accompanies most poetic instances of the Hive. In this sense, Plato's counter-poetic succeeds because, as the Cave evidences, the true idea's picture restricts pleasures to those that we should call intellectual. And the true idea's complexity augments its intended philosophical focus. We are so busy figuring out how it works, what it means, that we lose sight of rhetorical form — which is to say that we are not receptive to any appeals that might run counter to its visio-rational grain.

Plato intends that we see the bondage of others; we are not, however, to register our own enslavement to the dialectical process. We are prevented from sensing that the ground of any reasoning via pictures necessarily issues from imitation and, hence, merges with the poetic. Perhaps Glaucon expresses his sense of this paradox when he tells Socrates that *both* his "image" and its "prisoners" are "strange." This image's strangeness rises from the dissonance between intention and execution, ends and means. The Cave is painstakingly structured; it reeks of artifice. But if we bother with the paradox, then we are a prisoner. And while this sort of trick, borne of antirhetorical idealism, waxes and wanes depending upon the temper of the times, in every age there are minds that delight in it. When he made the true idea, Plato made it dangerous. If a person holds, as Plato does, that form is merely in the way of truth, at best a container from which we may pour a higher substance, then truly such a person is a worker who uses tools blindfolded.

Nonetheless, since the Cave has no predecessor, no poetical history that follows it into a philosophical text, it does what Plato asks of it. The Hive, on the other hand, is not as philosophically tractable. Hobbes and Milton, who were acutely aware of the emergence of a new idea of society and its definition of humanity, were troubled by the Hive when it was used naively as an instrument of reason. Both men recognized and explored the Hive's philosophical limits; they ask us to reject it as a model for human society. But such is the force of civilizational habit that, especially since the decline of rhetoric and the consequent diminishment of our understanding of verbal form, the true *idea* of the Hive has reasserted itself as nature, as unassailable *fact* in the most unlikely places and ways. An easy target for this criticism is the science of sociobiology, which its primary architect, Edward O. Wilson, contends is a rational inquiry into what he calls "the biological basis of social behavior."[21] Sociobiology assumes as fact and uses as a principle the analogy between human and insect sociality. And if I have thus far demonstrated anything from Rousseau and Plato, it is that any science — which is to say, any systematic inquiry — that naturalizes its metaphorical claims is an idealism and therefore needs careful scrutiny.

I am arguing that the true idea of the Hive is actually a poetic form that is used for philosophical purposes. I needed to spend some time making these distinctions, because the next chapter examines what the Augustans contribute to the symbol complex of the Hive and how Romanticism received these changes. Although Swift and Mandeville would not, I believe, have thought their insect analogies antipoetic or antitraditional, both men modernize an earlier formulation by subjecting it to the philosophical fable. In each instance an original form is recast so as to bring it in line with the empirical outlook and to improve its ability to picture the Europeans' new image of themselves. These experiments establish a powerful association between the fable, scientific speculation, and the insect analogy. Through its interest in psychological construction, Swift's fable of the spider and the bee becomes an important source of existential images. And because Mandeville's *Fable of the Bees* makes Milton's Pandemonium secular and natural, adapting it to sociological speculation, it guarantees that the alien society will be imagined entomologically. Far from eliminating the Hive, the Age of Reason gives it new life as poetic pictures that wield the authority of science.

3

THE HIVE, THE FABLE, AND THE

IMAGINATION OF SHADOW

The best way to insure against an obscene use of this philosophical tool [seeing the world as if through binoculars] is to ponder its theory, "Isolation." We always see things amidst their surroundings and generally perceive them according to what function they serve in that context. But remove them from that context and they suddenly become incomprehensible and terrible, the way things must have been on the first day after creation, before the new phenomena had yet grown accustomed to each other and to us. So too, in the luminous solitude of our telescopic circle, everything becomes clearer and larger, but above all, things become more arcane and demonic. . . .

In this way, the binoculars contribute both to our understanding of the individual, as well as to an ever deepening lack of comprehension of the nature of humanity. By dissolving the common-place connections and discovering new ones, it in fact replaces the practice of genius, or is at least a preliminary exercise. And yet perhaps for this very reason we recommend this instrument in vain. Do not people, after all, employ it even at the theater to heighten the illusion, or during the intermission, to see who else is there, thereby not seeking

the unfamiliar, but rather, the comfortable aspect of familiar
faces?
    Robert Musil, "Binoculars"

It all adds up to this: the fairy tale narrates a wish fulfilment that is
not bound by its own time and the apparel of its contents. In contrast
to the legend, which is always tied to a particular locale, the fairy tale
remains unbound. Not only does the fairy tale remain as fresh as
longing and love, but the demonically evil, which is abundant in the
fairy tale, is seen at work here in the present, and the happiness of "once
upon a time," which is even more abundant, still affects our vision of
the future.
    Ernst Bloch, "The Fairy Tale Moves on Its Own Time"

Context and Quandaries

Milton's Pandemonium reflects its passionate age, a time of political, religious, and stylistic extremity, when with violence and upon their own people Englishmen prosecuted opposed and uncompromising visions of order. Like Virgil, Milton uses the Hive to image and imprison the dark swarm, to subordinate its rebellious energies to a greater, and higher, order. However, unlike Virgil's prison, Milton's must also house Lucifer, his double, a willful singularity who like the crowd must be made to fit the cosmic plan. The consequence is a Hive that expresses its maker's ambivalence toward authority — toward, more specifically, the shapes through which the epic tradition obliges him to think and feel. Milton is thoroughly of his Age, but that Lucifer engages us more than any other Miltonic creation is no invention of Romantic yearning. Milton's Dark Prince, his maker raised to the power of a star, anticipates us: spiritually blinded by pride, bound by a cosmic legend, he rages within and against ancient symbols.

Pandemonium and Lucifer together form a complex symbol, which — though derived from classical and Biblical materials and thus involved with ancient and ultimate controversies — participates in and helps to shape the battle between the ancients and the moderns, an earthly struggle that from the early Renaissance to modernism affects the Hive's evolution. Although he is the heart of a hive, the monarch of fallen angels and so the foremost element of a divinely ordained collective instrument, through his passionate singularity Milton's Satan brings into sharper focus a version of the Hive that figures the individual as a solitary insect. If through the lens of Romanticism we pass the image of Satan imprisoned in Pandemonium, then take from this dark angel his divinity and agency, and cast him down without God into a modern human city, the result is Kafka's Gregor Samsa.

But between Satan and Samsa there are more than two centuries of profound cultural change and a series of vigorous reworkings of the Hive. Representative of these experiments is Jonathan Swift's solitary bee of *The Battle of the Books*. As I will detail below, although Swift uses *Battle* to defend the ancients against the moderns, key aspects of his strategy confirm that antiquity's cause has already been lost. Swift was a modern who chose to act in the interests of a literature whose worldview could not accommodate the emerging bourgeois subject. Therefore, in order to command the ancients and their symbols, Swift makes for them a new context. Swift's relationship vis-à-vis the traditional Hive recalls that between Virgil and Homer. Swift both requires the traditional Hive and feels obliged to honor its form. However, to possess the Hive Swift must excise it from the epic tradition — and to accomplish this he imitates Virgil's use of the fable, using its unique space to miniaturize and thus to domesticate both the symbols and the conflict that he would orchestrate.

The traditional epic is far more a problem for Swift than it was for Virgil. Pagan or Christian, the genre favors the grand gesture, monumental shapes, men, deeds. Such a dramatic scene requires old-fashioned beauties: a decorously elevated style, balance, proportion, symbolic congruence. Virgil excelled at these, and they agreed with both his purposes and worldview. The epic poet must equally dignify the frame and its contents, which he achieves above all through ornament gravely amplified. The epic makes princes of commoners and demigods of kings. (It is not only its antiquity that makes the literary epic an aristocratic genre.) Promotion, however, costs. The epic elevates on purpose; its *raison d'être* is not to dramatize the individual life, except as it contributes to a greater design. The traditional epic's office is to image forces and their effects on human beings, forces that are impersonal and of such magnitude that we sense them only through patterns of shared suffering. These are forces that because they transcend our knowledge exceed our control.

The classical epic does not survive the Age of Reason — but not because Westerners suddenly lost interest in either order or forces. To the contrary, the growing power of true science enabled Europe to conceive the first as a system of *mechanistic* natural laws that explained the second and promised their domestication. But rhetorical forms such as the Hive presented a special problem to these persons who were making a world safe for science. These aesthetically and cognitively habitual shapes expressed an antique psychology, referred to a collective rather than an individualistic model of the self. What follows is one way to state the challenge that old rhetoric raised to the moderns: Complex and socially significant thought cannot occur except through forms having these same qualities. And because such forms come into being over time, the foundation of most, if not all, were laid in antiquity. Therefore, the very tools that must be used to imagine the future are pervaded with old ways of thinking: innovation is a force exerted against the gravity of antiquity. As I showed earlier when discussing contemporary metaphors for the Internet, neither invention nor persuasion can be entirely severed from the past. And we may infer that these early moderns knew this more clearly than we, for they seem to have lavished nearly as much energy on rhetoric's reformation as they did upon understanding nature.

In *Novum Organum*, Francis Bacon — whom Richard Foster Jones observes "out[lined] the campaign which the moderns relentlessly carried on against the ancient through the next half-century"[1] — locates the problem of the "vulgar [read: rhetorical] mind" in the nature of words: "For men imagine that their reason governs words, whilst, in fact, words react upon the understanding; and this has rendered philosophy and the sciences sophistical and inactive. Words are generally formed in a popular sense, and define things by those broad lines which are most obvious to the vulgar mind; but when a more acute understanding, or more diligent observation is anxious to vary those lines, and to adapt them more accurately to nature, words oppose it" (112). To Bacon, words have agency: they "react upon the understanding." In themselves they have the power to oppose any attempt to "vary [the] lines" of popular thought. Educated in rhetoric, he thinks like a rhetor. Bacon neither believes that we may escape words nor means their agency metaphorically. He senses words, signs, and systems as shapes of power. To him they are necessary instruments because "the unassisted hand and the understanding left to itself possesses but little power. Effects are produced by the means of instruments and helps, which the understanding requires no less than the hand; and as instruments either promote or regulate the motion of the hand, so those that are applied to the mind prompt or protect the understanding" (107). So that language will serve his system of observational induction, an instrument complex enough to require subordinate instruments (Baconian science is a technology), Bacon calls not for the end of rhetoric but for a new rhetoric that will ensure that "axioms [will be] properly and regularly abstracted from particulars." He postulates a tongue so plain that it will have no traffic with argument, for "axioms determined upon in argument can never assist in the discovery of new effects [in nature]" (108). Bacon redefines truth and nature so as to place them into a new relation; his words show us the tendencies that, as they strengthen, increasingly separate the imagination from reason and the world as seen by science. In light of Robert Musil's suggestive comments about visual instruments that begin this chapter, Baconian rhetoric may be said to seek the "dissol[ution] of commonplace connections and [the] discover[y of] new ones." Through a contradictory move that is at least as old as Plato, for the sake of truth Bacon turns rhetoric against itself. He wishes to "dissolve" the psychological bond between his moment's forms and those of the past, to separate and make antithetical the psychology of logic and the psychology of persuasion. Through plainness, the first shall be rational; the second, because of its penchant for ornament and appeals to enjoyment, shall be irrational. The "genius" that Bacon would reduce, if not entirely "replace," is the core of what Kenneth Burke calls the "rhetorical motive": signification for its own sake, the cooperative play of the marketplace, and the passionate symbolic tumult of the "human barnyard."[2]

By about 1700, in England as well as on the Continent, belles lettres was well on its way to distinguishing itself from rhetoric and claiming for its own a new idea of the imagination. This process was of course much more gradual and uneven than can be detailed here. For instance, during this period, what we now think of as literature came to be and gained title to the imagination. A more complete picture of how this happened would include, in addition to what Bacon's thought heralded, factors such as increasing literacy and leisure time and advances in printing and bookmaking technology. Furthermore, the heart of such an inquiry would need to be an account of the bourgeoisie's formation and an explication of its peculiarly autonomous notion of the self. Because this chapter's focus is narrower, I shall assume some of these factors and processes and refer to others only when necessary. My subject is what happens to the Hive from neoclassicism to Romanticism, how this topos's traditional form is freed from the epic and what follows from this modernization. In this chapter, I will present the emergence of two of the Hive's modern versions, the "Self as Insect," and the "Insect as Other" — each of which is important enough to need treatment in its own later chapter.

Most interesting about the centuries that bracket the 1700 benchmark is the emergence of a new model of human being who is ready for a modern literary imagination and its appeals to the autonomous self, a psychology that is hungry for "new common-place connections." As Marlowe's Dr. Faustus (a minor Moses of the existential psyche) discovers, these connections do not yet exist. His narrative is a premonition that humans are outgrowing their Creator; his life and death give us a sight of the void at the center of things, a space that the next two centuries will attempt to fill. The psychological excesses of some of Shakespeare's characters more strongly anticipate and perhaps even help structure the West's emerging psychological capaciousness and appetite for personal experience, which together with the fruits of true science determine that between public role and private psyche there shall be antagonism. Bottom, for instance, a "low" character who in medieval drama exists only as a type, struggles with and exceeds his role on several levels. That Shakespeare can and chooses to draw Bottom — the bottom of the social order — with such life and to gift him with a complex and questing soul is a sign of things to come. In comparison, Lear and Macbeth are antiques.

It is Milton's Satan who unequivocally signals that the new human has arrived. At least as I have come to know it, Shakespeare's dramaturgy is humanistic and connective. His characters and his rhetoric work similarly: while both complicate and sometimes gesture beyond the old synthesis, this order's greater shape is still art's and human life's ultimate referent. In contrast, the pitch of Milton's Satan is higher than anything the Elizabethans achieved or would have valued. Milton makes Satan a self-contained cosmos of strident becoming whose essence more than conflicts with order and precedent: it is alien to all aspects of community. Thus, Milton brings to bear the whole of his learning and skill, all that he can muster from pagan and Christian antiquity, to force Satan's damnation.

What changed about the imagination between Shakespeare's time and Milton's was nothing less than its sources, prized subjects, and procedures of invention. Since the Greeks, most of the West's psychology, its life of feeling, lay on the surface of things, was largely inseparable from and mutually available as conventions, ornament. For the premodern West, rhetoric was teacher, guide, and translator; this system's complexities offered the self maps, models, and a vocabulary for thought, expression, action. Human nature and the individual self, the container and the thing contained, were by rhetoric meshed — each merged into the other and both were available and explicable to public and person alike. In the early-modern period this external collective psychology became pressured by the expansion of a sovereign self that would be neither defined nor constrained by any order external to itself. Room was made for this new model of the self at the top of consciousness: together old symbols and the soul began their inward journey.

The rhetorical imagination was, by our lights, public in its sources, procedures, and ends. This antique imagination of light and line I oppose (but by no means absolutely) to the modern imagination of shadow and suggestion. Poets inspired by the first, such as Dante, understood the self to be inhabited by and expressible through inherited forms. It is not that he or other poets like him did not recognize in themselves and their times feelings that exceeded and challenged the representational capacity of received symbols. To the contrary, only poets so at home with expressive form and supremely confident in their right and abilities to make it theirs could have so aggressively and successfully perfected and adapted the arduous gifts of Greece and Rome. What most distinguishes their imagination from ours is that it was embodied by and through symbols, characters, and narratives that were held in common. Far from recoiling from the light, these communal and conscious sources of the self gloried in it — they themselves were sources of a particular sort of illumination.

I do not mean to suggest that before *Paradise Lost* or *Clarissa* men and women lacked what we would recognize as an unconscious life, that they had nothing secret in them for art to excite and externalize. Pharaoh, for instance, dreamed of contrasting cows. Oedipus visited his mother in his dreams. Slumbering Scipio viewed the earth from afar and plotted the heavenly spheres. Lady Macbeth scrubbed at what was growing in the hidden places of her mind. But do notice the public nature of these literary dreams. Rather, I claim that during the rule of rhetoric, the empire of light, some, perhaps even many, of the processes and symbols that in us are *necessarily* unconscious were less so. Given that the premodern psyche was structured and functioned along lines more public than ours, how differently then appears our forebears' satisfaction with inherited forms, their attachment to antiquity, and their devotion to a model of invention that focused on *retractatio*. Far from signaling that the rhetorical mind was dulled by confinement within a venerated labyrinth, its expressive faculties suffocated beneath a moribund weight of tradition, these aspects of premodern art may well be signs that the self once enjoyed the sun and company.

The rhetorical imagination assumes that humans are social creatures whose being is best expressed through symbols that confirm the power and goodness of order and, hence, construct a reader whose identity is collective in its orientation. Because the modern, or Romantic, imagination defines the self as autonomous, distinct from both the city and nature, Romantic symbols and themes follow suit. Thus, the change from the rhetorical to the Romantic imagination was a shift in artistic emphasis from the perfection of communal forms that emphasize hierarchy and accord to the invention of ones built to image and gratify the sovereign self. A revolution, yes — but a revolution in and through form. And if there is one thing about changes in form that I have tried to show in this study, it is that novelty does not arise of itself, that it is the fruit of reworking. While the solitary and unaided understanding may indeed exceed what form allows, the act of communication returns the mind to social ground, commits the thinker to direct engagement with animated and willful structures, with mental entities that preexist and are external to the self. This is to say that the symbols that image and explore the Romantic self evolve much like their predecessors, gradually and not always predictably. Two truths of the evolutionary biology of metaphor are that every Age is one of innovation and that, out of the manifold novelties authored at any given moment, only a few survive and go on to prosper. We do not know exactly why some forms gain currency and others fade away — and, ironically, our ignorance of these matters grows as we approach our moment, in direct proportion to the amount of evidence. For the person who wishes clarity, certainty, and inevitability in argument, and who will not settle for any but clean lines of literary influence, the early-modern period begins an era of exceptional

frustration. Sweeping changes in belief, custom, and social organization; the multiplication of texts; the fall, dismemberment, and rebirth of
rhetoric; new aesthetics, genres, tastes, fashions, politics, and new science; an increasing number of writers of varied origins and agendas —
during this period all these factors and more collaborate, gather, enable,
and indeed force formal experimentation on a scale hitherto unknown.[3]

The Vision of Swift's "Secondary Address"

The classical Hive exemplifies symbols that display a *collective* figural
and psychological orientation. As demonstrated by my earlier discussion
of how Aeneas's view of Carthage works, within the Hive's space the
individual and collective are mutually defining: the singular and the collective essence cannot exist except in relation to each other. While it is
the singular observer's eye that constructs the scene, it is the city that
commands both the composition and our desire. In the classical tableau
the cityless self is drawn to the collective, which is *the* locus of longing.
And this longing suggests that a person's wholeness cannot be realized
except through union with the community. This style of analogy and the
metaphors that accord with it follow what Kenneth Burke titles a "traditional Rhetoric, [in which] the relation to an external audience [pos-
sessed of the old imagination and its collective sense of self] is stressed.
Aristotle's *Art of Rhetoric*, for instance, deals with the appeal to audiences
in this primary sense: It lists typical beliefs, so that the speaker may
choose among them the ones with which he would favorably identify his
cause or unfavorably identify the cause of an opponent; and it lists the
traits of character with which the speaker should seek to identify himself,
as a way of disposing an audience favorably towards him."[4]

Swift's bee in *The Battle of the Books* is an example of the second
and newer class of symbols, those that display an *individual* figural and
psychological orientation. *Battle*'s purpose is to defend the ancients
against the moderns. One should then expect Swift's rhetoric — his figural sources and their orientation and his analogical style — to be traditional. Some of it is, but careful examination shows that Swift alternates
between old rhetoric and elements of what Burke calls "a modern 'post-
Christian' rhetoric." In addition to the traditional conventions that are
necessary for establishing a "relation to an external audience," the post-
Christian [and postclassical] rhetor "must also concern [him- or her]self

with the thought that, under the heading of appeal to audiences, would also be included any ideas or images privately addressed to the individual self for moralistic or incantatory purposes. For you become your own audience, in some respects a very lax one, in some respects very exacting, when you become involved in psychologically stylistic subterfuges for presenting your own case to yourself in sympathetic terms" (38–39). The past (according to the Augustan fantasy of Roman greatness), its collective symbols and the golden accord that they imply, commands Swift's loyalty. He does not, therefore, *consistently* make himself his "own audience." But because he feels himself to be modern and is interested in creating a specific modern character, in *Battle* Swift experiments with "psychologically stylistic subterfuges," which Harold Bloom attributes to an "extraordinary perversity of imagination." Bloom argues that this sort of imagination "deliberately makes . . . [its author] . . . uninterpretable" and sees it as a stylistic connection between Kafka and Swift.[5]

Bloom is responding to those moments when, through the furious heaping of ironies, Swift overwhelms and negates the "norm" that makes satire work and civil communication possible. Here is Bloom on *Gulliver*'s conclusion: "What takes precedence here, the palpable hit at the obscenity of false human pride, or the madness of Gulliver, who thinks he is a Yahoo, longs to be a Houyhnhnm, and could not bear to be convinced that he is neither? As in *Tale of a Tub*, Swift audaciously plays at the farthest limits of irony, limits that make satire impossible, because no norm exists to which we might hope to return" (11).

While I do not find such moments either as uninterpretable as Bloom or interesting for quite the same reasons, I affirm their importance for an accurate estimate of Swift's motives and his considerable influence as a stylist and architect of modern letters. To me, these moments mark the eruption of a psychology that is impatient with and works against civil communication, the sort of discourse that Burke reminds us is epitomized by Aristotle's *Rhetoric*. This "traditional rhetoric" makes an "appeal to audiences in this *primary* sense: It lists typical beliefs, so that the speaker may choose among them" for purposes of identification (my emphasis). *Battle*'s "Preface" begins civilly with the traditional, primary appeal: "Satire is a sort of glass, wherein beholders do generally discover everybody's face but their own; which is the chief reason for that kind of reception it meets in the world" (397). Thus far we know how we should choose, with which camp we should identify. However, as soon as the speaker emerges armed with the first person pronoun, the ironies start their energetic accumulation. And once the "I" fixes on the organic body, the discourse turns toward the *secondary* appeal, a mode of address that is more private (what Richard Sennett would call "intimate") than the first, and at odds with more than conventional satire. In plain language, the speaker's wit becomes so savage and exclusive that the (traditional) satire's essential division between observer and observed is threatened with dissolution. Who among us, for instance, does not at one time or another (and especially when reading Swift) fear that one's "brain will endure but one scumming," that one should "beware of bringing [one's knowledge] under the lash of his betters?"

Thus made uncertain, our once reassuring position as knowing observer is further undermined by the following definition of "wit without knowledge": "it is a sort of cream, which gathers in a night at the top, and, by a skillful hand, may be soon whipped into froth; but once scummed away, what appears underneath will be fit for nothing but to be thrown to the hogs." While I suppose that we are allowed to imagine as ours that "skillful hand" that is doing the whipping, scumming, and throwing, the speaker has already spoken of himself as *the* agent of froth: "I have learned from long experience never to apprehend mischief from those understandings that I have been able to provoke; for anger and fury, though they add strength to the sinews of the body, yet are found to relax those of the mind, and to render all its efforts feeble and impotent." This speaker's confidence in his ability to render an opponent's (and perhaps any) mind "feeble and impotent" through provoking his opponent to "anger and fury" points directly at the spirited disputation of the spider and the bee, a contest between two modern psychological types.

I will presently examine this battle within *Battle* for what it tells us about Swift's idea of what makes an admirable modern psychology and so as to determine why he images it with the bee. Before I do so, however, let me examine another eruption of his "perverse," "psychologically stylistic subterfuge." Although I shall risk digression, it is helpful to clearly see this particular movement from traditional to modern rhetoric as a signature pattern in Swift. For this movement is a contest that Swift loves above all others: a spirited debate between two distinct voices, each of which is embodied in a character whose appearance and words express a distinct psychology and mode of verbal picture-making. The first voice is civil and of a piece with the conventional role of satirist. This voice's pictorial logic is rhetorical in the traditional sense: what is imaged refers to and derives its primary sense from the containing allegory. The second voice is decidedly less civil: its psychology exceeds and derives its vigor from opposing the satirist's role and values — the very conventions that make this sort of voice possible. This second voice has its own appetite — if you will, a "Baconian" soul — and seeks to affirm and gratify it through a more direct picture of and relationship with the world.

Like the one above, the brief satire below is also part of *Battle*'s front matter. Its topic is the causes of civil strife, and it begins with the primary appeal. The speaker's tone and rhetoric cooperate to invite us to stand above the fray, secure in a position that keeps our distance from and so guarantees our superiority to the "Republic of Dogs": "For, to speak in the phrase of writers upon the politics, we may observe in the Republic of Dogs (which in its original seems to be an institution of the many) that the whole state is ever in the profoundest peace after a full meal; and that civil broils arise among them when it happens for one great bone to be seized on by some leading dog, who either divides it among the few, and then it falls to an oligarchy, or keeps it to himself, and then it runs up to a tyranny" (398).

In this part of the satire Swift's irony stays within the boundaries of English neoclassical taste, which flourished during what Bonamy Dobrée tells us "might very well be called an age of attempted clarity, of trying to define the limits of reason, of seeking a balance that must from now on replace the old impossible harmony."[6] For the class to which Swift belonged and the betters they served, a skeptical humanism had effectively dampened Puritanism's fire; religion's fashionable warmth was more often than not supplied by Deism or one of its relatives. Because contemplating the implications of sin aroused enthusiasm, it was demoted to vice.

Notice what happens as *Battle*'s speaker continues: "The same reasoning also holds place among them [the dogs] in those dissensions we behold upon a turgescency in any of their females. For the right of possession lying in common (it being impossible to establish a property in so delicate a case) jealousies and suspicions do abound, that the whole commonwealth of that street is reduced to a manifest state of war, of every citizen against every citizen, till some one of more courage, conduct, or fortune than the rest, seizes and enjoys the prize; upon which naturally arises plenty of heart-burning and envy, and snarling against the happy dog" (398–99). The irony of the word "reasoning" commits the analogy to the secondary appeal, for what follows is far from reasonable: There are few creatures as embarrassingly irrational and unashamedly amorous as male dogs when excited by "a turgescency in any of their females" — and hungry dogs are not amorous dogs. Swift is parodying the simple logic of correspondence that makes allegory work. The restraint and precision of the satire's first element is not the second's interest, which is to kick *every* citizen where they live.

The speaker's initial purpose is to expose the engine of politics. But nothing new may be revealed through the commonplace that hunger is the universal source of disquiet that the vice of greed causes persons to channel and exploit. The speaker occupies and observes the "institution of the many" from a sovereign position that recalls both the structure and the function of the classical Hive. The implied distance between the speaker and his object of satire encourages thinking about people collectively, in terms of parties and factions. This distance helps keep the speaker's tone civil, his expression conventional. And since the reader may also imagine himself to be above the bone-wrangling mob, we may say that, within its limits, this opening satiric mode is inclusive, seeking to build and gratify a select community. As long as the speaker is content to keep his place in society, to remain consubstantial with his role as a satirist unfolding an allegory, his enjoyment of his own wit does not endanger propriety and threaten to alienate the reader.

In the satire's next element, however, the speaker abandons his post, approaches the fray for a closer look. In accordance with its subject and the speaker's proximity, this space is more *intimate* than the first. Thus, borrowing from Richard Sennett's *The Fall of Public Man*, I understand the movement of this speaker (who is obviously more interested by the spectacle of dogs mating than the playing out of his political allegory) as "the entrance of [a modern] personality into the public realm" of the fable's traditional space (219). The consequence is a second satiric mode whose "ideas or images," when compared with those of the first, are more "privately addressed to the individual self," which Sennett would call "intimate." And while this private address is "moralistic," it is hardly "moral" in the public and civic senses of the word. Nonetheless, the second mode does not eliminate the first. Because the second voice is conscious of itself as an anticonventional force, it needs its opposite in order to exist. It is, therefore, more accurate to say that the chord of "attempted clarity" and "balance" struck by the speaker's first tone is for a time inhabited by and forced to mingle with a dissonant, "incantatory" voice.

English neoclassical grace and humor spring from a Christianized mixture of Epicurean, Neoplatonic, and Stoic ideas and motives that is tempered by a stuffy nostalgia for simpler times and a worship of English common sense. This outlook of (somewhat arch) reasonableness insists that the previous century's excesses are anomalous. As a consequence, neoclassical art filters the world through forms that generate and reinforce a stance of restrained (and constraining) humanistic skepticism. The tone of Swift's second speaker does not admit to any such moderation and discards along with it the elegance lent by traditional rhetoric. While we may say that this voice remains skeptical because its speaker seeks a more direct and vital relation with the world, its philosophical stance is more private than public in its orientation. As much as is possible without entirely compromising *Battle*'s didactic motives, this second voice speaks to itself, springs from and expresses a passion for unmediated personal experience that renders moot the ideals of balance or harmony.

To borrow Musil's words, the first speaker's conventional and controlled allegory has "suddenly become [an analogy that sights an] incomprehensible and terrible" world. In the "luminous solitude of [Swift's naturalistic] telescopic circle, everything becomes clearer and larger, but above all, things become more arcane and demonic."[7] His second speaker "seizes and enjoys" his own wit's carnivorous perspicuity like "the happy dog" who by passion is attached to another in clear and public view. The humor is too sweepingly cruel to be naughty, too technical to be prurient. This wit is mature, but it lacks the resignation that makes Falstaff's wise. It is too solipsistic, too hateful of the body to be called Rabelaisian. And while it is sufficiently quirky, it is neither settled nor tender-minded enough to classify it as Montaignesque. There is something about this wit that recalls both sides of Dante, his savagery and his desire. But whereas the great Florentine's eyes tended upward, the gaze of Swift's speaker of the secondary address is transfixed by this world, one where flesh is the negation of both divine and dialectical transcendence. Dante saw Heaven as his prize, and he pursued it with medieval certainty and all the ardor of form; Swift's second speaker sees men through the lens of Baconian skepticism. Science has been let into the garden of similes: these men figured as horny dogs have been born in and for the marketplace. Their Beatrice is a bitch in heat.

This movement from primary to secondary address, this rhetorical shift from public-minded civility to private eccentricity, is accompanied by change from a communal, *rhetorical* way of seeing (which is also a way of not seeing) to another whose "theory is isolation" and whose power flows from details that are obtained optically and suggest a *mechanical* or *empirical* way of seeing. And if the reader thinks that I am sifting Swift's language too finely, then consider that the head dog of this satire's first part is described only generally, as "some leading dog." Because the speaker here works within his allegory's terms, it is neither necessary nor fitting to attribute to this animal anything resembling an internal state. In this initial mode any increase in understanding must come through *rhetorical* amplification: via the complication of a design that is extrinsic to the occasion's particulars. In contrast, the second part's top beast, "the happy dog," is dignified with a definite article and given his own state of being, albeit temporary, via the adjective "happy." Our knowledge has been increased through visual and naturalistic details: their referent is the phenomenal world and not the artificial space of allegory. Yet Swift is not abandoning art; he chooses to contain his visual experiments within the fable. For reasons that I will presently investigate, because Swift's optical experiments occur within the fable, instead of separating the dog from the man, it has the curious effect of confusing their essences.

There is something familiar and disturbing about this confusion of essences, a quality that, because it borders on the uncanny, may cause the reader to veer away from so close a look at Swift's Republic of Dogs. It is far more comfortable to treat it as an allegory told in a single voice, as a typical eighteenth-century utterance that has little connection with ourselves. This is why I wish to linger over this moment when Swift has his speaker step down from his sovereign position, when men and beasts are confused. Careful listening may recover a sense of "the way it must have been on the first day after [the] creation [of the modern self]," for this moment of Swiftian vision reveals that, far from being either divine or rational, man's essence is biological, a body over which character is thinly stretched and whose logic subtends the social realm. According to this model, human beings are by their nature incapable of bringing to fruition an ideal social order. Such a definition of the human and human society damns any persons who through an intimation of the ideal become awake to their animality: they will be equally oppressed by the way the world is and by the way it cannot be. In addition to diagramming how Swift will use the second address and its empirical seeing elsewhere in *Battle* (and later, in a maturer form, in *Gulliver's Travels*[8]), his vision of one "happy dog" shows us Romanticism's imminence and lays down a foundation for the existentialism that we see through Kafka's much darker confusion of the animal and the human.

Swift completes his (canine) satire on politics with a return to the staid panorama of civility, in the primary address. As eighteenth-century fable makers were wont to do, he leaves us with what sounds very much like a moral: "Again, if we look upon any of those republics engaged in a foreign war, either of invasion or defence, we shall find the same reasoning will serve as to the grounds and occasions of each; and that poverty or want in some degree or other (whether real or in opinion, which makes no alteration in the case) has a great share as well as pride, on the part of the aggressor" (399). Swift would have this dog fable's "scheme" reveal the "first ground of disagreement between" the ancients and the moderns. He means, of course, that we should see the moderns as suffering from intellectual want and subject to the vices that naturally follow — hence, their vicious attack on their betters. I shall indeed use Swift's scheme to interpret his Hive in *Battle*, but not quite as he asks.

The Battle between Moderns, and the Fable Explained

We need to understand Swift's bee, because the closer we approach our moment the more frequently the individual is figured as a solitary insect. Kafka, of course, looms in this argument's future. Bloom has already suggested a stylistic affinity between Swift and Kafka. And my discussion of the protoexistentialist aspects of Swift's secondary mode of address allows me to postulate an even stronger connection between them. The third and most obvious evidence of their relationship is that both Swift and Kafka use an image of the solitary insect to embody a psychology with which we are to identify. The fourth is that both formulations involve the fable.

From the rhetorical perspective, each literary genre involves a dis-

tinct mode of imitation and constructs a unique imaginary space. Ernst
Bloch, for example, has written about the fairy tale's space in such a way
as sheds light on how the fable works. In "The Fairy Tale Moves on Its
Own Time," Bloch defines the fairy tale by contrasting it with the legend. He observes that the legend "is always tied to a particular locale"
and that it refers to the past. It does not matter whether a legend "actually" happened, or if its "true" elements are mixed with fantasy. Like
its soberer cousins, the chronicle and the history, the legend's ultimate
ground is real space and time. The fairy tale, however, is a narrative of a
different order. "Pastness" (or for that matter, "futureness") and the uncertain flux of actual human relations have no place in this space. Indeed,
the fairy tale's characters and incidents are so conventional and abstract
that they exist only as functions that narrate "a wish-fulfilment that is not
bound by its own time and the apparel of its contents" (163). Although
Vladimir Propp's work on the structure of fairy tales demonstrates that
this sort of narrative is composed of elements, the psychosymbolic coherence of certain tales is so great that they are among the most durable
and well-traveled of stories. Arthur Waley tells us that "the earliest dat-
able version of the Cinderella story occurs in a Chinese book written
about 850–860 A.D."[9] Though the number of Cinderella-type stories argues against it having a single origin, one may imagine it following the
trade routes, changing "apparel" several times but never its wish nor this
wish's fulfillment. My point is that what distinguishes a fairy tale is an
irreducible core narrative that generates a distinct sort of space, one in
which objects, entities, and their actions work as a system to image and
satisfy an individual psychological fantasy.

The fable is similarly "unbound" and, especially in its Aesopic form,
generates space that, although different from the fairy tale's, is as distinct.[10] Like the fairy tale, the fable uses elements of the fantastic to augment, embody, and image aspects of experience that would otherwise
remain at the margin of consciousness. However, the fable is more a
typological incident than a narrative: it is a story so brief as to verge on
the tableau. Interestingly, one effect of this brevity is ambiguity. As a
perusal of Olivia and Robert Temple's excellent collection *Aesop: The
Complete Fables* makes abundantly clear, the traditional fable often requires an interpreter. The form's simplicity, then, is one source of its
power — which manifests itself as an overwhelming appeal to the reader's judgment. This provides, then, at least a partial explanation for both

the Augustans' near mania for the genre and the attention it has received from generations of illustrators. In his introduction to *Aesop: Five Centuries of Illustrated Fables*, John J. McKendry observes that:

> The fables lend themselves easily to illustration, for they are stories in which both actors and actions are simplified. The actors are sometimes humans, gods, or inanimate objects given the power of speech, but most often they are animals. The animals talk and act like humans whose behavior is shorn of any complications in order to emphasize a single characteristic. There are seldom more than three characters; most often there are two. If there are others, they usually act as a single group. The action also is straight-forward; there is usually one crucial act of crucial brevity, and there is rarely any great lapse of time. Conversely, although the fables are easy to illustrate, the illustrations do not explain themselves, and picture and story are bound together. Thus, the fables are best suited to book illustration; they do not lend themselves easily to treatment on the grand scale, in painting or sculpture. (5–6)

If the fairy tale's office is generalized as the imaging and playing out of commonplace *private* intuitions (*I* am a royal out of place; *my* parents are not my parents), then the fable's comparable office is to picture and complete minor commonplace *social* intuitions (the lazy starve; kindness is rewarded). The fable is a frame that simplifies, that "sh[ears away the] complications" of being for the purpose of emphasis. Whoever and whatever appears within its space is subordinated to "one crucial act of crucial brevity."

Similar to the Hive topos (which, as you will recall, I have discussed as a tableau), the fable positions its reader as an external observer and does so precisely. However, in comparison with the traditional Hive, the fable seats us closer to the action. Because the classical Hive was built to transmute a city into an organism, the space it imitates and structures is panoramic. The observer's distance from the object of figuration determines the topos's logic of simplification and its collective orientation. The fable's job is also to make a picture that images social abstractions, but these abstractions are conceived locally and, consequently, in a space that we sense as more intimate than the panoramic. The fable's pictorial locus is that place and moment where one or at most a few typological characters interact with a specific aspect of the world or with each other so as to reveal *elementary* social truths, the commonplaces of everyday life.

The space that the fable imitates is on the margin between what, in *The Hidden Dimension*, Edward T. Hall classifies as the "social" and the "public" spaces. Which is to say that we are positioned as an observer between seven and twenty-five feet from the characters and the locus of action. In real life, within this proximal range an observer may see most if not all of the body without sacrificing the ability to discern facial expressions and fine motor movements (114–25). We may confirm this range as proper to the fable by examining its typical illustrations. The overwhelming majority of such pictures show animals and humans in full. These images position us closely enough to witness character through expression and gesture and to hear conversation. Yet they place us far enough away to see the characters' relative sizes, positions, and bodily attitudes and to take in the crucial action as a whole. However fantastic the action performed or the behavior exhibited by persons, creatures, or things, the fable pictures it all modestly and always with uncompromising matter-of-factness. Hence, the form lends itself to the more homey variety of satire and comedy and not "to [artistic] treatment on the grand scale." The epic perspective and rhetoric — its psychology, characters, actions, and visual devices — are not generally appropriate for the fable: as modeled by Virgil, it is an excellent tool for extracting and domesticating epic similes. This also suggests a less obvious but more intriguing explanation for Swift's interest in the fable: that the genre situates the reporting consciousness close to an incident that cries out for judgment (if not for corrective action) surely tempts that part of Swift embodied by his modern, secondary speaker to enter, challenge, and thus to *modernize* the fable's antique and public space.

Since the fable positions us close to characters and actions, its logic of simplification is determined by its brevity and economy of description. The popularity of animals in fables reveals this logic at work. Animals of different species exhibit distinct appearances and behaviors that to human eyes appear definitive, leading to a metaphorically rich folklore that establishes the typological value of each animal and so helps determine its use. For instance, the fable of the tortoise and the hare images the social commonplace that speed is not everything in the game of life. In the actual world, the hare is built for speed but not endurance, and the converse is true of the tortoise. Within the fable's simplifying space, biology, because it determines observable action, is equivalent to character. The hare's and the tortoise's physical characteristics are transmuted into essences. In Aesop's universe you are what you do and — interestingly — according to H. J. Blackham, author of *The Fable as Literature*, if his fables teach "morality, it is not the morality of the Sunday school; rather, an open-eyed *Baconian* morality" (9; my emphasis). It seems, then, ironically, that the fable — which the eighteenth-century defenders of tradition valued for its antiquity and Swift chose as a weapon against change — may very well be the one ancient genre that works best with the moderns' empirical way of seeing and thinking.

In *Battle*, being is character and character is action. You are either with or against the ancients — and the satire would give us reason to side with antiquity. The situation is war, and combatants need ideological clarity, standards around which to rally. The honeybee is a fitting emblem for the good cause: no other animal type communicates quite the same qualities of purity, altruism, and social perfection, and none other has enjoyed so much sustained attention from so many esteemed poets. And Swift has further reasons to choose the bee. For one, he has the example of Sir William Temple, the patron of his early years, who in "On Ancient and Modern Learning" uses the bee to represent the ancients' useful and enduring purity in opposition to the ephemeral filth of modern "flies." However, Temple's rhetoric is prosaic and of the old school: his figures are ornaments to his thought, distributed rather than foregrounded and used as living emblems as Swift does in *Battle*. For example, in the third paragraph Temple informs us that modern "scribblers are infinite [in number], that like Mushrooms or Flys are born and dye in small circles of time" (4). He returns to this metaphor as part of the essay's conclusion:

> Now I think that nothing is more evident in the World than that Honour is a much stronger Principle, both of Action and Invention, than gain can ever bee. That all the Great and Noble Productions of Wit and of courage have been inspired and exalted by that alone. That the Charming Flights and Labours of Poets, the deep Speculations and Studies of Philosophers, the Conquests of Emperors and Achievements of Heroes, have all flowed from this one Source of Honour and Fame. . . .
> Avarice is, on the other side, of all Passions the most sordid, the

most clogged and covered with dirt and with dross, so that it cannot raise its wings beyond the smell of the Earth. (39–40)

Another reason for Swift choosing the bee as antiquity's defender is the model for Temple's figure of the bee: Seneca's analogy between the bee and the selective and combining intellect. Here is Seneca, who appropriately crowns his figure with a quotation from Virgil, lines from the tableau in which Aeneas sees Carthage as a beehive: "we should follow, men say, the example of the bees, who flit about and cull the flowers that are suitable for producing honey, and then arrange and assort in their cells all that they have brought in, as our Vergil says, 'pack close the flowing honey, / And swell their cells with nectar sweet.'"[11]

With such august backing, one would think that Swift, the defender of antiquity, would find the bee's use unproblematic. Swift, however, is a modern, and both his models' bees are synecdochic of the traditional Hive. This animal type cannot precisely image a character, a consciousness, for whom existence is synonymous with self-creation through direct and varied sense experiences (the antithesis of the spider's being, which as you will see is defined by its myopic self-absorption). The imitation of consciousness, the character, that distinguishes Swift's secondary address is learned but stridently and sometimes violently contrary to convention, versed in and comfortable with the old excellences but free to choose among them. This psychology, I am convinced, is to Swift a role, an experiment that he finds congenial because of its empirical (i.e., Baconian) core. Therefore, I conceive Swift's second voice as a writing toward a self, a method rather than a completely imagined character. Thus, it would be a mistake to confuse this processional consciousness with its creator. Despite his experiments, Swift's imagination remains one more of light and line than of suggestion and shadow: to him character is still more a public role than it is an essence generated by a private psychology. Swift's autonomous bee is an experiment in subject construction: he has this ancient image *perform* a condition of isolation that, because it is distinguished by fruitful mediation between past and present, is (in Swift's estimation) positive rather than negative. Swift's bee is, therefore, a subject under great tension. While its form and cultural alignment are traditional, its Being verges on the modern, depends upon the following interlocking notions: first, that unmediated (personal) sensory experiences may be had; second, that vision is the purest and, therefore, the most trustworthy sense; third, that percepts thus derived are true and universal; finally, that the reasoning built upon these personal, visual percepts will, therefore, also be true and universal. In sum, this modern consciousness cannot belong to a hive, a collective, conceived in either antique or naturalistic terms. Modern individuals must think and be for themselves, and they are joined to their kind only insofar as they do so. Seneca's and Temple's bee similes cannot image what Swift wants, because they refer to the bee as observed in nature and how this animal has been traditionally used by poets. To make his bee Swift must break with the past, and to do so he recapitulates Virgil's domestication of Homer's wild bees: he subjects an inherited form to the fable's simplifying space.

Like Milton's Satan (albeit considerably sweetened and miniaturized), Swift's bee does not fit its frame. Below is how the bee represents itself. Although its speech at this point alludes to antique models, the bee's individualism — its equation of Being with the capacity for unmediated experience and the freedom to choose for oneself — suggests a proto-existentialist psychology: "I am obliged to Heaven alone for my flights and my music; and Providence would never have bestowed me two such gifts, without designing them for the noblest ends. I visit indeed all the flowers and blossoms of the field and the garden; but whatever I collect from thence enriches myself without the least injury to their beauty, their smell, or their taste" (406). This bee gets its gifts of "flights and music" from "Heaven alone"; it lives to "enrich [it]self." Significantly, Swift's bee does not identify with any collective or communal principle until the end of its discourse, when its voice returns to the old-fashioned primary address.

Within the fable, I have asserted that action is character and character is Being. The autonomy of Swift's bee — strongest in those moments when it speaks in the secondary address — is an action that defines its Being as modern, but modern in a specific sense. His bee's Being (a pun that Swift could not have overlooked), its philosophical and moral essence, is antithetical to the spider's. The spider was also built to image a modern psychology, a negative one, whose qualities throw into relief what Swift wants us to find admirable about his bee. In contrast to the bee, the spider *cannot see clearly*, and even if he could it wouldn't matter. His web is a world "four inches round." One gathers that Swift believes, much like the Elizabethans, that a great passion sustained eventually affects the senses and ultimately the soul. This spider is more than choleric, paranoid — he is insane. He sees himself as a formidable mathematician and engineer and his home of dirty cobwebs as a "large castle." He thinks his learning superior to the ancients' (a negative autonomy that comes of prideful ignorance), and he shows himself to be blind to experience: he claims that he has "built [it all] with my own hands, and the materials extracted altogether out of my own person." Aroused by the same combination of pride, ignorance, filth, and body fluids that rarely fails to rouse his maker's ire, Swift's bee, transfixed and progressively invigorated by its own perspicacious wit, answers the spider's claim to a superior modernity: "You boast, indeed, of being obliged to no other creature, but of drawing and spinning out all from yourself; that is to say, if we may judge of the liquor in the vessel by what issues out, you possess a good plentiful store of dirt and poison in your breast; and, though I would by no means lessen or disparage your genuine stock of either, yet I doubt you are somewhat obliged for an increase of both, to a little foreign assistance. Your inherent portion of dirt does not fail of acquisitions, by sweepings exhaled from below; and one insect furnishes you with a share of poison to destroy another" (406). The pattern of opposed characters and psychologies that I noted in Swift's "Republic of Dogs" applies here and is clarified: Swift's bee begins in the primary address, in good taste and in accord with antiquity. It then moves to the secondary, much of whose vigor comes from depicting the spider as it is — a creature that feeds on other insects — which cooperates with what, above, Blackham calls the fable's "open-eyed Baconian morality." As earlier in *Battle*, here Swift's deft use of visual details evokes character and helps transmute a collective form — a topos dulled from use long before Temple felt obliged to repeat it — into a vigorous singular presence. The battle of *Battle* is, therefore, not exclusively between the ancients and the moderns. Swift uses this controversy (which by his time was an intellectual set piece) to image a contest between two types of modern perception and the Being each implies.

Swift is aware of his movement between types of address — and he trusts that we see it as well. He closes this dispute between the spider and the bee so as to recall both his models, Temple and Seneca. But he does it in such a way as to emphasize the tension between his solitary bee and its classical associations: "So that, in short, the question comes all to this; which is the nobler being of the two, that which by a lazy contemplation of four inches round, by an overweening pride, feeding and engendering on itself, turns all into excrement and venom, producing nothing at last, but flybane and a cobweb; or that which, by a universal range, with long search, much study, true judgement, and distinction of things, brings home honey and wax" (406). Of particular significance is that Swift orders his bee's allusions so as to move backward in rhetorical time, thereby focusing our attention on his final period. The next-to-last period, which describes the spider, refers to the passages from Temple's "Learning" that I examined above. (Swift feels free to mix his voice with his patron's, to sharpen the latter's rhetorical focus: Temple's abstract "small circles of time" become the Baconian "four inches round.") The final period honors Seneca with a well-made but conventional bit of rhetoric, a suspended construction that culminates in the nouns "honey and wax."

This last clause's traditional elegance makes a strong primary appeal, which to Swift's eighteenth-century readers would suggest meaning of a "universal range." Part of this structural achievement is a powerfully rhythmic closure that announces the fable's moral. And who better than Aesop to interpret it?: "As for us the Ancients, we are content with the bee to pretend to nothing of our own, beyond our wings and our voice, that is to say, our flights and our language. For the rest, whatever we have got, has been by infinite labor and search, and ranging through every corner of nature; the difference is, that instead of dirt and poison, we have rather chose to fill our hives with honey and wax, thus furnishing mankind with the two noblest of things, which are sweetness and light" (407–8). As I have established, left to its own devices, Swift's bee lives by and for itself. It enjoys a degree of freedom and agency, an autonomy of existence, beyond that allowed to Aesop and his fellow ancients. After all, each of these entities serves the collective; each is similarly engaged by and satisfied with filling his hive with "honey and wax" (an interestingly commercial activity), substances that are intended for the edification and illumination of "mankind." By making the bee the ancients' totem, Aesop definitively links it with a collective essence that conflicts with Swift's positive image of psychological modernity. Although complicated by characterization, witty dialogue, and naturalistic details, Swift's fable is true to its class. Despite a closure that forcefully affirms convention and a stabilizing interpretation by no less than Aesop, the tale's meaning remains ambiguous. That Swift does not, and perhaps cannot, resolve this contradiction is understandable; that he foregrounds it is courageous. He is on the cusp of vast rhetorical and psychological changes, and a large part of his verbal power and his interest to subsequent generations stems from imaging the tensions that define the modern character.

Although the modern self modeled by Swift's bee is — relative to its cultural context — autonomous, resistant to inherited forms and an unexamined rhetorical way of seeing, we should not think that this modern notion of the human is any less artificial than the one it superseded. Indeed, not only do the aspects of *Battle* that I have analyzed here demonstrate that the modern psychology is a construct, they show that this psychology (which is, after all, an imitation and amplification of a *social* intuition) was made from inherited forms through an arduous process of reworking. Like Virgil before him, Swift needs the bee for his own uses. But while the Roman used the fable to make a natural city of a swarm, which in retrospect does not seem to be a tremendous figural leap, Swift wishes to image an individual consciousness whose Being suggests a degree of independence from both nature and culture — in that his bee may wander, experience, and choose as it pleases. Though its origin is Roman, by placing Seneca's figure into a fable and giving it the power of the second address, Swift changes its figural orientation from the collective to the individual.

We know that the fable simplifies, which is an action that focuses and emphasizes through *redaction*. Among several things, redaction means to reduce (as in "to boil or strip down to essentials," "to miniaturize") and the acts of exposition and translation. Virgil, for instance, depends upon the fable's redactive powers when, in *Georgic* 4, he *reduces* Homer's wild bees, thereby making an admired but primitive simile available for his *exposition* (he wishes to expose and amplify the bees' collective way of living, their social perfection). Virgil is thus able to direct the *translation* of Homer's naturalistic language and its precosmopolitan psychology into an ornamented allegory that expresses a paradigmatically *Roman* essence. I emphasize "Roman" because the model of human society that Virgil wishes to find in Homer and in the natural hive is almost certainly not "in" either: at most the hierarchical accord that subtends the Virgilian Hive of peace is their suggestion, one potential among many. We might then say that the fable helped Virgil to conceive his desire through its "discovery" in Homer and in nature and then to image it in the form of a topos. Swift uses the fable similarly, to conceive a desire through an inherited form, Seneca's, and then to reduce, expose, amplify, and translate this antique synecdoche into an entity that can mediate between the rhetorical and the modern psychology. When we read Seneca's figure as a Roman utterance, at most it may be said to *suggest* Swift's self-creating bee. It is through the fable that Swift is able to de-emphasize the Roman figure's collective orientation and emphasize the suggestion that he will then image. So powerful is this picture of a human being as an insect that of Swift's creations only Gulliver is better known. But Gulliver has been brightened, restored to full mental health and given over to the writers of children's books: he ceases to be Gulliver. Swift's bee, however, is a subtler and, ultimately, a more resonant thing. Not only does it survive, it flourishes to become the reigning devil, the dark commonplace, of a host of modern fables.

Some Consequences of Reason's Fables

Although we have studied the Hive topos as a reworking of a literary form first published by Homer, it is clear that part of the excellence of Virgil's natural city is that it closely refers to the actual beehive. Seneca's figure, a synecdoche of Virgil's Hive that focuses on only one of its model's aspects, is at a remove from nature. Together this focus and distance enable Seneca to more directly picture individual humans as solitary bees. Swift's redaction of Seneca takes this process of denaturalization and individuation one step further. Swift's bee is doubly removed from nature; hence, Swift may use it to image a consciousness whose relationship with all determinate "collectives" (natural law, artistic precedent, and society) necessarily involves a process of observation, judgment, and choice — a process that makes sense only if one is positioned so as to clearly and dispassionately view options. More specifically, to Swift and his ideological circle this positioning was a conscious *self*-positioning that enabled a particular sort of seeing and thinking. In the following passage from *Spectator*, number 1, Joseph Addison dramatizes this self-positioning through the character of "Mr. Spectator," an obviously artificial consciousness whose relationship with society illuminates part of what Swift accomplishes with his bee: "Thus I live in the world, rather as a spectator of mankind than as one of the species; by which means I have made myself a speculative statesman, soldier, merchant, and artisan, without ever meddling with any practical part in life. I am very well versed in the theory of an husband or a father, and can discern the errors in the economy, business, and diversion of others, better than those who are engaged in them; as standers-by discover blots, which are apt to escape those who are in the game. . . . In short, I have acted in all the parts of my life as a looker-on" (2325). Even though Swift's observing bee is noticeably more engaged by and, therefore, directly involved with what he sees than is Addison's Mr. Spectator by the social "game," it is highly significant that both characters are presented to us as artificial visual instruments that enable the same perspective and process of observation, judgment, and choice. Of equal importance is that both characters also display the same tension between the individual and the collective: their shared artificiality is a costume for an emerging psychology that is defined by its isolation from the collective. Because Addison's Mr. Spectator does not — at this moment, anyway — engage with the past, he has less stake in the future than Swift's bee; he can afford to be more playful. Perhaps because he lacks the solidity of an entomological analog, if Mr. Spectator survives his moment he does so only as an essayist's stance, a stylistic spectre. Swift's bee, however, because it attempts more and engages with the Hive, is of greater consequence. For one, Swift's experiment effectively sunders the image of the bee from both its natural and its rhetorical ground, clarifies as one of its potentials an essence of "bee-ness" — an abstract power of wandering and gathering — that may be *assigned*, transferred to objects quite different from any Swift chose to imagine.

For example, when discussing the consolations of his addiction in *Confessions of an English Opium-Eater*, Thomas De Quincey pictures an opium-bee that "extracts its materials" from roses, which is both a traditional poetic symbol and a bee's natural food. Although I have not yet located unequivocal evidence that this analogy directly alludes to Swift, that Swift's bee flies "straight away to a bed of roses" after discoursing with the spider at least suggests allusion. But the most interesting aspect of De Quincey's opium-bee is that, in addition to gathering from roses, it does the same from "the soot of chimneys" (47). Grevel Lindop, the editor of the Oxford World's Classics edition of *Confessions*, glosses this soot-gathering: "in 1856 De Quincey added a note explaining that bees often entered Lakeland chimneys to take the soot left by wood or peat fires" (240). I am certain that only a Romantic, and only one as original as De Quincey, could have conceived a symbol of a bee that values equally the natural and the made, the nectar of flowers and the excrement of flame. However, in that Swift's bee is an experiment in consciousness that stands equally as spectator of nature and culture, I strongly suspect that even De Quincey could not have imagined the powers of opium as he does — vitalizing it with an abstract bee-ness — were it not for what Swift had already accomplished in *Battle*.

That Swift was singularly present in Romantic minds is more clearly demonstrated by John Keats.[12] In his letters on negative capability, which number among the most representative literary documents of his generation, Keats felt obliged to directly answer Swift's fable of the spider and the bee — and he does so in such a way as helps explain why among his fellow Romantics the Hive's evolution slows. In a letter written to J. H. Reynolds, dated 19 February 1818, whose subject is the "voyage of conception" made possible through "delicious diligent idleness," Keats counters Swift's preferred modern self with his own, which he figures through the spider reimagined: "Memory should not be called knowledge — Many have original minds who do not think it — they are led away by Custom — Now it appears to me that almost any Man may like the Spider spin from his own inwards his own airy Citadel — the points of leaves and twigs on which the Spider begins her work are few and she fills the Air with a beautiful circuiting: man should be content with as few points to tip with the fine Webb of his Soul and weave a tapestry empyrean — full of Symbols for his spiritual eye, of softness for his spiritual touch, of space for his wanderings, of distinctness for his Luxury."[13]

It is significant that Keats frames his spider with an attack on memory as it is understood within the traditional system of rhetoric. To the ancients and their admiring moderns such as Swift, memory was a storehouse of *public* (and, therefore, necessarily conventional) forms that inspired the poet and guided invention. A model or convention committed to memory tended to direct the imagination's processes along visible and civilizing channels. The Hive as Keats understood it was, of course, one such convention. Keats's quarrel is, therefore, not with the ancients per se but with what he calls "Custom" — the stultifying worship of antique forms — which he sees as the enemy of freedom and originality. It is clear that Keats associates both the figure and the character of Swift's bee with unoriginality, for it is this insect's opposite, the spider, that Keats elevates as a novel example of creativity that is open to

"almost any man." In opposition to Swift's elitist, Baconian self perfected through the excellences of the ancients' "enrich[ing] . . . flowers
and blossoms," Keats's ideal self assumes a Being that is creative and
genuine in direct proportion to its freedom from custom and its sensitivity to a *personal* spirituality. Keats's answer to Swift makes clear that
the rhetorical imagination and its aesthetic of light and line has been
replaced by the same suggestive and inward beauties that Swift anticipated and sought to counter.

For Keats the wellspring of Being is at once internal and cosmic: for
the civilizing neoclassical dialectic between the self and the ancients he
substitutes an osmotic merging and flow of creaturely feeling between
the soul and nature. Culture has no place in this equation; each person
must make his or her own rhetoric: "spin[ning] from his own inwards
his own airy Citadel. . . . [made from] the fine Webb of his Soul and
weave[s] a tapestry . . . full of Symbols for his spiritual eye." Rhetorical
memory, "Custom," the common denominator of old-fashioned civil
society and the author of shared procedures of making and enjoyment,
no longer plays a role in self-creation: from "his own inwards" Keats's
modern generates personal symbols for his private "spiritual eye." Swift's
Baconian empiricism, because it begins with appearances that are apparent to all, pursues truth through reason and works against private symbols and any psychological variety that falls outside established character
types. Keats's model of Being and theory of creativity is anti-Baconian,
irrational — and he is aware of its powers for social disruption. However, unlike Swift and his circle, Keats champions that "the Minds of
Mortals are so different and bent on such diverse Journeys." He allows
"that it may at first appear impossible for any common taste and fellowship to exist," but reassures us that "common taste and fellowship"
are natural (rather than learned and earned, as in Swift's cosmos) because "Minds would leave each other in contrary directions, traverse each
other in Numberless points, and all [*for* at] last greet each other at the
Journeys end" (*ERW*, 1221; bracketed text in original).

Keats's natural tendency toward community — a gentle and utopian
democracy of the spirit — requires that debate, the very heart of the
process of Baconian socialization, must be cast out of the garden: "Man
should not dispute or assert but whisper results to his neighbour, and
thus by every germ of Spirit sucking the sap from mould ethereal every human might become great, and Humanity instead of being a wide

heath of Furse and Briars with here and there a remote Oak or Pine, would become a grand democracy of Forest trees" (1211). In place of the active and elite intellectuality — the rhetorically enabled *wit* — of Swift's ideal modern, Keats offers a receptiveness to feeling and a passivity before natural inspiration and a new definition of nobility: "Now it is more noble to sit like Jove than to fly like Mercury — let us not therefore go hurrying about and collecting honey-bee like, buzzing here and there impatiently from a knowledge of what is to be arrived at: but let us open out leaves like a flower and be passive and receptive — budding patiently under the eye of Apollo and taking *hints* [the suggestions that we have located in inherited forms?] from every noble insect that favors us with a visit — sap will be given us for Meat and dew for drink" (my emphasis). We are to be, then, modern lilies of the field, spiritual and rhetorical vegetarians: nature will give us "sap . . . for Meat and dew for drink" (1211).

Bathed in the rhetorical imagination's dreamless light, Swift's bee "enrich[es]" and perfects itself through the wisdom of ancient books. In answer to this winged symbol of industry and tradition, Keats announces his own: the thrush. This symbol is native and unburdened by the weight of the past. Because it is a bird, the thrush is far more our biological kin than the insect: its warm blood, intelligence, and voice evoke entirely different associations and require a different sort of identification. No matter how Swift imagines his bee, it cannot escape its synecdochic association with Nature's beehive and antiquity's picture of the city-as-hive. In contrast, the thrush is solitary and wild. Keats's sensitive spider, who on this day of idleness is receptive to wisdom because he has "not read any Books," learns from this wild bird to "fret not after knowledge" because "song comes native" and "he's awake who thinks himself asleep."[14] But it would be wrong to confuse this thinking sleep as creative torpor. Unlike the Augustans, the Romantics looked first to Nature and natural language for their inspiration, an emphasis that inverts the Christian synthesis's hierarchy of poetic value. To the rhetorical imagination, art is superior to and improves nature. Indeed, to the rhetorically trained, art *is* nature. Swift, for example, despite his Baconian leanings (an attitude toward perception that if freed from method anticipates Keats's "Life of Sensations Rather Than of Thoughts"[15]), adheres to the old model of creation: one makes the new through *retractatio*, the learned engagement with and adaptation of inherited forms.

The Romantic imagination, however, gives Nature creative agency. The poetic activity thus becomes more a transcription of a single mind's intimate overhearing of patterns extrinsic to the social sphere than a public performance in a theater of humanistic language and intuition. Romanticism dethrones the old confidence in mastery. It replaces a refereed focus on light and line and desire for the cosmopolis with an aesthetic of shadow and suggestion, a longing for the infinite — both external and internal — unmediated by Custom. What the telescope did for Milton's art, the dream does for the Romantics: a new sensibility and rhetoric rises from and chronicles an individual's awakening to the word through an innate sensitivity to extralinguistic patterns. In a letter to his brothers, George and Tom, Keats famously defines this sensitivity: "at once it struck me, what quality went to form a Man of Achievement especially in Literature & which Shakespeare posessed [*sic*] so enormously — I mean *Negative Capability*, that is when man is capable of being in uncertainties, Mysteries, doubts, without any irritable reaching after fact & reason." (Keats's emphasis).[16]

Keats's letters on negative capability demonstrate that the English Romantics felt the Augustans to be their negation: a worldview, an aesthetic, and, especially, a psychology to be opposed with an alternative. No wonder, then, that the Romantics had little use for the fable, which the Augustans valued for its antiquity, its characterologically driven space, and its capacity to image social intuitions. Indeed it seems that nearly all of the neoclassical literati translated and wrote them.[17] However, of these many fables only Bernard Mandeville's *The Fable of the Bees* comes close to matching *Battle*'s influence over the Hive's modern formulations. In *Battle* Swift models for his inheritors two new and powerful literary tools: the self imaged as an autonomous insect and a solitary insect essence abstract enough to be transferred. As I have mentioned, Kafka owes Swift a debt, but so do Nietzsche, Hardy, Sartre, and many others. While the tones of contemporary analogy that evoke a character's isolation through the image of a solitary insect may strike us as Aeschylean or Shakespearean, the thought and technique behind such an utterance — the real source of its rhetorical power — is almost certainly Swift's.

Though less than Swift's, Mandeville's contribution to the symbol complex of the Hive is substantial: a picture of human society's opposite as a sentient insect society. Like Swift, Mandeville uses the fable to modernize an inherited form. However, because his focus is wider than Swift's and he wishes to satirize his time's obsession with attacking vice, Mandeville chooses more ambitiously. To the fable's simplifying and inherently satirical space he subjects that most sinful of Hives, Milton's Pandemonium. Through the fable's agency, Mandeville deflates and secularizes Milton's epic simile, using Satan himself, as it were, to make a picture of human nature. The imaginative consequences of this reworking turn out to be quite different from what Mandeville or his vitriolic opponents could have predicted. The Age of Reason decried and sometimes had the book burned.[18] How different Mandeville's reputation a century-and-a-half later: in *Capital* Marx titles him "an honest and clearheaded man" (304). Given Marx's utopian mind, we may speculate that he understood *Fable* as a model of social speculation, a powerful instance of philosophical projection far more attuned to the realities of European modernity than Plato's *Republic* or even More's *Utopia*. Interestingly, in the twentieth century this sort of social speculation would become literature, a subgenre of science fiction that we might call the "alternative history." And indeed Mandeville's *Fable* is an alternative history of humanity, one that shows the development of a race of sentient insects into our species's antithetical equivalent.

On its surface, *Gulliver's Travels* is more obviously a source book for images of alien societies than Mandeville's *Fable*. Swift draws each culture with a draftsman's eye, doling out generous helpings of bizarre and alien customs, arts, languages, philosophies, sciences, and religions. Nonetheless — like the beast fable — each of these alternative societies boils down to an isolated and magnified aspect of the human. Each race of beings is a measuring device, a lesson in a textbook of true ideas that is dressed as a romance. One does not, therefore, get the sense that any of these geographically isolated types will ever leave their Plinean space and enter ours. In contrast, the fabulous space occupied by Mandeville's "Grumbling Bees" overlaps and interweaves with our own.

Swift and Mandeville use the fable's powers of magnification differently and for different ends. More accurately, Swift is not content with the fable's proximal limits. He augments his seeing and his satire through an imitation of microscopic vision. Gulliver's views of the Brobdingnagian body, for example, clarify that Swift's most urgent purpose is to shame every one of us into humility. Viewed as a whole, judged as an example of eighteenth-century satire, Gulliver is an excellent but nonetheless conventional satire on the vice of pride. Take the contrast between the Yahoos and the Houyhnhnms, for instance. Although one gathers that Swift sees in the Yahoos' animality an immediacy of being and a freedom that is denied the Houyhnhnms (who are, after all, sentient *domestic* animals), these beast men are meant to shame us — as are, I think, the Houyhnhnms. Although their rationality and manners are more attractive than the Yahoos' civilization of gibbering and excrement tossing, this society is no less extreme — it, too, is a warning against enthusiasm.

Mandeville also cautions us against enthusiasm; but when it comes to attacking vice, he takes a more original path than Swift. Mandeville thinks shame is hypocritical, that "Private Vices [have] Publick Benefits." He proposes to tell us what we "really are," "to shew, that these Qualifications [the passions], which we all pretend to be asham'd of, are the great support of a flourishing Society" (77). *Fable* is the story of a "Hive" of "Insects [that] lived like Men, and all / Our Actions they perform'd in small" (63). This Hive is a miniature England, and, like its larger counterpart, its greatness and prosperity require that the manifold private vices — sloth, lust, avarice, and pride, to name only a few — be practiced for the public good. For instance, according to Mandeville, avarice is the motivation for hard work; and vanity, that "Minister of Industry," employs millions in needless production.

Little England that it is, this Hive of human insects, ignorant "that Perfection here below / Is more, than Gods can well bestow" (69), dares to grumble, to cry "brazenly, / Good Gods, had we but Honesty!" Jove hears their grumbling and "with Indignation moved, / At last in Anger swore, he'd rid / The bawling Hive of Fraud, and did" (70). The consequence is a "vast and sudden . . . Alteration" — a transformation that echoes Milton's description of shrinking devils:

> the Signal giv'n,
> Behold a wonder! they but now who seem'd
> In bigness to surpass Earth's Giant Sons
> Now less than smallest Dwarfs, in narrow room
> Throng numberless, like that Pigmean Race
> Beyond the Indian Mount, of Faery Elves,
> Whose midnight Revels, by a forest side
> Or fountain some belated Peasant sees,

Or dreams he sees, while over-head the Moon
Sits Arbitress, and nearer to the Earth
Wheels her pale course; they on their mirth and dance
Intent, with jocund Music charm his ear;
At once with joy and far his heart rebounds.
Thus incorporeal Spirits to smallest forms
Reduc'd thir shapes immense.
(*PL*, 1.776–90)

Here Milton shows us that the power of evil only reduces those who wield it. But he also compares this power and its effects to the "dreams" of "some belated peasant." Milton is not suggesting that Satan's power is a fancy of ignorant dreams; he is saying, rather, that when unalloyed with reason and holy writ the imagination makes a "wonder" of evil, unwittingly collaborates with humanity's Adversary.

Mandeville secularizes Pandemonium, demoting its sin to vice: he makes it human. He inverts its meaning by arguing that vice is essential for a happy polity: "Thus every Part was full of Vice, / Yet the whole Mass a Paradise" (67). His Hive's "Alteration," however, mirrors Pandemonium's "wonder": what was once extensive and powerful is made quite the opposite. The effects of virtue are many, and at first they are good. Prices drop. Justice and health prevail: the courts close, the lawyers pack up and leave, physicians save lives by letting nature cure. Public servants serve their public, forswear bribery and influence peddling, and live on what they earn. The clergy imitate Christ. Mandeville's analog to the "belated Peasant['s]" unalloyed imagination is the social commonplace that social health is directly proportional to the virtue of its citizens. He shows its untruth thus: in the absence of vice, this once rich and powerful nation of insect-men begins a progressive decline. Having no armies abroad and no foreign policy, commerce stalls. Satisfied with the gifts of "Kind Nature" and content with "their homely store," these insects no longer want or produce anything inessential: companies and whole industries leave. "So few in the vast Hive remain; / The Hundreth part they can't maintain / Against th' Insults of Numerous foes." The Golden Age of the remaining and virtuous bees is marred by war. They are victorious, but "many Thousand Bees were lost." And since these insects are now "Hard'ned with Toils, and Exercise / They counted Ease it self a Vice; / Which so improved their Temperance; / That, to avoid

Extravagance, / They flew into a hollow Tree, / Blest with Content and Honesty" (75). Mandeville, a physician, has used the fable as a sociological petri dish. Into a healthily vice-ridden society, like ours in every respect except scale, he has introduced a pathogen, virtue, an ideology that can destroy nations because it eliminates individual differences, because it changes weak and contentious moderns into beings who, according to the moral, belong in a Hesiodic tale.

Mandeville does not, however, conclude his fable with the "vain Eutopia[n]" image of insect-men transformed into angelic honeybees. These remaining bees who leave their now near-empty city for a hollow tree do so for ideological reasons: they are still sentient and they are battle-hardened. In "Remark (X)," Mandeville, always the uncompromising realist, casts the Spartans as modern England's antithesis. Mandeville admits to their virtue and martial prowess but observes that "there never was a Nation whose Greatness was more empty than theirs" (254). Although the Spartans "were indeed both fear'd and esteem'd Abroad" and enjoyed "perfect equality" among themselves, their lives were barren of comforts. And (to apply Mandeville's reasoning) because they were reared in the absence of vice, free from its stimulation and the opportunities it makes for self-actualization, we may infer that one Spartan's thoughts and desires were much the same as another's. The consequence of such mental homogeneity is the individual's diminishment, a most un-English condition. Mandeville makes the point several times that no English citizen would "submit to the Harshness of" this life, that to do so one would need to be brought up Spartan. In that the Spartans are more and yet definitely less than us, they are Mandeville's type for a profound social otherness.

Obviously Mandeville's Sparta, the antithesis of our pluralistic and tolerant nation of pleasure-seeking individualists, does not precisely fit what the natural hive brings to mind: a rustic community of industrious, naturally domestic *animals* who are aggressive only when threatened. The Homeric connection between bees and warriors is the obvious counter-image to this peaceful community, but Mandeville's choice to explain his virtuous bees through Plutarch's Spartans rather than Homer's Achaians or any one of Virgil's several entomologically figured peoples suggests that he wants to steer clear of the epic, of its nostalgic, heroic mode of picturing. *Fable of the Bees* is an exercise in speculative social engineering, and Mandeville wants to keep it that way. Its conceptual product is a Rousseauean true idea, a society that is our equivalent but also our opposite. The qualities that distinguish the Spartans align with and enrich the poem's concluding and sovereign image: a race of sentient super-insects who live *out there*, in nature's alien space. In this respect, Mandeville is the sovereign interpreter of and conduit for Milton's Pandemonium; he is the doctor who delivered to Conrad, Wells, and a host of other romancers the Other as Insect.

4

THE OTHER AS INSECT

*The long corridor that ringed the old inn like a square
hoop was so jammed with people that one could not pass.
They were waiting in front of a door, excited, crowded
together in an irregular circle, in the empty center
of which there stood a guard. Others kept coming,
and the corridor filled like a clogged conduit. There was
the rustling sound of whispers, angry and astonished.
The crowd had its own language, different from the
language spoken by each of those people. It resembled bees
buzzing, or growls. Words were lost, leaving a collective
noise; individual moods were lost, leaving a collective,
dangerous one.*

   Meša Selimović, Death and the Dervish

The insect society has always suggested Otherness, but it was not until Europe's nineteenth century that this difference began to be widely thought of as absolute, essential. While early modern thinkers, such as Hobbes and Milton, anticipate this division between human and insect sociality, their world was still marked by the aesthetics and values of Christian antiquity. This worldview held that in itself order was good and was so in direct proportion to its intensity. The more (order) the better — in both senses of the phrase. Nature was seen as another of God's books, and by dint of a single and interested Creator its creatures were joined to us and us to them. Just as Nature abhorred a vacuum, so it opposed dissonance and asymmetry; everything had its proper place in the Great Chain of Being. Because we aspired to an image of its politics, we saw the natural beehive as kin. Rhetoric not biology, analogy rather than blood, tied us to this living allegory, which signified visually in a language that all could understand. Consequently, as long as the old ideas maintained their power, the Hive's allegorical possibilities were almost entirely restricted to positive formulations. Even Milton — and after him, Mandeville — who rejected the natural hive as a model for human society, did not disagree that its organization was admirable.

Why then over the course of the nineteenth century do we increasingly see such a radical change in the Hive's implications? By themselves, contact with new lands, strange peoples, and foreign customs cannot be held responsible. Europe was long since used to such novelties — and neither capitalism nor colonialism, nor even their combination, were unique to either this century or Protestant Europe. Yet it is not until the Hive is adapted to nineteenth-century Europe's stories of conquest, brought to bear upon alien (un)natural settings and asked to describe the work of modern empire, that we begin to see the Other — especially its sociality — figured almost exclusively through the Hive and in such a way as blurs the ancient distinction between the beehive and the ant heap.

Mandeville's separation of the human from the natural hive announces that the city's divorce from the insect society impends, that their division will rise from a wrangle about essence understood biologically. Mandeville argued that England's greatness issued from "private vice"; his message: if you listen carefully to what the ancients insisted was a complex and perfect harmony, you will hear the truth of its dissonance. Virgil felt this disharmony, but he was Roman and, hence, understood it as a contrast between two discrete collective modes that should be expressed through distinct insect metaphors. The first is Aeneas's initial view of Carthage. This version of the Hive is civilized, orderly, and future oriented and finds its expression through the metaphor of the beehive and its traditional language of golden light. The second is the picture of the Trojans provisioning their ships with the spoils of Dido's betrayed and broken city. Here Virgil uses the Hive to image barbaric energy, the opposite of progressive order, and abstraction clothed in the dark flesh of ants. While we do, of course, register the differences between these images, we also feel their intersection. For the modern mind the poles of light and darkness clarified by Milton's Pandemonium have moved toward a common center. The consequence is a poetically significant confusion — one that expresses an ambivalent opinion of society, which frequently finds its voice through the image of the ant heap. The root cause of this metaphoric shift is Darwinism's retranslation of the book of nature. On a scale infinitely larger than Mandeville could imagine, Darwin makes an image of a disharmonious harmony that encompasses both culture and nature. Through Darwin's lens the immutable accord of sacred creation loses its sentience, becomes subject to time and a blind struggle over the things of brute flesh: sustenance, territory, mates.

It is not, however, the picture of nature as warlike that makes Darwinism different from earlier theories. Virgil, for instance, in his *Georgics*, speaks of humanity's relationship with nature as a martial struggle. For the sake of intellectual economy, I will reduce Darwinism's revolution to the redefinition of two interrelated terms: complexity and perfection. Darwinian complexity is defined by modern Europe's idea of the self and unfolds over time. The initial part of this idea is, of course, a continuation and projection of Enlightenment values, which are themselves descended from humanism. It is this idea's latter part, that organic complexity is the product of changes that accumulate over time, that is new. When combined, these two principles — the first a measuring device and the second a mechanism — give to morphological difference a wider and more extreme significance. Simplicity of form becomes a priori evidence of antiquity and, if need be, inferiority. Barbarism, for example, which for the ancients was mostly a matter of language, is easily naturalized by the evolutionary thinker. Hence, a paradox. Although Europeans now shared their flesh with other creatures and cultures, the nature of existence itself seemed to mandate essential difference.

Second, and most important, Darwinism redefined perfection. Under the old plan, which reflected the Creator's Will, the universe was complete, an all-encompassing design already achieved. Each creature was perfect in itself, and creation's variety formed a sacred and harmonious whole. In contrast, Darwinism saw the universe and its parts as in a process of physical becoming. Perfection was relative, to be realized differently by each type of creature over time and through the agency of natural selection. Thus, although all creatures are subject to law as in the sacred universe, the court of Darwinian nature rules in favor of strength and follows a constitution of increasing specialization.

The irony is that at the same time humans joined the rest of creation they began to conceive the differences between species and peoples as absolute. For the first time, it became possible to picture an Other that was natural and unconnected with the mythoreligious patterns of the past. Ready to fuel this imaginative breakthrough was the accumulating work of insect watchers, who as early as 1586 were beginning to see the beehive as a distinctly nonhuman society.[1] Mandeville's Spartan bees reflect some of this thinking. And certainly Spitzner's discovery in 1788 that the honey bee dance was related to the activity of nectar gathering (which indicates an insect-specific language) demonstrates that entomologists were busy making a new picture of the insect realm, a world that had little to do with ours.[2] It is no wonder, then, that the social insects began to signify in a new way: suggesting a new sort of alterity, one natural and yet highly organized. Empowered by the blessing of science, it was not long before the poetic picture of the insect society became the sovereign image of human civilization's nonhuman equivalent.

During the last decades of the nineteenth century, from its familiar ground of describing "us" the Hive was, so to speak, put to work in the colonies describing "them" and the changes wrought in "us." To Europeans of the time, among the most disturbing aspects of the colonial encounter was the potential that the civilized soul (the orderly, Christian bee of northern climes) would be seduced by the savage ant heap — or, worse, that the superior hive itself might become corrupted, weakened, and fall through its instruments' contact with barbarian races. The result was new versions of the Hive that helped to forge and articulate what has turned out to be a durable and highly expressive linkage between the ancient form I have been discussing and the psychic consequences of our global ambitions and their more unfortunate practices. Relatedly, around this same time the Hive finds itself assigned even farther afield, serving as the template for the West's first truly alien threat.

Although an experienced colonizer, the Europe of Joseph Conrad's day was not prepared for the consequences of sustained cultural contact within a frame of economic, technological, and socioethical progress. Increasing population, the rising literacy and expectations of the working class, and immigration merely complicated the equation further. The time for utopian experiments seemed to be past, and social Darwinism was increasingly attractive as explanation and biological justification for a system of differences that was increasingly felt to enclose and warp the human spirit. There was a growing sense that society was out of control, that the emerging technological bureaucracy was itself a threat, an unnatural force capable of shaping us and even the future according to its mechanistic purposes.[3]

Conrad's *Heart of Darkness* displays many of the late colonial period's obsessions and anxieties. Like Hardy's great novels of social change, *Heart* is both conservative and groundbreaking, confirming the past and its forms and yet anticipating and giving shape to emerging psychologies. This novel shows us two different views of and insect images for the subjects of the colonial situation. Each of these images alludes to and to a degree reworks one or more of our antique models. Yet each also redefines what the Hive means, maps some of its evolutionary possibilities. The first such image comes soon after Marlow's arrival in Africa. He has steamed upriver thirty miles to his company's "station," where he is to be briefed and prepared for further movement into the interior. For the first time in the novel, we have a clear view of the colonial enterprise. Our interpretative frame is the Hive: "At last we opened a reach. A rocky cliff appeared, mounds of turned-up earth by the shore, houses on a hill, others with iron roofs amongst a waste of excavations hanging to the declivity. A continuous noise of the rapids above hovered over this scene of inhabited devastation. A lot of people, mostly black and naked, moved about like ants" (18). Although its presence is subtle, the Hive's perspectival logic is at work in this passage. Marlow is on the deck of a ship, viewing the station and these workers from a distance. From this position, Europeans and Africans appear to be equally part of an anthill of activity. We know this because Marlow classifies all these figures as "people." The only distinction he makes between them is to observe that the majority of these "ants" are "black and naked." He is not yet close enough to discern the crucial difference in status and power between whites and blacks. Once ashore, however, he looks about, and finds himself on a descending path (the direction is significant; this space is organized by an infernal geometry). Marlow soon discovers a "file" of starving, chained Africans forced at gunpoint to carry earth by a uniformed native. In the same breath Marlow describes this native ironically — as "one of the reclaimed" — and unironically — as "the product of the new forces at work" (19). Obviously Conrad thinks of colonialism as an order that shapes human beings just as it does other "raw material" (a term he uses to refer to the African laborers).

"Instead of going up . . . [Marlow now] turn[s] . . . and descend[s] . . . to the left" and moves through a blasted landscape cut by ravines filled with mechanical refuse. He makes it to the forest's shade but there enters what he calls the "gloomy circle of some inferno" (20). In these woods "black shapes crouched, lay, sat between the trees, leaning against the trunks, clinging to the earth . . . in all the attitudes of pain, abandonment, and despair . . . this was the place where some of the helpers had withdrawn to die." Marlow's descent, his getting lost in a wood, and the reference to "some inferno" all allude to Dante's *Commedia*. In this respect *Heart*'s rhetoric looks to the past, is built from a series of reworkings in the classical mode, to include figural inversions. For example, whereas Dante reserves the image of the insect and its social structure for Paradise, the conclusion of his speaker's journey, Conrad begins Marlow's with its infernal equivalent. This outpost is no shining city. Indeed, it is the opposite of what the city should be. Significantly, in this African ant heap Marlow quickly discovers that his adversary is neither nature nor the savage, but civilization released from all limits, a society whose laws are bureaucratic procedures and whose soul is Mammon. Conrad himself observed the colonial machine at work in the Belgian Congo. No wonder, then, this novel's association between Europe's African colonies and literature's dark swarm.

In addition to their evocation of literary antecedents, together these passages from *Heart* express a version of the Hive unique to the latter half of the nineteenth century — namely, a humanmade society that has antihuman tendencies, a bureaucratic, dehumanizing machine. Everywhere Marlow sees men working in the heat even to the point of death, and to no apparent human (i.e., rational) purpose. Hence, the figure of the anthill, which in this context signifies mindless, ceaseless activity.

Conrad holds in reserve his second insect image, that of the beehive, which suggests an order more organized and yet, within this dystopian frame, more threatening. (Bees, of course, have stings, and thus far Conrad's native "ants" act more like the gentle European variety than, for instance, the voracious African army ants.)

Like his first use of the Hive, the beehive image he deploys near the end of his tale echoes and inverts key moments of the *Commedia*. Marlow is on the deck of a riverboat, looking out into the blackness of the jungle. The deathly ill Kurtz is down below. Soon these Europeans are to be on their way downriver and away from the force that Conrad equivocally suggests that they have both created and awakened.

> On the hill a big fire burned, illuminating fitfully a crooked corner of the station-house. One of the agents with a picket of a few of our blacks armed for the purpose was keeping guard over the ivory, but deep within the forest red gleams that wavered, that seemed to sink and rise from the ground amongst confused columnar shapes of intense blackness showed the exact position of the camp where Mr. Kurtz's adorers were keeping their uneasy vigil. The monotonous beating of a big drum filled the air with muffled shocks and a lingering vibration. A steady droning sound of many men chanting each to himself some weird incantation came out from the black flat wall of the woods as the humming of bees comes out of a hive, and had a strange narcotic effect upon my half awake senses. I believe I dozed off leaning over the rail till an abrupt burst of yells, an overwhelming out-break of a pent-up and mysterious frenzy, woke me up with bewildered wonder. (63)

In this passage, by merging the Hive with the atmospherics of night and the jungle, Conrad places us *inside* a whole and functioning non-European — and therefore nonhuman — sociality: we are surrounded by the "black flat wall of the woods" and are therefore more highly subject to its terms than while at the Company station. There, Marlow is not yet inside the order that he observes from a distance and figures as an ant heap. He sees the Company's work in terms of digging, a senseless parody of civilized industry, and thinks its product mere garbage, dying and corrupted Africans. In the ant heap, the force of colonialism is an external pressure that works from the outside in. It treats the body as a commodity, disciplining and using it up.

Because the Company station is geographically and sociologically closer to Europe than Kurtz's shadowy domain, and its inhabitants therefore more strongly subject to the colonial machine, it would seem that to go upriver, farther into the jungle, would be to leave colonialism behind. But the darkness into which Marlow travels is meant to signify more than just a non-European condition. While journeying upriver does indeed bring Marlow into contact with the Other, I am convinced that this jungle Hive is meant in part to signify the psychology of colonialism.

Whereas the Company ant heap passage is the product of sight, this jungle Hive is evoked by sound. This conversion of a visual into an auditory structure harks back to an aspect of Milton's Pandemonium that has important consequences for the Hive. As part of the rhetoric necessary for taking on Dante and inverting his prized topos, Milton treats hearing as antithetical to seeing. Light has spiritual associations and rational efficacy, but hearing is how we make "darkness visible." In the night, a weird sound dominates the sensorium even more completely than does an arresting sight during the day. Additionally, perhaps because we may focus our eyes and not our ears, and since in comparison to the first the latter are unreliable, unlike the visual perception, the aural's source is difficult to locate. Hence, sound more than sight evokes mystery. And if unusual and complex enough, such as the noise of Kurtz's admirers, a sound affects us with a singularly brooding, thrilling immensity, one in which body is rendered useless and the mind opened to direct psychological assault.

The jungle Hive's atmosphere of antiquity, mystery, and threat is evoked by words that fill the ear and, through their suggestion of magic, mesmerism, and oriental excess, attack the will: "monotonous," "muffled," "droning," "incantation," "humming," "narcotic." Marlowe has been lulled into a "narcotic" sleep by the "steady droning" sound of "many men chanting each to himself." As in the majority of contact narratives, human-being-ness is equal to Western-style individuality. Hence, tellingly, Marlowe describes this sound's author as "men," as individuated beings ("men chanting each to *himself*," my emphasis) only so long as he is able to imagine them in individual action. Once the sound passes through the "black flat wall of the woods," it becomes a communal voice possessed of an agency and a purpose greater than any human being can either wield or fathom. What Conrad has done here is really quite amazing. He turns the Hive inside out. Instead of descriptive language subordinated to a visual structure, here the Hive's structure is contained and entirely defined by its "content." Conrad is thereby able to dehumanize, demonize, and empower Kurtz's "adorers" without literalizing their society through detail, which, within the frame of alien contact, would commit him to the path soon to be taken by H. G. Wells.

Rather than making his Hive's strangeness visible, which would to some extent require him to open it up to empirical speculation, Conrad chooses instead to psychologize this dark energy. This he accomplishes by style, by the manner in which, for instance, he figures the "sound of many men chanting each to himself" as the "humming of bees." By constructing its sentence so as to emphasize the way in which the sound "came out" of the jungle, he removes from this voice any residual imputation of individuality, as well as raises it to the status of a natural condition such as the darkness of night or the wind. The lack of punctuation in the long first period, reinforced by the sonorous, rhythmic "as the humming of bees comes out of a hive," subordinates sense to sound. The affect here is complex, occult — but I do not think that Conrad wishes for Kurtz's "admirers" to have the power of magic. If they seem to, it is Marlow's doing — for, after all, *Heart* is an old salt's yarn.

I would, however, emphasize that Conrad empowers these Africans by collectivizing them to such a degree that they cannot signify except as a corporate subjectivity, which is alien precisely because it resists assimilation by Europe's "complex machine." Hence, we are to read this subjectivity as a nonhuman entity. Perhaps, additionally, these bees are meant to suggest an order antithetical but equivalent to the invasive colonial bureaucracy and its parent civilization. If so, then in a sense their corporate sentience gives us sight into the colonizers' collective soul.

Marlow's state at this moment offers a further clue to the psychological direction that Conrad chooses for his bees. Marlow is neither fully conscious nor, most importantly, in a position to see Kurtz's "admirers." If he cannot see, he cannot know — and vision equals power in the Hive's charged space. In fact, Marlow is not even on African soil. He is "half awake" on the deck of a boat (a complex symbol of European mobility and material and intellectual superiority) looking into the forest, seeing the "red gleams that wavered, that seemed to sink and rise from the ground amongst confused columnar shapes of intense blackness." He is kin to Milton's "belated Peasant [who] sees, / Or dreams he sees" (*PL*, 1.782–83) and is thus prey to the jungle's "narcotic effect[s]." He is Odysseus lashed to a mast and listening to the Sirens.

Heart of Darkness thus announces two important variations of the Insect as Other. The first, as I have already mentioned, is an order that is humanmade but antihuman, dehumanizing. Its "product" is psychic distortions, grotesque ideas, words, and actions that suggest an inward alterity. The second variation is a Hive that is nonhuman and therefore natural, but alien. There is a satisfying symmetry to how these variations work and, accordingly, to their distinct products. The first is Faustian: humans use their knowledge to make monsters and so become monsters themselves. The second is also Faustian, but with a crucial and generative twist: we use our knowledge blindly and consequently stumble upon the Other.

Conrad does wish to distinguish between these versions of the Other as Insect, however, for he leaves one with the impression that the native African Hive is one of or perhaps all the following things: the effect of Kurtz's overreaching, the brooding, anti-individualistic nature-soul of Africa, and an "insider's view" of the colonial ant heap. Conrad's most important contribution to the Hive's development, however, has to do with how he psychologizes the Other, linking it with the internal rather than the external world. The idea that the Hive expresses a collective, social intelligence greater than the sum of its elements is, of course, not new: Homer assumes this in his *Iliad* 2 bee simile, and Virgil makes it explicit in *Georgic* 4 when he merges the images of the beehive and the city. But Conrad gives this idea a gothic — or I should say, a Miltonic — twist that quickly becomes part of the Hive's stock rhetoric.

Considering how we currently understand and use the Other as Insect, H. G. Wells is perhaps even more influential than Conrad. No text before or since *The First Men in the Moon* — published in 1901, two years after *Heart of Darkness* — so powerfully clarifies the linkage between the social insect and the alien. Wells was not by any means the first writer to imagine extraterrestrial life, but his predecessors, such as Lucian, Cyrano de Bergerac, and William Dean Howells, did not have either the tools necessary to construct a convincing nonhuman civilization or, more importantly, the inclination. Their aliens are pretty much humans in costume, grotesques, or ambulatory moral illustrations. And though Wells's moonmen, the "Selenites," end up in the latter two categories, he begins his novel with the clear intention that they and their hierarchical, communal society will be absolutely alien. This intention is a signal development in the Hive's history. For in contrast to his predecessors and even to Jules Verne, Wells so heavily draws upon what science says about social insects in themselves, as a distinct object of study, that he is able to use this body of specialized knowledge as a new compositional template. Hence, at least for a while, he is able to counter the considerable force of literary habit.

Marjorie Hope Nicolson also senses something new in Wells, which she helpfully describes as "an idiom and a point of view . . . that is foreign to me. Perhaps I have lived too long with the old tales and have flown to the moon and planets too often in antiquated vehicles but in company of mariners whose imaginations were unfettered by overexact knowledge of technological possibilities of moon rockets and space ships. Something has gone that I miss. Something has entered that I do not sufficiently appreciate."[4] When compared with the "imaginations" of present-day "cosmic voyagers," Nicolson finds those of pretechnological fantasists "unfettered." Perhaps these writers were, as she says, unburdened by "overexact" technical knowledge, but it is also true that most of them had a philosophically complex social vision to demonstrate. Furthermore, at least one historian of utopia has found it to be so pervaded with the discussion of science that he wrote a scholarly book on the subject.[5] I agree with Nicolson that Wells's novelty rises from a substitution of one "idiom" for another. But I also think that we may appreciate Wells's contribution a bit more than Nicolson does by seeing what his technological limits mean and, especially, what undergirds them.

Although Wells's art, like Verne's before him, enjoys dressing up romance conventions in scientific garb, his idiom is far less ornamental than his master's: it is the exhaust from a substantial engine of reworking. In contrast to Verne, for whom the future was a nineteenth century with better toys, when at his best Wells does nothing less than change the way that inherited natural symbols may signify. He alters the tenor of invention, shifts the imagination's source of pattern from literature to science. However, because his science functions as an assumed and unifying theory similar to how the Parisian social system works in, for example, Balzac, Wells's experiments are not entirely revolutionary.

Nevertheless, because the focus of the Wellsian idiom is a theory of nature rather than a theory of humanity, he gives us a new representational template for the Other. He teaches literature how to make a picture of what until then only science knew how to represent: namely, how radically the insects differ from ourselves. Science alone could give the imagination the details and authority necessary for expressing this insight. But because this "scientific" realism springs from an eccentric view of the universe, one in which the human realm is diminished, placed within and made subject to a fully secular cosmos, it has an unintended, generative effect. While his fictions have the power to picture the unknown and the Other to a degree and in a detail impossible in the traditional novel, the science in them asserts itself palpably, strangely. It makes itself felt as a self-interested, alien system.

We register Wells's science as a character of sorts, a brooding presence that is at odds with the traditional romance's guarantee that all will work out in the end. It is this presence, I am convinced, that anticipates and helps to articulate the dystopian tone that marks even the twentieth century's brightest utopian fantasies. What I mean to suggest, finally, is that it is this dystopian presence that actually disconcerts Nicolson. The Wellsian "point of view" that Nicolson finds alien is just that. More than just a tool for imagining the Other (Conrad's use of the Hive), the character of science in Wells is its own creature. It implies, if not demonstrates, that the very system that alone defines us as "modern" is no longer in our employ. Providence, whose object was the soul, is now Science, and thus the progress of all pilgrims is realized through and defined by the machine with the most moving parts.

In *The First Men in the Moon*, the novel aspects of Wells's scientific realism are strongest soon after we arrive. Rather than reworking only inherited forms so as to produce a traditional, human-centered allegory, he simultaneously experiments with an allegory derived from the science of entomology. Below is our first sight of a Selenite, as related by Bedford, the narrative's Ishmael and reluctant Watson to the overreaching inventor-scientist, Cavor. Our heroes have lost their ship, and after watching to their horror a huge "mooncalf" "wallow[ing] past . . . smashing a path amidst the scrub" of fungus trees: "By contrast with the mooncalves [eighty feet high, two hundred long] he seemed a trivial being, a mere ant, scarcely five feet high. He was wearing garments of some leathery substance so that no portion of his actual body appeared — but of this of course we were entirely ignorant. He presented himself, therefore, as a compact bristling creature, having much the quality of a complicated insect, with whip-like tentacles, and a clanging arm projecting from his shining cylindrical body-case" (511–12).

In this passage, the word "ant" seems first to signify only the difference in size between the mooncalf and its shepherd, but Wells means it more literally. This creature has "much the quality of a complicated insect." It possesses "whip-like tentacles," and its "clanging arm project[s] from his shining cylindrical body-case." Beyond tapping into the same colonial anxieties expressed by Conrad's versions of the Hive, this creature also evokes domination, the insect, and the machine. We see a hint of this merging of social, entomological, and mechanical alterity in Marlow's view of the Company station ant heap, but once we get upriver, Conrad reserves his insect analogies for the non-European.

Bedford and Cavor are not immediately captured, but driven by hunger they eat some of the fungus that surrounds them. They become drugged and awake in a cell far below the Moon's surface. They know that the Selenites have imprisoned them, for after having seen the mooncalf shepherd and just before eating the drugged fungus, they had discovered one of the Selenites' tunnels, nearly falling into it when its massive cover suddenly opened. They then crawled to a place from which they could peer into the shaft and were transfixed by what its size implied about its makers:

> For a time that stupendous gulf of mystery held us so that we forgot even our sphere [lost spaceship]. In time as we grew more accustomed to the darkness we could make out very small dim illusive shapes moving about among those needle-point illuminations. We peered, amazed and incredulous, understanding so little that we could find no words to speak. We could distinguish nothing that would give us a clue to the meaning of the faint shapes we saw.
>
> "What can it be?" I asked; "what can it be?"
>
> "The engineering! . . . They must live in these caverns during the night and come out during the day."
>
> "Cavor!" I said. "Can they be — *that* — it was something like — men?" [referring to the mooncalf shepherd]
>
> "*That* was not a man." (514)

As in the case of Marlow's sight of the Company station, behind this view from above is both the Hive's perspectival logic and an inversion of an antique paradigm. As these men suspect, below them is an entire and new civilization. And as they soon discover, it is a civilization that is comparable to an insect society. Intended or not, Wells's inversion of Dante is clever. Because this civilization is on the moon, like Dante's Heaven it is above the earth. Yet, because it is subterranean, it is in the position of Hell. As in the *Commedia*, on the moon knowledge and vision are synonymous. But Wells's narrative is nonredemptive. The Selenites are not angels and their city is no Celestial Rose. Thus, Bedford and Cavor's first sight of the Selenite realm is very like blindness: they peer into a "darkness . . . [in which they] could make out very small dim illusive shapes moving about among those needle-point illuminations." Echoed as well, but also inverted, is Dante's language about the impossibility of expressing in human speech the glory of Paradise. Bedford narrates: "We peered, amazed and incredulous, understanding so little that we could find no words to speak. We could distinguish nothing that would give us a clue to the meaning of the faint shapes we saw."

Thus far Wells manages to keep the literary Hive at bay, using its riches sparingly. An involved entomological allegory has his attention, one that enables him to construct a society that is absolutely hierarchical and whose members are morphologically shaped for their various duties. We discover such details through a series of radio transmissions sent from the moon by Cavor, who was left for dead by Bedford during a violent escape. Despite his injured condition and his having killed a number of Selenites, rather than being "instantly slain," it appears that Cavor is favored. Accompanied by a group of Selenites (two of which he notices have distinctively "larger heads and smaller bodies" than their peers), Cavor receives what he desires most: entrance into the moon's interior.

It turns out that his big-headed companions are members of a Selenite caste that specializes in thinking. And Cavor radios that the Selenites' physical variations are almost without limit. Bedford comments on Cavor's report:

> I have endeavoured to indicate the very considerable differences observable in such Selenites . . . as I happened to encounter; the differences in size, hue, and shape were certainly as wide as the differences between the most widely separated races of men. . . . But within the moon practically unsuspected by me, there are, it seems, a host of variations. The moon is indeed a kind of super-anthill. But in place of the five distinctive types, the worker, soldier, winged male, queen and slave of the ant-world, there are amongst the moon-folk not only hundreds of differentiations, but, within each, and linking one to the other, a whole series of fine gradations. And these Selenites are not merely colossally superior to ants, but, according to Cavor, colossally, in intelligence morality and social wisdom, higher than man. (595)

Cavor speculates that the moon's lower gravity has allowed a range and quality of adaptation denied earthly insects. But, once within their city and while on his way to his "hexagonal cell," Cavor finds himself examined by a crowd of these creatures. His description of this event alludes to yet another of our models, Milton's Pandemonium, and does so more openly than the reader has yet seen in the novel. Apparently the writer's relationship with the Hive is changing along with Cavor's understanding. Here Wells begins to shift his ground of invention from the scientific to the literary.

At the bottom of "an enormous cylindrical space . . . a quarter of a mile across . . . was an incredible crowd. Suddenly and violently there was forced upon my attention the vast amount of difference there is amongst these beings of the moon":

> Indeed, there seemed not two alike in all that jostling multitude. They differed in shape, they differed in size! Some bulged and over- hung, some ran about among the feet of their fellows, some twined and interlaced like *snakes*. All of them had the grotesque and disqui- eting suggestion of an insect that has somehow contrived to bur- lesque humanity; all seemed to present an incredible exaggeration of some particular feature; one had a vast right forelimb, an enormous antennal arm, as it were; one seemed all leg, poised, as it were, on stilts; another protruded an enormous nose-like organ beside a sharply speculative eye that made him look startlingly human until one saw his expressionless mouth. One has seen the punchinellos made of lob- ster claws — he was like that. The strange and (except for the want of mandibles and palps) most insectlike head of the mooncalf-minders underwent astounding transformations; here it was broad and low, here high and narrow, here its vacuous brow was drawn out into *horns* and strange features. (596; my emphasis)

The description continues, but the words "snakes" and "horns" are worth reflecting upon. Their Biblical connotations mark this scene's poetic alignment, one confirmed by its conclusion, the sound made by this gathering: "All about me were eyes, faces, masks, tentacles, a leathery noise *like the rustling of beetle wings*" (598; my emphasis). To me at least, this sound alludes to lines 767–68 of *Paradise Lost*, book 1: "Thick swarm'd, both on the ground and in the air, / Brusht with the hiss of rustling wings."

The more we read about the Selenites, about their strange variety, the more Wells invites us to fear them. The invisible distortion of the psyche that fascinates Conrad is in Wells made visible. Indeed, here as in many of his other narratives, physical difference is the primary indicator of alterity. But I do not think that it is natural, human variety that Wells fears. In the following passage he continues down the path opened up by his use of Biblical language, departing even farther from the relatively pure entomological allegory that has thus far kept his aliens alien. From a purer sort of invention he now shifts to the mode of social allegory so that he may criticize modernity's "technical" sort of "education." Wells is not speaking against science; rather, he vigorously opposes altering the human enterprise and the person to meet its needs.

Cavor has discovered how the Selenites achieve their physical variety and through it a seamless fit between form and social function. And it is Cavor's knowledge that transmutes our fear of the Other into ambivalence about our society and the selves that it creates:

> The making of these various sorts of operatives must be a very curious and interesting process. I am still much in the dark about it, but quite recently I came upon a number of young Selenites confined in jars from which only the forelimbs protruded, who were being compressed to become machine-minders of a special sort. The extended "hand" in this highly developed system of technical education is stimulated by irritants and nourished by injection while the rest of the body is starved. Phi-oo [Cavor's Selenite translator], unless I misunderstand him, explained that in the earlier stages the queer little creatures are apt to display signs of suffering in their various cramped situations, but they easily become indurated to their lot; and he took me to where a number of flexible-limbed messengers were being drawn out and broken in. It is quite unreasonable, I know, but these glimpses of the educational methods of these beings have affected me disagreeably. I hope, however, that may pass off and I may be able to see more of this aspect of this wonderful social order. That wretched-looking hand sticking out of its jar seemed to appeal for lost possibilities; it haunts me still, although, of course, it is really in the end a far more human proceeding than our earthly method of leaving children to grow into human beings, and then making machines of them. (604–5)

Second only in horror to the cruelty of this "technical education" is Cavor's rationalization of it. He is a modern Gulliver whose pronounced naivete, like his forebear's, progressively becomes a symptom of madness. Although Cavor tells us that "that wretched-looking hand sticking out of its jar seemed to appeal for lost possibilities . . . [and] haunts me still," he decides that this method of deforming children to suit their place in society is "really in the end a far more human proceeding than our earthly method of leaving children to grow into human beings, and then making machines of them."

This passage lifts the Selenites' entomological curtain and reveals them to be an instrument of social criticism. They may be super-insects, but their society is now to be read as one possible conclusion for our own. At this point in the story Wells plays one of his two favorite hands, placing center stage his distrust of science unbound, of reason allowed all things in the name of a progress defined in mechanical (i.e., technological) terms. Even though Cavor may not know it, from this moment on he is narrating a descent into Hell.

At the heart of this Hive, like Satan enthroned in Pandemonium, sits the "Grand Lunar." As part of a procession that brings to mind the paintings of Hieronymous Bosch, Cavor is carried to see him. The Selenite threat has gone beyond the alien. These beings are now demonic, fully Milton's creatures, right down to a reference to Catholic architecture:

> Imagine the largest hall you have ever been in, elaborately decorated with blue and whitish-blue majolica, lit by blue light, you know not how, and surging with metallic or livid-white creatures of such mad diversity as I have hinted. Imagine this hall to end in an open archway beyond which is still a larger hall, and beyond this yet another and still larger one, and so on. At the end of the vista a flight of steps, like the steps of Ara Coeli at Rome, ascends out of sight. Higher and higher these steps appear to go as one draws nearer their base. But at last I came under a huge archway and beheld the summit of these steps, and upon it the Grand Lunar *exalted on his throne*. (61; my emphasis)

The situation and language evoke Milton's image of Satan enthroned in Pandemonium, exponentially amplifying the results of contact with the Other: "High *on a Throne* of Royal State, which far / Outshone the Wealth of Ormus and of Ind, / Or where the gorgeous East with richest hand / Show'rs on her Kings barbaric Pearl and Gold, / Satan *exalted* sat . . ." (*PL*, 2.1–5; my emphasis).

Physically, the Grand Lunar is little more than a brain; he is the logical conclusion of the path down which Wells sees science taking us:

> He was seated in a blaze of incandescent blue. A hazy atmosphere filled the place so that its walls seemed invisibly remote. This gave him an effect of floating in a blue-black void. He seemed at first a small, self-luminous cloud, brooding on his glaucous throne; his brain-case must have measured many yards in diameter. . . .
>
> At first as I peered into the radiating blaze, this quintessential brain looked very much like a thin, featureless bladder with dim, undulating ghosts of convolutions writhing visibly within. Then beneath its enormity and just above the edge of the throne one saw with a start minute elfin eyes peering out of the blaze. No face, but eyes, as if they peered through holes. At first I could see no more than these two staring little eyes, and then below I distinguished the little dwarfed body and its insect-jointed limbs, shrivelled and white. The eyes stared down at me with a strange intensity, and the lower part of the swollen globe was wrinkled. Ineffectual-looking little hand-tentacles steadied this shape on the throne. . . . I saw that the shadowy attendants were busy spraying the great brain with a cooling spray, and patting and sustaining it. (611)

Part Oriental despot like Milton's Satan (Cavor seats himself before it in "Turkish fashion") and part Kurtz realized exponentially and fattened on power, the Grand Lunar questions Cavor about the Earth and its creatures. One human aspect interests him most, the degree to which our bodies fit our occupations. Do individual Earthlings, he seems to ask, serve society *completely*? Are they even able to do so? He is measuring humanity's vulnerability as a species:

> He talked with his attendants, as I suppose, upon the strange superficiality and unreasonableness of (man), who lives on the mere surface of a world, a creature of waves and winds and all the chances of space, who cannot even unite to overcome the beasts that prey upon his kind, and yet who dares to invade another planet. During this aside I sat thinking, and then at his desire I told him of the different sorts of men. He searched me with questions. "And for all sorts of work you have the same sort of men. But who thinks? Who governs?"

I gave him an outline of the democratic method.

When I had done he ordered cooling sprays upon his brow, and then requested me to repeat my explanation conceiving something had miscarried.

"Do they not do different things then?" said Phi-oo.

Some I admitted were thinkers and some officials; some hunted, some were mechanics, some artists, some toilers. "But *all* rule," I said.

"And have they not different shapes to fit them to their different duties?"

"None that you can see," I said, "except perhaps their clothes. Their minds perhaps differ a little," I reflected.

"Their minds must differ a great deal," said the Grand Lunar, "or they would all want to do the same things."

In order to bring myself into closer harmony with his preconceptions, I said that his surmise was right. "It was all hidden in the brain," I said; "but the difference was there. Perhaps if one could see the minds and the souls of men they would be as varied and unequal as the Selenites. (685)

In effect, Cavor has told the Grand Lunar that human beings are technologically primitive, ill-adapted socially and occupationally, and divided by nature.

We are supposed to reject the Grand Lunar's "surmise" that the "minds and souls of men . . . [are] as varied and unequal as the Selenites." But we do not do so. For we know that the Selenites are a way to see what is "hidden in the [human] brain." And the Selenite Hive gives us more than just a view of how the human soul is distorted through social inequality and technological education. Their model of social perfection is a view of our psychological future, of a society founded upon the engineering, the corruption and control of the mental variety natural to our species.

Although soon overpowered by an older idiom, Wells's application of the entomological allegory to the utopian romance virtually creates what we now call "hard" science fiction.[6] Even though we never see the Grand Lunar's legions invade the Earth — unlike Wells's Martians, who stride through English streets in 1898 and soon catch their death of cold — the Selenites quickly and permanently house themselves in one corner of our literature. Among their offspring are the murderous and planet hungry "bugs" of Robert Heinlein's *Starship Troopers* and the all-assimilating Borg, who periodically threaten the security of Star Trek's United Federation of Planets.

But Wells's Selenites are only one of his two important experiments with the Hive. The other predates Cavor's discovery of the Grand Lunar's government by five years. Although earthly, not only does it occur in a space separated from civilization, an island, similar to its heavenly version it also signifies manufactured alterity. I am referring to the scene in *The Island of Dr. Moreau* wherein Prendick enters the realm of the beastmen. First the approach, which, appropriately, raises the spectre of infernal ground:

> The path coiled *down* abruptly into a narrow ravine between two tumbled and knotty masses of blackish scoriae. Into this we plunged.
>
> It was extremely dark, this passage, after the sunlight reflected from the *sulfurous* ground. Its walls grew steep and approached one another. Blotches of green and crimson drifted across my eyes. My conductor stopped suddenly. "Home," said he, and I stood on a floor of a chasm that was at first absolutely dark to me. I heard some strange noises and thrust the knuckles of my left hand into my eyes. I became aware of a disagreeable odor. (55–56; my italics)

And now Prendick's sketch of the beastmen's Hive from without and his fuller description of its interior:

> The place was a narrow passage between high walls of lava. . . . I hesitated — had half a mind to bolt the way I had come — and then, determined to go through with the adventure, gripped my nailed stick about the middle and crawled into the little evil-smelling leanto after my conductor.
>
> It was a semicircular space, *shaped like the half of a beehive*, and against the rocky wall that formed the inner side of it was a pile of variegated fruit, coconuts and others. Some rough vessels of lava and wood stood about the floor, and one on a rough stool. There was no fire. (55–58, my italics)

These passages bridge the narrative's movement from chapter 11 to chapter 12, the physical and narrative center of this twenty-two chapter novel. So powerful are the implications of the divide between the upper and lower worlds and the force of classical precedent that Wells dramatizes the value of this barrier and its crossing by structuring his fiction around what amounts to a *nekuia*.

Perhaps Wells's language participates in habits he is unconscious of, but given the description of Prendick's descent and Wells's later, clear allusions to Milton in *Men in the Moon*, we may assume that he was familiar with Dante and Milton. In contrast to the *Men in the Moon*'s Hive, however — which draws its power and clarity from an entomological (i.e., scientific) allegory that for a moment eclipses the ancient patterns — this half-Hive is subtler, what we might call adjectival rather than substantive. Some force is subduing *Moreau*'s Hive.

Because *Moreau* predates *Men in the Moon*, one could argue that the differences between their Hives shows Wells discovering and then perfecting his new version, moving from a nascent to a fully voiced form. But to argue this alone would be to overlook two larger rhetorical issues, both of which have to do with changes in the code of literary realism that affect how the Hive will be used in the twentieth century. First, even by Wells's time the modern Hive's various formulations, and consequently their uses, were already being influenced by a heightened sense of the insect's alterity — both as a natural symbol and as a convention. By this I mean that, even while inventing science fiction, Wells has difficulty making the insect society as understood by science (the entomological template) a stable substitute for the antique. Hence, for example, the unresolvable tension and awkward movement between scientific detail and poetic allusion in *Men in the Moon*. In sum, the more detailed and accurate our scientific knowledge about the insects, the less useful this understanding is for the allegorist. Significantly, that this proposition informs Wells's fiction indicates that Darwinism's simpler analogies are by this time in retreat. Wells's inheritors will, therefore, find themselves having to invent their own "natural" entomological templates in order to claim the authority, the realism, of science.

The second issue of realism that helps subdue *Moreau*'s Hive is that Wells felt, correctly, that the overt painterly descriptions and foregrounded literary allusions of nineteenth-century "high" realism would conflict with his "plain" style, an amalgam of three "truthful" modes: travel writing, journalism, and the popular science article. This does not mean that his writing eschews the literary. I have already established, for example, that he uses the riches of Dante. But he does so quietly. Wells's difficulties with allusion help us to understand his versions of the Hive, but they are also important to us because they reveal the general conditions under which the Hive's subsequent reworking will take place. In the main, despite the Hive's continued and considerable presence as a habit of thinking in the twentieth century, writers will no longer be able to use the antique poetic form of the Hive as freely and *openly* in realistic fiction as was once common practice. Relatedly, except for the fabrications of genre fiction and occasional resurrections of involved Darwinistic allegory (as in sociobiology), what the twentieth century comes to think of as realism works to camouflage — but not to eliminate — the Hive.

As we move into the twentieth century, whether authorized by literary tradition or science, when wielded too visibly outside of specific genres the Hive arouses suspicion. Writers require its terms, its ways of seeing the world, but the topos must be carefully managed. One reason: the Hive's poetic forms align us with an inheritance and modes of visible and historically resonant ornament and allegory that we no longer quite know what to do with. Second, we moderns no longer wish to believe that the Hive accurately expresses the essence of our social order. For example, the appeal of the unabashedly allegorical speculation epitomized by Maurice Maeterlinck's *The Life of the Bee* begins to fade with the passing of the Bergsonian vogue and is nearly muted through what Juan Antonio Ramírez, author of *The Beehive Metaphor*, describes as "the proliferation of negative ideas that have been associated with the beehive since the Second World War." According to Ramírez, "The idea of a people or nation that functions like a superorganism and before which personal individuality disappears was emphasized by the Nazis." Not only did "the defeat of the fascist powers" fail to revive the Hive's former appeal, the cold war "saw an attenuation of the 'positive' connotations associated with the social insects, and very few people have dared to advocate the resurrection of the beehive as a symbol of political activity" (24). Indeed, with few exceptions it is not until postmodernity that we begin to see the Hive's "'positive' connotations" reassert themselves in Western literature — and even here the comparison of an ideal human society with an insect society is rarely attempted outside of the fable.[7] Apparently, while we seem comfortable with viewing other cultures, rural life, or even our future according to the Hive's terms, in our civilized, metropolitan social order we no longer seem to see the quality of organization that the Hive was built to represent. Nor, more importantly, does the modern individual prefer to think of himself or herself according to the Hive's social categories, as either a worker or a drone, or even as a queen. All of these are castes in the strictest sense, implying that the self is defined by and subject to the social order — and any model of subjectivity that equates the "good life" with self-sacrifice and service to others is antithetical to the current Western notion of what it is to be autonomous and therefore human.

Since Wells's Hives lie just on our side of the divide between the antique/rhetorical forms of the Hive and its contemporary/scientific versions, I must go back a few generations to find a version of the Hive equivocal enough to give a clarifying perspective. The tableau with which Balzac concludes *Père Goriot* will serve, for Balzac means it to function simultaneously as a visible, poetic figure and as a natural expression of modern, individualistic psychology. Its doubleness probably arises from Balzac's society being poised between a still viable neoclassical past and an emerging democratic future.

Having just buried the body of his mistress's father (on borrowed money and in a pauper's grave), for the first time Eugene Rastignac sees Paris as a whole. Although his idealism has been eroded, his ambition remains undiminished:

> Rastignac, now all alone, walked a few paces to the higher part of the cemetery, and saw Paris spread out along the winding banks of the Seine, where the lights were beginning to shine. His eyes fastened almost hungrily on the area between the column in the place Vendôme and the dome of the Invalides, home to that fashionable society to which he had sought to gain admission. He gave this murmuring hive a look which seemed already to savour the sweetness to be sucked from it, and pronounced the epic challenge: "It's between the two of us now!"
>
> And as the first shot in the war he had thus declared on Society, Rastignac went to dine with Madame de Nucingen. (263)

His position above the city and his (mock) heroic challenge evoke the scene of Aeneas looking down upon Carthage. And like Virgil's underworld and Dante's Celestial Rose, access to this "murmuring [or buzzing] hive" is controlled by women. Mysterious and dangerous though it may be, Rastignac's Paris is feminine, a collective mother/resource from which (at least in the hero's imagination) a future of greatness may be "sucked" — hence, the form of our hero's "epic challenge," a dinner date with somebody's well-connected wife.

This novel was written for an audience whose members, because they were bourgeois, we may assume recognized and were gratified by Balzac's allusion to Virgil, a poet familiar to every European schoolchild of the time. But while these readers were modern enough to recognize the classical Hive's limitations as both a model for society and a way of seeing, because their society was far more traditional than ours, we may assume that they were more sensitive than we are to how and why Virgil used the Hive topos's powers of simplification and its associations with domestication. As you will recall, when Aeneas figures Carthage as a beehive, both he and the city are reduced to essences, which the Hive's structure relates through a simplifying antithesis. Virgil's tableau of Carthage surveyed reminds us of the poem's epic frame (a narrativized fate that drives and domesticates Aeneas, making him Roman through dutiful suffering) and prepares us for the city's undoing. Aeneas is beekeeper and Carthage is the Hive — and obtaining honey in the early nineteenth century was as violent as in Virgil's day. Because a practical moveable-frame beehive would not become available and popular until the latter part of the 1900s, the honeybee colony had to be cruelly smoked and their combs ripped out along with their young.[8] Thus, the Hive's simplification and opposition of Aeneas and Carthage makes good and appropriately sober poetic sense: this tableau is in harmony with both Virgil's and the *Aeneid*'s worlds.

In contrast, there is dissonance between the Hive and *Père Goriot*, because in a realistic context the Hive tends to *over*simplify. Balzac knows that the sprawling and magnificently complicated Paris of *La Comédie humaine*, a synecdoche for and the sum of European civilization, cannot be pictured by the traditional Hive. He also understands that, through reducing the relationship between Rastignac and Paris to an opposition between the individual and the collective, the Hive implies exactly the old-fashioned, heroic action that in "modern" Paris leads one to destruction. Because the implied analogy, "Paris is a beehive," is neither precisely a description of Rastignac's consciousness nor entirely the lens through which Balzac would have us see *our* Paris, the Hive topos lies on the fiction's surface as a testament to a shared culture. But it is also a sign that antique patterns are the stuff of romance, dangerous if taken too seriously by the social climber. Finally, Balzac would also have us see Paris, our social reality, as more than the sum of any rhetoric or representation, to include his own impressive realism. In a novel that is as consistently bare of consciously poetic metaphors as it is cluttered with objects, in a narrative whose author is not shy about telling us how to think and feel, the presence of this antique and therefore *visible* Hive is significant, especially since it serves as the conclusion of a narrative that demands both closure and a sequel. In sum, if we read it as a diagnosis of his moment's consciousness of order, then Balzac's Hive signals that while the forms of the past are still available and meaningful, their signification as visible structures is changing.

Nevertheless, that Balzac treats the Hive as a rhetorical (public) form, thereby enriching his fiction by what strikes me as a traditional act of *retractatio*, suggests that he still owns imaginative stock in the typological culture that Wells feels is behind him. Balzac understands the Hive to be artificial in the artistic sense; he therefore uses its *form* obviously, as a conventional device through which, among other things, we gain a sense of what Paris is not. In *Moreau* Wells treats his Hive as natural in the scientific sense: it is an inartistic and passive substance, as a resource not unlike the animals who by bad science have been reworked into things less than either man or beast. Considering that his fiction holds the process of reason to be greater even than the practice of science, it is ironic that Wells deals with the Hive as he does. Instead of confronting it as a representation that embodies a social theory, he deals with it by simply assuming this theory to be fact. This is not to say that he is unaware of the Hive as a literary form, for he consciously adapts it. Rather, my point is that he does so by attempting to derhetoricize it, to transmute it from featured allegory into quotidian backdrop.

Moreau's Hive is incomplete because the beastmen are. Their society is too disorganized, primitive, and herdlike to mesh well with a complete deployment of the Hive topos. In contrast to the Selenite Hive, this half-Hive is part of the visual *background*, to function, as it were, nearly off the screen of our formal radar. I suggest that Wells attempts to do with the language of visual description something similar to what Conrad more easily accomplishes with sound when creating his African bees — namely, to invoke the Hive without overtly featuring its structure, for visible artistry would conflict with the style of Marlow's telling and spoil Conrad's dark and lapidary exploration of colonialism's psychological import. As fantastic as its containing narrative may be, the half-Hive of *Moreau*'s beastmen marks an important step toward a naturalized version of the Hive that soon becomes the rule in realism. True enough, Wells's lunar Hive is so fully expressed and allegorically amplified that, in a sense, its structure becomes reality. But this sort of realism is ephemeral, for it contradicts what Balzac's Hive has already announced: when expressed visibly, in the old manner, the Hive and the social order that it embodies are no longer adequate to our experience of life as it is actually lived.

Between Balzac and Wells a general "law of proximity" emerges that comes to determine to what degree the Hive may be formally voiced: *The stranger, or "farther away," a fictional world is from the facts of the present moment — spatially, temporally, culturally — the stronger and more visibly the Hive may appear.*[9] I do not, however, mean to suggest that contemporary writers who deal in the "world as it is" are in every circumstance forbidden by their intuition of the law to use an apparent, or voiced, form of the Hive. Rather, when they have need of the Hive's unique and indispensable office, more often than not, they feel as a force the rightness of the Hive's unvoiced, naturalized form.

Aldous Huxley's *Brave New World* further illustrates the modern writer's ambivalent relationship with the Hive as a voiced form. This novel describes a not-too-distant future in which social planning has been carried to a scientificized extreme. The family, romantic love, self-determination, democracy, waste, war, and unhappiness have all been eliminated by human engineering in the service of the state. Human beings are manufactured by cloning, then chemically tailored and strenuously educated for a specific caste and occupation. These citizens spend their lives in service to a state whose stability depends upon making sure that every citizen is happy contributing to the common weal. Toward this end, private desires are not tolerated, all leisure time is spent in forms of elaborate consumerism, and any residual individualism is controlled with a mood-altering drug known as "soma." In 1932, the year the novel was published, no doubt its technological projection was received as being considerably more fantastic than it now appears. Yet the novel does not exactly feel like science fiction. In the 1930s Russia was in the grip of Stalinism, Europe was everywhere churning with a nationalistic spirit quickly ripening into Fascism, and the scientific monster that Wells first clearly saw in the moon was now out in the open at home. Huxley, therefore, needed his dystopia to be a "this-topia" — to strongly resonate with its moment. Hence, although he borrows heavily from science fiction, he is careful with how he uses its style of Hive.

He cannot, as was at this time already customary in the science fiction pulps, draw too heavily upon an entomological analogy. If he did, the resulting scientific allegory would be received as too alien for serious social criticism; it would force him into a generic corner that would limit his art as well as his audience. For similar reasons, Huxley cannot overly use the poetic Hive, which he nonetheless requires because only this conceptually and visually potent form will provide him with an image of a social order that is excessively organized and hierarchized, and therefore antihuman. He solves his dilemma by easing into the language of the Hive. He begins by using it suggestively. The Hive is so powerful a habit that he may assume its presence and depend on our familiarity with it for a while, thereby reserving its explicit deployment until a crucial and dramatically significant moment.

The novel begins with a tour of the "Central London Hatchery and Conditioning Center." This "squat grey building" is a metaphor for this society, our future. From this locus of social planning emerge engineered human beings ready for work. After human eggs are fertilized and then "budded" (multiplied) on the ground floor, they go to the basement where in a "tropical" darkness they are moved along an assembly line. At appropriate intervals, according to what place its adult form shall play in society, each embryo is shaped by being either exposed to or denied chemicals and oxygen. To a group of students touring the facility, Mr. Foster, the center's director, explains how fertility (i.e., the potential for social instability presented by natural passion and its consequences) is managed:

> in the vast majority of cases, fertility is merely a nuisance. One fertile ovary in twelve hundred — that would really be quite sufficient for our purposes. But we want to have a good choice. And of course one must always leave an enormous margin of safety. So we allow as many as thirty per cent of the female embryos to develop normally. The others get a dose of male sex-hormone every twenty-four metres for the rest of the course. Result: they're decanted as freemartins — structurally quite normal . . . but sterile. Guaranteed sterile. Which brings us at last . . . out of the realm of slavish imitation of nature into the much more interesting world of human invention. (13–14)

This passage is the first clear indication that Huxley is working from an entomological template. These "freemartins" are this society's equivalent of the social insect worker caste, which consists of infertile females.

As the novel progresses, Huxley continues to remind us of this society's not-rightness, of its "insectness" — a quality that pervades every aspect of this world, to include the sound of its machines. The passage below suggests that the philosophical substance of insectness, which traditionally has resided in a social order, is for Huxley more distinct and attributable than for Wells. Hence, the outlook expressed is entirely twentieth-century and, interestingly, confined to a series of nouns used as adjectives: "The machine shot into the air. Henry accelerated; the humming of the propeller shrilled from hornet to wasp, from wasp to mosquito. . . . He took his foot off the accelerator. The humming of the screws overhead dropped an octave and a half, back through wasp and hornet to bumble bee, to cockchafer, to stag-beetle. . . . Henry kept his eye on the revolution-counter; when the needle touched the twelve hundred mark, he threw the helicopter screws out of gear. The machine had enough forward momentum to be able to fly on its planes" (72–73). The helio-plane's occupants, Henry and Lenina, are flying to Stoke Poges to play "Obstacle Golf." As they pass over the English countryside, "Lenina look[s] down through the window in the floor between her feet." The narrator takes this opportunity to tell us that "at Brentford the Television Corporation's factory was like a small town." Lenina says to Henry: "They must be changing the shift." And now the narrator takes over completely, for our perception of this social order as alien, as insectlike, is now to be embodied in a comparison that transcends these characters: "Like aphides and ants, the leaf-green Gamma girls, the black Semi-Morons swarmed round the entrances, or stood in queues to take their places in the monorail tram-cars" (74–75). We have just taken a further and definitive step into a familiar geography.

The moment of figural recognition comes when Bernard, an individualist in a collectivist social order (hence the novel's Christ figure), is found out: the hatchery director declares Bernard "an enemy of society." From this point on, this human hive begins to aggressively show itself to be more insect than human. Huxley now asserts the Hive topos more clearly. Finally, this social order is figured according to the long-anticipated old model — but the view is not from without:

The hands of all the four thousand electric clocks in all the Bloomsbury Centre's four thousand rooms marked twenty-seven minutes past two. "This hive of industry," as the Director was fond of calling it, was in the full buzz of work. Every one was busy, everything in

ordered motion. . . . From the Social Predestination Room the escalators went rumbling down into the basement, and there, in the crim-
son darkness, stewingly warm on their cushion of peritoneum and
gorged with blood-surrogate and hormones, the foetuses grew and
grew or, poisoned, languished into a stunted Epsilonhood. With a
faint hum and rattle the moving racks crawled imperceptibly through
the weeks and the recapitulated aeons to where, in the Decanting
Room, the newly-unbottled babes uttered their first yell of horror
and amazement. . . .

Above them, in ten successive layers of dormitory, the little boys
and girls who were still young enough to need an afternoon sleep
were as busy as everyone else, though they did not know it, listening
unconsciously to hypnopaedic lessons in hygiene and sociability, in
class consciousness and the toddler's love-life. . . .

Buzz, buzz! The hive was humming, busily, joyfully. Blithe was
the singing of the young girls over their test-tubes, the Predestinators
whistled as they worked, and in the Decanting Room what glorious
jokes were cracked above the empty bottles! (174–75)

From the basement we move upward, tracing the path of human engineering, moving from the past into the future until we emerge in a space
of joyful workers whose labors are unified by music — but there is no
standing outside and above this Hive. Huxley puts us in its midst. Thus,
we cannot quite occupy the traditional position of visual sovereignty
over the collective, because, rather than a structured view-from-above
and movement from the outside in, this description is a tour of a labyrinth, a cutaway view of this technological Hive. Although the manner in which this picture functions (details accumulate until the insect
analogy is enabled) recalls Aeneas's view of Carthage, our movement
through it is mediated by the machine, which merges with the narrator's
voice. Hence, the Hive's axial organization is evoked as much by our
feeling that this machine, its processes, and this voice are wrong as by
any precise imitation of visual structure.

In that this passage serves as the novel's physical as well as narrative
center and its themes are time and becoming ("the moving racks crawled
imperceptibly through the weeks and the recapitulated aeons"), we
should think of it as Huxley's reworking of the *nekuia* of *Aeneid* 6,
wherein the spirits of the righteous dead are reborn into Roman bodies,
the dutiful components of Imperium. Thus, in Huxley's description of

"the newly-unbottled babes' . . . first yell" as one "of horror and amazement," perhaps we hear something of Aeneas's query to his father Anchises, when he sees those many souls crowding together to be reborn:
"But, father, must we think that any souls pass aloft from here to yon
sky, and return a second time to sluggish bodies? What means, alas! this
their mad longing for light?" (557). I also sense the influence of Wells's
picture of Selenite education, for it is in "bottles" that these human em-
bryos are shaped to fit their respective societal niches. Further, Dante is
also present, in the way that music is used — but his Celestial Rose is
more distant from Huxley's dystopia than is Virgil's underworld locus
of regeneration. For if this society alludes to one of the two world cities
that haunt the West's images of order, its type is the pagan rather than
the Christian Rome.

Don DeLillo (who, to my mind, is more a modernist than a postmodernist) builds upon the Hive that Wells establishes and Huxley advances. Below is a passage from *White Noise* that I have selected for two
reasons. First, more clearly than either the beastmen's half-Hive in *Moreau* or the labyrinthine hatchery in *Brave New World*, it illustrates that
when viewed from *within*, the Hive tends to be expressed obliquely, is
coded so as to remain in the background. While its affect is meant to be
felt, its structure is not to be seen directly. This makes visual sense, for in
the modern novel of life-as-lived a visible Hive would intrude — it is a
marker of an alterity and an allegorical style that has been turned over
to the fantasists. Also, because the alignment of DeLillo's Hive is "demonic," I mean for it to show that the minimally voiced, or "camouflaged," Hive still follows the older, fully voiced mode's polar tendencies.
Just as when visible, the invisible Hive tends to be either angelic or demonic, or even mixed — a condition that becomes more common as we
approach our moment.

In the only way possible in DeLillo's America, when his Everyman,
Jack Gladney, wishes to restore his sense of being and his connection
with his fellow human beings, he sets out, family in tow, to the shopping
mall. The adventure of shopping, Gladney's restoration and expansion
of self, occurs as a single, organic, rising action that begins once he and
his family are inside "the Mid-Village Mall, a ten-story building arranged
around a center court of waterfalls, promenades and gardens" (84). We
are inside the modern Hive (the *nekuia* become suburban cosmos), a
ten-story, manufactured theater of "transaction." Gladney defines this

space as childish, feminine, irrational, one whose exact customs are alien. Like Dante, he needs a guide. In this instance, his children — who, along with his wife, Babette, are "puzzled but excited by [his] desire to buy" — eagerly present themselves as such. Raised by television, Gladney's children are veritable demons of consumption, native scouts in the suburban spiritual wilderness that is their world:

"When I could not decide between two shirts, they encouraged me to buy both. When I said I was hungry, they fed me pretzels, beer, souvlaki. The two girls scouted ahead, spotting the things they thought I might want or need, running back to get me, to clutch my arms, plead with me to follow. They were my guides to endless well-being" (83). The narration now widens to take in the life of this Hive, an orgy of commodified experience that reunites Gladney with his (anti)culture:

People swarmed through the boutiques and gourmet shops. Organ music rose from the great court. We smelled chocolate, popcorn, cologne; we smelled rugs and furs, hanging salamis and deathly vinyl. My family gloried in the event. I was one of them, shopping, at last. They gave me advice, badgered clerks on my behalf. I kept seeing myself unexpectedly in some reflecting surface. We moved from store to store, rejecting not only items in certain departments, not only entire departments but whole stores, mammoth corporations that did not strike our fancy for one reason or another. There was always another store, three floors, eight floors, basement full of cheese graters and paring knives. I shopped with reckless abandon. I shopped for immediate needs and distant contingencies. I shopped for its own sake, looking and touching, inspecting merchandise I had no intention of buying, then buying it. I sent clerks into their fabric books and pattern books to search for elusive designs. I began to grow in value and self regard. I filled myself out, found new aspects of myself, located a person I'd forgotten existed. Brightness settled around me. We crossed from furniture to men's wear, walking through cosmetics. Our images appeared on mirrored columns, in glassware and chrome, on TV monitors in security rooms. I traded money for goods . . . I was bigger than these sums. . . . I felt expansive, inclined to be sweepingly generous. (83–84)

We are in a cathedral of consumption, a Pandemonium freed from fear and God's plan, an electrified Vanity Fair. Gladney gorges himself on his "fancy," on images of himself, thereby filling, finding, and locating himself anew. The transforming, growing Gladney reports that "brightness settled around me." His disregard for "sums" (reason, consequences) makes him feel "expansive . . . inclined to be sweepingly generous," in tune with his surroundings.

As the climax of this transfiguration, while the Gladneys eat yet "another meal" amid the swarm and spending, the narrative voice disengages from the protagonist's consciousness to offer a summary view of the American Hive: "A band played live Muzak. Voices rose ten stories from the gardens and promenades, a roar that echoed and swirled through the vast gallery, mixing with noises from the tiers, with shuffling feet and chiming bells, the *hum* of escalators, the sound of people eating, the human *buzz* of some vivid and happy transaction" (my emphasis). Similar to the tour of Huxley's hatchery, we are denied a traditional, external view of the Mid-Village Mall. Hence, the Hive's axial structure remains in the visual background. Its commingled affects of community and otherness, however, are evoked by the narrator's voice as it joins and rises with the noise and other voices. This rising action gives structurally significant direction to the narrator's voice as it pulls away to take in the larger picture of the "voices [that] rose ten stories" and merged into "a roar that echoed and swirled through the vast gallery." This rising and merging of sound is the hidden armature upon which the narrator's unifying perspective is built. In this sense the antique Hive's office of establishing a view from above is fulfilled. Behind the narrator's voice stands the writer, and behind him is the Hive topos, perhaps only as a habit, as a sense of structural rightness. But the Hive is nonetheless present and formative.

The necessity to work one's way toward a fully voiced expression of the Hive indicates that this topos has become peculiar, difficult to manage. This is the case largely because the humanistic motives and anthropomorphic trajectory of the antique, poetic Hive have been assumed and altered by science. Also, as I have already suggested, democratic individualism does not much care for how the Hive pictures the individual vis-à-vis the social order. The ancients saw the natural hive's order as a perfect embodiment of reason and balance, treating it as a living symbol from which a principle could be extracted and applied. They understood it more philosophically than we, but without losing sight of its rhetorical character, its beauty, its made-ness. Today, even though we still see in the natural hive an ideal order, outside its natural context it is often felt to be extreme, to suggest social oppression and the diminishment of the individual. Science has helped us to realize just how alien this order really is. Our scientific knowledge of the natural hive has thus affected how we may use it poetically, for, like it or not, to use the Hive directly in the old manner is to paint the figured object with insect-specific qualities. Because science has given the modern imagination a philosophical perspective from which to view human beings and insects similarly, biologically and socially, in comparison with our prescientific predecessors we take the Hive's metaphorical terms much more literally.

How, then, when a contemporary writer needs to figure an order as being alien, collective in nature, and highly intelligent, does he or she do so without forcing it into the entomological template? In *Jurassic Park*, Michael Crichton faces exactly this problem. Since his dinosaurs must be alien, aggressive, and more organized than a herd but less so (and differently) than an insect colony, he must moderate the Hive's tendency to make insectlike whatever it figures. His solution is to combine the technique of "suggestive delay" that I pointed out in Huxley with alternative metaphors for the collective. In chapter 1, I stated that Homer had discovered three of the four ways to figure a crowd: as a natural force, an animal herd or flock, or an insect swarm. All these modes suggest sociality, but none as intensely as the Hive. Crichton understands his options and applies them: he uses two herd metaphors (one mammalian and another avian) to leaven his presentation of the Hive.

Even though the island and its genetically resurrected dinosaurs are soon to be carpet bombed, so as to account for each and every carnivore, in vampire-slayer fashion a group of characters searches out the velociraptor's nest. During the approach, there is the requisite evocation of infernal ground: "The ground was hot, Gennaro thought, as he walked forward. It was actually *hot*. And here and there mud bubbled and spat up from the ground. And the reeking, sulfurous steam hissed in great shoulder-high plumes. He felt as if he were walking through hell" (376). Once the characters are underground, lying "on a concrete ledge . . . about seven feet above the floor," they are in a position to survey from above the nests below. They detect "at least thirty raptors [of various ages]. Perhaps more." Grant (the novel's manly hero-scientist) pronounces this hatchery to be a "colony": "there were three nests, attended by three sets of parents. The division of territory was centered roughly around the nests, although the offspring seemed to overlap, and run into different territories. The adults were benign with the young ones, and tougher with the juveniles, occasionally snapping at the older animals when their play got too rough" (387). Although Crichton has just used the word "colony" in a biological frame, he does not immediately or explicitly develop its insect associations. He has already revealed these carnivorous dinosaurs to be highly intelligent, so much so that they have come to symbolize our opposite, an alien "master species" that, if allowed off the island, will quickly supplant human beings. But he does not want to express their sociality according to the entomological template, not only because he subscribes to the current "dinosaurs were big birds" theory, but also because the Hive analogy suggests civilization, which for his purposes is an unnecessarily complex state of organization. (After all, these velociraptors are long-dead "barbarians" resurrected for the entertainment of a modern "Rome" that has been corrupted and weakened through its technology.) Hence, Crichton describes these dinosaurs as mammalian parents socializing their young into a pack structure.

This scene has all the features necessary for an evocation of the Hive. Crichton places his observers in a visually sovereign position, looking down upon an organized alien collective. Most importantly, to destroy their enemy, these observers must understand them. The human race's salvation depends upon a successful search for a pattern, whose elements of near discovery and dinosaur counting allow Crichton to heighten suspense and to slow the Hive topos's emergence. The summit of this period of crucial surveying is a description of the nest closest to the humans, which Crichton uses to foreground the "good" (and old-fashioned) science of direct and purposeful observation. Through Grant's consciousness we see the return of the "dinosaurs are birds" model: "In the phosphorescent green glow of the night-vision goggles, Grant peered down into the room from the ledge, looking at the first nest. It was made of mud and straw, formed into a broad, shallow basket shape. He counted the remains of fourteen eggs. Of course he couldn't count the actual shells from this distance, and in any case they were long since broken and scattered over the floor, but he was able to count the indentations in the mud. Apparently the raptors made their nests shortly before the eggs were laid." (388). Now Crichton has us thinking of these "raptors" as birds. But Ellie, another scientist, has also been watching, and she notices something significant in how the raptors "arrange them-

selves spatially." She says to Grant, "No, look. Look for yourself. Watch
the little ones. When they are playing, they tumble and run every which
way. But in between, when the babies are standing around, notice how
they orient their bodies. They face either that wall, or the opposite wall.
It's like they line up." Grant's response reveals the Hive's presence: "I
don't know, Ellie. You think there's a colony metastructure? Like bees?"
And her rejoinder confirms its nature as camouflaged. "No, not exactly,"
she said. "It's more subtle than that. It's just a tendency" (389). Admittedly, these characters have no psychology outside of scientific speculation — but their limits highlight the Hive's naturalized presence in the
imagination. These observers have had the entomological template in
mind since first looking down upon the raptor nursery, but Crichton
does not need nor wish to make it explicit. Although he borrows its
traditional, poetic structure and its essential attributions of hierarchy and
otherness, Crichton has Grant use the Hive instrumentally, as a theory
rather than an analogy.

Crichton-the-romancer wishes for his characters to "discover" the insect analogy in nature. Hence, Crichton has Grant wildly mix his biological metaphors so as to get at the Hive: the scientist's speculation runs
directly to the possibility that this "colony" of warm-blooded reptiles
has insectlike characteristics. On cue, Ellie suggests that this collective
orientation is a "kind of communication." "Grant was thinking the same
thing. Bees could communicate spatially, by doing a kind of dance. Perhaps dinosaurs could do the same thing" (390). Because Crichton wishes
to combine the Hive's attribution of alterity with the current theory that
dinosaurs were more like modern birds than reptiles, he has his characters explain this behavior as migratory in nature.

This instance serves to remind us of several things concerning the
Hive topos as we now tend to use it. First, the Hive and its language
are present at least as a potential whenever a collective is observed from
above. Second, the Hive topos's office and associations are indispensable
when it comes to figuring an alien order, especially a threatening one.
Third, the Hive has become so associated with insect-specific qualities
that its management may require both the technique of delay and its
moderation through alternative metaphors for the group. It seems, then,
that a technology of sorts for representing the collective has grown up
around the Hive. Despite its antiquity, its stubborn tendency to manifest
itself as apparent structure (which at every turn threatens naked alle-

gory), and the seeming limits imposed upon it by the entomological template, more than simply surviving the civilization that made it, the Hive has flourished and multiplied.

Finally, Crichton's Hive reminds us that the topos is a way of knowing. It is psychologically present in his characters and available to them as a shared design, which they use as an instrument for understanding the external world. For the Hive's major tradition is a series of variations and complications of a basic tableau that views the collective from the outside. According to this model, the Hive is both alien and external to us. However, complementary to the "external" tradition, which reaches its climax in the Insect-as-Other subtopos, is another tradition, a series of formal experiments that have been conducted in order to represent what it is like to live *inside* the Hive. And whereas the Hive's major tradition has followed the Western imagination on its journeys into progressively alien spaces, its complement, the Self-as-Insect subtopos, has taken the opposite path. Anticipated by Shakespeare, announced by Swift, and present as an aspect of Marlow's experience of Africa's strangeness, the Self-as-Insect's trajectory is inward; its office is to make visible the Hive's effects upon the individual psyche.

THE SELF AS INSECT

*So very tempting to want to distribute the entire world
in terms of a single code. A universal law would then
regulate phenomena as a whole. . . .*

*Unfortunately, this doesn't work, has never even begun
to work, will never work. Which won't stop us continuing
for a long time to come to categorize this animal or that
according to whether it has an odd number of toes or
hollow horns. . . .*

*All utopias are depressing because they leave no room
for chance, for difference, for the "miscellaneous."
Everything has been set in order and order reigns. Behind
every utopia there is always some great taxonomic design:
a place for each thing and each thing in its place.*

Georges Perec, "Think/Classify,"

Zeus to Tutor: *They [the flies of Argos] are a symbol. But
if you want to know what the gods did, look around you.
See that old creature over there, creeping away like a beetle
on her little black feet, hugging the walls. Well, she's a
good specimen of the squat black vermin that teem in
every cranny of this town.*

Jean-Paul Sartre, The Flies

The Hive topos's primary office is to picture social order, to define by mutual contrast the human individual and the organized collective. This topos's core is an imitation of a visual experience, that of surveying a group from a sovereign position. From this *external* position, the observer may apprehend the group as a whole, now simplified. The visual field is then divided into two antithetical regions, which (along with their contents) are interpretable according to a code of proximity and similitude. This process of interpretation then enables the observing consciousness to attribute otherness to the observed collective. And depending upon a collective's degree of organization and its ethical alignment, it tends to be figured as either an angelic beehive or a demonic ant heap.

But the Hive topos has another office, an alternative and, as to its most significant assumptions, a comparatively recent view of the collective — one from *within*. Because this version of the Hive topos involves the figuration of the individual as an insect, I call it the "Self as Insect." Swift's bee in *Battle of the Books* is an important step toward this variation of the Hive, which finds its perfection in the character of Kafka's Gregor Samsa. But though solitary, because Swift's bee defends the inherently superior ancients against derivative moderns, it is aligned with and is an honorary citizen of an angelic collective. For Swift, the ancients' "society" (in several senses of the word) is entirely good, and he persuades us to join it through satire, a genre that in his hands cannot accommodate either the ambiguities of identification or the dangers to the self that stimulate Conrad's tentative exploration of the demonic Hive's interior in *Heart of Darkness*.

In *Heart*, even though Conrad favors an external, sovereign view of the colonial system, his interest in how the colonial system shapes the psyche causes him to experiment with the traditional Hive, to modify its grammar of relative position and proximity. Marlow's physical journey from the Company station to Kurtz's outpost is also a psychological movement into the dark Hive of colonialism. Accordingly, I compared Marlow's primarily visual and external figuration of the Company station as an ant heap with the ambiguous "atmospherics" of his night aboard ship, when "half awake" he stares out into the impenetrable jungle, "narcot[ized]" by the collective sound of Africans chanting somewhere just beyond the "black flat wall of the woods."

However, even though this moment suggests what it is like to be part of the Hive, subjected to and threatened by its all-encompassing, anti-human order, Conrad stops short of an explicit use of the Self as Insect topos, for that would require him to figure *individuated* Europeans — certainly Kurtz and perhaps even Marlow (the object of our identification) — as insects. This Conrad would not do, I believe, because it would further complicate the notion of European cultural superiority and problematize his novel's essential dramatic opposition between the autonomous Marlow and the demonic collective, thereby exactly predicting the attitude toward society that undergirds Sartre's brand of existentialism and the antithetical poetic he uses to express it. Yes, Conrad does generally object to colonialism; however, the fact remains that to him Africa and its inhabitants are a geography for testing the European soul. Like Marlow, Conrad requires an Africa that has no meaning except as a collective Other. While Marlow does physically enter the Hive and feels its dark seductions, as long as he does not become corrupted (lose his objective, rational stance) or, worse, entirely "go native," psychologically he remains external to it. It is Marlow's job to come perilously near the heart of the demonic Hive, to be tested by it, and yet remain uncontaminated.

Nevertheless, because he criticizes the "new forces" of colonialism, Conrad presents his Africans more sympathetically than his Europeans — a strategy that is complicated by the mediation of Marlow's consciousness. For example, Marlow's description of "the place [near the Company station] where some of the [native] helpers had withdrawn to die": "black shapes crouched, lay, sat between the trees, leaning against the trunks, clinging to the earth . . . in all the attitudes of pain, abandonment, and despair" (20). Our sympathies are engaged, but only generally. Marlow does not — and, perhaps, is unable to — individuate these Africans: he represents them as "black shapes," the embodiments of abstract "attitudes." I sense that because Marlow must control his identification with the Africans, he limits his entomological metaphors. He is willing to travel into the heart of darkness, but, tellingly, it is not in his character (or in his interests?) to transcend it through the spirit expressed by Gloucester's famous simile, whose sentiment anticipates how Kafka will use the Self as Insect to represent the modern condition: "As flies are to wanton boys are we to th' gods, / They kill us for their sport."[1]

Similar to Marlow, Gloucester represents human beings in such a way as to arouse our general sympathies: as vulnerable to a power that they do not understand and cannot resist. However, unlike Marlow, exactly because he does not wish to distinguish between men but rather between gods (power) and men (the powerless), Gloucester figures his sufferers as flies. This choice allows him to attribute to human beings a collective existence that connotes neither meaningful organization nor agency. And because the gods are the sadistic (and therefore inhuman) actors in this tableau, we do not conclude that we flies are loathsome. We are simply stupid and helpless before powers over which we have no control.

Shakespeare thus reminds his inheritors that, in addition to its usual job of expressing hierarchy and corporate strength, through the substitution of one insect image for another, the Hive topos may be adjusted so as to express vulnerability within an uncertain cosmos. In this sense his flies may be said to return us to an aspect of Homer's and Virgil's experiments with the form that are easily overshadowed by the Hive's strong tendency to oppose subject and object. For instance, in the fourth *Georgic*, Virgil impresses upon us the bees' fragility when, right after a Homeric description of their valor in battle, he states, "These storms of passion, these conflicts so fierce, by the tossing of a little dust are quelled and laid to rest" (1.203). These bees may indeed be mighty warriors, but they are nonetheless miniature beings, easily harmed by even "the tossing of a little dust."

As I pursue the Hive's development into our time, it is helpful to keep its affective aspect in mind. First, it would not be wise to hold that our predecessors were less aware than we are of everything that *their* metaphors can do. And second, since its invention the Hive topos has never ceased to tell us that there is a connection of feeling between ourselves and other creatures, one that extends beyond the shared capacity to suffer. Although I would ultimately ground this feeling in our species's capacities for identification and imaginative sympathy, I must observe that the metaphoric operation often serves as the rails over which these capacities travel in order to achieve expression. My argument: when we figure ourselves as bees or flies, even though we may intend it only as a matter of speaking, we have also, however implicitly, figured insects as human beings. Because the metaphoric image rises from the merging of two dissimilar essences, even a structure as antithetical as the Hive topos, which I have established as containing and using metaphor for more complicated ends, cannot entirely negate the elemental reciprocity of the trope. All a writer can do is harness this reciprocity or, if need be, either camouflage it or direct the reader's attention elsewhere.

In general, the traditional, external form of the Hive topos does not tend to encourage individuated identification and its attendant affective dimension. This is so in part because, unlike the internal mode, which works toward identification and thus favors the use of either solitary or small groups of asocial insects (most usually flies or cockroaches, but sometimes also butterflies, moths, and beetles), the external requires a collective, hierarchical vehicle. And identification — at least the affective sort I have in mind — with a collective is difficult to achieve for modern Europeans. Of course, the most important factor to be considered when evaluating the meaning of any insect analogy is the poet's intentions. If, as in the case of Gloucester's simile, a writer uses a *group* of flies rather than a beehive to symbolize the collective, while we should probably go ahead and interpret his analogy as an instance of the Hive's external mode, we should also be open to the possibility that part of what is being communicated falls within the Self as Insect's orbit. Because the Hive is a structure that establishes and distributes power according to the nature of specific symbols, the degree of organization implied by a particular insect image can clarify the species of a particular simile — thereby helping us to notice and to evaluate not only the affect of mixed forms, but also authorial intention at an exceedingly fine level.

Because images of disorganized or solitary insects may be used to figure the intimate group or an individual, in contrast to images of the colony, they tend to compel our personal identification. Hence, not only are such images uniquely suited for evoking feelings of isolation, vulnerability, disgust, pity, and compassion, they are also more psychoanalytically potent than the traditional versions of the Hive. They are useful for arousing an apprehension of what we call the uncanny.

To paraphrase Freud, by "uncanny" I mean that particular species of the frightening at whose core is something familiar that we wish to repress.[2] Gloucester's fly simile expresses our helplessness before the cosmos and also paints a very disturbing picture of the Divine. It is conceivable that persons who believe in a Supreme Being enjoy their powerlessness before Him, but such enjoyment would surely depend on repressing the possibility that His (or their) will is capricious or downright mean.

Indeed, part of what is involved in most instances of Self as Insect is what Freud might call the mind's "primitive" capacity for animism: as when we interpret the appearance of similarity as identity. According to him, "an uncanny effect is often and easily produced when the distinction between imagination and reality is effaced, as when something that we have hitherto regarded as imaginary appears before us in reality, *or when a symbol takes over the full functions of the thing it symbolizes*" (221; my emphasis). When we figure, for example, a city as a beehive, the symbol remains a manner of speaking. It is never really adequate to its object; we cannot simply accept the beehive as a biologically accurate representation of human sociality. While we easily grasp the beehive's allegorical possibilities, human and insect societies are different enough that, if one wishes to make an entomologically "authentic" analogy, one must reinterpret the human element. One may do this in two ways. First, one may imaginatively distance oneself from the human world so that it is entirely reduced to a principle synonymous with our experience of the insect colony, such as "expansion." We see this in the simile by Lewis Thomas: "Nobody wants to think that the rapidly expanding mass of mankind, spreading out over the surface of the earth, blackening the ground, bears any meaningful resemblance to the life of an anthill or a hive." Or, as in Huxley, one can construct a human society along insect lines.

While neither of these techniques for authorizing the use of the Hive — distancing oneself from a human collective or shaping its government to agree with an insect model — is modern, their extremity is decidedly so. Thomas doesn't view a city from a hill and through a poetic convention: he surveys the Earth from orbit and posits a "meaningful resemblance" between human civilization and "the life of an anthill or a hive." Similarly, Huxley does not ornament his dystopia with insect associations either gathered through allusion or presented as analogies: he builds it from an entomological blueprint. More importantly, however, the extremity that unites both techniques assumes true biological affinity between humans and insects, which simply would not have occurred to, for instance, Shakespeare. If we assume that the Archbishop of Canterbury's bee simile from *Henry V* expresses an important aspect of how Shakespeare understood the beehive's relation to human society, then, much like Virgil before him, the Bard sees "honey-bees, / [as] Creatures that by a rule in nature teach / The act of order to a peopled kingdom" (1.2.187–89). Hence, because to Shakespeare the insect colony expresses an *ideal* of order that must be *general* if it is to be lived by creatures as different as bees and humans, he does not strain to imagine his "peopled kingdom" as a beehive: by nature they are analogically so, and this nature (as opposed to the nature of King Lear or Macbeth) is God's nature. To clarify: while Shakespeare's ideas about the Hive cannot be summed up by how his characters use it, my point is that, unlike ours, the Elizabethan worldview was prescientific. In contrast to ours, their ideas about sociological kinship were entirely shaped by and expressed through custom and inherited artistic forms.

However, that Elizabethan society was much more poetical than ours does not mean that its people were any less rational than we are — especially when on the subject of metaphor. It is in this light that we should consider the following passage, which continues the one above. Here, the Archbishop of Canterbury is addressing the young King Henry V. England is on the eve of war with France; Scotland is rebelling. About to receive the French representative, Henry wants to know whether he may safely divide his forces so as to prosecute his rights on the continent. Taking his lead from Exeter's comparison between national coherence and music, the Archbishop uses the beehive as a heaven-approved grid, as a system of correspondences that illustrates that the righteous human commonwealth, England, will hold together because it is God's Will:

> They have a king, and officers of sorts,
> Where some, like magistrates, correct at home;
> Others, like merchants, venter trade abroad;
> Others, like soldiers, armed in their stings,
> Make boot upon the summer's velvet buds,
> Which pillage they with merry march bring home
> To the tent-royal of their emperor;
> Who busied in his [majesty] surveys
> The singing masons building roofs of gold,
> The civil citizens kneading up the honey,
> The Poor mechanic porters crowding in
> Their heavy burthens at his narrow gate,
> The sad-eye'd justice, with his surley hum,
> Delivering o'er to executors pale
> The lazy yawning drone.
> (1.2.190–204)

The Archbishop has merged human and insect characteristics, but only to a point. It is not his purpose to argue that men are bees; rather, he wants to show King Henry that in ways that matter men and bees naturally participate in a Divine order and according to their place in the chain of being.

While the Archbishop's simile does indeed anthropomorphize the beehive, there is no sense about this figure that the "symbol [of the bee-hive has] take[n] over the full functions of the thing it symbolizes." Hence, there is nothing "uncanny" about this model of human society. What is familiar about it — variety encompassed by and rendered co-operative through just law — we do not all wish to repress. As we enter the twentieth century, however, this sort of poetic and *rational* allegory gives way to its opposite: a scientifically authorized but nonetheless *irrational*, animistic style of insect allegory, one that employs the uncanny as an agent of social commentary.

As a general rule, when a person is figured as an insect,[3] the insect symbol may indeed be said to threaten to "take . . . over the full functions of the" person, and far more so than when a collective is figured as an insect colony. I think this is so for three interrelated reasons. First, unlike a city's complexity, a person's is not visually apparent. Second, a single human being is much smaller in relation to his or her surroundings than a city; hence, he or she is much more easily reduced by distance to the apparent size of an insect. Third, because a human being is physically much more vulnerable than a collective, he or she possesses a psycho-logical dimension, an emotional life, denied any corporate entity. While an individual insect is not usually thought to be sentient, its small size and physical vulnerability mean, finally, that the individual's relationship to social power may be summed up by it much more accurately and to-tally than a city is by an image of a beehive.

For instance, when at the end of *Père Goriot* Rastignac looks down upon Paris and sees it as a hive whose honey he will take, certainly Balzac (and probably Rastignac as well, for he really is only working himself up for yet another round of social climbing) does not believe that Paris can be summed up by the symbol of the beehive. However, we get an en-tirely different sense when, in *The First Men in the Moon*, in the middle of his involved and somewhat tediously detailed entomological allegory, Cavor, the novel's misguided scientist and part-time narrator, tells us about the Selenites's peculiar sort of "technical education."

This moment is distinguished by its gruesomeness, but on an ethical, emotional level it reminds us of the cruelty and self-serving attitude that undergird utilitarian education and its motives. On a more specific and personal level, however, the affect of "that wretched-looking hand sticking out of its jar" is uncanny. It is this passage's locus of feeling because its unconfined state contrasts so strongly with the rest of the organism, whose suffering must be unimaginable. In its educational context, this hand thus reminds us of what teachers and parents in particular must repress, namely their own memories of public education: the many years of confinement and discipline marked above all by the lack of choice, the trauma of being shaped for purposes not yet glimpsed, much less understood.

Wells achieves this intensity of affect because he focuses on a single creature and its suffering. While he could have accomplished much the same without lingering over this solitary "wretched-looking hand sticking out of its jar," he chooses rightly, for this moment is where his allegory strikes closest to home. As I shall demonstrate below, Kafka, working in and extending the same mode, achieves something even greater and more revealing about the crushing effect that society has upon the lone individual.

As Freud teaches us, because the child cannot distinguish between reality and the imagination, the world the child inhabits is pervaded with animistic notions. These notions are bound up with fantasies of control and power, for it is also during this time that the child's sense of and relationships with various social powers are formed. So it should come as little surprise that a child's relations with insects are informed by these same issues of power and the imagination. To a child especially, in the insect society is found not only the perfection of order, and a frightening strength in numbers, but a fascinating vulnerability as well. The natural hive or colony is composed of tiny creatures that by parental example we are often encouraged to regard as valueless and that, if we choose, we may easily kill.

I also think that the obvious physical differences between humans and insects, especially to children who are so much smaller and weaker than the adults who alternately care for and punish them, suggest a difference in Being from which originates the attitude that because insects are of a "lesser" order they *deserve* crushing. Toward the isolated insect we seem to exhibit this attitude even more strongly. Much more so than the colony, the isolated insect is a natural object of identification (a dramatic and emotional resource that informs Gloucester's fly simile). Hence, again in comparison with the colony, the isolated insect much more easily and intensely evokes both our pity and our cruelty, feelings we similarly find — or discover missing in ourselves — in our contact with the disorganized insect group.

Something of the attitude that insects should be crushed informs Victor Frankenstein's address to his creature, when they finally meet face-to-face for the first time since the night of its creation: "'Devil,' I exclaimed, 'do you dare approach me? And do not you fear the fierce vengeance of my arm wreaked on your miserable head? Begone, vile insect! Or rather, stay, that I may trample you to dust! And, oh! That I could, with the extinction of your miserable existence, restore those victims whom you have so diabolically murdered'" (83). In order to put his "Devil" (double) into a category that is at once utterly alien and physically vulnerable, Frankenstein refigures him as an insect, thus enabling him to imagine himself towering over his physically superior adversary. Under the circumstances, this analogy sounds ridiculous, and no doubt Shelley means it this way. She would draw attention to the scientist's essential character flaw. In language reminiscent of Gloucester's simile of the flies, the "monster" tells us that to Frankenstein life is something to "sport . . . with."

In order to figure something or someone as an insect, we must imagine ourselves in a position superior to it. In Frankenstein's case, his language would have him looming above his nemesis like a god. In Gloucester's metaphor, human beings are figured as the middle term in an ascending order, positioned below the gods "who kill us for their sport." These are indeed different analogies, but not in the ways that matter, for Frankenstein employs a generic category, "insect," which presupposes singularity. Gloucester uses a more specific and plural one, "flies." However, each analogy's sense derives from the Hive topos's structure; and more importantly, both employ natural symbols that attribute to their respective objects a similarly noncooperative and therefore vulnerable essence.

In contrast to the image of the insect society,[4] those used by Gloucester and Frankenstein have the capacity to suggest that an object or a person is outcast(e), even loathsome. To one degree or another, both the image of human beings as flies and a humanoid reduced to a "vile insect" seek to arouse our disgust and, at least in Gloucester's analogy, our pity. While it is true that in the case of the fly image our disgust has foundation, it is nonetheless a fact that both vehicles work toward it. It seems, then, that there is a relationship between the sort, or nature, of alterity we sense about an object and the degree of its symbol's sociality. If the object in the observed, and therefore alien, position is collective, as is the rule with the primary form of the Hive topos, while this object may arouse fear, it may also suggest the ideal. It therefore almost never evokes the uncanny. In contrast, when the regarded object is singular, or a disorganized group, its very isolation and/or lack of order seems to mark it as being unclean. Even the locusts, who have always been a singularly destructive pest, and which the Bible reminds us "have no king,"[5] are not associated with an outcast state. In fact, far from being vermin, they are kosher.

Like its parent topos, the Self as Insect is a structure whose meaning is to a degree independent of any particular metaphor. However, the fly and the cockroach are the images most commonly used with it because, to human eyes, (1) they are unorganized and therefore defenseless, (2) they display an obvious interest in filth, (3) they are sometimes all too irritatingly present in our homes, and (4) unlike the bee and the ant they do not seem to have larger, admirable goals beyond feeding and reproduction. For these reasons I believe it is common to picture Gregor Samsa as a cockroach, even though Kafka ambiguously calls him *ungeheueres Ungeziefer*, which means "monstrous vermin." According to Stanley Corngold:

> Kafka was an amateur of etymology and very likely aware of the original sense of those haunting "*un-*" words, "*ungeheureres Ungeziefer*" . . . into which Gregor is transformed. "*Ungeheuer*" connotes the creature who has no place in the family; "*Ungeziefer*," the unclean animal unsuited for sacrifice, the creature without a place in God's order.
>
> Hence, the apparent realism with which Kafka describes the vermin should not conjure for the reader an insect of some definite kind. This would be to experience the vermin the way the cleaning woman does, who calls him "old dung beetle!" But "to forms of address like these Gregor would not respond"; they do not reflect his uncanny identity, which cannot be grasped in an image.[6]

Corngold has in mind Freud's theory of the uncanny, which establishes that the uncanny (the *Unheimliche*, "unhomely") "is in reality nothing new or alien, but something which is familiar and old-established in the mind and which has become alienated from it only through the process

of repression. This reference to the factor of repression enables us, furthermore, to understand Schelling's definition of the uncanny as something which ought to have remained hidden but has come to light"
(Freud, 217). This idea is peculiarly applicable to *The Metamorphosis* because, although Gregor Samsa's *physical* change is disturbing and aspects
of his life as an insect are disgusting, the story is not "about" these
things. They are not its source of power. Rather, the story is a transcript
of an uncanny "becoming." It is a machine that not only makes visible
the psychic price of adult responsibilities, but also reveals what lies beneath the bourgeois family's supposed closeness and economic interde-
pendence. In both respects, what emerges is at once impossibly strange
and yet familiar, "frightening [because it] . . . leads back to what is
known of old and long familiar" (195).

Kafka's primary instrument for showing this uncanny becoming is the
process of Gregor adapting to his new body. Soon after he wakes to
discover "himself changed in his bed . . . lying on his back hard as armor
plate . . . [with] his many legs, pitifully thin . . . [and] waving helplessly"
(3), his mother, worried that he will miss his train, knocks on the door
to his room and calls to him. When he answers, he notices that his voice
has changed: "What a soft voice! Gregor was shocked to hear his own
voice answering, unmistakably his own voice, true, but in which, as if
from below, an insistent distressed chirping intruded, which left the
clarity of his words intact only for a moment really, before so badly gar-
bling them as they carried that no one could be sure if he had heard
right" (5). His mother does not notice the change, and we are told that
"the wooden door must have prevented . . . [it] from being noticed" (6).
But this explanation is not meant to be convincing, for it belongs as
much to Gregor as to the narrator, and neither is reliable. It is significant
that he speaks first to his mother. Among all his family members, one
would think that she would notice such a change in her son's voice. But
she does not. This exchange through the door suggests at least the following: that Gregor is still in the first stage of his metamorphosis, that
even before his change he was already estranged from his family and,
finally, that all concerned prefer to repress anything out of the ordinary,
anything that might interfere with their tenuous hold on their class
status. And Gregor participates in this repression, for even though he
does not wish to admit it, his family's overriding concern is that he get
to work.

Part of the story's genius lies in Kafka's restraint: he does not begin by making monsters of the family or a total fool of Gregor. The family is used to living above their means. And after his father's "business disaster," Gregor has taken up the slack by becoming the family's breadwinner. After a time, however, "they had just gotten used to it, the family as well as Gregor, the money was received with thanks and given with pleasure, but no special feeling of warmth went with it any more" (27). Although less loving than we would like, this family is normal, and by all appearances, Gregor is a good son. But he is also neurotic. His obsession with his job (which becomes comic and then pitiable) and his conviction that his family cannot survive without him together suggest that he suffers from what Freud might call "pathological narcissism." This malady amounts to an overdeveloped conscience. That is, the "special agency" that "stand[s] over against the rest of the ego, which has the function of observing and criticizing the self and of exercising a censorship within the mind, and which we become aware of as our 'conscience'" (Freud, 211) has in Gregor achieved an unhealthy independence. In that Gregor's conscience moves him only toward duty, part of what his new body signifies is that such a use of a human life is not really human at all.

Soon after Gregor discovers himself changed and speaks with his mother through his room's closed and locked door, his office manager arrives. He wants to know why Gregor "didn't catch the early train" (10). The manager speaks to Gregor through the locked door, informing him of his disappointment: "I intended to tell you all this in private, but since you make me waste my time here for nothing, I don't see why your parents should not hear too. Your performance of late has been very unsatisfactory; I know it is not the best season for doing business, we all recognize that; but a season for not doing any business, there is no such thing, Mr. Samsa, such a thing cannot be tolerated" (12). This time when Gregor responds, his voice is no longer human. The manager asks his parents, "Did you understand a word . . . that was the voice of an animal" (13). The family calls for a locksmith and a doctor, but even though Gregor notices that they no longer understand his words, he does not grasp what is happening to him. He feels better but does not see his "improvement" as a sign that he is getting used to his body, that he is becoming more and more *unheimlich*: "But Gregor had become much calmer. It was true that they no longer understood his words, though they had seemed clear enough to him, clearer than before, probably because his ear had grown accustomed to them. But still, the others now believed that there was something the matter with him and were ready to help him. The assurance and confidence with which the first measures had been taken did him good. He felt integrated into human society once again and hoped for marvelous, amazing feats from both the doctor and the locksmith." Not only does Kafka present Gregor's condition as progressive, he also identifies its source. Gregor's disease is rooted in a crisis of belonging. At issue is his state of social "integrat[ion]." His place in his family and his place at work are equally dependent upon his ability to carry out his duty. His duty, his ability to earn money, is thus the sum of his adult identity. And he hates this identity, this self. In a sense, then, his psychological progress as an insect is a regression. Overnight Gregor has gone from provider to dependent, from adult to infant.

As the narrative progresses, so does his disorder. When they see him, his manager and parents react to his appearance with obvious disgust. And when given some of what had always been his favorite drink, milk (by which Kafka signifies Gregor's repressed desire to again become a child), he finds that he no longer cares for it. Thus far his sister exhibits a somewhat reluctant compassion for him, and when she realizes that his tastes in food have changed, "she brought him a wide assortment of things, all spread out on an old newspaper: old, half-rotten vegetables; bones left over from the evening meal, caked with congealed white sauce; some raisins and almonds; a piece of cheese, which two days before Gregor had declared inedible. . . . In addition to all this she put down some water in the bowl apparently earmarked for Gregor's use" (24). Gregor is now aware that he has his own bowl, like an animal, but does not care. He is hungry and, tellingly, it is the old cheese (which, technically speaking, is rotten milk), that "immediately and forcibly attract[s] him ahead of all the other dishes." The completeness of his gustatory metamorphosis is strikingly visceral: "One right after the other, and with eyes streaming with tears of contentment, he devoured the cheese, the [old, half-rotten] vegetables, and the [congealed] white sauce; the fresh foods, on the other hand, he did not care for; he couldn't even stand their smell, and even dragged the things he wanted to eat a bit farther away."

The narrator himself (but, importantly, not the reader) begins a retreat from Gregor, which is first noticeable in the following passage. Significantly, this passage treats the changes in how Gregor sees:

Often he lay there [on his "cool leather sofa" beside the door] the whole long night through, not sleeping a wink and only scrabbling on the leather for hours on end. Or, not balking at the huge effort of pushing an armchair to the window, he would crawl up to the window sill and, propped up in the chair, lean against the window, evidently in some sort of remembrance of the feeling of freedom he used to have from looking out the window. For, in fact, from day to day he saw things even a short distance away less and less distinctly; the hospital opposite, which he used to curse because he saw so much of it, was now completely beyond his range of vision, and if he had not been positive that he was living in Charlotte street — a quiet but still very much a city street — he might have believed that he was looking out of his window into a desert where the gray sky and the gray earth were indistinguishably fused. (29)

Here Kafka presents in visual terms what I have called Gregor's "crisis of belonging." While still a member of human society, Gregor would look out this window with a "feeling of freedom." The fact that he would "curse" the hospital that blocked his view indicates that he longed for an even greater perspective, one more sovereign and powerful. Obviously his adult identity of dutiful earning was never sufficient. Now what had once impeded his vision, the hospital, is no longer even visible. I take this structure to be a sign of the modern state, its institutions public as well as private, which together confine and shape Gregor like the Selenite in its jar. Gregor cannot anymore distinguish even the difference between the earth and the sky. Ironically, the process that made him into a creature of absolute psychological alterity has also made him this social order's logical and ultimate product. Freedom (which suggests at least the potential for inward rebellion, even if it is expressed only as vague dissatisfaction) is at best a "remembrance of a feeling," but his perceptions are so altered that he may no longer even apprehend that a *something* stands between him and seeing, that it and its institutions are a hated impediment to his sovereignty. In this passage Kafka reminds us that to be human one must be free: he suggests that our humanity is eroded by a lack of perspective and that even our desire for perspective may be extinguished by an unexamined life of conformity.

The Metamorphosis is a parable, not a strict allegory, that borrows from the fable, for it seeks to express a general social problem or condition rather than to comment on specific incidents, ideas, or personages. And a major source of its richness is the Self as Insect topos, which allows us to so fully and emotionally identify with Gregor that it is his family (and by way of extension modern society) and not he that ends up in the nonhuman position. All the characters in this story are shown to be empty, distorted by an oppressive petit-bourgeois existence, and thus to a degree they share Gregor's disorder. However, Gregor's vulnerability grows along with his insectness; his obliviousness ripens into instinctual behavior. He is "forgetting [even] his human past" (33). Consequently, as he becomes progressively less and less human, losing the power to speak and see as a man, and to feel except as a lower organism, Gregor also loses the power of moral choice.

As Gregor becomes more *unhuman*, his family, and his father in particular, exhibits increasingly *inhuman* behavior toward him. In Gregor's eyes his father, too, has undergone a physical transformation, one that Kafka also intends to evoke the uncanny: "Gregor turned his head away from the door and lifted it toward his father. He had not really imagined his father looking like this, as he stood in front of him now . . . [he] should really have been prepared to find some changes. And yet, and yet — was this still his father? Was this the same man who in the old days used to lie wearily in bed when Gregor left on a business trip?" (37–38). Gregor's father has been transformed into a uniformed giant. And just before Gregor is chased by him, the narrator tells us that Gregor is "staggered at the gigantic size of the soles of his [father's] boots" (38). Clearly, Gregor is seeing his father as a child might — hence this scene's peculiarly wrenching familiarity. In a rage, his father begins throwing apples at his son, and "one . . . literally forced its way into his back" (39). Gregor is paralyzed with a "startling, unbelievable pain." Only Gregor's sister, Grete, intercedes to prevent his murder.

As the days wear on, Gregor's wound begins to fester and the family falls on harder times. The apartment is expensive, but they cannot move out because of Gregor. Even his sister's compassion for him cools. Their maid has left, to be replaced with a lower-class domestic, an old cleaning woman who is not afraid of Gregor. She treats him as she would a household pest, once even attempting to crush him with a chair. His family fills his room with junk and furniture, for they are now renting a room to three strangers. Gregor hardly eats anymore and spends all his time in his filthy room. When he emerges, wishing to better hear his beloved sister playing the violin for the boarders, they see him and vacate without payment. This is the context for the novel's final transformation. Grete chooses to no longer recognize Gregor-the-insect as having once been human, as being her brother. She turns on him because she feels that his disorder impedes her burgeoning youth with all its vague prospects: "'My dear parents,' said his sister and by way of introduction pounded her hand on the table, 'things can't go on like this. Maybe you don't realize it, but I do. I won't pronounce the name of my brother in front of this monster, and so all I say is: we have to get rid of it. We've done everything humanly possible to take care of it and to put up with it; I don't think that anyone can blame us in the least'" (51). Here the opposition between the human and the insect is clearly drawn; its terms are moral. In preparation for her brother's extermination, Grete, once Gregor's protector, now separates him from his name. He is no longer "Gregor," he is an "it." In effect, she pronounces him dead, for she, and her family along with her, choose no longer to even pretend that they identify with Gregor. Grete states that "we've done everything *humanly* possible to take care of *it* and to put up with *it*" (my emphasis). The irony is obvious. Even though they know what they are about to do is wrong, blameworthy because of its inhumanity, at this moment the Samsas become moral "monsters," expressive of the soullessness and the blindness that we associate with the insect. In Freud's language, their "function" has been "take[n] over" by what they have chosen to repress, by what Gregor symbolizes: a hated alien presence, a physical reminder of what they do not wish to know about their lives.

The Self as Insect topos is frequently used for such illuminating reversals, as a way of measuring and making visible the degree of a character's human-being-ness.[7] And such moments usually involve an evocation of the uncanny, for they return us to our childhood experiments with insects, incidents of contact between ourselves and creatures uniquely different from and vulnerable to us. At least for myself, in my memories of such things, I do not find much to be comfortable about. And I strongly suspect that writers who use the Self as Insect are quite aware that it resonates with this sort of recollection. When outside parental control and presented with a colorful beetle or a hill of ants, whether a child chooses to forbear or to kill, this "primal scene of the sidewalk" still impresses itself on his or her mind. It is our first taste of what it means to have absolute power and, through identification, what it is to suffer from it.

Graham Greene, for instance, in his novella *The Third Man*, uses a version of the Self as Insect to show us what's inside (or lacking in) Harry Lime, what becomes of someone given opportunity in the absence of just law. Rollo Martins, a writer of pulp Westerns and Lime's schoolyard chum, has been invited by Lime to come to Vienna to write for his "pharmaceutical" business — which, as it turns out, is no more than Lime black-marketing adulterated penicillin. Martins arrives to find himself in a city that has been split into "zones" by the occupying victors of World War II. (Thus, Greene means it to symbolize the whole of postwar Europe.) Martins arrives just in time to attend Lime's funeral, but he soon suspects that his friend has faked his death. He sets out to find him, at first working around and then later aiding the police, who are also after Lime. Near the end of the story, Lime sets up a meeting with Martins at the "Great Wheel," a Ferris wheel set in "the Russian zone where the Prater lay smashed and desolate and full of weeds, only the Great Wheel revolving slowly over the foundations of merry-go-rounds like abandoned millstones, the rusting iron of smashed tanks which nobody had cleared away, the frost-nipped weeds where the snow was thin" (307). For an hour in the cold Martins waits for Lime near the Wheel. He notices the "few courting couples . . . packed together in a single car of the wheel and revolv[ing] slowly above the city, surrounded by empty cars. As the cars reached the highest point of the wheel, the revolutions would stop for a couple of minutes and far overhead the tiny faces would press against the glass" (369). In many ways Martins is a failure. Greene makes him an American type, naive and a bit of a fool, personally and culturally unprepared for the consequences of the war and Europe's tired divisiveness. But he is a better man than many, one unused to making categorical distinctions between persons, and this we may tell even by how he sees. Although the couples in the cars at the top of the wheel are culturally and spatially distant from him, he perceives their faces and thinks of them only as "tiny." Although by itself this detail is meaningless, Greene is preparing us for the narrative's most significant visual moment, an instance of the Hive topos that juxtaposes the author's subtle allusion to Gloucester's flies with Lime's extreme figuration of human beings as "dots."

Lime finally shows up — whistling. He "came [toward Martins] with his amused deprecating take-it-or-leave-it manner." The narrator, the detective Calloway, now interrupts the tale to offer his view of Harry Lime, which in its own way is as mistaken as that held by Martins. To Martins,

Harry is the best friend he ever had, a person he had loved and admired since they were boys; Calloway sees him as a rather agreeable crook who finally crossed the line: "Don't picture Harry Lime as a smooth scoundrel. He wasn't that. The picture I have of him in my files is an excellent one: he is caught by a street photographer with his stocky legs apart, big shoulders a little hunched, a belly that has known too much good food for too long, on his face a look of cheerful rascality, a geniality, a recognition that *his* happiness will make the world's day" (370; Greene's emphasis). Lime "tips" (bribes) the woman in charge of the wheel, so that they may have a car to themselves. The view-from-above that the Great Wheel provides is the narrative's only moment of wider visual perspective, and Greene is sensitive to the connection between seeing and power that the Hive formalizes. As the car begins to rise, Lime remarks that the Viennese no longer have the money to get themselves private cars on the Wheel. The narrator is careful to keep us on our toes when it comes to Lime: when "He looked out of the window . . . at the figures diminishing below," we are told that his expression "*looked like* [one of] genuine commiseration" (my emphasis).

As the car continues to rise, a disillusioned Martins bitterly queries Lime: "Have you ever visited the children's hospital? Have you seen any of your victims?" Lime responds: "'Victims?' he asked. 'Don't be melodramatic, Rollo. Look down there,' he went on, pointing through the window at the people moving like black flies at the base of the Wheel. 'Would you really feel any pity if one of those dots stopped moving — for ever? If I said you can have twenty thousand pounds for every dot that stops, would you really, old man, tell me to keep my money — without hesitation? Or would you calculate how many dots you could afford to spare? Free of income tax, old man. Free of income tax.' He gave his boyish conspiratorial smile. 'It's the only way to save nowadays'" (371). Martins is discovering just how conscienceless his friend has become, how far Europe's disorder has allowed him to go. (Greene probably has Conrad's *Heart of Darkness* in mind, for there is a character in the novella named "Kurtz.") When accused of killing children for profit, Lime's defense belies his chummy manner and all but the "conspiratorial" aspect of his "boyish . . . smile." In so many words, he says to Martins: for such profit, Rollo, you would do the very same thing. Namely, to "calculate" the value of "dots . . . [one] could afford to spare."

If Martins is a type for the naive, well-meaning American, then Lime is his antithesis: the American cut loose from all restraint, free to do as he pleases in an old world that, broken by war, is vulnerable to and hungry for the new way and its abundant new money. Lime has become fully a creature of this new old world, one in which, he tells Martins: "nobody thinks in terms of human beings. Governments don't, so why should we? They talk of the people and the proletariat, and I talk of the mugs. It's the same thing. They have their five-year plans and so have I" (372). Lime makes no distinction between either democratic or socialist motives, between his methods and the policies of nations. And he has a point. Everyone is in on "it," so why should he "feel any pity" for persons about whom their own governments do not care?

Lime is certainly more than a "smooth scoundrel." He imagines himself a Nietzschean hero, poised above the "flies of the market place."[8] But when he measures himself against the people below, he cannot see them as living things, as even the "black flies" that the narrator represents "moving . . . at the base of the Wheel." Although he seems to fancy himself as such, Lime is no Zarathustra, no prophet. Greene signifies this by reserving the fly image for himself and having Lime push the Self as Insect topos to an unfortunate and geometric extreme: to him, other human beings are mere "dots." Greene thereby shows Lime's "truth" (the truth of the "new" man and the old new Europe) to be inhuman, abstract accounting. Like Gregor's family, except more consciously and therefore gratuitously, Lime has chosen to become a moral monster. Disorganized and vulnerable, the Viennese are indeed flylike: they live amidst garbage and rubble and on the victors' handouts. However, it is Lime who ends up being the "insect." He is a cruel opportunist who Greene shows living, and then dying, in the sewers like some "monstrous vermin" — in this instance, like a rat.

Kafka and Greene similarly portray modern society as an overwhelming and oppressive force. In the manner of an experiment, they pit the lone individual and antique humanistic motives against this modern "spirit of the hive." Because this universe is nonredemptive, the human being is unevenly matched against the principle of society. Hence, this sort of contest works itself out in terms of what Northrop Frye calls the "descending mode."[9] Such a literary science proceeds from terms that produce a negative drama, one that therefore resonates with the Hive's demonic polarity. Kafka, in particular, features this negativity by emphasizing the isolated insect's obliviousness and vulnerability.

Yet, as undeniably oppressive as the social order is in Kafka, its opposite is nonetheless present. We are, for instance, able to perceive and indeed to precisely measure the Samsa family's wrongness because we measure it against an ideal of domestic affinity. In this sense *The Metamorphosis* may be said to affirm the value of and the human need for not merely "society" in the abstract, but more specifically for a society of mutual understanding and loving relations. Furthermore, by making Gregor an insect, Kafka would also have us recognize our connection with the rest of creation (an important extension and focusing of the Romantic sensibility that I discussed through Keats's program of "negative capability"). Our sympathy for Gregor matures into compassion in step with his metamorphosis. But the ethical problem raised by our willingness to feel for an insect what we sometimes may withhold from a human being is not lost on Kafka. It is an intentional irony that we feel most deeply for Gregor only when he has ceased to be human, and especially when Grete turns on him. At this moment we feel more for Gregor as an abused animal than we would for a suffering human being. From this point of the story there is little difference between how his family sees him and how we see him, which is Kafka's way of suggesting that we, too, may have become inhabited by a symbol.

This is to say that more than just insectness is transferred at this moment: the locus and nature of uncanniness shifts as well. Before his family (a synecdoche for society at large, including the reader) metamorphoses into moral insects, Gregor is the *Unheimliche*. His isolation, vulnerability, and refusal to recognize either his true condition or his complicity in it make apparent aspects of the individual human condition that we prefer to repress. By "complicity" I mean that in some respects Gregor longed for his transformation, wished to be reduced to an entirely dependent, infantile state that would prevent him from continuing a hated adult existence. Yet it is not his desire for regression that disturbs us. Nor is it even this desire's physicalization via the insect image that we find uncanny. Rather, it is the creaturely enjoyment that Gregor takes in adapting to his insect body — which to my knowledge is a process never before documented — that bears out Freud's insight. Gregor's *becoming* an insect is a special instance of the frightening at the heart of which is a familiar urge toward self-infantilization and a fear of its consequences.

Importantly, when insectness is transferred from Gregor to the family/social order, it is an abstract entity that is now rendered uncanny.

Because the familiar-frightening quality that we discover in Gregor's inevitable, horrifying, but pleasurable adaptation to his insect body now belongs to his family — a collective — the "familiar" aspect of ourselves revealed by this unindividuated uncanniness has to do with our behavior as part of a group. Our reading now reflects back upon the Samsa family's process of transformation, which although muted until the all-important moment of transference, now springs into relief. Gregor's uncanniness, which has dominated our interest until now, fades. We sense now that our identification with the family includes us in a more general but even more damning critique.

Sartre, whose existential subject and way of seeing largely epitomize European modernism's primary tradition, takes metaphor as seriously as Kafka. However, because his model of Being is antagonistic (similar to Conrad's) rather than affective (like Kafka's), Sartre's Hive is quite different from Kafka's. Sartre knows that to figure a person as an insect or any other nonhuman creature or object involves an act of dehumanization. Philosophically, this act enlists the person so figured into one or more nonhuman categories, forcing upon that person a demeaning fellowship that obscures human uniqueness and, hence, the nature of freedom.[10] We may assume that Sartre recognizes the philosophical and aesthetic importance and the potential of the Self as Insect topos, for it is the reigning analogy of *The Flies*, a rewriting of Aeschylus's *Eumenides*. But since he, unlike Kafka, thinks that freedom is possible only when the individual consciously *accepts* alienation, which in his philosophy is the very source of human-being-ness and power, his use of the Hive topos follows a more Nietzschean path. And he intends that any attribution of the uncanny should follow suit, for it is the mass, society, that he condemns. He pictures society as enjoying its blindness, as fairly wallowing in its intellectual infantilism and superstitious barbarism. Instead of allowing, as Kafka does, that the self may *become* alienated from the social order, Sartrean existentialism asserts as a principle that humans are by *definition* singular, self-defining.[11] Moreover, according to this model not only society but nature is alien and inimically opposed to humankind. Hence, any unexamined, or assumed, social or natural sense of belonging is illusion, an instrument and symptom of self-enslavement. The true person, the fully human self, is so only to the degree that he or she realizes and accepts this double and absolute alienation. Action, then, issues from a will-to-power that is oddly uninformed by historical and social facts.[12]

Revealingly, in *The Flies*, while the citizens of Argos are described as "black beetles" (51) and are conflated with the flies that plague their "dead-and-alive . . . carrion city" (58), Orestes, the hero, is never figured as an insect. This detail is significant, because even though the unenlightened Orestes who enters the city of Argos is shown to be just as much a slave to ignorance as the Argites, Sartre dissociates him from the Hive. Sartre does so because the unenlightened Orestes's primary function is that of observer — he is a philosopher in the making, a less complicated Marlow. As such, even before Orestes discovers his freedom, his separateness from the collective, he anticipates the office of the insect analogy's sovereign observer to such a degree that, in order to avoid contradiction later, Sartre does not permit him to use the figure until after his transformation. Philosophically, Orestes has come to Argos to become free so that he may choose his path; rhetorically, he is here to learn how to use metaphors so that he will not be used by them; and in terms of our argument, his purpose is to obtain title to the Hive topos, to claim for himself its particular way of seeing.

In the original, soon after his return from the Trojan war, Agamemnon is murdered in his bath by his Queen, Clytemnestra. Their son, Orestes, commanded by Apollo, then kills her. But even Apollo cannot absolve him of this crime against nature. Hence, he is pursued by the Furies, ancient female spirits who seek to avenge his mother's blood. The play opens in the Delphic sanctuary of Pythian Apollo, where Apollo and the Furies establish their respective characters and alignments toward Orestes. But the bulk of the action occurs in Athens, where Orestes's fate is to be decided by a jury of citizens. After hearing the evidence, the twelve-member panel is evenly split. So the judge Athena casts the deciding vote for absolution. The Furies are enraged and must be persuaded — bribed, actually — to accept the verdict. Athena persuades them to cease their wandering and hounding and to live beneath the Acropolis as the city's domestic guardians.

Sartre's version has Orestes return to his native Argos after only recently learning his origin, for soon after Agamemnon's murder Aegistheus, the usurper, had him exiled. Orestes was so young at the time (three years of age) that he grew up not knowing himself. But now he is here to determine his "path." He explains his desire to his sister, Electra, to whom he has just revealed his identity and who urges him to flee: "Try to understand. I want to be a man who belongs to some place, a man among comrades. Only consider. Even the slave bent beneath his load, dropping with fatigue and staring dully at the ground a foot in front of him — why, even that poor slave can say he's in *his* town, as a tree is in a forest, or a leaf upon the tree. Argos is all around him, warm, compact, and comforting. Yes, Electra, I'd gladly be that slave and enjoy that feeling of drawing the city round me like a blanket and curling myself up in it. No, I shall not go" (91; Sartre's emphasis). This city that Orestes figures as a "warm blanket" is anything but. Aegistheus reigns absolutely, and to keep power he has the entire populace turn out once a year for a ceremony in which the unquiet dead are "released" from their mountain cavern. Even though the ceremony is a fabrication, so great is the city's and Aegistheus's guilt for Agamemnon's unavenged murder that they actually believe that the spirits descend upon and harry them. This day of meaningless confession and socially enforced madness is Sartre's picture of what comes of "belong[ing without choice] to some place, [of being] a man among comrades." He means it as an allegory whose barbarity and unashamed superstitiousness is supposed to evoke the sort of "collective" uncanniness that we have seen Kafka use to describe the Samsa family. Sartre would have this scene confront us with our complicity in, public justification of, and enjoyment in suffering. Orestes observes, but is not part of this madness. However, Sartre shows him to be blind as well. Our hero, who has thus far lived a life of wealth and travel, can think of belonging only as slavery. But since he does not yet grasp that he, too, is a slave and is, therefore, ignorant of this condition's true price, he is unaware how ironic his figures are.

Sartre wants us to see that Orestes misunderstands, indeed romanticizes, the condition of slavery and to connect his wrong thinking with his flawed and unconsciously ironic organic metaphors. In an effort to elucidate how his imaginary slave feels about his position in "*his* town," Orestes makes the following analogies: "as a tree is in a forest, or a leaf upon the tree." He is blind to what the slave, the trees, their leaves, and the forest all have in common: they all may be owned. While it is true that they live, their being is incomplete, less than human, only one step above dead matter.

For Sartre, the metaphoric function is the very source of the chimeras of false membership; confusing the symbol with reality is to become illusion's slave. Freedom, true human-being-ness, thus begins with rejecting inherited, unexamined symbols. Hence, the crucial moment of *The Flies* occurs when Orestes, having asked for and received a sign from

Zeus, realizes that he must make his own choices and pursue a life that he alone makes:

> *Electra* [*apprehensively*]: No, Philebus [Orestes's Athenian name], don't be stubborn. You asked the gods for orders [about whether to leave Argos or to stay]; now you have them.
> *Orestes:* Orders? What do you mean? Ah yes, the light round that big stone. But it's not for me, that light; from now on I'll take no one's orders, neither man's nor god's.
> *Electra:* You're speaking in riddles.
> *Orestes:* What a change has come on everything, and, oh, how far away you seem! Until now I felt something warm and living around me, like a friendly presence. That something has just died. What emptiness! What endless emptiness, as far as the eye can reach! [He takes some steps away from her.] Night is coming on. The air is getting chilly, isn't it? But what was it—what was it that died just now?
> *Electra:* Philebus — (92–93)

Philebus, the enslaved self that was Orestes, has died. This person was defined by his need to belong; thus, with Philebus also passes away that illusory "something warm and living" that he had felt "around" him like a "friendly presence." In its place is nothing, an "endless emptiness." Suddenly free from the mediation of symbols, Orestes's first perception is his state of absolute singularity, his isolation from everything and everyone that he once imagined himself to be close to. Sartre dramatizes this state by having Orestes "take . . . some steps away from" Electra.

Until this moment Orestes has only wished to be close to his sister and to belong to Argos. Now he sees his relation to the city and its people differently. He tells Electra: "I must go down — do you understand — I must go down into the depths, among you. For you are living, all of you, at the bottom of a pit. [*He goes up to Electra.*] You are *my* sister, Electra, and that city is *my* city. *My* sister. [*He takes her arm.*]" (93; Sartre's emphasis). Philebus/Orestes wished to be possessed; he was acted upon. Now Orestes is the possessor; agency is his. He approaches Electra and claims his relation to her physically (he takes her arm) and through language (he renames her with a repetitive use of the possessive pronoun: "You are *my* sister . . . *My* sister"). He similarly chooses to claim Argos, which at first he calls "*my* city." Furthermore, and most importantly, his sense of placement vis-à-vis Electra and Argos has changed. Because he knows himself to be distanced from them, he speaks of them as "living . . . at the bottom of a pit" — they are equivalent to the "strange prisoners" who are chained in Plato's cave, unaware that outside their "pit" there is a world of light and self-determination.

Orestes's moment of enlightenment is also a moment of choice, of knowing, in fact, that one has already chosen. But more than merely claiming his birthright and his city, he chooses to save them from themselves. He will "go down into the depths, among" these blind and fallen people.[13] Like Greene's Rollo Martins and Harry Lime, we are to know Orestes by how he sees. Electra, who is frightened by his transformation, asks Orestes what he intends to do. He invites Electra to gaze with him down upon Argos: "there it lies, rose-red in the sun, buzzing with men and flies, drowsing its doom away in the languor of a summer afternoon. It fends me off with its high walls, red roofs, locked doors. And yet it's mine for the taking; I've felt that since this morning. You, too, Electra, are mine for the taking — and I'll take you, too. I'll turn into an axe and hew those walls asunder, I'll rip open the bellies of those stolid houses and there will steam up from the gashes a stench of rotting food and incense. I'll be an iron wedge driven into the city, like a wedge rammed into the heart of an oak tree" (93). The new Orestes uses metaphors differently than the old. Before he knew himself and the uncompromising nature of freedom, he wished to become part of something, to merge with an order greater than himself: to become a tree in a forest, a leaf on a tree, one citizen among many. Now, however, any such order is the Other. The organic metaphor of the tree, for instance, is now an external and passive substance whose Being is to be violently altered. It is to be split by Orestes the "iron wedge." The new Orestes figures himself only as made things, tools: instruments whose office is to shape the sleeping "dead and alive" cosmos according to human will.

Orestes stands in Aeneas's place, Argos in Carthage's. Aeneas sees Carthage's towers as "confront[ing]"; Orestes speaks of Argos as "fend-[ing] me off with its high walls, red roofs, locked doors." And, because of the past's presence in all our minds, predictably, appropriately, there are insects in Argos as well: "there it lies, rose-red in the sun, buzzing with men and flies."[14] For my purposes, this is the play's most significant moment — but not only because it echoes the insect analogy of the play's title. The new Orestes exists only as long as he ensures his difference and thereby keeps his distance from nature and society — and Zeus as well. For as we discover, Zeus is merely a servant — indeed perhaps even the creation — of "dead and alive" humans' desire to be enslaved by symbols. The first act's establishing stage directions name Zeus the "god of flies and death." Now while Zeus may have sent this plague of flies in response to his worshipers' desires and is, therefore, a servant of human wishes, he is no less a character of presence. Zeus wishes Orestes to leave Argos, tempting him to turn from the existential path. At every opportunity it is he, Zeus, who insists upon figuring the Argives as insects.

Interestingly, Zeus also uses the insect analogy instrumentally. For instance, when asked by Orestes's companion and teacher, the Tutor, what the flies signify, the disguised Zeus tells him: "They are a symbol. But if you want to know what the gods did, look around you. See that old creature over there, creeping away like a beetle on her little black feet, hugging the walls. Well, she's a good specimen of the squat black vermin that teem in every cranny of this town" (55). Zeus would have the Tutor see these people as less than human, unworthy of consideration. Perhaps he hopes the Tutor will so instruct Orestes. One would think that as part of his new role the *Übermensch* Orestes would oppose himself to Zeus and his language just as surely as he has defined himself against his old self and its/his analogically expressed longing for enslavement. But this he cannot do absolutely, for it is the nature of the Sartrean free person to transcend and so tower above it all.

Sartre's definition of what it is to be human assumes a division between subject and object, individual and collective essences that makes his existentialism nearly a different species from Kafka's. Kafka moves us to hate what the Self as Insect implies; Sartre awards it to the free human like a diploma. This contradiction of a former slave enslaving others with a metaphor — if it truly is a contradiction — is revealed when Orestes speaks to Electra of "his city": "there it lies, rose-red in the sun, buzzing with men and flies." Although he does not, as is Zeus's practice, use metaphor to mix their substances, he nonetheless speaks of men and flies as existing on the same level and unified by a common activity. In sum, Orestes has difficulty seeing humans and flies as other than interchangeable, a confusion that may be attributed as much to his spatial sovereignty as to his philosophical position. Indeed, the two are inextricably related.

Although Sartre and Kafka agree that the Self as Insect topos is indispensable to picturing the modern condition, that our sympathy for Gregor is channeled through and controlled by his figuration as an insect suggests that, in contrast to Sartre's position, Kafka believes that at some fundamental level suffering joins us to the rest of creation. Kafkian suffering is at once more amorphous and pervasive than the Sartrean; it is an inescapable and shaping pattern that cannot be directly grasped. Hence, if it were possible for him to tell us what he thinks of Sartrean existentialism, I suspect that he would at the very least express reservations about Sartre's insect analogy. Indeed, since *The Metamorphosis* is a parable singularly concerned with what it means to see another as an insect, I would not be surprised if Kafka were taken aback by Orestes's almost offhand assumption that it is his right to use the Hive as he wishes, that he regards this ancient and ethically loaded metaphor as merely one among many instruments available for the prosecution of his will.

However we may disagree with his use of the Self as Insect, Sartre reminds us that the Hive topos is intimately connected with the fantasies of power that undergird action and give us title to the objects that we act upon. But given the dialectical nature of the Hive, its tendency to manifest itself in antithetical complements, it should not then surprise us that the image of the insect as powerless, loathsome, and virtually inanimate is far from the last word on the subject. An individual roach is certainly vulnerable, but it is also a member of a species that is admirably durable, and even courageous. However, these virtues are alloyed with, perhaps even stem from, blindness. Kafka himself suggests as much. In her essay "The Impossibility of Being Kafka," Cynthia Ozick quotes from one of Kafka's letters written in 1920. His subject is the "Jew-hatred" of his fellow citizens of Prague; he is thinking about leaving his city: "I've spent all afternoon out in the streets bathing in Jew-hatred. . . . *Prašive plemeno* — filthy brood — is what I heard them call the Jews. Isn't it only natural to leave a place where one is so bitterly hated? . . . The heroism of staying put in spite of it all is the heroism of the cockroach, which also won't be driven out of the bathroom" (80).

A fine example of the cockroach used as a symbol for the alienated person and to evoke the bittersweet stubbornness of life may be found in Tewfik al-Hakim's play, *Fate of a Cockroach*. Al-Hakim seems almost to be answering Kafka's letter, for the drama's central crisis involves a cockroach in a bathroom. *Fate* is a thematically complicated and strongly allegorical drama about three distinct orders of beings — ants, cockroaches, and human beings — whose shared sentience goes unrecognized because of differences in size. The play's first act treats the insect realm. We are introduced to the King of the cockroaches, his wife the Queen, and a few of their subjects. Soon we discover that this King is self-appointed, because unlike the ants, who are naturally bureaucratic and therefore a continual threat despite their relative smallness, the cockroaches are by nature free, unable to organize themselves even in the interest of self-protection. They have no government, and according to the King, his species's "characteristics" may be reduced to the principle of "every cockroach striv[ing] for his daily bread" (3). Thus, his self-appointment, for no cockroach takes orders from another.

The King's experiments with hierarchy and his courtly pretensions satirize monarchy. And the cockroaches as a species are similarly used, for the way that their nature mingles freedom with selfishness exposes the dangers of a society founded solely upon self-interest. However, al-Hakim intends for these roaches to be more than allegorical functions. They think and feel similarly to human beings and even develop a religion to explain our actions, which to them occur on such a scale as to be mysterious. And in their realm as in ours, especially when it comes to explaining the inexplicable, there is disagreement. In this instance, the Priest and the Savant (both also self-appointed) draw different conclusions from the Priest's "miraculous" rescue from the ants:

Savant: Have the gods ever listened to you?

Priest: Naturally.

Savant: When was that?

Priest: Once, I was lying ill in a corner when I saw the armies of
ants approaching. I was certain that I was done for. I called upon
the gods with a prayer that came from the depths of my heart.
Suddenly I saw that something looking like a large dark cloud full
of water had descended from the skies and swooped down upon
the armies of ants and swept them quite away, clearing them off
the face of the earth.

Queen: How extraordinary!

Savant: The scientific composition to this cloud is well known: it
consists of a network of many threads from a large piece of
moistened sacking.

> *King:* Neither the cloud's origin nor yet its scientific composition is
> of interest. What is of importance is who sent it down and wiped
> away the ants with it.
> *Priest:* Speak to him, O King, and ask him who sent it down from
> the sky and with it destroyed the armies of the ants. Who? Who?
> *Savant:* That is a question that science cannot answer. However, I
> very much doubt the existence of any connection between this
> priest's prayer and the descent of this cloud. (16–17)

Beyond poking fun at both reason and religion, al-Hakim uses this
conversation to show how one's place in the scheme of things controls
vision and hence the very terms by which understanding is pursued.[15]
His instrument in this regard is one of the literary cockroach's subtler
offices, that of evoking a species of blindness that we associate with extraordinary gustatory contentment. Sartre, as I have mentioned, uses the
fly for a similar purpose. But there is something unique about the cockroach in this regard, which another instance from a very different text by
the Scottish fabulist Alasdair Gray shall make clearer. In "Time Travel,"
a retired physicist — who has gone a bit mad from mathematics and solitude — speaks of those people who still reject his discovery of a unified
field theory. He tells us that "my discovery [that everything is connected
to everything else] angered many people by proving that loneliness is a
convenient form of ignorance" (123). These people, whom he first titles
"hearty pragmatists," he then figures as cockroaches: "People with this
self-centered view cannot be faulted. They want to be nothing but cockroaches in the larder of the universe, so have no interest in the rest of
the palace." The speaker is both far from ignorant and terribly lonely,
so there is unconscious irony in his pronouncement that "loneliness is a
convenient form of ignorance." And I think that Gray is suggesting that
the intensity of the speakers' work in physics has made him into something of a cockroach, for in a sense his interest in the "larder of the universe" has been so great that he has no time or inclination to take an
"interest in the rest of the palace" of human existence.

Like al-Hakim, Gray uses the cockroach to signify a peculiarly human
sort of near-sightedness that stems from our need for physical as well as
metaphysical certainty.[16] And certainly there is some of this need in Gregor Samsa as well as his family, which may be yet another factor for why
we tend to recall Gregor as a cockroach. Therefore, for this and other

reasons, we may observe that in modern literature, the cockroach subtly connotes a degree of human-being-ness that is rarely discovered in other insect symbols.[17] Al-Hakim knows this about his roaches and therefore complicates their nature, moving them closer to the human by further exploring the causal relationship between what one sees and how one thinks.

These creatures are like us in that they not only apprehend their sentience but discuss it among themselves. And, again very much like human beings, they use their self-awareness — which the playwright delicately shows to be a precious faculty — for lesser ends; namely, to favorably distinguish themselves from all other creatures, especially the ants:

> *King:* [Unlike the ants] . . . we are certainly in no need of food, of the storage of food, or of war.
> *Savant:* And so we are superior creatures.
> *King:* Without doubt. We attack no living creature; we harm no one. We do not know greed or the desire to acquire and store things away.
> *Queen:* Are there no creatures superior to us?
> *Savant:* No, we are the most superior creatures on the face of the earth.
> *Queen:* That's right, and yet we suffer because of those other, inferior creatures.
> *Savant:* Inferiority is always a cause of trouble, but we must be patient. We cannot bring those creatures who are lower than us up to the same standard of civilization as ourselves. To each his own nature, his own environment, and his own circumstances. The ant, for instance, is concerned solely with food. As for us, we are more concerned with knowledge.
> *Queen:* Knowledge?
> *Savant:* Certainly. These long whiskers we have we do not use only to touch food. Very often we touch with them things which are not eaten, merely in order to seek out their nature, to discover their reality. (20–21)

The Savant's notion that roaches are "more concerned with knowledge" than food is comical, because he has just finished advising the King that if he wants to form an army of roaches for a raid against the ants, then food is the only means of assembling enough of them. And once assembled, the Savant himself admits that they would merely fill their bellies and go their separate ways. Yet al-Hakim also, and tenderly I might add, shows that these roaches are not entirely slaves to their bellies: they possess curiosity, taking an aesthetic and intellectual pleasure in experience for its own sake.

Unfortunately, it is curiosity that leads the King to investigate the bathtub, which the Savant has tantalizingly described as "a vast chasm — probably a large lake . . . that . . . is sometimes without water, at others full of water. . . . [And when dry] it has a very beautiful appearance. Its sides are smooth and snow-white — as though strewn with jasmine flowers" (14). The King falls into the empty tub but cannot escape because of its walls' smoothness. The very quality that brought him pleasure now threatens his survival. But despite the fact that no one can aid him, he continues trying to scale the tub's walls — while above him his wife cries her grief, the Savant rationalizes, and the Priest prays.

The second act opens in the same apartment, but in the human realm. It is early morning and Adil, a hard-working, hen-pecked worrier ripe for a crisis of Being is called to the bathroom by his wife Samia, who wants him to kill the roach. These humans are in no way aware of the roach's sentience, which makes the drama all the more affecting. For while we know that the King is suffering along with the rest of the roaches, through ignorance the human characters are free to make of him and his struggle what they will. As we shall presently see, Adil gives cosmic significance to the roach's struggle: in Orestian fashion he claims it as a symbol for existence. But al-Hakim would have us view this "symbol" more modestly and pointedly: as a projection of Adil's otherwise repressed will-to-power.

As I read it, the situation that grows out of Adil's fixation upon the roach is meant to satirize Sartrean existentialism, most pointedly its tenet that the "free" and therefore "fully" human person is able to transcend social and biological determinants and thus cannot help viewing, is even entitled to view, all other unenlightened creatures instrumentally. Adil sees the cockroach and becomes so intent upon its struggle that he refuses to kill it. But it is not compassion that he feels for the cockroach. Rather, he sees its stubborn, repeated attempts to escape as a drama of self-reliance, as an experiment in "will-power":

Samia: Am I going to have my bath?
Adil: Go ahead! Have I stopped you?

Samia: And the cockroach?

Adil: I am responsible only for myself.

Samia: Which means that you intend to leave it like this inside the bath?

Adil: I think it's better to leave it as it is so that it can solve its problem by itself.

Samia: Are you joking, Adil? Is this a time for joking?

Adil: On the contrary, I'm being extremely serious. Do you not see that it's still trying to save itself, so let's leave it to try.

Samia: Until when?

Adil: We cannot — either you or I — decide when. That depends upon its will-power — and up until now it has shown no intention of discontinuing its attempts. Look! So far it is showing no sign of being tired. (37)

Samia quickly loses patience with her husband's strange behavior and, intent on getting her bath so that she may go to work, she leaves to get the insecticide. Adil locks himself in the bathroom and begins speaking to the cockroach, warning it, encouraging it: "They want to kill you with insecticide. Don't be afraid — I'll not open the door. Stick to it! Stick to it!" (38).

Kafka's influence becomes apparent when the phone rings. It is their employer. Samia's concern is getting to work and what her boss will think of her and her husband. She converses with her employer about her husband's problem, and the company doctor is dispatched. A little later, instead of a "locksmith," as in *The Metamorphosis*, she talks about getting a carpenter to break down the door. In this instance, the parallel between the Kafka and the al-Hakim is expressed by the family's desire to use an external agent to penetrate the transforming subject's private space.

Adil remains oblivious to his wife. During her telephone conversation, according to the stage directions, Adil is "engrossed in watching the cockroach. He makes gestures to it as he follows it climbing and falling down; by sighs and miming he expresses all his emotions and concern" (40). Just as Kafka's Gregor becomes progressively more insectlike, so does Adil identify more and more strongly with what he sees in the struggling roach. He begins by watching only, then for a while he speaks to it, and now "by sighs and miming he expresses all his emotions and concern." It is as if his human psychological complexity is being replaced by a pathologically intense motive to identify with an insect, the least of God's creatures — but, sadly, the terms of this identification are determined by his position as distant observer within the Self as Insect's structure. Through this change in Adil's psyche al-Hakim shows us that the single-minded pursuit of metaphysical certainty is itself a source of blindness.

Key to understanding the playwright's meaning are Adil's and Samia's antithetical personalities and how the domestic situation ensures their conflict. Importantly, as in *The Metamorphosis*, we are to grasp this scene's immorality by virtue of its opposite. Our fantasy of and longing for a loving family, which together have their source in the inherited patterns that Sartre rejects, are here unspoken but necessary elements of the drama. The play allows no Sartrean a priori rejection of the family, society, or nature; for good or ill the characters must make their choices within and according to their roles.

Samia is selfish, money-hungry, shrewish. Adil, who is much more sensitive and contemplative than his wife, has been psychologically beaten by her. The constant, unendurable tension at home, a meaningless job, and the prospect of a tedious, penurious future combine to threaten his sanity. He cannot escape, so he casts his imagination upon the first object with which he can identify. As for Samia, she has no love for anyone but herself and reveals her true feelings for her husband by how she classifies him: in an echo of that moment when Grete denounces her brother, when irritated by his refusal to open the door, Samia refers to Adil as "a creature." She also calls him a "parrot," for so great is his preoccupation with the roach that Adil merely "automatically echoe[s] her words" (41). As with both *The Metamorphosis* and *The Third Man*, this drama's mode is one of "descent." Adil, who has long felt himself to be trapped and watched, replicates this pattern — except now he is the watcher and hence a torturer. But he is not actively so. We never get the sense that he understands himself to have title to agency. Thus, it seems that we should not blame him for his inaction's results, for we have seen that his nature is such that he can only be dehumanized by forces outside of his control. Nevertheless, even as we allow him victim status, we still hold him culpable for allowing the King unnecessary suffering. Al-Hakim is walking a thin line here: on the one hand, because he is preparing for a Kafkaesque transfer of insectness, he has Adil's culpability decline quickly and in direct proportion to his increasing vulnerability. On the other, he needs Adil to be responsible for choosing an interpretation of the roach's struggle that satisfies his desire for power at the same time that it justifies his weakness. This particular "cosmicification" of the cockroach enables Adil to proceed as if his failure to act according to societal norms (i.e., with compassion) is right.

To underscore and develop this critique, al-Hakim now brings in the company doctor who, after attempting to understand Adil's behavior psychoanalytically (another occasion for satire), also begins to see the roach's struggle as emblematic of the "struggle of life." Al-Hakim's point throughout is that human beings all too frequently use suffering — which should arouse our sympathy, consequently binding us to our fellow creatures and to each other, and most importantly moving us to compassionate action — as a screen upon which to project our personal anxieties and rationalizations. The roach is just a roach trying to get out of a tight spot, and because the reader knows him to be sentient we alone are sensitive to what he must be feeling. But Adil will not or cannot see the roach other than as a key element of a symbolic drama that he seems unwilling to disturb, perhaps because he himself has invented it. Adil stands in the same position vis-à-vis the King as the Queen, Priest, and Savant. But while they desperately wish to help but cannot, Adil can but chooses not to. The playwright hereby suggests that Adil's compulsion to watch without taking action makes him much more of an insect than the roaches. Al-Hakim drives home this point by presenting as genuine Adil's distress because he is "unable to attain the magnificent level reached by the cockroaches" (67). There are several levels of irony here. First, Adil feels that he cannot "attain" the level of an insect, and yet he has — but not in the way that he desires. Second, he thinks that the cockroach exists on a "magnificent level." He says this of a creature so small that it thinks a bathtub is a lake and so much a slave to its gut that despite its intelligence it is prey for the much smaller ant. Yet another, broader irony is that in this universe cockroaches and human beings are nearly psychologically identical but incapable of recognizing the fact. Thus, the roaches make gods of us and we make symbols of them.

In the end, the cook Umm Attiya, runs the bath; the King is drowned and then flicked into a corner. When the ants appear to carry him off, they, together with their dinner, are eliminated with a wet rag. Although stimulated by the roach's death, we cannot say that Adil grieves. He merely shifts his pathologically intense identification to a new object, the "extraordinary discipline" of the ants. It is only after all these creatures are cleaned away that he seems capable of a fully human response:

he curses the cook. At this moment I sense that Adil could recover his humanity. But, unfortunately, as if a switch has been thrown, Samia, who so long as the doctor (a company representative) was present had at least attempted to restrain her bad nature, once again begins rudely ordering Adil about, treating him as a thing. When thus again confronted by the unchanged facts of his loveless marriage and his meaningless existence, he withdraws into a strange silence, only to break it by screaming at Samia that her demands are "Understooooood!" What is "understooooood" the playwright does not, wisely, make entirely clear. But the play's last line suggests that Adil now clearly recognizes his desire for extermination, for complete erasure: he calls for Umm Attiya to "bring the bucket and rag and wipe me out of existence" (76).

Like his models Kafka and Sartre, al-Hakim treats the Hive philosophically. Fully aware that the Hive topos's power issues from its division of the world into antithetical and necessarily simplified categories, al-Hakim uses it to show us the blindness and cruelty that attends the conversion of living things into symbols, into mere instruments. For example, that Adil sees the roach only instrumentally, as a symbol of struggle, and consequently makes no attempt to alleviate its suffering, suggests that he is incapable of compassion. Even though he strongly identifies with and claims to admire the cockroach, as soon as it is dead, without pause or reflection he turns to another object so that he may continue his voyeuristic study of the "struggle for life" (69). *The Fate of a Cockroach* thereby suggests that the "thought experiment," an instrumental use of metaphor that we have located in Plato and identified as important to Mandeville's experiment with sociological projection (and which Sartre evidences is one of the Hive's most common modernist applications), is inherently flawed as a means of investigating the meaning of the self and its relationship with the cosmos.

But al-Hakim takes issue with more than the implications of Sartre's instrumental seeing: he would have us question Sartre's insistence that right action necessarily issues from a condition of existential isolation. In this regard, consider that even though Adil is not physically transformed into a symbol of alienation, like Gregor Samsa he nonetheless and progressively loses perspective on the symbolic process *because of and in direct proportion to the degree of his existential condition*. Instead of being moved toward Sartrean freedom by his isolation, Adil falls prey to the unconsidered symbol. And because he cannot know the symbol as a convention that blocks or determines his vision, his psychology becomes that of a disengaged observer — a role that, because it deprives him of agency, only ensures that his suffering will continue. Adil's descent into pathology thereby confronts us with an aspect of the Hive topos that Sartre would repress. Not only does Adil's personal version of the Hive allow him to play god, it makes him the type of god appropriate to a cosmos that we hope does not exist. Adil models a supreme being who, if he sees us at all, either does not understand our suffering or care about it.

Adil's God (Adil-as-God?) returns us to the universe of Shakespeare's Gloucester, for there is a distinct possibility that the god(s) might even take pleasure in our struggle. This is a view shared by Thomas Hardy. He expresses it thus in *Tess of the D'Urbervilles* with the image of Tess and Marian laboring in the swede-field of Flintcomb-Ash:

> The swede-field in which she and her companion were set hacking was a stretch of a hundred odd acres, in one patch, on the highest ground of the farm, rising above stony lanchets or lynchets — the outcrop of siliceous veins in the chalk formation, composed of myriads of loose white flints in bulbous, cusped, and phallic shapes. The upper half of each turnip had been eaten off by the livestock, and it was the business of the two women to grub up the lower or earthy half of the root with a hooked fork called a hacker, that it might be eaten also. Every leaf of the vegetable having already been consumed, the whole field was in colour a desolate drab; it was a complexion without features, as if a face, from chin to brow, should be only an expanse of skin. The sky wore, in another colour, the same likeness; a white vacuity of countenance with the lineaments gone. So these two upper and nether visages confronted each other all day long, the brown face looking up at the white face, without anything standing between them but the two girls crawling over the surface of the former like flies. (281)

This scene may be interpreted as a version of our familiar tableau. We are placed above Tess and Marian and are invited to see them as two insects, in this instance, as flies. But these flies are crawling over an immense, featureless brown *face*, and above them, equally huge, but "in another colour [is] the same likeness; a white vacuity of countenance with the lineaments gone." The earth and the sky are represented as gods, but their faces are "vacu[ous]," "featureless." They have no eyes with which to see the girls' sufferings, and are thus, perhaps, oblivious to them. But since these girls are "crawling over the . . . [brown god's face] like flies," Hardy implies that at any time they might be crushed or brushed away by a larger and impervious force.

Based upon the examples above, all of which are resonant with the descending mode, I would generalize that to be figured as an isolated insect and/or to become a subject of the social order guarantees that one will be dehumanized and then exterminated. However, these same instances also suggest that — when reframed as a calculating and uncompassionate psychology associated with the role of disengaged observer — the quality, or essence, of insectness is to a degree separable from the insect image. Kafka, for instance, makes especially clear that this psychology may be transferred from the "insect" to one or more human characters, an aspect of the Hive that Sartre did not seem to allow for. It then follows that there may be alternative uses of the isolated insect, ones that do not determine that to be an insect is to be either blind (a slave: absolutely determined by and subject to the Hive of sociohistorical conditions) or a moral monster (free, a master: divorced from and external to the cultural whole).

These thoughts are a preface to a consideration of two culturally distinct responses to the Sartrean Hive that are distinguished by an interest in exploring a socially constructed and *approximate* universal identity rather than one self-realized, transcendent, and absolute.[18] Instead of assuming that one may, in Sartrean fashion, stand outside society and history and thereby acquire a "true" identity, Kobo Abe's *The Woman in the Dunes* and A. S. Byatt's *Morpho Eugenia* illustrate a post-Sartrean — which is to say, a postmodern — model of the Self as Insect and its role in narratives of identity formation. Unlike Sartre's Orestes, characters in these texts must remake themselves without the advantage of an uncorrupted (i.e., antisocial and *simplified*) perspective. In the absence of visual sovereignty, character is discovered and shaped gradually and within the confines of affective relations; thus, right action must be determined and taken within the social Hive — and not without ambivalence. Hence, in comparison with the sovereignty promised by Sartre's model, the self-determination realized within the postmodern Hive is modest, but more human in scale and more achievable.

POSTMODERN VERSIONS OF

THE SELF AS INSECT

*Primitive beekeeping consisted of little more than
providing the hives, and killing the bees (for instance by
plunging the hive into boiling water) to get the honey and
the wax. In ancient Egypt, smoke was used to drive bees
from their hive, and by ancient Roman times bees were
fed. At some time in the Middle Ages, beekeepers devised
a form of protection to wear when handling their hives.*

*Until the sixteenth century, a significant age for the
honey bee, the beekeeper's calendar remained virtually
unchanged; in early summer he caught and hived the
swarms which issued; in late summer he killed the bees
in most of his hives, cut out the combs, and strained
the honey from the wax; and in the fall, if necessary,
he provided food in the remaining hives, which he
overwintered. Burning sulphur was commonly used for
killing the hives.*

*Little was understood as to what went on inside the
hive, for the events there could not be seen.*

Gordon F. Townsend and Eva Crane,
"History of Apiculture"

*Mead was the ideal nectar of the Scandinavian nations, which they
expected to quaff in heaven out of the skulls of their enemies; and, as
may reasonably be supposed, the liquor which they exalted thus highly
in their imaginary celestial banquets, was not forgotten at those
which they really indulged in upon earth. Hence may be inferred the
great attention which must have been paid to the culture of the bee in
those days, or there could not have been an adequate supply of honey
for the production of mead, to satisfy the demand of such thirsty tribes.*
    Edward Bevan, *The Honey-bee,* quoted in
    T. Michael Peters, Insects and Human Society

Provisional Definitions of Modernism and Postmodernism

The term "postmodern," which first appeared in literary criticism in
the late 1950s "to lament the levelling off of the modernist movement," [1]
has since become the accepted (but highly contested and variously defined) title for a new sensibility that arose during the Cold War — for
my purposes — in reaction to the psychology and aesthetic epitomized
by Sartrean existentialism. As I have discussed, Sartrean existentialism
conceives each human being as a singular and self-defining entity to
whom both culture and nature are alien and inimically opposed. The
true person, the fully human self, is so only to the degree that he or she
realizes and accepts this double and absolute alienation. Action, then,
issues from a will-to-power that transcends all things external to the Cartesian *cogito*: especially suspect are inherited symbols and aesthetic systems (for example, the Hive and rhetoric) and all sources of intuitive
or local knowledge, affiliation, and pleasure, such as the body, family,
community, and native geography. Like the subject it posits, Sartrean
existentialism is viable in direct proportion to the degree to which objects external to the *cogito* are simplified and kept separate. It is apparent,
therefore, that when used as an aesthetic base Sartrean existentialism is
peculiarly subject to exhaustion.

Steven Connor, author of *Postmodernist Culture,* recognizes the aesthetic limits of Sartrean existentialism — albeit at a remove. His focus
is literary modernism, whose exhaustion, he observes, is widely considered to be an essential precondition for the experiments that led to what
we now classify as postmodern literature. In Connor's view, the failure of modernism was the inevitable product of its emphasis on self-

sufficient form and what he calls its "subjectivism." Connor generalizes that modernist texts display an "aesthetic of authorial detachment, in which the author . . . removes himself, god-like, from the work." He argues that modernism's "aesthetic of extreme artistry" determines that "the work of literary creation [which images and furthers the work of self-creation] . . . can now no longer be represented as the humble sub-jugation of the will to the task of representing the world [as in realism], or conforming to a body of aesthetic precepts [to include inherited con-ventions such as the Hive]." And Connor's further observations about modernist art reiterate what I have been saying about Sartrean aesthet-ics and subject formation: "the [modernist] commitment to produce a work of art that will know no other rules but its own, and will transform the vulgar contingency of worldly relations into purified aesthetic terms, requires an extremity of vigilance, knowledge and mastery on the part of the artist, who is now divine artificer rather than humble workman" (107–8). The process through which Sartre's Orestes becomes fully hu-man hinges upon and dramatizes exactly the "extremity of vigilance" that Connor describes. It is through "knowledge" of his existential con-dition that Orestes gains "mastery" of himself and an instrumental ("purif[ying]") perspective on metaphor, thereby becoming his own "di-vine artificer" with power over a passive and inferior creation.

Clearly, this model of an isolated and unitary self divorced from his-tory and culture no longer speaks to how many people feel themselves to be in the world. For example, one of our moment's defining aesthet-ics, multiculturalism, is only one aspect of a notion of Being and a model of *complex* identity (a self created through a negotiation between global and local systems and objects of identification) that are both resonant with the facts of globalization. This is not to say, however, that either the existential subject or modernism's universalizing claims have been supplanted. As will be demonstrated through a close examination of two culturally distinct but rhetorically similar postmodern versions of the Self as Insect — the first used by Kobo Abe in *Woman in the Dunes*, and the second by A. S. Byatt in *Morpho Eugenia* — the Sartrean/modernist existential subject has been accepted in a variety of cultures as an arma-ture for the formation of postmodern identity, but not unconditionally. In place of narratives that reduce the world to fuel for existentialist epiphany and artistic transcendence of the local — for example, James Joyce's *Portrait of the Artist as a Young Man* — Abe's and Byatt's similarly detail Orestes's domestication. The protagonists of *Woman* and *Morpho* are remarkably similar: each is an alienated and rational observer — significantly — an *entomologist* who through experience and love comes to recognize and to accept a more limited but richer existence. Although they differ as to particulars, Abe and Byatt agree that to be fully human is to belong to a Hive, that — like it or not — the full sweetness of life must be obtained through relations with others and in dialogue with inherited symbols and other cultural patterns.

Sartrean Existentialism and the Challenge of Orestes

Sartre, however, attempts to get his poetic honey the old-fashioned way, by killing the Hive. Like his early modern predecessors and Plato before them, Sartre wants the power of inherited aesthetic forms — but he would have it poetry-free. As I have discussed, Sartre's method is to use the Hive technically, as philosophically as possible — which is to say without either reducing the human-being-ness of others or submitting to the poetic object's aesthetic invitations.[2] However, Sartre does not entirely succeed on either count. Even though Orestes's sovereign view of Argos, the collective, enables him to perceive it as alien and to define himself against it, this act of definition nonetheless commits him to a relationship with his opposite. By this I mean that, although using the Hive involves categorization — a rational operation that enables an attribution of essence and difference — any such logical extension of the Hive's structural implications remains grounded in a primal and equivocal analogy between human and insect, self and Other. And since analogy tends to merge the substance of its constituent objects, definition within the Hive's charged space is mutual. Even as the sovereign observer constructs the Other with his or her gaze, by its very nature the Other, albeit passively, reciprocates.

The presence of and resistance to the Other defines Orestes, whom Sartre envisions as superior Everyman, the type for a man unyoked from any and all inherited associations and memberships except for those he chooses. The new Orestes knows metaphor to be illusion. Hence, he commands it; he stands beyond narrative and, therefore, must make his own path. Because Orestes is truest to his nature when in the position of uninvolved observer, however, Sartre is keenly aware that his new man is in danger of agential impotence, ethical bankruptcy. Unless Sartre gets

Nietzschean Orestes down from his hill and into society, he will remain a social nonentity who, in the final analysis, may not be all that human. Hence, Sartre defines the existential life as one of action, the sort that is both *necessarily* good and socially efficacious. In this sense Orestes embodies Plato's motive to domesticate the crowd through a philosophized poetic. Although it embodies a motive that now seems reactionary, Sartre claimed that his poetic was revolutionary and expressed a universal psychology.

Sartre claims for existential humans a universal potential and the title to it, both of which he establishes in the Cartesian *cogito*, which to him is the only absolute certainty available to all persons. To Sartre, without foundation in the *cogito*, "all views are only probable, and a doctrine of probability which is not bound to a truth dissolves into thin air" (*HE*, 51). In a move that seeks to bridge the gap between subjectivism and praxis, Sartre further claims that the existential "subjectivity we have thus arrived at, and which we have claimed to be truth, is not strictly an individual subjectivity, for . . . one discovers in the *cogito* not only himself, but others as well. . . . the man who becomes aware of himself through the *cogito* also perceives all others, and he perceives them as the condition of his own existence" (51). Universalism, perhaps — but only on the existentialist's terms and to the existentialist's advantage. Even though Sartre claims that the existential state is the "universal human condition," a seemingly rock solid foundation for connection between human beings, he nonetheless requires for his system an Other that is absolutely different from and qualitatively inferior to the existential subject. Orestes perceives the Other only as "the condition of his own existence." "It" is at his service; "it" is an instrument of self-making. The Sartrean Other is not even a reflection, however inverted, of the existential subject, for any such mirroring implies at least the potential for some order of reciprocal relations. Even though the "the man who becomes aware of himself through the *cogito*" may "reconstitute within himself the [Other's] configuration" (53), the reverse is unthinkable.

But Sartre has more than philosophical reasons to reject the self that "becomes" via what he considers some vague reciprocal relationship with the Other. More specifically, as pertains to figurative language, reciprocal "becoming" implies that poetic analogies have agency. The problem is, therefore, both rhetorical and philosophical: while the rational analogy contributes a certainty and clarity to Sartre's project, the poetic tends to blur boundaries, suggesting that we must settle for *approximate* knowledge and relations. To assent to poetic mediation, then, would commit one to a skeptical, pragmatic stance toward any absolute human universal. Indeed, the participants in such a mutually defining and, therefore, approximate relationship would have to act in spite of and, indeed, according to their different and partial understandings. Because limits would have to be accepted, considerations of difference and an ad hoc way of making knowledge would take center stage. Because the Cartesian *cogito* reserves power entirely for the seeing subject (who, below, Sartre identifies as European), it could not serve as the ultimate ground for ethical conduct during such approximate encounters.

Sartre is the antagonist *par excellence*: self and Other, subject and object, must remain distinct, opposed. According to Zygmunt Bauman's summary of Sartrean ego-formation, the "ego is born of self-knowledge . . . [that] is triggered by the gaze of the Other: a scrutinizing gaze, evaluating gaze, 'objectifying' gaze. The Other looks upon me as an object. . . . This is not so much discovery, as being discovered; an assault which prompts my resistance. My 'awakening' to myself (if Sartre used that phrase) would be unthinkable unless as an act of resistance. I can become a self, an ego, only when gathering my strength *against* the Other" (Bauman's emphasis).[3] Yet, in apparent contradiction to this model of the self that seems to oppose the very possibility of a *practical* universalism, because Orestes's Being must be one of socially significant action, Sartre forces the issue. His instrument is simplification. He purifies the actors as well as the terms of their contact.

In order to ensure philosophical consistency and, consequently, a rational ethics, Sartre categorically denies the formative importance of any factors external to the *cogito*. The determinate powers of culture, class, race, gender, and other such constructions, he calls either "historical situations" or "configurations." And he dismisses these categories because, to him, human-being-ness in any "situation" is by definition a resistance to and a transcendence of such constructions. Consequently, Sartre is able to claim for the existential subject fantastic powers of understanding that are in perfect alignment with his will: "every configuration [is sufficiently similar that] even the Chinese, the Indian, or the Negro, can be understood by the Westerner." By "can be understood," Sartre means "that by virtue of a situation that he can imagine, a European of 1945 can, in like manner, push himself to the limits and reconstitute within himself the configuration of the Chinese, the Indian, or the African. Every configuration has universality in the sense that every configuration can be understood by every man. . . . There is always a way to understand the idiot, the child, the savage, the foreigner, provided one has the necessary information."[4] To be fair, we must note that Sartre himself reminds us that the "universality of man," which is grounded in the "absoluteness of [individual] choice[,] does not do away with the relativeness of each epoch." However, frankly, I do not think that Sartre is particularly interested in either this "relativeness" or, especially, what his own resistance to this concept's implications suggests about his philosophy's ethical limits.[5]

The aim of Sartre's project is ethical action grounded in personal autonomy and obtained through the acting-out of philosophical categories, especially those that precisely define and control social membership. Hence, the insect analogy's attraction and special challenge to a thinker like Sartre, who wishes to deploy it as a purely rational instrument (i.e., free from the natural and therefore "irrational" merging of essences). For when this analogy is expressed in language, presented as a verbal picture, its seemingly unmediated representation of the world evokes, at least in potential, a complex of psychohistorical and aesthetic habits. Because this complex preexists any particular formulation, it is present to the audience as an ideology: it resists its elimination. Our appetite for the poetic Hive's honey cannot be reasoned away.

Despite his revolutionary stance, Sartre has also tasted this honey. For instance, the Hive's singular importance to *The Flies* suggests that Sartre has been influenced by his predecessors. He places the Hive topos exactly where one would expect it, based on these predecessors, making it the visual and dramatic center for Orestes's definition of himself in relation to the collective. However, the presence and placement of the Hive are not the whole of Sartre's negotiation with this topos's history. Because of Sartre's philosophical and scientific outlook, the problems posed by the Hive require an *antiaesthetic solution*, one that will break with the past and nullify the topos's iconic, imagistic office (the irrational complement to its rational, categorical powers) — thereby enabling its instrumentalization. Sartre must wrest the Hive from the poets — but since he refuses to meet them on their own ground, his conquest must be through dialectic.

In order to avoid traditional poetic reworking (*retractatio*, allusion,

direct artistic engagement with authored aesthetic acts), Sartre emphasizes the only proven alternative: he alters the Hive's context. In a single
powerful stroke he would shift the Hive topos's rhetorical alignment
from the literary to the philosophical. Here Sartre's problem is analogous to that faced by the defense attorney who, in an earlier example, I
imagined as having to deal with the undeniable presence of an object
that to the jury looks like and therefore "is" the murder weapon. According to Bachelard, the object exerts "fascination," an irrational and poetic
appeal. Because, for our purposes, the Hive's picture is an object, like the
defense attorney Sartre cannot unmake his material adversary. Instead,
he must change the nature of its appeal, transform it from a locus of
resistance to one's will into the will's instrument.

To Sartre, human society, the Hive, is the very source of illusion. He
regards it much as the dystopian Wells does, except more extremely.
The human realm is impure, a dehumanizing order from which, especially when in its midst, we must remain separate if we are to retain our
human-being-ness, our power and title to act. Having defined society
in this way, it easily follows that, for existential subjects to act inside the
Hive without losing themselves to it, they must never cease to bear
within them the attitude that they first grasped when, standing beyond
and above the collective, they came to know it as the Other. According to this design, because power is truth and truth is only to be had
by seeing the Hive from outside, of necessity, then, the Hive cannot
produce its own solutions. Because it cannot know itself (which is the
province of the isolated sovereign subject), it cannot save itself. Of
consequence, then, this design summons up figures from the past: the
prophet, the lawgiver, the Christ — or in their absence, the philosopher.
The Hive is benighted, passive: it is "dead and alive" matter needing the
master's hand — and this goes for all persons in it who do not have
the advantage of Orestes's perspective. Thus, Sartre does not transcend
the irrational and affective aspects of persuasion. Instead, he follows a
familiar path. Sartrean existentialism is an (anti)rhetoric that evokes and
harnesses a fantasy of special knowledge and mission: the Christian myth
of the soon-to-return Redeemer. Ironically, the appeal of this drama of
individual enlightenment and self-sacrifice energizes and authorizes his
exposure and dismissal of the Hive's poetic history and implications.

Sartre helped define his age and was, therefore, entirely of it. Hence,
to his drama of the secular Christ, he adds the appeal and the sanitizing

office of modern science. Orestes's way of seeing is a familiar nexus: it combines an instrumental attitude toward language and an individual assumption of power and the title to wield it. And part of this nexus's familiarity derives from its claim to scientific authority.[6] Because Sartrean existentialism derives so much from Cartesian seeing, the office of his "free" man generally overlaps that of the Hive's sovereign, observing consciousness. But more importantly, this office resonates with the scientist's perspective, a relationship that is made clearer by again returning to Lewis Thomas's orbital view of the Earth: "Nobody wants to think that the rapidly expanding mass of mankind, spreading out over the surface of the earth, blackening the ground, bears any meaningful resemblance to the life of an anthill or a hive."[7] Thomas is consciously using the Hive as a visual instrument; it enables him to conceive as a whole and over time all persons and their various activities. He is aware that the Hive used thus reduces human-being-ness, renders meaningless all factors except those that further our grasp of the mass's definitive action of expansion. We have, then, a humane voice that thinks inhumanely because it *sees* inhumanely. Hence, the sentence's conversational strategy: the speaker pretends to find distasteful the hard truth born of scientific sight. This is a gesture of mock resignation to the reality of a disinterested and secular cosmos. Beneath the humanistic concern is a "like it or not, this is reality, folks" attitude: "nobody wants to think that . . . the expanding mass of mankind . . . resemble[s] the life of an anthill or a hive." However, because we are seeing through his scientific eyes and by means of a structure that feels natural (the Hive), we sincerely wish to think of our species as an insect colony. We, too, want to be tough-minded, to see the truth revealed by and to share in the power of this "unique" perspective.

Even though he neither pretends to be taken aback by how he sees nor puts us into orbit, Sartre tempts us similarly with a way of seeing that is just as fantastic but meant to be even more provocative. Both Thomas and Sartre assume that the truth of the human condition may be grasped only by separating oneself from the human Hive and viewing it from an exterior and sovereign position. Hence, their similar acceptance of and delight in an absolute universalism of the eye that they intend to be scandalous, a quality that each believes contributes to his thought's veracity. Furthermore — and this helps to explain their reliance upon Cartesian-style visual instruments — Thomas and Sartre share the same intellectual will-to-power. This will-to-power assumes that neither apology nor limit is required for either its methods or conclusions, for it is offered to us *as* science: the necessary unfolding of an objective, value-free getting-at-the-truth that we can neither ignore nor contradict — unless we care to join those below us in the "pit" of ignorance.

Sartre is clear about the mass's unenlightened state — and despite (or perhaps because of) Thomas's biological perspective, his estimation of it is not all that different. Both men hold that knowledge and power are united in the seeing subject, whose powers arise from a sovereign position that is discovered and communicated through the Hive. Not only does Thomas's language enable us to think of human action on a global scale, it also asks us to conceive of all actions in our visual field, observed as well as implicit, as aspects of a single organization whose philosophical essence is a natural and therefore *unconscious* "expansion." This estimation's affinity with Sartre's thought is obvious. Although by way of extension we are implicitly part of the "rapidly expanding mass of mankind, spreading out over the surface of the earth, [that is] blackening the ground," not only are we physically separate from this action, we are thereby made aware of its inexorable and probably self-destructive nature. Our individual (self)consciousness, our sovereign capacity to see, to know, and thus to judge the whole as philosophically distinct, sets us apart from the mass below.

I have spoken several times of the Hive topos as an "intermediate" form, one that combines the poetic/imagistic office of metaphor and the rational powers of the argumentative topos. Once again this knowledge is useful, for even more explicitly than Thomas, Sartre deals with the Hive as just such a form. While observing Argos, "*his* city," from the sovereign position, Orestes struggles to keep the Hive's vehicle and tenor apart, to see flies as flies and persons as persons. As one agent of his attempt to favor the Hive's conceptual office at the expense of its poetic capacity, he asserts biological — *scientific* — accuracy by distinguishing between humans and flies. If you consider this expression of Sartre's scientific motive relative to the discussion in chapter 2 about anxiety and the true idea, you will notice that he presents Orestes's seeing as natural in the same manner as Kelly, Birkerts, and Daley. Like them, Sartre *projects* the Hive's categorical genius upon the world. When informed by this strategically naive theory of vision, the eye becomes an instrument through which we "discover" in nature what we already know must be there. All four of these writers desire a "big picture" that both guards them from and enables them to pronounce upon what makes them anxious. But Sartre is distinct from these others, for he *knows* that his fears are aesthetic. More specifically, he wishes to undermine the humanistic office of literature, to replace it with his own lesson that we are simultaneously similar to and yet distinct from Others. Affective and approximate similitude implies a notion of freedom that allows for factors external to the *cogito*; Sartre must defend philosophy.

Among my argument's essential principles is the idea that each step in the Hive's development — how it is reworked by a particular writer — is determined by the choices of earlier writers. Of course, how a writer understands and deploys these inherited choices is inflected by factors supplemental to those expressed through the Hive's genealogy. But at the core of each new version of the Hive are essential elements derived from one or more inherited aesthetic patterns; thus far no formulation has entirely broken with the past. And though the dialectic of invention is now less precisely known than during the rule of rhetoric, more diffuse in nature and variously realized in our literature than in our forebears', the old rules still apply. Contemporary writers still must work from their predecessor's materials. And because of Sartre's still-considerable presence, in order to renew and adapt the Self as Insect, it is with his model of the existential sovereign subject and its antisocial, scientifically informed view of the collective that many writers feel obliged to contend.

Kobo Abe's *Woman in the Dunes*: Domestication by Landscape

Sartre's version of the Self as Insect remains psychologically potent and aesthetically significant because his Orestes is the type for a condition of human-being-ness marked by clarity of purpose and absolute freedom. Because this sort of being issues from the Cartesian experience, it depends upon psychic isolation, which is guaranteed only by physical separation and emotional independence from others. Hence, Kobo Abe represents the protagonist of *Woman in the Dunes*, Niki Jumpei, as pathologically suspicious and a poor reader of social conventions and institutional obligations.

At the start of *Woman*, Jumpei, a thirty-one-year-old schoolteacher and amateur entomologist, thinks that his relationship with society is direct. But we may call it simple, for the social order is alien to the Orestean type: it is his enemy and usually female. For Orestes to have congress with society outside a strict and unequal subject/object relationship is to put his freedom at risk, to imperil his title to action, his masculinity — in sum, to threaten the foundation of "true" human-being-ness.

Jumpei shares his city apartment with a woman but feels no attachment to her. Neurotic, lonely rather than self-sufficient, he prefers to spend his free time studying insects. On August holiday, Jumpei boards a bus, leaving behind the city and the irritations of his relationship and job. His destination is a remote coastal area of Japan distinguished only for its sand dunes. His ambition is to discover and name after himself a species of insect. Apparently he is so divorced from his body, from nature, that he conceives of reproduction as naming. He would beget abstractly, via an exercise in biological nomenclature.

Jumpei disembarks at a "commonplace, rather poor village" on the edge of the dunes and sets out on foot. Although he walks through the hamlet, he pays no attention to its citizens, for "sand and insects were all that concerned him" (8). An outsider, a modern, Western-educated urbanite, he is the village's antithesis. In George Eliot's words, he is not at all disposed to "look with loving pardon at [the] inconsistencies" of the village, its people, and their cooperative way of life.[8] As he proceeds, he notices that even though the road and the sand on either side of it rise, the houses remain on the same level — they are "sunk into hollows scooped in the [progressively rising wall of] sand" (9). Near the top of the slope, Jumpei observes that it must be "at least sixty-five feet down to the tops of the houses." Elevated and isolated thus, he is in the sovereign position. "In amazement, [he] peer[s] down into one of the holes" and asks himself, "What in heaven's name could it be like to live there?" Through his eyes, the village "resembl[es] the cross-section of a beehive . . . sprawled over the dunes. Or rather the dunes lay sprawled over the village. Either way, it was a disturbing and unsettling experience" (10).

The differences between Jumpei's and Orestes's view from above are worth considering. Orestes is empowered by his sovereign sight of Argos. In a moment he becomes fully Socratic: he knows himself, grasps the common person's blindness as well as its cure. Therefore, his descent into society is strategic, voluntary. Further, Orestes is perfect and recognizes himself as such. It is the world and not he that needs changing. In contrast, Jumpei registers his view from above as "disturbing and unsettling." Abe thus unequivocally blocks the Hive's tendency to empower the sovereign observer. Although existentially isolated, Jumpei gains nothing from his sovereign perspective, no insight into himself or the life of the village he observes. One gathers that his tendency to see others as different and inferior has long since desensitized him to the implications of this sort of seeing. What Jumpei wants is simplicity and control; like al-Hakim's Adil, he finds these by observing the insects' struggle for existence.

Just as in A. S. Byatt's *Morpho Eugenia*, the second postmodern text I address, in *Woman* the Orestean archetype is represented as a male entomologist, who is subjected to and changed by being and acting within a human Hive. Denied the simplicity and power of the sovereign perspective, he is forced to revise his sense of order, priorities, and definition of freedom. This domesticating process suggests that, for the inheritors of the Sartrean worldview and its symbols, the social Hive is no longer an entirely alien order absolutely inimical to human-being-ness and thus in need of the sort of revolution demanded by Sartre. Indeed, although *Woman* and *Morpho* are existentially inclined, when I compare their philosophical ambition and dramatic scale with those expressed by *The Flies*, I sense pragmatic modesty, a project less absolute, strident, and universalizing. Moreover, rather than assenting to Sartre's dictum that ethical choice begins with rejecting the world, both writers agree that it is Orestes, the sovereign observer, the scientist, who in congress with others must discover meaning for himself in the midst of the social Hive's limits and uncertainties. Also, since the postmodern entomologist's choosing and acting is grounded in a particular place and is informed by a sense of relations with others rather than entirely generated by the implications of spatial separation, any implied universal principles ultimately derive more from the Hive's poetic, affective powers of analogy than from those rational and categorical. If you would recall the diagram of Thomas's and Virgil's views from above, you will note that the Sartrean, universalist view is kin to the scientific and global, whereas the postmodern is aligned with the poetic and local.[9]

To return to *Woman*: having established Jumpei's existentialism, his psychological difference from the village Hive, Abe casts him into it. In the early evening of his first day in this strange landscape of sand and buried houses, the entomologist meets a villager who, once determining that Jumpei is not "from the government," agrees to find a place for him to stay for the night. Jumpei is taken to "one of the cavities on the ridge of the dunes at one end of the village" and climbs down a rope ladder into it (22).

At the bottom is a house and a young woman. He discovers that she is all alone, that her husband and daughter had been buried in the sand by a typhoon a year ago. Jumpei finds the situation awkward and titillating. He is unsure how to take their forced intimacy (the house is small) or how much he should help the woman, who spends the night clearing the sand off and from around the house. They shovel the sand into cans and then transfer it to baskets that are periodically lifted to the surface. He shovels for a while but soon wants to quit. The woman continues. We overhear him thinking her behavior to be "quite like . . . a beetle['s]," an attribution of insectness that, although authorized by the narrative's vocabulary of insect images, reminds us that Jumpei's sense of existence depends upon the assumptions that he is superior to and categorically distinct from others, including this woman, whose name he has not even bothered to ask.

However, his passionate interest in the meaning of existence makes him interesting to us. We share his bewilderment at the woman's acceptance of her lot, which he understands as "exist[ing] only for the purpose of clearing away the sand" (39). She agrees with his estimation but seems not to entirely grasp his meaning, for she tells him, "we just can't sneak away at night, you know." His Sartrean reaction exposes his metropolitan, Western-style values (which his own life hardly expresses, an irony to which he is blind): "Yes you can. It would be simple, wouldn't it? You can do anything if you want to." While continuing to shovel, the woman explains herself, summing up the traditional communal psychology that Abe opposes to the Sartrean: "The village keeps going because we never let up clearing away the sand like this. If we stopped, in ten days the village would be completely buried. Next it will be the neighbor's turn in back. See, there."

Jumpei goes to sleep befuddled and irritated. In the morning he finds the rope ladder gone and himself prisoner. He cannot climb the steep sand wall, and after beating the woman with a towel he interprets her passivity and silence as evidence that she is part of a conspiracy. His figuration of himself as "some famished mouse" who has "been lured by the beetle into a desert from which there [is] no escape" (50) again expresses his sense of categorical difference from the woman. And a prisoner he is.

He discovers that he will not receive food or, more importantly, water unless he works, fills the "lift baskets" with sand on a nightly basis, thereby joining, quite against his will, the village's battle against the relentless sand.

Jumpei does not have any intention of remaining in what, during an escape attempt, he refers to as a "slave hole" (176). But even though he gets free (having made and successfully used a cloth rope and makeshift grappling hook), while working his way quietly through the village, his thoughts register how much his time working and sleeping with the woman has changed him. Where before he could not fathom what sort of life could be lived at the bottom of these holes, he now can "easily understand how it was possible to live such a life." As he proceeds, he mentally catalogs the domestic and human contents of the holes he passes, which he thinks "terrifyingly repetitive . . . like the beating of the heart" (177). Although he still fears the villagers as captors, and even though he occupies his initial sovereign position above the village, Jumpei no longer views them as insects. But he certainly has no intention of rejoining them.

The village dogs scent him. He is pursued, becomes trapped in quicksand, and is rescued then returned to the woman's hole. After a period of illness and depression, he again makes peace with the woman. For the first time, he feels an ineffable connection with her when "suddenly a sorrow the color of dawn well[s] up in him" (207). His human-being-ness grows apace with his sense of this Hive as home. Even though he is not yet conscious of it, growing in him is the capacity to care about this woman and her people.

In the confines of this hole/home, subject to what he once thought of only as a "monotonous existence enclosed in an eye" (63), forced to join a community and to cooperate with a companion who is now his lover, Jumpei's Orestean psychology becomes interwoven with the villagers' contrasting way of being. This is not to say, however, that Jumpei's modern, existentialist self is entirely remade or extinguished by his new circumstances. Thoughts of escape rarely leave his mind. Nonetheless, he comes to better understand his companion's and the villagers' psychology and thus his own.

During a conversation with his lover about the immoral and probably illegal sale of the inferior local sand to outsiders for use in concrete, Jumpei achieves his first conscious insight into this social Hive's collective psychology. He begins to recognize that the village's communal ethics are legitimate because its people are located in and psychically bound to a specific geography. This ethic of place contrasts with his metropolitan inclination toward abstract and universal standards, which he understands primarily as laws that are imposed from above instead of generated from circumstance:

> "Don't joke! It would be a fine mess if you mixed this sand with cement — it's got too much salt in it. In the first place, it's probably against the law or at least against construction regulations. . . ."
>
> "Of course, they [the villagers] sell it secretly. They cut the hauling charges in half too. . . ."
>
> "That's too absurd! Even if half price were free, that won't make it right when buildings and dams start to fall to pieces, will it?"
>
> The woman suddenly interrupted him with accusing eyes. She spoke coldly, looking at his chest, and her attitude was completely different.
>
> "Why should we worry what happens to others?"
>
> He was stunned. The change was complete, as if a mask had dropped over her face. It seemed to be the face of the village, bared to him through her. Until then the village was supposed to be on the side of the executioner. Or maybe they were mindless man-eating plants, or avaricious sea anemones, and he was supposed to be a pitiful victim who happened to be in their clutches. But from the standpoint of the villagers, they themselves were the ones who had been abandoned [by the government to the encroaching sand]. Naturally there was no reason why they should be under obligation to the outside world. So if it were he who caused injury, their fangs should accordingly be bared to him. It had never occurred to him to think of his relationship with the village in that light. (222–23)

Suddenly confronted with the affective claims of human beings whom he no longer sees as completely Other, Jumpei gains perspective on himself and his situation. He reinterprets his "relationship with the village [by the] . . . light" of imaginative contrast. Because this operation is intuitive, informed more by feeling than reason, he is able to see the villagers as simultaneously alien and similar. Obviously, his earlier habit of scientifically analogizing the villagers as insects no longer serves. Although his appeal to law and ethics suggests that one part of him still inclines toward the simplicity and extremity enabled by the antithetical categories of Sartrean seeing, he now begins to grasp the existence and power of a *feeling* relationship. Jumpei begins to consider that human-being-ness (to include his own) may be socially constructed, and therefore may be various and yet comparable without diminishment. He understands that the villagers' outlook, their difference from him, is the product of their locatedness, which he is beginning to share.

It is *Woman in the Dune*'s conclusion that most strongly suggests that Abe is responding directly to the Sartrean armature. Since Jumpei's imprisonment, when not shoveling sand, he has been consumed with fantasies of escape. After his flight and recapture, he builds a device he calls "Hope," a baited bucket with a trick lid set in the sand. Its purpose is to catch a crow so that he may tie a note to its leg and have his words delivered to the outside world. But Hope doesn't net the expected result. After several weeks of waiting, while again changing the bait in vain, Jumpei decides to thoroughly check the trap's operation. He scrapes away the sand, removes the cover, and discovers that it contains about four inches of potable water. Stunned and excited, he speculates that the difference in temperature and water content between the surface of the sand and the region below caused his crow trap to "act . . . as a kind of a pump, drawing up the subsurface water" (233). How he first thinks of this event confirms his Orestean inclination: he values his discovery of water as a tool for gaining independence from the villagers. However, his emotional reaction is more complex; Abe unfolds it so as to clearly answer Orestes's discovery of self and purpose through his sovereign view of Argos.

This key section of the novel mimics the Hive topos's phenomenological operation. Abe first establishes his formulation's visual structure; he then explores its psychological consequences. The first passage below suggests that the truth of oneself and the human condition may be had only within the collective, only when deprived of modernity's *scientifically* universalizing sovereign perspective. Abe inverts the Sartrean pattern:

> The fact that he was still just as much at the bottom of the hole as ever had not changed, but he felt quite as if he had climbed to the top of a high tower. Perhaps the world had been turned upside down and its projections and depressions reversed. Anyway, he had discovered

water in this sand. As long as he had his device the villagers would not be able to interfere with him so easily. No matter how much they cut off his supply, he would be able to get along very well. Again laughter welled up in him at the very thought of the outcry that the villagers would make. He was still in the hole, but it seemed as if he were already outside. (235)

Jumpei feels that his world, his perspective on things, has been "turned upside down": the world's *"projections and depressions reversed."* Jumpei means "projections and depressions" in the physical sense, yet Abe anticipates the changes that his protagonist will soon undergo as a consequence of this inversion of Sartrean seeing by asking us to consider "projection" and "depression" more abstractly, as positions that enable a certain visual tableau and thus determine particular sorts of human-being-ness. He indicates as much by concluding the paragraph with Jumpei's meditation on the connection between position and one's comprehension and *judgment* of pattern. This section's first two sentences announce the movement of Jumpei's mind from a Western-style scientific way of seeing order (one informed by a universalizing system of definition through antithesis) to one more intuitive and artistic (an outlook that assumes and seeks a beauty in a design that allows a place within it for the human): "Turning around, he could see the whole scene. You can't really judge a mosaic if you don't look at it from a distance. If you really get close to it you get lost in detail. You get away from one detail only to get caught in another. Perhaps what he had been seeing up until now was not the sand but grains of sand." In order to "see the whole scene" of his existence, Jumpei does not need high ground. All that he must do is "turn[ ] around," thereby making himself the center of this particular locale, which now may serve as a microcosm of the whole. One might argue that Jumpei's language recapitulates Sartre's requirement that in order to know the whole one must "look at it from a distance." But here neither Jumpei nor Abe means "distance" in the geographical sense, for to be placed thus vis-à-vis the collective tends to enable the illusion of subject/object opposition and the consequent attribution of alterity to the collective. The conventional sovereign position gives the Orestean subject power over the world and the title to use it because it simplifies. Since this type of observer cannot be privy to finer details (the Hive topos builds upon the eye's limitations as well as its powers), he fills them in by extrapolating from what his isolation and singularity imply. Significantly, this operation confirms Bauman's summary of Sartrean ego-formation, which I have already examined.

We know that Jumpei now begins to favor artistic seeing over the scientific, because he thinks of "the whole scene" of himself surrounded by sand, sun, and struggling human beings as a "mosaic." And because a mosaic is a picture made from the shaped but otherwise unconverted substance of a place, from the bones of the earth, Jumpei's figuring the world thus suggests an aesthetic intuition that is practical, elemental, located rather than ideal.

This particular aesthetic rises from a seeing that Abe believes is free from the mediation of visiophilosophical instruments, those verbal devices that augment and shape perception and, thus, feeling and knowledge. Jumpei confirms his release from the effects of such forms: he compares his earlier way of seeing to the distortion produced by "eyes [fitted] with magnifying lenses" (236). His feeling now is that to see in the instrumental, Sartrean manner is to be unaware of the relationship between things, to be "concerned . . . only with curiously exaggerated details: nostrils in a thick nose, wrinkled lips or smooth, thin lips, spatulate fingers or pointed fingers." He recalls that when "he looked very closely at those parts alone he would feel like vomiting," which suggests that Abe considers Sartrean seeing unhealthy and unnatural. To Jumpei's former eyes, habituated as they were to the distortion of magnification, details (the content selected or manufactured by this type of vision) were understood automatically and solely through their unfavorable measurement against abstract perfection. Hence, "everything seemed tiny and insectlike." But now that he perceives differently, Jumpei decides, "if the chance occurred for him to renew his relationship with [the persons in his past], he would have to start all over again from the very beginning. The change in the sand corresponded to a change in himself. Perhaps, along with the water in the sand, he had found a new self."

New though his self now may be, and in the face of thinking in terms of "renew[al]," "relationship," and "change," Jumpei remains an outsider. Since his psychology was formed in the Westernized metropolis, his present circumstances and experiences cannot entirely remake him. And one of the novel's greatest pleasures is its convincing psychological realism, which in large part stems from Abe's refusal to assert any such absolute and therefore improbable rebirth. Even after realizing his "new self," Jumpei continues to think of escape. These thoughts accompany his scientific outlook, which, even though it continues as part of his psychology, is gradually sublimated and transformed. Now expressed through his interest in perfecting Hope, his Sartrean tendencies have a life-giving focus, one that is energized by what at times seems almost a selfless desire to understand. Indeed, even though he continues to find it difficult to admit his new feelings even to himself, he is changed by the routine of life in the hole and his proximity to the woman.

She becomes pregnant; there are complications and she must be taken to a hospital. As she leaves, the woman looks at Jumpei "beseechingly with eyes almost blinded by tears and mucus until she [can] see him no longer." He "look[s] away as if he [does] not see her" (238). Abe does not explain why Jumpei "look[s] away" from the woman he has impregnated, but that he notices that her eyes are "almost blinded with tears and mucus" suggests that his new and old selves and their respective ways of seeing are contending. The word "tears" indicates that Jumpei registers the woman's emotions, while "mucus" points toward scientific magnification, the instrumental sort of seeing that here for the last time so blatantly asserts itself.

Curiously, even though the woman is "hauled up by rope," the villagers have let down the rope ladder and left it there. Jumpei touches it, climbs it. "Circling around the edge of the hole, he climbed to a spot where he could view the sea." From this position, when he turns around, he can see the dust he supposes is made by the three-wheeler taking the woman away. But he does not leave. Instead, he notices his shadow moving at the bottom of the hole near the water trap. His shadow(self) focuses his awareness on Hope, and he sees that it has been damaged. He climbs back down to repair it. And because he now knows that he may leave when he wishes, and wants to tell someone, preferably the villagers, about his water trap, he decides that "he might as well put off his escape until sometime after that" (239).

Jumpei's actions after climbing the ladder demonstrate the degree to which his old Sartrean outlook has been integrated into its opposite. The entomologist's ambivalence, expressed by his coldness toward the woman and his telling himself that he may leave when he wishes, is now more a matter of surface than essence. To make Jumpei's new essence visible, Abe shows him "circling around the edge of the hole" (238), circumambulating his affective "mosaic," which is now his world, its defining microcosm.

As you may recall, I argued earlier that in order to preserve his human-being-ness, his power and title to action, once inside Argos, Orestes must retain undiminished within him the scene of his existential rebirth — as if fixing the scene to his eyes and using his original view from above as an instrument of simplification. Jumpei, who discovers his "new self" while a prisoner in a hole and singularly bereft of visual sovereignty, similarly carries with him into the other world the essence of his rebirth. Having "climbed to a spot where he could view the sea," a landscape whose chaotic substance and lack of boundaries would otherwise make it antithetical to his hole in the sand, Jumpei observes that it "too was a dirty yellow." He sees little difference in *color* between the sea and the sand, which suggests that he is now making aesthetic, connective analogies instead of rational and antithetical ones. The trajectory of his psychological change, then, is contrary to Orestes's, whose rebirth issues from a visiospatial partitioning of the world. Hence, if we break with Abe's assumption that Jumpei now sees naturally and interpret this color analogy as a sign that Jumpei is projecting a pattern upon the world, then this pattern and its implications are of an order and intensity distinct from Orestes's sovereign inclination toward contrast. Even the air outside Jumpei's hole "did not taste as [he] expected . . . [it] only irritated his throat" (238–39), a bodily reaction that recalls the way that his old way of seeing used to nauseate him. Furthermore, Jumpei now reiterates the same movement that defined his initial breakthrough in understanding and feeling: he "turn[s] around" — and when he does he sees "a cloud of sand r[ising] on the outskirts of the village." As he does with the sea, he automatically perceives this cloud as part of the affective mosaic, thinks it is "probably the three-wheeler with the woman" (239).

What more should we make of this "mosaic"? More specifically, in what sense is Jumpei's new way of seeing and being in the world non-Western? Admittedly, it is rather beyond this study's scope to fully engage with the complicated issue of a Japanese-specific aesthetic, which is the probable source of Abe's counter-Sartrean armature. Also, it is risky to thus generalize from any single text, especially one like *Woman*, whose author obviously commands Western conventions. However, I would place *Woman* at the intersection of two overlapping traditional Asian aesthetic patterns, one pictorial and the other narrative, which posit similar images of the good life. The first may be represented through Sung dynasty landscape painting, and the second through the story of the traveling, spiritually seeking civil servant who, like Jumpei, finds in the isolated village a microcosmic center that balances human and nature within a specific landscape.

Sung dynasty painting, which James Cahill calls "the age of full maturity of Chinese painting," [10] visualizes what may be called Chinese "nature humanism." For instance, in Fan K'uan's *Traveling among Streams and Mountains*, a work that Cahill regards as the "supreme monument of the period," human figures are placed in a monumental landscape rendered in exquisite detail. But since K'uan used the calligrapher's rather than the painter's brush, the realism of *Traveling* is quite distinct from that communicated by Western landscapes. Cahill observes that "the world of the painting seems neither to reflect faithfully the physical universe nor to overlay it with a human interpretation" (34). This calligraphic style does not know the twin artifices of Western-style realism: single-point perspective and what we now might call the "photographic mode" of similitude.

Although human beings and their works are diminished in scale, they are nonetheless essential for *Traveling*'s completeness. When combined with the unaffected but visible brushwork, this compositional strategy suggests that although nature exists independently of humans, they share a common substance because both are made in the same *manner*. The existence of human beings is thus confirmed without either individual characterization or explicit allegory. (In this regard it is instructive to compare Brueghel's scenes of village life.) In *Traveling*, humankind's being in nature is simply that: nature is neither object nor backdrop. Moreover, between humans and nature there is no struggle, either represented or implied. If the picture may be said to evoke a sense of difference and thus isolation, then this tension arises between viewer and image. It is resolved by contemplation. Time spent with *Traveling* evokes a sensation similar to Jumpei's new sense of the world as a unifying, unconscious mosaic. The picture's flatness — by Western standards — only contributes to this sense of the whole as a complex and yet unaffected *design*.

It is similarly valuable to think of *Woman* as modeled upon the ancient narrative of the wandering, enlightenment-seeking civil servant who discovers new life and meaning in the country. This story originates in China, but because of the extensive cultural relationship between China and Japan, it should be treated as native to each people.[11] *Woman* may be said to evidence this story's influence, for even though Jumpei resists belonging to the village, accepting his place in its "mosaic," it is the inherited Asian pattern and not Sartre's universalizing existential outlook that finally emerges as correct. Yet this native pattern does not entirely eliminate Western influences. Because Jumpei's integration into a holistic relationship with humans and nature is forced, Abe is able to comment upon the unhappy effects of Western-style urbanity without idealizing its opposite, the village. Jumpei remains a modern. Although *Woman* stages a contest between ways of seeing — the modern and alien versus the traditional and native — and asserts the latter's superiority, its conclusion does not escape the existentialist frame. It appears that Abe's opponent is the type of modernity represented by Sartre, not the idea of modernity per se.

When compared with Byatt's, Abe's response to Sartre is more reactive, yet more accepting. We should therefore classify *Woman* as an *emergent* postmodern text and position its version of the Self as between al-Hakim's and Byatt's. Certainly, that Abe wrote *Woman* in the early sixties, a period dominated by existentialist aesthetics, helps explain both the sheer presence of Orestes and the novel's desire to mesh existentialism with native patterns. It is also worth considering that Western-style individualism and scientific seeing are foreign additions to Japanese culture, and thus may serve Abe as powerful symbols for alienation. Moreover, *Woman*'s mythological simplicity suggests its kinship to both the texts that I have discussed as being paradigmatic to existential literature, *The Metamorphosis* and *The Flies*. Abe so directly engages with Sartre because, like al-Hakim, he feels himself more an observer of than a participant in the Western tradition. This perspective makes Orestes more visible and answerable than is the case for later Western writers such as Byatt. But I should note that although *Woman*, like *Fate of a Cockroach*, is obviously influenced by Kafka, in contrast to al-Hakim, who writes in the direct light of *The Metamorphosis*, Abe chooses to stay on the edge of its pattern, borrowing only general characteristics for the construction of an existentialist fable that, although distinctly Japanese, anticipates key elements of the postmodern outlook.

My reading of *Woman* allows at least the following observations. First, the novel suggests that the Hive topos makes cross-cultural sense. This is to say that it may signify in non-Western texts, and may even be a cross-cultural fixture of the mind. If this potential exists, then it is due to the Hive's psychophysiological grounding in visual experience. Second, the novel illustrates that the Hive's artistic implications are similarly deployable within Western and non-Western narratives. Abe, for instance, uses the Hive topos in ways that closely parallel those I have been discussing all along: namely, to make visible the relationship between the individual and the collective and to evoke the ethical and psychological problems that arise from socially constructed seeing. Jumpei's eyes serve as a screen upon which Abe displays an evolving series of projections, thereby externalizing psychological content to which the entomologist himself may be blind. At first these projections are scientific, Sartrean. But they become progressively mixed with and leavened by an affective, poetic way of seeing. Third, since *Woman* demonstrates that the Hive is socially inflected, it follows that at a finer level we cannot entirely account for all its versions through the West's mutually defining antithesis of angelic and demonic paradigms. Indeed, *Woman* evidences that the Hive may be as complex and meaningful when determined by a worldview that assumes an embedded identity as when generated by the Western classical model, one that emphasizes the sovereign subject's separation and difference from the collective.

Although I have selected and dealt with non-Western texts so as to shed light on the Western tradition (*Fate of a Cockroach*, *Woman in the Dunes*), the above observations suggest that the Hive could serve as a mechanism for cross-cultural psychological comparison. Because the Hive imitates an actual experience and its structure derives from the way that the eye works in all cultural circumstances, the topos might be explored for its value as a mental benchmark. Indeed, I have used the Hive thus when discussing Virgil's domestication of Homer's bees. Although the West may claim Homer, his poetry expresses ideas of being, cooperation, and action that are far more alien to us than Virgil's — and perhaps Homer's psychology is even more distant from us than that expressed by Abe's native counter-armature, which seems to share some affinity with twentieth-century existentialism. But my task now is to bring the Western Hive up to date and to close this argument, which I shall do by way of Byatt's *Morpho Eugenia*. Familiar ground does not guarantee simplicity, however. The postmodern Self as Insect is no less complicated than Abe's, for as I shall show in *Morpho*, Byatt's response to Sartre also employs a native armature synthesized from earlier patterns.

A. S. Byatt's *Morpho Eugenia*:
From Marriage Plot to Postmodern Honeymoon

Similar to Jumpei, Byatt's entomologist, William Adamson, wanders into a trap, a social Hive baited with a libidinal object. Having lost almost everything in a shipwreck while returning from ten years exploring the Amazon and collecting insects there, Adamson is invited to Bredely Hall by its owner, Harald Alabaster, with whom he has corresponded but whom he has never met. At Bredely, Adamson meets Alabaster's family and is particularly struck by the eldest daughter, Eugenia. But as he notes in his journal, their "stations are unequal" (15). Eugenia's family is landed aristocracy; Adamson is the able son of a successful butcher, has no money of his own and no prospects without patronage. However, since Alabaster has a passion for collecting and conversation, he employs Adamson to order his collection of insects, help educate his younger children and, later, to debate with him the ideas he is developing for a book. Adamson thus gains limited access to Eugenia — but his status in this household is carefully determined. For a time his passion for her (for her beauty and the conventional although intense romance it seems to promise) must remain unexpressed.

But he has another passion, one whose familiar terms will enable me to get at *Morpho*'s central themes, which are quite familiar to an observer of the poetic Hive: the relationship between how one sees and character and, of course, the self's relationship with the social order. In this fiction, at least for those unbound by title and money, character establishes the verity of one's affective bonds, which in turn determine one's fate.

Byatt tells us that as a boy: "William trained his eye in the farmyard and amongst the bloody sawdust of the slaughterhouse. In the life he finally chose, his father's skills were of inestimable value in skinning, and mounting, and preserving specimens of birds and beasts and insects. He anatomised ant-eaters and grasshoppers and ants with his father's exactness reduced to microscopic scales" (10). As Abe does when discussing the microscopic way of seeing that Jumpei associates with his old self, Byatt here uses the microscopic view to establish the Sartrean instrumental outlook and lay the ground for its attendant ethical problems. Abe and Byatt agree that mechanically augmented vision detaches one from the Hive's affective pattern, aligns one with the scientific outlook and its instrumental notion of metaphor. In the words of Adamson's journal, the microscopic view makes one into a "stupid giant." From its subject the sovereign perspective exacts a substantial price: "purposefully intelligent beings" appear "incomprehensible" — which is to say that the human/nature "mosaic" is visible but does not signify, because its sense cannot be discerned from a distance and by an unconnected observer.

The structural diagrams of Thomas's and Virgil's views-from-above that appear in this argument's introduction help illuminate this trade-off's ironies. While distance indeed enables sovereign subjects to see the whole and its order, they grasp only what they see. Any percepts except those either purely visual or generated from the observer's singularity (the *cogito*) are simply unavailable. Because he lacks any context for or alternative to his simplified view from above, Orestes cannot grasp his own "incomprehensibility" — hence this quality's projection upon the object, and in a manner anticipated by Kafka's treatment of insectness. In sum, this model of blindness, repression, and transference distinguishes the literary responses to Sartre's Self as Insect. Appropriately, the writers who choose this model are interested in epistemological limits instead of their transcendence or denial. Because these writers, so to speak, contain Orestes as well as his negation, they are able to simultaneously affirm and question what perception by its very nature seeks to deny, its absence. They are able to accept the Sartrean proposition that *seeing is being* and yet deal with the visual act as a symbol, as a form that may be reworked.

Once Adamson had "walked in a state of religious anxiety, combined with a reverence for Wordsworth's poetry, looking for signs of Divine Love and order" and wrote "of the wonders of divine Design" (11). But this "changed when he began collecting" (10). He began to see the world as constituted by discrete objects whose value issued from their place in an abstract system, one whose reassuring structure could relieve the anxiety that accompanies learning one's place in an organic, local mosaic. What Adamson once saw as "the furious variety of forms," he now considered "a mask, [an] enhance[ment of an] underlying and rigorous order." His daily journal wherein he used to "examin[e] his conscience . . . gave way insensibly to the recording of" visual details and relations scientifically understood. Byatt reports that to Adamson, the "world [now] looked different, and larger, and brighter, not water-colour washes of green and blue and grey, but a dazzling pattern of fine lines and dizzying pinpoints" (11). Appropriately and in keeping with his new-found sovereign perspective, Adamson's "ruling passion" ceases to be his con-

science and the anxious struggle for faith and becomes: "the social insects. He peered into the regular cells of beehives, he observed trails of
ants passing messages to each other with fine feelers, working together
to shift butterfly wings and slivers of strawberry flesh. He stood like
a stupid giant and saw incomprehensible, purposefully intelligent beings building and destroying in cracks of his own paving stones. Here
was the clue to the world. His journal became the journal of an ant-
watcher . . . and began to intermingle a rapt, visionary note with practical
sums for outfitting, for specimen boxes, with names of ships, with useful
addresses" (12). Adamson's journal reports a shift from a religiopoetic
way of seeing to one more scientific. For the labor of writing himself
into a (local) mosaic that binds into one God, human, and nature, he
begins to substitute a (global) quest for transcendence that is enabled
and determined by the Hive's visiospatial terms. His microscopic seeing
is a way of traveling that presages his escape from England, his expedi-
tion to the New World — a new Eden for a new Adam.

Adamson's microscopic view of the ants enables him to perceive them,
their "building and destroying," as "purposefully intelligent." He embraces this perception as "the clue to the world." Yet, this clue is "incomprehensible." Even though he has struggled to exchange the seeming
freedom and epistemological security of alienation for the limits and
anxiety of belonging, he seems to have never really escaped the human
mosaic. His years in Brazil, his shipwreck and rescue, his acceptance into
Bredely Hall — this is the stuff of Romance, allegories, fairy tales — and
Adamson senses as much: "Understanding daily life in Bredely Hall was
not easy. William found himself at once detached anthropologist and
fairytale prince trapped by invisible gates and silken bonds in an en-
chanted castle. Everyone had their place and their way of life, and every
day for months he discovered new people whose existence he had not
previously suspected, doing tasks of which he had known nothing" (35).
His attempts to simplify his life by travel have led him here, to a fairytale castle whose ways, we might say, he finds "incomprehensible." He is
aware that Bredely Hall is highly organized and hierarchical, but does
not yet grasp what Byatt lets us know subtly and frequently: he is trapped
in what amounts to a giant insect colony. When he visits Lady Alabaster, a "hugely fat" woman who spends her days reclining and pampered
in her chambers, Adamson senses that "this immobile, vacantly amiable
presence . . . [is] a source of power in this household" (31). She is the

center of a class-bound female society. Her husband, Harald, keeps to his hexagonal study, worrying over his arguments against a disinterested cosmos. It is from his wife, mysteriously, that orders flow to the many servants, some of whom Adamson discovers one morning when he rises early. As if to remind us of the entomologist's present blindness, it is Byatt who supplies the insect analogy: "William, running downstairs at six, found a very different population from the daylight one — a host of silently hurrying, black-clad young women, carrying buckets of cinders, buckets of water, boxes of polishing tools, fistfuls of brooms and brushes and carpet beaters. They had come like a cloud of young *wasps* from under the roof of the house, pale-faced and blear-eyed, bobbing silently to him as he passed" (57; my emphasis).

His penury and unexpressed desire do not continue to be the only factors that keep him at Bredely. He marries Eugenia and takes his place as part of the household. But he never loses his sense of inhabiting a "between-world" and soon feels himself to be extraneous. He spends his time tutoring the children and is coming to know Matilida Crompton, the children's teacher and the only other member of the household who shares his liminal state, class origins, and critical intelligence. About the time of his first child's birth, Adamson, Crompton, and the school-age Alabaster children begin an "organized ant-watch." The several colonies of different species of ants on the estate are mapped, and at Crompton's urging he begins writing their natural history.

Now, "in the hot days just after midsummer," the various incomprehensible threads of his life at Bredely begin to intersect. The ant Queens and their suitors were nearing the time for their nuptial flight, and Adamson by now suspects his nature to be "drone-like":

he was hard put to it not to see his own life in terms of a diminishing analogy with the tiny creatures. He had worked so hard, watching, counting, dissecting, tracking, that his dreams were prickling with twitching antennae, advancing armies, gnashing mandibles and dark, inscrutable complex eyes. His vision of his own biological process — his frenzied delicious mating, so abruptly terminated [by Eugenia's ready conception], his consumption of the regular meals prepared by the darkly quiet forces behind the baize doors, the very regularity of his watching, dictated by the rhythms of the nest, brought him insensibly to see himself as a kind of complex sum of his nerve-cells and

instinctive desires, his automatic social responses of deference or required kindness or paternal affection. *One* ant in an anthill was neither
here nor there, was dispensable, was nothing. This was intensified,
despite his recognition of the grimly comic aspect of his reaction, by
the recording of the fate of the male ants [who died soon after their
one flight, whether or not they consummated with a Queen]. (116;
Byatt's emphasis)

With her usual care Byatt prefaces this report with a phrase — an intellectual pun — that guides our interpretation: Adamson is beginning to
"see his own life in terms of a *diminishing analogy*" with the ants. By this
Byatt means that Adamson allegorizes himself, feels less and less difference between himself and the ants: he perceives as fading in himself the
powers and the certainty of the sovereign perspective. However, because
he holds fast to this perspective's instrumental notion of metaphor, he is
threatened by its most powerful rational superstition: the terrifying possibility that the insect analogy is literally true, that he himself or any
other person is "nothing" to the collective. In his natural history, titled
"The Swarming City," Adamson considers the Hive analogy thus: "The
terrible idea — terrible to some, terrible, perhaps, to all, at some time or
in some form — that we are *biologically predestined* like other creatures,
that we differ from them only in inventiveness and the capacity for reflection on our fate — treads softly behind the arrogant judgement that
makes of the ant a twitching automaton" (131; Byatt's emphasis). For-
merly his passion, an object whose Otherness once served him as a release from anxiety and as a locus of order, the Hive is now Adamson's
nemesis. It already occupies his dreams; now it invades his philosophy. When taken literally, which is to say biologically (as Lewis Thomas
does) the insect analogy's implications erode the foundations of Orestean
free will and human-being-ness. And this is an apprehension that Byatt
would have us share, for in *Morpho*, character, motive, and the Hive's
shaping force converge.

When asked by an interviewer from *Salon* to comment about writing
Angels and Insects (from her answer one may assume that Byatt is talking
about *Morpho*), Byatt tells us that the novel "didn't have a plot for a long
time — it was just this metaphor, which is a very simple one but works"
(1). She further states that her characters and their choices are "*driven* by
the story and the metaphor" (2; my emphasis). Byatt's use of the word

"driven" is significant, for her picture of the Hive in *Morpho* as an oppressive order that forces the hero's growth and escape is rooted in her
experience of formal education. When I asked her, "What is it that draws
you to the beehive?" she recalled the unpleasantness of boarding school:
"I started on hives and anthills with an interest in my own terror of the
social, as a result of boarding school. I think it was in Coleridge that I
found the image of the single consciousness of the antheap. Certainly it
was the fear of the collective that took hold of me — mixed with a curiosity about how these things worked. I'm not sure that it [fascination
with the insect metaphor] was primarily literary." Adamson's experience
of the Hive is also primarily extra-literary: it is his *biological* attraction to
Eugenia that drives him to her and binds him to the Alabaster collective.
However, Adamson knows that he is more than his biology and is thus
aware that he is being compelled by only one part of his being. This
sense of doubleness — his sense of himself as both subject and object —
prevents his assimilation and opens a window for escape.

Adamson's discovery that his children are not his own, the product of
an incestuous relationship between his wife and his brother-in-law, reveals Bredely's demonic alignment. If our hero is to survive, to grow, he
must leave. He does so through the intercession of and accompanied by
Crompton. With her he has developed a relationship that, because it is
more intellectual than fleshly, strikes us as more adult, more *human*, than
what he had with Eugenia. This relationship between equals further appeals to us because it resonates with the still-determinate Romantic fantasy of the soul mate. The sheer fact of the soul mate's existence implies
that maturation is a relationship quest: a spiritual and middle-class analog to the gentry's incestuous strategy for maintaining their class and its
property.

It is my conceit that in several respects *Woman* and *Morpho* are children of the same father, Jean-Paul Sartre. And like all gifted children,
their relationship with parental authority is complex and not without
antagonism. Like *The Flies*, these texts are similarly concerned with the
psychological effects and ethical implications of enhivement. Hence,
both foreground the Self as Insect. However, since in a manner of speaking they tell us what happens to Orestes after he comes down from his
hill, they must modify the Hive's Sartrean form. In this sense *Woman*
and *Morpho* may be seen as supplements to Sartre, completions of his
pattern. Yet, as has been my business to establish, these texts are not

merely so. They are reworkings of more than just the Sartrean armature, and in many of their particulars they differ radically. For instance, even though both define the self in such a way as to work within the existential frame, Abe and Byatt conceive of human-being-ness, the collective, and the relations between them quite differently — and these differences have important narrative consequences.

In comparison with Adamson's, the curve of Jumpei's narrative is simple, probably because Abe has the advantage of a clear antithesis between native and alien social models. Jumpei enters, is transformed by, and then remains in the Hive, reconciled to life with a woman selected for him. One has the impression that his unnamed companion could have been any youngish female of the village. Adamson, however, enters Bredely, rejects its "queen," and then departs wiser and with his proper and *chosen* mate. Because Byatt works entirely within the Western tradition, images of hierarchy and social embeddedness (especially when used to evoke a gothic atmosphere) can only threaten the self's diminishment or death. Hence, in her narrative the consequences of choice are graver than in Abe's. Jumpei must choose between a located and affectively significant life and urban alienation, but for Adamson the options are life or death. Once he knows about his wife's incestuous relationship, one gathers that the animus between himself and the violent Edgar must find its expression. Life equals escape.

Since true human-being-ness in *Woman* derives from accepting one's place in a particular and located mosaic, through contemporary Western eyes Abe's notion of freedom might be called "negative." By this I mean that in order to belong Jumpei must accept a passive, contemplative way of being. And since this notion of freedom is contrary to the active "being-in-the-world" required by the Orestean archetype, Abe is able to end his narrative as he does, with Jumpei "acting without acting." Both this particular idea of freedom and sort of action are alien to the characters in *Morpho* with whom we are to identify. While Eugenia may be secure in her place within the Bredely mosaic, her character is biologically determined by a social order that seems to possess a mysterious and superhuman agency. To belong to Bredely, to submit to the rule of tradition and inherited wealth, is to be assimilated, reduced as a human being. If Eugenia seems less human than Adamson and Crompton, it is because she is.

Moreover, again because she is working entirely within the Western tradition, to one degree or another Byatt must assent to the following: our anxieties about belonging, of being owned and constrained; the commonplace view of the social order as oppressive; and the psychological potency of the Orestean archetype. And because this archetype is a fully functioning myth (by which I mean that it is not generally known even to exist, which gives it special power), it is especially difficult to imagine beyond it.

Byatt senses as much. And since it is with a myth that she must contend, she requires a counter-armature equal to the task. Similar to Abe's strategy of drawing upon powerful native patterns, for the construction of her counter-armature Byatt employs that most British of narrative paradigms, the marriage plot. However, she is not confident that by itself the marriage plot may contend with a myth of subjectivity as potent as Sartre's without spoiling her tale. Her solution? In opposition to the Sartrean armature and its undergirding narrative of the Christ (according to which the self's transformation is accomplished by death), and because *Morpho* is interested in a sustainable life of feeling in *this* world rather than a dramatic act of sacrifice, Byatt merges the marriage plot with the myth of Orpheus and Eurydice.[12] This synthesis of ascendent marriage plot and descendent myth allows for the dangers of the underworld without an unhappy ending.

Still, Byatt carefully tempers the closure enabled by this effective fusion of classical and native-English stories. The final pages of *Morpho* have Adamson and Crompton on the deck of a boat sailing through the night toward the New World. Byatt tells us that "this is a good place to leave them, on the crest of a wave, between the ordered green hedgerows [of England], and the coiling, striving mass of forest along the Amazon shore" (182). However, Byatt is not actually ready to leave them, for she has the captain enter and present Adamson with a "curiosity," a monarch butterfly that one of the sailors has found in the rigging. Crompton "observes to William and Captain Papagay that the wings are still dusty with life. 'It fills me with emotion' she says. 'I do not know whether it is more fear, or more hope. It is so fragile, and so easily crushed, and nowhere in reach of where it was going. And yet it is still alive, and bright, and so surprising, rightly seen.' 'That is the main thing,' says Captain Papagay. 'To be alive. As long as you are alive, everything is surprising, rightly seen.' And the three of them look out with renewed interest at the points of light in the dark around them" (183). It is important that Adamson and Crompton are not, at this moment, alone on this starlit deck. The Captain's presence (a benign father figure, a saint of traveling?) negates the possibility of closure-via-embrace — the marriage plot's own form of biological determinism. Instead, the Captain's words enable a reinterpretation of one of the novella's key symbols, the butterfly. The novella's final focus is thereby refined: once associated with Eugenia, confinement, and the Hive, the symbol of the butterfly is renewed. It is now "surprising." Papagay ensures that this symbol is "rightly seen" as a figure for a life, a mode of being that is genuine and vital because one lives it at the intersection of science and poetry, realism and Romance. This butterfly is simultaneously an instance of *Danaus plexippus* and the self whose nature is traveling.

This situation and its symbols, however, are pictured ironically. In order to get at what makes *Morpho* and its version of the Self as Insect postmodern, I must push my interpretation further. The Romantic situation (a loving couple viewing the stars while on a cruise) is narratively appropriate, but Byatt's forceful use foregrounds its artificiality. Byatt's equivocality extends to Adamson's and Crompton's relationship: while it is considerably more intellectual (i.e., modern) than Adamson's marriage with Eugenia, like the one it supersedes this modern relationship's foundational attraction is biological. But this moment cannot be reduced to satire. Byatt's personal ironization of love in all its forms is distinguishable from her technical use of irony. To clarify: this moment's layered meanings simultaneously express the narrator's opinion of love and reiterate the text's postmodern relationship with inherited forms. At work here — but not necessarily in harmonious concert — is a singular reporting consciousness (an entity that to me feels like the child of George Eliot and Virginia Woolf who has been reading Swammerdam and Darwin for their metaphors) and a postmodern attitude toward the symbol. *Morpho*'s plot presents this butterfly as a substantive — but the shifting dissonance between conventional narrative, the perspicacious, wry, and yet loving narrating voice, and Byatt's quietly massive style generates an animating context. Byatt uses science and the English novel to play a sort of jazz in the Victorian key. Her style is improvisational: its intense vigilance is made fluid through a simultaneity of rejection and acceptance that publishes its postmodern alignment. Bathed in this jazz the butterfly's significance as a symbol for the traveling self is marvelously complicated. Adamson and Crompton are not singular Orestean wanderers. Domesticated by love, they are fellow travelers: separate selves who through biological coercion, a shared economic need, and intellectual choice form an artificial and provisional entity. And Papagay's involvement suggests how different this entity is from that suggested by the conventional notion of love: although he is not one of the lovers, significantly, Papagay shares their way of seeing.

Our release from focusing on the monarch lends pleasure to the three's mutual and yet individuating act of "looking out with *renewed* interest at the points of light in the dark around them" (my emphasis). Something old has been reinvigorated. Significantly, these "points of light" are not the stars that lovers are so fond of regarding. They are instead "phosphorescent animalcules, the Medusae [a kind of jellyfish, like the beehive a singular and yet composite organism], swimming with tiny hairs, presenting a kind of *reverse image* of the lavish star soup" (182; my emphasis). Adamson, Crompton, and Captain Papagay are poised between the micro- and macrocosms, each of which echoes the other — but, again, it is the visual evidence of life that receives their "renewed interest," not the "profound, blue-black [sky], spattered with the flowing, spangled river of the Milky Way." Adamson seems to have discovered a way to view the cosmos through its smallest forms without artificial magnification and hence without either anxiety or separation and its attendant sense of fumbling giantism. This inversion of his earlier way-of-being is congruent with that moment in *Woman* when Jumpei feels that his perspective on things, his world, has been "turned upside down," that its "projections and depressions [have been] reversed." And similar to the consequences of Jumpei's change, Adamson now seems to enjoy an outlook that, while it emphasizes the connective work of aesthetic intuition over the divisive precision of science, does not accept antagonism between poetry and science, feeling and reason, reading and traveling. Indeed, Byatt suggests a way of seeing that holds as complementary poetic intuition and scientific process. Adamson's silence at this moment may be read as a confirmation of this "new" science, for Adamson breaks with his usual habit by not providing his companions with facts about these living lights. These we are given by the narrator.

Unlike Abe's entomologist, however, Adamson does not have to go it alone during his crucial shift from one sort of seeing to another. It is Crompton, playing Eve to her cerebral Adam, who enables her man's seeing. Together, as I have said, she and Adamson form a greater and — because it combines biological coercion and intellectual affinity — peaceful whole, a condition that is further suggested by the nature and order of their reactions to the monarch. We have seen that the butterfly "fill[s]" Crompton "with emotion[s]" of fear and hope, but this admission is a response to and a completion and humanization of Adamson's factual statements. This movement recapitulates the novel's philosophical domestication of Sartre: "It is the Monarch, says William, excited, Danaus Plexippus, which is known to migrate great distances along the American coast. They are strong fliers, he tells Matilda, but the winds can carry them hundreds of miles out to sea" (183). In addition, as if to nail down her point about Adamson's and Crompton's unity, Byatt represents their final speeches to each other within a single paragraph. This practice deviates from the conventional indentation that is her practice elsewhere in the novella, to include the first of what Byatt calls "two more pictures," the scene in which Adamson takes leave of Eugenia. In this picture, Adamson confronts Eugenia with the unnaturalness of her relations with her brother and the absoluteness of their parting. Here, as I have mentioned, the dialogue is conventionally indented, and therefore especially contrasts with the form Byatt chooses for the second and final picture. The effect of this shift in form is one of separation from what has occurred, a sense that we and the characters we have come to care about occupy a new space and may look forward to happier prospects.

The Hive's Affective Future

Like all of the narratives using the Self as Insect that I have presented in this and the previous chapter, *Morpho* examines what it means to exist within the Hive rather than above it. Byatt's primary means of representing the psychological consequences of and creative response to Adamson's enhivement is a series of verbal pictures that chart his maturation, his discovery of and adjustment to an existence defined by a relationship founded upon mental and physical affinity. These pictures also provide her with a language that makes visible a particular order of mental action; they are a symbol system that extends her analysis of the visual act's ethical and psychological implications. Hence, as with all the texts that I have examined in this argument — and given Byatt's motives — we have no need to wonder why we again find the Hive exactly where it should be.

In the course of this argument, among other things, I have tried to show that the Hive topos is itself a special sort of seeing, a gestalt and a process by which the mind constructs the self and Other in relation. It is thus an object deserving its long history of reworking and our attention. Further, our analysis of the Hive's development after the dissolution of rhetoric's official rule suggests that at present our topos evokes two distinct ways of imagining oneself in relation to the collective: the Other as Insect and the Self as Insect. These versions of the Hive are antithetical procedures for construing the world, and each is roughly congruent with a specific outlook that favors a particular analogical mode. I have formalized these two analogical modes with contrasting paradigms: the *instrumental* (which either denies metaphor or attempts to make it a mere tool — either way this mode works from the separation of subject and object, and thus favors contrast and hierarchy) and the *affective* (a way of construing the world through metaphor's capacity for mutual definition and the merging of substances). Even though most writers tend to mix these two analogical modes, reflection upon the modern instances of the Hive suggests that the Other as Insect, the view of the collective from without, tends to favor the instrumental mode, whereas the Self as Insect is in sympathy with the affective.

Now I move up the scale of forms so that I may speak of the Hive as an idea complex: While it is true that the conception of the Hive I am presenting has narrowed to a contrast between two antithetical models accompanied by opposing analogical tendencies, this focus is not without its value, for it illuminates what is currently the Hive's most viable region. Of this complex's two "post"-rhetorical modes, the Self as Insect is the most active, largely because the modern subject feels himself or herself to be contained, defined, and pressured by the social realm, the human Hive, to a degree heretofore unknown. The experience of standing outside the social Hive now seems a bit naive and old-fashioned, and perhaps difficult to imagine. Hence, it is to the Self as Insect that we must look if we are to make any estimate as to the Hive's further progress in the West.

Since I am now engaged in prognostication, it is fortunate to have the perspective of Byatt's *Morpho Eugenia*, for this novella suggests that the Hive's development is proceeding as it always has: by the recovery and reworking of inherited models. Moving back down the scale of forms, I have established that because of the power of the Sartrean pattern, in order to use the Hive topos as the scene for a newer form of the existential *Bildung*, Abe and Byatt must each create what I have called a "counter-armature" — an aesthetic and philosophical mechanism whose purpose is Orestes's re-rhetoricization. Both writers do so by drawing upon alternative, culturally specific paradigms. I have described Byatt's formulation as a combination of myth and marriage plot, and have read *Morpho* accordingly. However, *Morpho* exhibits another characteristic that — while it cannot, of course, enable us to predict exactly what forms the Self as Insect shall take in the future — nonetheless marks one of its possible developmental paths and its source.

J. M. Coetzee shows us where to direct our attention. In his review of Byatt's *Babel Tower*, Coetzee shows a fondness for the term "literary ventriloquism," which he applies to Byatt several times — and not, one gathers, without pejorative implications. On the one hand, Coetzee applauds her for moments in *Babel Tower* when the "voice of their culture speaks through" her characters.[13] Yet he also feels this same quality to be a weakness: "*Babel Tower* is a novel of ideas, and many of its situations — the activities of the commission, for instance — are contrived as occasions for the discussion of ideas. Not only does the new Parisian structuralism come up but also advances in the sciences: in genetics, biochemistry, animal psychology, linguistics, computer science. To an extent these conversations bring to life the intellectual excitement of the mid-1960s. Nevertheless, in the end one is left puzzled. Much of the science is now outdated: What can Byatt's motive be for devoting so many pages to it?" (18). Indeed, *Babel Tower* is a novel of ideas and several of them have to do with science. Since most of Byatt's fictions are distinguished by the quality of their intellectual reconstruction, I am not sure that I follow all of Coetzee's reservations. In particular, I am puzzled by his puzzlement about Byatt's interest in "science [that is] now outdated." If *Babel Tower* is "about" the intellectual life of a certain time, and the science discussed is of that period, then in what sense is this science "outdated"?

Problem or not in *Tower*, Byatt's attention to Victorian science is one of *Morpho*'s most engaging aspects. Indeed, Coetzee seems to like *Morpho* more than *Tower*, but he does remark that the novella "allow[s] Byatt to do more high-Victorian ventriloquizing." This statement seems to undercut his comment that *Morpho* "shows Byatt at her satiric best in a world that is textual (Darwin, Tennyson, Lewis Carroll) rather than real, a world that she is at home in and reproduces exactly" (19). I have read Byatt perhaps more carefully than Coetzee, for I know that her genius is for irony more than satire. Be this as it may, my point is that effective satire and irony equally require a presence of mind superior to what suffices for "ventriloquizing." I will not address the problem raised by Coetzee's assumption that text may evoke anything other than a "textual" world. However, I will respond to the idea that Byatt "reproduces exactly" the "high-Victorian" moment. The truth of Byatt's reconstructive genius in *Morpho* is that it *imitates* rather than "reproduces" its object. And I mean imitation in the antique, writerly sense: the use of inherited form as a means for establishing and reworking essences.

Byatt's attention to Victorian ideas is not simply a means for evoking a mood or anticipating what will please the doily and Masterpiece Theater set. I submit that in *Morpho* Byatt is *using* the high-Victorian moment, its science in particular, to image and deploy an outlook that makes current — which is to say *postmodern* — sense.[14] Byatt would answer the Sartrean pattern with a theory of existence and a way of seeing that together synthesize what modernist Orestes would keep separate: science and imagination, the instrumental and the poetic modes of apprehension. Byatt is a modern who *chooses* to journey into an uncertain but exhilarating future — and so is Adamson. She sets this novella of ideas in the Victorian moment because she requires aspects of its psychology that may be recovered only through literary form. In sum, I argue that Byatt wishes to move forward, to imagine, as it were, "around" Sartre's psychic and aesthetic bulk — and that to do so, since she cannot imagine the future, she has no choice but to reimagine the past.

To reiterate: I sense that *Morpho* works toward and in its conclusion posits as ethical a way of seeing that combines without reduction or hierarchy the scientific and poetic modes. If I were to follow Coetzee too closely, I would be forced to hold that this way of seeing is anachronistic, the capstone to an act of literary ventriloquism. But there is another way to think about what Byatt — and postmodernism in general — is doing with "outdated science" and subject positions. I suggest that Byatt's double attitude toward the object is a theory of the symbol that is recoverable only *through* the act of literary ventriloquism. Her evocation of ideas at such a fine level should therefore be studied as a form of intellectual mimesis. Who or what, then, is she imitating, and why?

There is one moment in particular that suggests both the author of

Byatt's chosen theory of the symbol and what we should make of it —
and he is neither precisely Victorian nor English. In the days before his
marriage, during a conversation with Harald Alabaster about God and
natural design, Adamson is privy to Alabaster's refutation of a passage
by Darwin wherein he talks about how the eye's excellence tempts us to
believe in a Creator. In this scene Alabaster plays the old-fashioned defender of an interested cosmos and Adamson the doubting modern, pro-
ponent of an orderly but Godless nature. Alabaster says:

> Now, Darwin, in his passage on the *eye*, does seem, does he not, to
> allow the possibility of a Creator? He compares the perfecting of the
> eye to the perfecting of the telescope, and talks about the changes
> over the millennia to a thick layer of transparent tissue, with a nerve
> sensitive to light beneath, and he goes on to remark that *if* we com-
> pare the forces that form the eye to the human intellect *"we must sup-*
> *pose that there is a power always intently watching each slight accidental*
> *alteration in the transparent layers."* Mr. Darwin invites us to suppose
> that this intently watching power is inconceivable — that the force
> employed is blind necessity, the law of *matter*. But I say that in matter
> itself is contained a great *mystery* — how did it come to be at all —
> how does organisation take place — may we not after all come face
> to face in considering these things with the Ancient of Days? (41;
> Byatt's emphasis)

Harald Alabaster is something of an old fogey. Even to him his version
of the argument-by-design seems a bit tired. However, it is Adamson's
and not Alabaster's way of seeing that Byatt tests, finds wanting, and
modifies. Furthermore, it is Adamson not Alabaster who represents our
modern, Sartrean scientific outlook. It is Alabaster — the voice of a fading philosophy — who, contra-Darwin, insists that poetic analogy has a
place in scientific investigation. Alabaster's awareness that "in matter itself is contained a great mystery" anticipates Adamson's later mode of
seeing, which is the focus of *Morpho*'s concluding picture. If Adamson's
instrumental seeing is Sartrean and his "rightly see[ing]" its correction,
then, far from being "outdated," Alabaster's science, his attitude toward
metaphor, is at the core of Byatt's answer to Sartre. Is, then, Alabaster
postmodern?

Byatt's ventriloquism is a means of getting at a psychology that helps
her to imagine what would otherwise be impossible — a non-Sartrean

way of being: organicism. This non-Sartrean outlook grew up in opposition to and then was supplanted by the exact and unequivocal sort of science that undergirds the Sartrean pattern. Keeping in mind that *Morpho* is a response to Sartre and that Adamson is an Orestean type, through Alabaster's quotation of Darwin we overhear Maurice Maeterlinck: "we must suppose that there is a power always intently watching each slight accidental alteration in the transparent layers."[15] Again, perhaps there is more to Byatt's "literary ventriloquizing" than Coetzee knows.

In a passage from *The Life of the Bee*, a work that mingles — to our taste rather curiously — natural history, organicism, and scientificized theology, Maeterlinck points out what comes of the "eye draw[ing] near" to the Hive:

> It comes to pass with the bees as with most of the things in this world; we remark some few of their habits; we say they do this, they work in such and such fashion. . . . And then we imagine we know them, and ask nothing more . . . we see the constant agitation within the hive; their life seems very simple to us, and bounded, like every life, by the instinctive cares of reproduction and nourishment. But let the eye draw near, and endeavour to see; and at once the least phenomenon of all becomes overpoweringly complex; we are confronted by the enigma of intellect, of destiny, will, aim, means, causes; the incomprehensible organisation of the most insignificant act of life. (45–46).

As if he senses the rise of the Orestean type, Maeterlinck invites us — *the Orestes in us* — to "draw near" the Other; as it were, to come down from our hill, but to leave there the way of seeing that issues from and depends upon the *cogito*. Because Orestes discovers himself through a sight of the Hive from afar, it "seems [to him] very simple," a locus of "constant [irrational] agitation" and a space wherein being is "bounded . . . by instinct." Because he carries within him this originative sight, even when near "the enigma of . . . life," its "complex[ity]" escapes him. To unreformed Orestes any "act of life" external to his own is merely an agent against which he must contend, an aspect of the "dead and alive" substance awaiting the potency of his will. Perhaps, then, the true "high-Victorian" of *Morpho* is Adamson before he finds true love, for his instrumental outlook — an earlier guise of which Maeterlinck endeavors to correct — derives from a Marxism unalloyed by the lessons of the twentieth century. Hence, its ecological blindness and illiberal humanism.

Maeterlinck proposes that we accept that even the "least phenomenon" is "overpoweringly complex," its organization "incomprehensible." How, then, may the singular subject "confront" an "enigma" of this order and survive? His solution is Byatt's: in order to "see rightly" we must apprehend things as both similar to and distinct from ourselves; rather than reject, we must accept and value the enchantment of the world that analogy alone enables. In the following passage, Maeterlinck renames analogy "illusion" and argues that "the faculty of admiring which an illusion may have created within us will serve for the truth that must come, be it sooner or later. It is with the words, the feelings, and ardour created with ancient and imaginary beauties, that humanity welcomes to-day truths which perhaps would have never been born, which might not have been able to find so propitious a home, had these sacrificed illusions not first of all dwelt in, and kindled, the heart and the reason whereinto these truths should descend" (323). Although "ancient and imaginary beauties" such as the Hive are not the truth, the "faculty of admiring" that they arouse in us may pass as such. Maeterlinck tells us that these "beauties" will be inevitably and happily supplanted by something grander, but nearly a century has passed since he wrote these words and still we wait for its advent. Or, rather, those of us who are not poets wait — for the sum of this entire argument is that the truth of things is neither in the future nor something that we may expect to descend from above. Instead, as demonstrated by the long history of the Hive, the illusion that passes for each age's truth is continually emerging from inherited beauties that are embodied in form and by dint of a process that only begins with admiring. Admiration evokes the desire to imitate, and imitation is the genius of *retractatio*, the way we draw honey from the Hive of language. Viewed thus, this getting of honey is natural to our kind — essential, really, for, as our postmodern writers remind us, the Hive is home. We are like bees, tirelessly and together converting last spring's rhetoric into new white comb.

NOTES

PREFACE

1 Honoré de Balzac, *Père Goriot*, 276.
2 Arthur Zajonc, *Catching the Light*, 5.
3 Giambattista Vico, *The New Science*, 88.
4 Jules Michelet, *The Insect*, 52.
5 Michel Foucault, *The Order of Things* (abbreviated as *OT*), 43.
6 Ernst Mayr, "Cause and Effect in Biology," 26.
7 Martin Heidegger, *Early Greek Thinking*, 14.

INTRODUCTION: THE ALPHABET OF THE BEES

1 Dennis L. Dollens brought to my attention the exceptional passage by Nietzsche that I have quoted in the epigraph. He has also several times mentioned to me "Motown bee songs," a family of the insect analogy that has yet to be described and cataloged. For an engaging and thoughtful introduction to Goethe's theory of light and color, see pp. 188–216 of Zajonc, *Catching the Light*.
2 Lewis Thomas, "Social Talk," 108.
3 Virgil, *Aeneid*, rev. ed., 2 vols., trans. H. R. Fairclough, 1:271. Unless otherwise indicated, all passages from the *Aeneid* and the *Georgics* are taken from these volumes.
4 *Collections of the Massachusetts Historical Society*, ser. 4, vol. 7 (recatalogued as vol. 37), frontispiece.
5 George D. Watt, *Deseret Alphabet, 2nd Reader*, artist unknown. (New York: Russel Brothers, 1886). Perhaps to no other religion are the symbols of the honeybee and the beehive as important as they are to Mormonism. Unfortunately, I have not had time to research and report on this fascinating use of the insect metaphor.
6 Fatbeehive, Inc., http://www.fatbeehive.com (30 August 1998).
7 La Colmena, Plaça de l'Angel, 12, Barcelona.
8 Beehive Technologies, Inc., http://www.bzzzzzz.com (30 August 1998). This same abstraction of the hive metaphor may be conceived three-dimensionally, employed as the ultimate organizational scene or principle. For instance, Jorge Luis Borges begins "The Library of Babel" (in *Labyrinths: Selected Stories and Other Writing*) with the following definition of the universe: "The universe (which others call the Library) is composed of an indefinite and perhaps infinite number of hexagonal galleries" (51). It is in one of these hexagonal spaces that the unnamed narrator was born. And it is in this library, which the speaker describes as "*a sphere whose exact center is any one of its hexagons and whose circumference is inaccessible,*" that he will die (52, Borges's italics). Although speaking of the universe/Library through Pascal's argument of God, Borges's speaker sums up the beehive as a symbol for an order of signs that anticipates our current fantasies and fears about the World Wide Web: "*The Library is unlimited and cyclical*" (58, Borges's italics). Further, Borges's vision of the universe as a labyrinth of signs subordinated to the hexagon and its associations anticipates elements of A. S. Byatt's sense of the cosmos, which I suggest in chapter 6. Finally, how do we understand Borges's image of the Library/universe as a circular system

of hexagons? Gaston Bachelard suggests that "when a thing becomes isolated, it becomes round, assumes a figure of being that is concentrated upon itself" (*Poetics of Space*, 239). This statement sheds light on Borges's universe, for it contains everything and is therefore absolutely isolate. Hence, the fusion of the Scholastic definition of God (a circle of infinite circumference whose center is therefore everywhere) with the sign of the Hive. This arresting image defines Being as a labyrinth of signifying spaces that, because of its very completeness, exists absolutely and yet does not: this labyrinth is simultaneously entirely made and yet eternally under construction.

9   Beehive Productions, http://www.beehivepro.com (30 August 1998).
10 Beehive Telephone Companies, http://beehive.net (30 August 1998).
11 Ralph Waldo Emerson, "The Poet," 455.
12 Karl Marx, *Capital*, 163.
13 Emily Dickinson, "Awake ye muses nine, sing me a strain divine," 11–14.
14 Jonathan Swift, *Gulliver's Travels and Other Writings*, 112.
15 Mary Shelley, *Frankenstein*, 83.
16 Kafka calls Gregor "*ungeheueres Ungeziefer*," which Stanley Corngold translates as "monstrous vermin." According to Corngold, "'*Ungeheuer*' connotes the creature who has no place in the family; '*Ungeziefer*,' the unclean animal unsuited for sacrifice, the creature without a place in God's order" (Corngold, introduction to *The Metamorphosis*, xix).
17 Samuel Gompers and Herman Guttstadt (attributed), "AFL, Some Reasons for Chinese Exclusion. Meat vs. Rice. American Manhood against Asiatic Coolieism. Which Shall Survive?" Rosanne Currarino, scholar of labor history, kindly provided me with this and other similar references.
18 George Lakoff and Mark Johnson, *Philosophy in the Flesh*, 102–11.
19 Wolfgang Kohler, *Gestalt Psychology*, 39.
20 As will become clearer, the Hive is both a figure of speech (a particular arrangement of words) and a figure of thought (a form of ideas). Parallelism is an example of the former: "I came, I saw, I conquered"; and metaphor of the latter: "my love is a rose." This combination of figural characteristics means that the Hive may be present as a structural principle even when its tableau is less than fully presented. In *De Oratore* 3.52.200, Cicero observes that "there is this difference between the figurative character of language and of thought, that the figure suggested by the words disappears if one alters the words, but that of the thoughts remains whatever words one chooses to employ." He is speaking of pure instances of each of these categories. Now even though the Hive combines the offices of the figures of speech and thought, to a degree it shares metaphor's capacity to exist independently of any particular arrangement of words. As I shall make clearer, whereas the function of metaphor and similarly "pure" figures of thought is a natural aspect of the mind's workings, the Hive is more of a habit, one whose structurally generated meaning grows out of our experience of the world.
21 Corbusier, *When the Cathedrals Were White*, 89–90; Corbusier's emphasis. Further, although David E. Nye is incorrect to imply that the view from the top of a skyscraper was humankind's first experience of the Hive's perspectival tableau (and was thus, by way of extension, responsible for its attendant entomological metaphor),

his discussion of the Empire State Building's psychological and aesthetic consequences is revealing. See his *American Technological Sublime*, 100–108. Of particular interest is his clear discussion of how this view evoked feelings of "mastery." He classifies this experience of the city-as-pattern as an aspect of a larger aesthetic nexus he calls the "geometrical sublime," which fairly describes what students of the beehive began to see in it starting, it is reasonable to suppose, in the late Renaissance. A seventeenth-century anticipation may be seen in the following passage from Sir Thomas Browne's *Religio Medici*, which merges classical, Biblical, and mathematical valuations of natural order. The passage emphasizes the fascinating qualities of miniature life and, by way of extension, insect behavior and architecture: "Indeed what Reason may not go to school to the Wisdom of Bees, Ants, and Spiders. . . . what wise hand teacheth them to do what Reason cannot teach us? Ruder heads stand amazed at those prodigious pieces of nature, Whales, Elephants, Dromedaries, and Camels; these, I confess, are the Colossus and majestic pieces of her hand: but in these narrow engines there is more curious Mathematicks" (quoted in Marjorie Hope Nicolson, *Science and Imagination*, n. 155). Before Nature was searched for its "Mathematicks," the beehive was admired for its social architecture alone. That is, before the rise of the quantified natural sciences, the beehive was largely associated with a natural (and in some instances a supernaturally sanctioned) civic perfection rather than one spatial or artificial, one that could be represented by numbers. Hence, seeing in the beehive's physical structure an expression of nature's mathematical "soul" is an early sign of the modern outlook that, for our purposes, Sartre brings to its absolute and final dramatic fruition.

22 All passages from *Paradise Lost* (abbreviated as *PL*) are quoted from *Complete Poems and Major Prose*, edited by Merritt Y. Hughes.

23 Homer, *The Iliad of Homer*, translated by Richmond Lattimore, 16.641–44. Unless otherwise indicated, all passages from the *Iliad* are from this translation.

24 *King Lear*, 4.1.36–37.

25 Henry David Thoreau, *Walden*, 674.

26 Sylvia Plath, "Stings," lines 60–65.

27 I learned of Virgil's contrasting ants and bees from an unpublished article by Andre Stipanovic, which he kindly made available.

28 Quoted in Becker, *When the War Was Over*, 200–201.

29 In *Next of Kin* the primatologist Roger Fouts reports that Washoe — a female chimpanzee he helped to raise and teach, who learned elements of American Sign Language — when removed from her human family and placed with her own kind for the first time, referred to them as "black bugs." Fouts writes that "Washoe loved to squish black bugs. They were the lowest form of life, as far beneath human — and therefore herself — as anything that she could think of. Along with everything else she had learned from her foster family, Washoe had apparently absorbed the lesson of human superiority" (121–22). I am not sure that Fouts is correct in his assessment that Washoe's figuring of the other chimpanzees as "black bugs" is necessarily *human* in origin. Humans and chimpanzees appear to share an instinct for complex social hierarchy and language (spoken as well as gestural), an intense visual faculty, and the capacity to make analogies (a fundamental principle of memory-based behavior; see Fouts, 156–59). It is therefore arguable that Washoe came to her analogy naturally.

While this line of speculation does not make an "archetype" of the Hive topos, it does, however, suggest that the Hive's structure emerges from the contact between the world and our (largely) visually based categorical faculty. Also relevant to this line of speculation are Fouts's observations about how other cross-fostered chimpanzees classified themselves in response to or through sorting photographic images, 160–62. At least to me, this sorting of images into categories of human and Other seems to involve the same sort of reasoning as Washoe's hierarchical "black bug" analogy. Hence, this analogy may be a simplified version of the hive metaphor.

1. FROM HOMER TO VIRGIL

1 Jules Michelet, *The Insect*, 130.

2 George Eliot, *The Mill on the Floss*, 181.

3 For a succinct and lucid discussion of the Homeric simile, see Martin Mueller, *The Iliad*. Mueller's comments about Homer's cinematic qualities are particularly relevant to our study: The *Iliad*'s "seeming digressions and endless descriptions are, like still shots or slow-motion sequences, moments of heightened suspense" (109). Mueller also confirms the *Iliad*, book 2 bee simile's aesthetic importance to the whole and helpfully defines its local narrative function: "The most elaborate simile cluster in *The Iliad* occurs in book 2 when the marshaling of the army on the plain of Skamander is expressed through a sequence of five similes. This unique cluster expresses not only the sheer mass of the army but also *the process by which the confused multitude is turned into an orderly force*" (111; my emphasis).

4 J. M. Redfield observes that in the *Iliad* "dominant simile families are at the edge of civilization: a point of liminality and conflict." See his *Nature and Culture in the Iliad*, 113–14.

5 John Keegan, *A History of Warfare*, 3–12, 196, 237–54.

6 Although Joseph Farrell does not treat *retractatio* specifically, it is nonetheless central to his discussion of classical allusion, which is well worth knowing. See his *Vergil's Georgics and the Traditions of Ancient Epic*, 3–25. Also see Davis P. Harding, *The Club of Hercules*, 8–19; and W. F. Jackson Knight, *Roman Vergil*, 73–77.

7 The notion that my object's structure is consistent across a range of translations is central to this argument. Later in this chapter I will redefine my tableau as a *literary topos*, a mental shape that organizes verbal experience between the level of the sentence and the level of narrative. Since a form like the Hive is established almost entirely by a visually informed order of elements and their spatial relationships, its core structure is largely independent of generic, linguistic, and cultural limits. Consequently, the translator and the poet use the literary topos similarly: the first to structure translation and the second as a template for invention. And given the recent emergence and vigorous growth of a translation-driven world literature, it is important that we come to understand the Hive and its topical kin.

8 Hesiod, *Works and Days*, 61–68.

9 498–502. Wilkinson uses this passage as a lens for examining Virgil's politics and patrimonial concerns. See his translation, 30. For a fuller and yet still accessible treatment of the poem, also by L. P. Wilkinson, see *The Georgics of Virgil: A Critical Survey*. Useful for thinking about how Virgil uses the pastoral landscape and its conventions to image cosmopolitan concerns is Eleanor Winsor Leach's *Vergil's Eclogues:*

Landscapes of Experience. Although this volume treats the *Eclogues* rather than the *Georgics*, Leach's analysis helps the reader to grasp the pastoral foundations of Virgil's art, which in turn clarifies the all-important symbolic aspect of his realism. In this regard I heartily recommend approaching the *Aeneid* as the culmination of a process: through, first, the *Eclogues* and then the *Georgics*. Indeed, the heart of my argument about the poetic relationship between Homer and Virgil hinges upon an act of *retractatio* that occurs in Virgil's fourth *Georgic*. I submit that Virgil takes on Homer gradually, selectively. This cumulative approach to Virgilian intertextuality helps illuminate Virgil's choice of Homer's bee simile as the hinge for his engagement with the Greek epic's local forms. I have also found sections of Joseph Farrell's learned analysis of Virgilian allusion, *Vergil's Georgics and the Traditions of Ancient Epic* similarly helpful (3–96, 207–72). In particular, I have come to value his observation that allusion in Virgil is a strategy that enables the reader to participate in the poetry's construction, a process that he calls a "creative dialogue" (62). He also surveys the critical debate surrounding the nature of allusion in Virgil and is singularly clear about the importance of understanding this practice through the rhetorical vocabulary of the time.

10 For an exhaustive discussion of *giantomachia* in Virgil, see Philip K. Hardie, *Virgil's Aeneid: Cosmos and Imperium*, 85–119. Although not as explicitly featured as other topics in the book, Hardie's treatment of how Virgil structures epic space is worth reading. In particular, see 219–37, wherein Hardie discusses the relationship between philosophical system and representations of space. His focus in this section is Virgil's imitation of Lucretius, which is most illuminating.

11 In his *A Handlist of Rhetorical Terms* (52–53), Richard Lanham quotes Ong at length and recasts the latter's distinction between logical and literary topoi as one between "formal" and "material" commonplaces.

12 The single most helpful English translation of Aristotle's *Rhetoric* remains Lane Cooper's *The Rhetoric of Aristotle*. For his commentary on the argumentative topoi, see pp. xxiv–xxv of the introduction. In this volume, Aristotle discusses the most universal topoi (143–47) and provides us with an annotated list of those more specific (154–72). In his own right, Cooper obliges the reader with a descriptive analysis that lays out the work's plan and the organization of the topics (xxxvii–xlvii).

13 Lanham's distinction between "formal" and "material" topoi is a version of the useful but sometimes overly analytic division between "form" and "content" that seems to preoccupy twentieth-century criticism. I take this distinction between form and content to mean that, on the one hand, the general topoi are "pure" *containers*, abstract forms that may be "filled" with, and thus are empowered to order, almost any matter; and that, on the other, the literary commonplaces, which are ceremonial or generic set pieces, are "pure" *content*. Such a distinction tends to break down in literary practice, because few writers deal with inherited forms as mere content that may be simply repeated verbatim. Even in the Western epic tradition, one in which for many centuries the Homeric texts were treated as quasi-religious objects, poets felt comfortable with vigorously reworking inherited set pieces. For example, if one compares Homer's "Shield of Achilles" (*Iliad* 18) with Virgil's "Shield of Aeneas" (*Aeneid* 8), one sees that this "material" topos's content is considerably altered. With the possible exception of bureaucratic titles and customs, probably the most persis-

tent and justifiable use of unaltered material topoi in modern life is to be found in religious discourse, especially in oral delivery, because much more than written language, spoken performance tends toward and indeed invigorates formula. For instance, when speaking about or interpreting the language of the King James Version of the Bible, American Protestant literalists will use Elizabethan pronouns and verb forms, claiming even that this style of English language is God's language.

14 Walter Ong, quoted in Lanham, *Handlist*, 152–53.

15 This wonderfully suggestive phrase is not Curtius's. It belongs to Ferdinand Brunetière (*ELLMA*, 609), about whose thought Curtius wrote his doctoral dissertation. Peter Godman quotes Brunetière and discusses Curtius's relationship with him and others in the epilogue to *ELLMA* (599–653).

16 Here I am making a distinction between a "strategy of arrangement" (the overall plan of a composition) and the schemes (the "figures of form"), such as climax or parallelism. Although we may speak of the former as a convention, as when we divide a novel into chapters, unlike the scheme of climax, which is general and exceedingly flexible (in that it may be used to structure a sentence as well as an entire work), the logic of any strategy of arrangement is unique to a particular work. Thus, in comparison to the scheme, the strategy of arrangement is at once more artificial and more limited.

17 Quintilian, *Institutio Oratoria*, vol. 3, 7.6.1.

18 Corbett, 441.

19 Homer, *The Odyssey*, trans. A. T. Murray, vol. 1, 381.

20 *Iliad*, 18.606–7.

21 Sennett quotes this passage from Joseph Rykwert, *The Idea of a Town* (Cambridge, Mass.: MIT Press, 1988), 59.

2. FROM DANTÉ TO MILTON

1 Dante Alighieri, *Paradiso*, 31.1–12. Unless otherwise indicated, all passages by Dante in Italian and their translations are from Mandelbaum's three-volume translation, which I abbreviate as follows: *Inferno, Inf.*; *Purgatorio, Pur.*; *Paradiso, Par.*

2 For a discussion of Lucretius's theory of life-seeds and its significance to Virgil, see Philip K. Hardie, *Virgil's Aeneid: Cosmos and Imperium*, 219–37.

3 A lucid treatment of this signal change in the Christian West's idea of and relationship with nature is Marjorie Hope Nicolson's *The Breaking of the Circle*. For a more contemporary interpretation of cultural change, see Michel Foucault's *The Order of Things*.

4 Kenneth Burke, *Counter-Statement*, 58; my italics.

5 John Milton, *Paradise Lost* (abbreviated as *PL*), 231 n. See Rebecca W. Smith, "The Source of Milton's Pandemonium," *Modern Philology* 29 (1931): 187–98.

6 John Milton, *Defensio Prima* (First Defense), 87.

7 The term "unexercised" I take from Milton's *Areopagitica* (abbreviated as *Areo.*) This term neatly summarizes his belief that a leisurely, or timid, Christianity is not genuine. Milton writes: "I cannot praise a fugitive and cloistered virtue, unexercised and unbreathed, that never sallies out and sees her adversary, but slinks out of the race where that immortal garland is to be run for, not without dust and heat" (729).

8 C. M. Bowra, *From Virgil to Milton*, 198–99.

9 Simone Weil, *The Iliad, or The Poem of Force*, 3; Weil's emphasis.

10 Thomas Hobbes, *Leviathan*, 225–28.

11 In "The Bee-Simile Once More," John T. Shawcross provides several interesting examples of sixteenth- and seventeenth-century demonic bees. Of particular significance is Richard Hakluyt's image of Turks — Asiatic infidels — as swarms of bees opposing the rescue of Christians held in Alexandrian fortresses. Shawcross offers evidence that Milton read Hakluyt and was influenced by him.

12 In *Three Elizabethan Pamphlets*, ed. G. R. Hibbard, 13.

13 Fredric Jameson, *The Political Unconscious*, 87.

14 Burke, *Counter-Statement*, 58.

15 The offices of clarifying ideas and making a mental picture are Aristotelean notions of the metaphor. I am arguing that contemporary arhetoricality encourages the Hive's ideological function, which, though visual, is nonetheless distinct from its rhetorical/artistic expressions.

16 Quoted by Antony Beevor, *Stalingrad, the Fateful Siege*, 176.

17 Julia Conaway Bondanella translates "des notions justes" as "accurate notions." However, "true idea" better suits my interpretation of Rousseau. In this part of the *Discourse on Inequality*, Rousseau is laying down an absolute base for further reasoning, hence my selection of "true" rather than "accurate." And the ambition and force of Rousseau's reasoning seems to exclude the tentativeness of the word "notion."

18 Bachelard, *Poetics of Space*, xxxii.

19 For an important reading of *The Republic* that treats the Allegory of the Cave as the dialogue's "center," see John Sallis, *Being and Logos*, 444–55.

20 Bachelard, *Psychoanalysis of Fire*, 21–41.

21 Edward O. Wilson, *Sociobiology*, 4.

3. THE HIVE, THE FABLE, AND THE IMAGINATION OF SHADOW

1 Richard Foster Jones, *Ancients and Moderns*, 48.

2 Kenneth Burke, *A Rhetoric of Motives*, 23.

3 Richard Sennett's *The Fall of Public Man* is an invaluable explanation of why, during the eighteenth and nineteenth centuries, a notion of experience as collective and public was eclipsed by one individual and personal. Regarding the effects of the rise of literacy on European culture and psychology, see Elizabeth L. Eisenstein, *The Printing Revolution in Early Modern Europe*, and Lucien Febvre and Henri-Jean Martin, *The Coming of the Book*.

4 Burke, *Rhetoric of Motives*, 38.

5 Harold Bloom, introduction to *Modern Critical Views: Jonathan Swift*, 10.

6 Bonamy Dobrée, *English Literature*, 16.

7 Musil, "Binoculars," 83–84, 86.

8 See Marjorie Hope Nicolson's *Science and Imagination* for a deservedly influential discussion of the microscope and *Gulliver's Travels*.

9 Quoted in Iona and Peter Opie, *The Classic Fairy Tales*, 158.

10 I have found H. J. Blackham's *The Fable as Literature* to be an extremely useful history and analysis of the fable. Less accessibly written but more encyclopedic is *History of the Graeco-Latin Fable* by Francisco Rodríguez Adrados. I have had the advantage of only volume one of this multivolume work, which treats the fable from its origins through the age of the great Hellenistic collections. I understand that volume two is now available.

11 Seneca, "On Gathering Ideas," 277, 279.

12 My thanks to Debra Roy for pointing out this important connection between Swift and Keats.

13 John Keats, letter "To J. H. Reynolds, February 19, 1818," in *English Romantic Writers* [abbreviated as *ERW*], 1211.

14 Keats, "What the Thrush Said," *ERW*, 1151, lines 9–10, 14.

15 Keats, letter "To Benjamin Bailey, November 22, 1817," *ERW*, 1208.

16 Keats, letter "To George and Tom Keats, December 21–27, 1817," *ERW*, 1209. The reader will profit by Walter Jackson Bate's analysis of negative capability, which Harold Bloom has excerpted in *Romanticism and Consciousness*, 326–43. Indeed, the volume as a whole is an excellent companion to English Romantic texts. A superlatively clear estimate of the West's rediscovery of the sublime — indispensable background for understanding Romanticism — is supplied by Marjorie Hope Nicolson's *Mountain Gloom and Mountain Glory*. A historical perspective on Romantic criticism will be had through Jerome J. McGann's *The Romantic Ideology*. In this book McGann analyzes how Romantic ideology has shaped its critical reception; his ideas are, therefore, a useful antidote to, in particular, Bloom's psychological ahistoricity — which has deeply influenced my own thinking.

17 Please see Mark Loveridge, *A History of the Augustan Fable*. Though modest in length, this volume excellently treats both the context and the details of its subject. It evidences that for the Augustans the fable was far from a minor genre. The bibliography is top shelf.

18 Phillip Harth, introduction to *The Fable of the Bees*, by Bernard Mandeville, 14.

4. THE OTHER AS INSECT

1 In 1586 Luis Mendez de Torres published "the first description of the queen bee as a female that laid eggs." Before Mendez, the beehive was still entirely understood in Greco-Roman terms, as a city ruled by males. Although the ancient model would retain most of its power until the twentieth century, Mendez's correct sexing of the queen bee is a significant break with the past. For a more complete narrative of how we came to our present understanding of the beehive, see Gordon F. Townsend and Eva Crane, "History of Apiculture" (in *History of Entomology*, 387–406). Although dated in some respects, this collection of articles is an authoritative introduction to a range of entomological disciplines. Unless entirely historical, each article begins with a brief but well-researched topic-specific history, and all responsibly survey the appropriate literature.

2 Townsend and Crane, "History of Apiculture," 398.

3 For a strongly stated and, hence, useful account of the cultural consequences of the Industrial Revolution, please see Karl Polanyi's *The Great Transformation*. Polanyi defines the "complex machine," physically and sociologically, somewhat as Lewis Mumford does in *Technics and Civilization*, 3–7, 107–267. Polanyi argues that the complex machine converts everything into a mechanistically explicable and, hence, useful substance: "Machine production in a commercial society involves, in effect, no less a transformation than that of the natural and human substance of society into commodities. The conclusion, though weird, is inevitable; nothing less will serve our purpose: obviously, the dislocation caused by such devices must disjoint man's

relationships and threaten his natural habitat with annihilation" (42). As I shall presently illustrate, the changes in the Hive during this period clearly show that the complex machine's transformative threat was keenly felt.

4 Marjorie Hope Nicolson, *Voyages to the Moon*, 251.

5 The book, one well worth looking through, is Nell Eurich's *Science in Utopia: A Mighty Design*. Even though Eurich makes utopia a focus, until Verne and Wells the overlap between this sort of fantasy and the "cosmic voyage" surveyed by Nicolson in *Voyages to the Moon* is substantial. Thus, Eurich offers an equally valuable but distinct treatment of much of Nicolson's terrain.

6 Although many would claim Jules Verne as the inventor of science fiction, as I have endeavored to express above, his science is distinct from Wells's. Verne indeed complicates the adventure story with science, but science plays second fiddle to the old forms and possibilities, and thus never emerges as a system. In contrast, science in Wells is more complete and powerful, serving as foundation as well as ornament. (As suggested by my analysis of Mandeville's *Fable of the Bees*, a traditional form may be given new and more urgent life through the empirical motive.) How science inflects Wells's relationship with the Romance may be similar to how colonialism affects Conrad's relationship with the same.

7 In chapter 6, I shall attend to A. S. Byatt's *Morpho Eugenia*, which resurrects an organicist notion of the Hive. Because organicism synthesizes instead of opposes the scientific and poetic theories of the symbol, it serves Byatt as a base for her postmodern version of the insect analogy.

8 *Père Goriot* was published in 1834, forty-two years after François Huber's invention of the "leaf beehive" in 1792, which was made of wooden frames and opened like a book for easy bee observation and honey collection. Even so — and despite several improvements over Huber's design — it was not until Lorenzo Lorrain Langstroth's design, which he patented in 1852 and described in his highly influential *The Hive and the Honey Bee*, that the artificial beehive became popular and modern apiculture was born. In Balzac's day, domestic bees were still kept in traditional beehives. When honey was collected the colony was "smoked and choked . . . mercilessly" and "the honey was extracted by removing the honeycombs [thereby killing] . . . the numerous larvae that might still have been alive" (Ramírez, 24 – 35).

9 This law is an extension of what I have already titled the Hive's "aesthetic code": *That which is proximate to me and also my size is like me, and (therefore) that which is distant from me and different in size is unlike me.* This code is a perspectival logic that makes proximity the index of similitude.

5. THE SELF AS INSECT

1 *King Lear*, 4.1.36 – 37.

2 Sigmund Freud, "The Uncanny."

3 I begin this section discussing the uncanniness of the *individual*-as-insect because the formulation better expresses our moment's psychology and hence aligns more obviously with Freud's ideas than does the "collective" sort of uncanny. I shall take up the "collective" as a special source of the uncanny, below, when treating Kafka and Sartre.

4 Aristotle was impressed by the bee's cleanliness (*History of Animals*, 9.40.626a). To

the ancient Hebrews the beehive's product connoted purity. In the Bible, the sweetness of God's law is measured in terms of honey: "How sweet are thy words unto my taste! Yea, sweeter than honey to my mouth" (Ps. 119.104, KJV). During the Middle Ages, the skep was used to represent the Virgin Mary. The probable source of this association between Mary and the hive is Virgil, who in the fourth *Georgic* claimed that the bees "indulge not in conjugal embraces, nor idly unnerve their bodies in love, or bring forth young with travail, but of themselves [without the male] gather their children in their mouths from leaves and sweet herbs" (211). Because the skep was a "home" for the bees, I suspect that it also connoted domesticity, the female sphere. Its conical shape may even have suggested the female breast, which late-Medieval iconographers were not shy about picturing. Certainly, these associations with purity, virginal femininity, and the breast help explain the skep's popularity as an icon of advertizing. In this argument's introduction I cite and briefly discuss some examples.

5 "The locusts have no king, yet go they forth all of them by bands" (Prov. 30.27, KJV). Of the ant, Proverbs says, "Go to the ant, thou sluggard; consider her ways, and be wise, which, having no guide, overseer, or ruler, provideth her food in the summer, and gathereth her food in the harvest" (Prov. 6.6–8, KJV). It is worth noting that when figuring cooperation the author of Proverbs, who represents the ancient Hebraic tradition, conceives of the locust and the ant similarly. According to Proverbs, both species lack rulers but are nonetheless cooperative, which we have long known is not true of ants. This use of the insect is closer to Homer's view than to Virgil's, for, like the speaker of Proverbs, Homer uses insects — bees, wasps, and flies — primarily to signify swarming, an essence to which any suggestion of cooperation is subordinate. In contrast, the Attic Greeks, like the Romans after them, were disposed by their urban, hierarchical outlook to make finer distinctions between insect species. It seems that, while the archaic poet saw in the insect an analog to the human clan or band, the classical poet tended to discern in the same natural pattern a metaphor for social division and monarchal hierarchy. (See Aristotle, *History of Animals*, 9.40.624a–627a; and Plato, *Republic*, 552a–d.) This is not to say, however, that after the founding of the city-state the social insect is used only for imaging the urban condition. Rather, the old capacity remains — but to it is attached related newer meanings. Interestingly, I have yet to discover in either Sumerian or Egyptian literature an equivalent to Virgil's city allegory of *Georgic* 4, which undergirds his further experiments with the form and determines much of the Hive's later development in Western literature. In two Mesopotamian texts, *Atrahasis* (the story of the world destroyed by flood) and *The Epic of Gilgamesh*, for instance, human beings are figured as dragonflies, an insect symbol even less evocative of cooperation than the Hebraic locusts. (See Stephanie Dalley, *Myths from Mesopotamia*, 33, 109.) In this light, it would be quite interesting to establish and then to compare with the classical Hive the insect analogies native to India and China.

6 See Corngold's introduction to his translation of Kafka, *The Metamorphosis*, xix. Unless otherwise noted, all passages by Kafka are from this translation.

7 Until this moment I have generally used the word "humanity" or something similar to signify the state of being a person. Because this argument's remaining pages address the Hive's development within and against the Sartrean existential frame, for

"humanity" I shall substitute the term "human-being-ness," which I have borrowed from Sartre. However, he means it more technically than I do, for I wish "human-being-ness" to express both the state of being human and the notion that one is human in direct proportion to his or her capacity for "identification," by which I mean imaginative sympathy with and hence compassion for a person or creature other than oneself. Kafka, I would argue, favors this "identificatory" definition of the human — and, indeed, it is crucial for the all-important transfer of insectness in *The Metamorphosis*. By this light, Kafka may be said to be the author of an *affective* strain of existentialism that parallels and challenges Sartre's *antagonistic* variety. Because Sartre's existentialism stems from a further rationalization and individuation of German idealist philosophy, it succeeds only through eliminating the irrational and affective qualities of human-being-ness, qualities that, in contrast, Kafka believes are both natural to our species and essential for our individual and social well-being. As I shall presently discuss, because Sartre would have a rational, philosophically consistent ethics, he insists that the human is entirely self-creating, emerging from and sustained by the Cartesian *cogito*. This recipe for self-creation presumes that a person is able to stand apart from the mass and, therefore, may view all things exterior to the *cogito* as illusion, secondary in terms of formative power. As I read him, Kafka does not at all believe in this sort of self-creation. Nor does he share Sartre's obvious will-to-power and his sense of entitlement to action, elements of Sartrean existentialism that I shall also treat presently.

8 When making Harry Lime and revealing his character at the Great Wheel, Greene may have had in mind Friedrich Nietzsche's parable of the *Übermensch* among the "flies of the market place" (*Thus Spake Zarathustra*). In this parable, Nietzsche speaks negatively of the world revolving around the inventors of "new values," ideas that he considers dehumanizing. Greene seems to share some of Nietzsche's suspicion of new values, because he ironizes them. However, perhaps because of the disturbing ethicopolitical implications of Nietzschean excess, I sense that Greene does not totally agree with the Superman's attitude toward the masses, for Zarathustra's language is consonant with how Lime appears to think of himself vis-à-vis the rest of humanity: "Even when you are gentle to them they still feel despised by you: and they return your benefaction with hidden malefactions. Your silent pride always runs counter to their taste. . . . Before you they feel small, and their baseness glimmers and glows in invisible revenge. . . . Indeed, my friend, you are the bad conscience of your neighbors: for they are unworthy of you. They hate you, therefore, and would like to suck your blood. . . . Flee, my friend" (165–66). One does get the impression that there once was something unusual about Lime, a freedom and a power that later became corrupted exactly because he did not, as Zarathustra advises, "flee" the marketplace. But also about Lime is the character of the "actor," who "has spirit but little conscience of the spirit. Always he has faith in that which he inspires the most faith — faith in himself. Tomorrow he has a new faith, and the day after tomorrow a newer one" (164).

9 On page 54 of *Anatomy of Criticism* Frye observes that narratives tend to unfold in either a comic (ascending) or a tragic (descending) mode. And since there tends to be consonance between the symbolic "container" (a given mode or plot) and its "contents" (incidents, characters, rhetorical forms), the Hive topos's angelic and de-

monic formulations follow suit. For Kenneth Burke's discussion of the relationship between the "container and the thing contained," see *A Grammar of Motives*, 3–9.

10 Sartre would classify the act of figuration per se as an instance of idealism, which, if not understood as such, amounts to an occurrence of false consciousness. He would have us know and use metaphor only instrumentally, as a tool — and to apply its office only to the nonhuman. He understands clearly that metaphor is possible only if its objects are first perceived as essences that, as in the case of the Hive topos, are formulated by treating appearance as reality. Because metaphor defines/creates its objects dialectically, it is thereby able to "yoke" them together in the service of an image, which is a defining and external order. In a sense, then, metaphor "conscripts" its object into the "membership" of the image. Hence, because of his insistence upon the uniqueness of human-being-ness, Sartre would probably classify the specific act of figuring a human as an act of "materialism" rather than "idealism." This is the case because to Sartre any pattern or attribution that is not chosen by the individual "reduce[s] him to an object" — which he would have us know as the sin of every other philosophy except existentialism: Existentialism "is the only one which gives man dignity, the only one which does not reduce him to an object. The effect of materialism is to treat every man, including the one philosophizing, as an object, that is, as an ensemble of determined reactions in no way distinguished from the ensemble of qualities and phenomena which constitute a table or a chair or a stone" ("The Humanism of Existentialism," 51; hereafter cited as *HE*.) For more about Sartre's definition of and problems with poetry, see pages 5–17 of his *What Is Literature?* Of particular interest is how he regards the poetic image, what he calls the "phrase-object" (10). He speaks of it as a "magical" — and therefore irrational and self-interested — motive that opposes the speaker's purposes.

11 Because existentialism is a broad philosophical movement that explores and articulates a particular and yet extremely various aesthetic, we should keep in mind that Sartre's version is distinct. For example, he classifies himself as an "atheistic" rather than a "Christian" existentialist and goes on to situate himself within a narrow philosophical lineage (*HE*, 34–35). See also Maurice Friedman's introduction to *The Worlds of Existentialism*. Friedman defends existentialism through carefully defining Sartre with and against his fellow existentialists. Hence, my use of the qualifier "Sartrean." Nevertheless — and despite Jean Wahl's warning that Sartre probably can't be nailed down because his "philosophy is one of the incarnations of problematism and of the ambiguity of contemporary thought" (25) — I shall use Sartre to represent an entire worldview. I do so because he is existentialism's defining figure — but also because the extremity of his terms enforces a division between subject and object that necessitates a peculiarly isolated concept of the human. As I shall explain below, this notion that we are human only to the degree that we are free to choose is predicated upon a fantasy of freedom that resonates strongly with both the Hive topos's construction of a sovereign observer and the traditional, male writing persona. When this persona and its implicit definition of the human are challenged by a new aesthetic, one that does not accept that human-being-ness is solely predicated upon self-definition (one that accepts the reality and, hence, the influence of external/inherited patterns), the Self as Insect topos is reworked accordingly.

12 The first part of chapter 6 treats this and related subjects as they bear upon postmodernism's assent to and revision of Sartre's ahistorical universalism.

13 I find this to be the play's least convincing moment, because Orestes's salvific motive seems to contradict the terms of his enlightenment. It seems more in character for him to simply walk away. Sartre was aware that his philosophy was charged with being a doctrine of "desperate quietism." In response, Sartre claimed that to know that one exists is to recognize that Being is no more and no less than a series of choices, of which inaction is one; hence, action is unavoidable. Furthermore, Sartre theorizes that existential persons are inclined toward right action, praxis (the active establishment of freedom for all), because their being is diminished if all are not equally and absolutely free to pursue their individual "plans."

14 In the original: *"bourdonnante d'hommes et de mouches" (Les Mouches*, 75).

15 Al-Hakim's existentialism is far closer to Kafka's than to Sartre's, for in contrast to the way Sartre's cosmos works, that shared by the first two writers in no way allows for one to stand apart from social or natural patterns. For them, human-being-ness is an unavoidable mix of determinism and self-determinism, of social and biological facts, the nearly inexpressible human longing for the other, and our drive to see around the corner of existence. And because, according to this gentler existentialism, one is inseparable from one's fantasies and cannot be said to exist outside of one's role, right action or its opposite manifests itself conventionally (i.e., pathetically, passionately). One's choices are, therefore, never absolutely one's own; hence, responsibility is to one degree or another distributed, shared. Sartre asserts that true being is beyond what the Hive topos images and evokes (the overlapping terms and constraints of the natural and social orders), but al-Hakim suggests that any such claim is as much a product of the Hive as any other. In this sense his perspective anticipates the ethical ground of what Zygmunt Bauman calls the "postmodern perspective" (see Zygmunt Bauman, *Postmodern Ethics*, 3–12, 33).

16 Although Shakespeare and Hardy similarly use the fly to attribute something of this same sort of blindness to larger forces and consequences — Gloucester when describing our relationship to the gods, Hardy when picturing Tess and Marian hacking turnips at Flintcomb-Ash — the cockroach is its most powerful vehicle. The reason is probably a combination of its domestic ubiquity and its sometime obliviousness to danger when feeding. Unfortunately, given the paucity of literature on the poetic value of insects in general, this footnote is probably the only word on the subject.

17 This statement is problematized by the Russian–Eastern European tradition. With the exception of a few postmodern texts — for instance, Vollman's *You Bright and Risen Angels* — in Anglo-European literature, one insect species tends to be primary in any given text. And if there is more than one, then they are hierarchized. This also seems to be the case in Russian realism. However, since the publication of *The Insect Play* (1923) by the Čapek brothers, a pluralistic version of the insect analogy has come to light, one that allows for the equal and extreme anthropomorphization of a variety of different insects. Victor Pelevin's *The Life of Insects* is an excellent contemporary example. His version of the Hive topos enables him to express the personal and yet shared vulnerability of individuals who are suspended between an oppressive past and the uncertainties of a free market future. Pelevin's characters live in an ontological limbo; their psychological and social uncertainty is dramatized through physical indeterminacy: human beings are and are not insects. This postmodern version of the Hive inspires and cooperates with a fabulous space in which human

beings act out a series of fables unified by a single vision of how insects live: within each fable Being is defined by immediacy and colored by a sense that the individual is nothing in the greater scheme of things. The fable frame permits the author to represent the human condition as victimization by overlapping social and biological forces. The reader is left with the feeling that human life is all the more valuable by dint of its fragility and ephemerality.

18 My use of the word "approximate" as a desirable aspect of a pragmatic and human-istic outlook is derived from Yi-Fu Tuan's *Cosmos and Hearth*, especially pp. 133–88. Although Tuan considers himself to be a "high Modernist," and therefore opposed to postmodernism, his theory that Western-style liberal "cosmopolite" culture serves as an armature for the world's only sustainable future has many persuasive aspects. One of these is his idea that the modern cosmopolite requires a complex identity, one that issues from multiple "hearths" rather than a single hearth. He reasons that while the native hearth may serve as the locus of specific identity, the international-ized city must provide the terms for an *approximate* universal identity. Because Tuan's model of subjectivity places multiplicity at the core of Being, it departs radically from the Sartrean pattern, which proposes that true Being is *absolute* and universal. As I will demonstrate in the next chapter, Tuan's multiple-hearth subject is exactly what Kobo Abe and A. S. Byatt show us how to construct.

6. POSTMODERN VERSIONS OF THE SELF AS INSECT

1 Andreas Huyssen, "Mapping the Postmodern," 234–43.

2 In *What Is Literature?* while establishing what to him is the absolute and necessary difference between prose and poetry (like Plato, Sartre has a problem with poets, with verbal enjoyment for its own sake), Sartre claims that the poetic "attitude" withdraws from language its instrumental potential. The poet does not use lan-guage; he is used by it. "For the poet, language is a structure of the external world" to which he gives himself. "The poet is outside of language. He sees words inside out as if he did not share the human condition." In contrast, the prose writer, whom Sartre calls "the speaker": "is *in a situation* in language . . . he is surrounded by a verbal body which he is hardly aware of and which extends his action upon the world." To the speaker, language is "domesticated," "useful conventions, tools which gradually wear out and which one throws away when they are no longer ser-viceable" (7–8; Sartre's emphasis). Yet, Sartre's antirhetorical stance is far less origi-nal than his emphatic style implies. And despite his problem with poetry, we may classify his system's "mood" (the quality of its implicit dramatism) as Romantic. What is important about his thought in this matter, however, is his insistence that language that acts in and upon the world be free from ornament and wild (i.e., undomesticated) metaphor. Even though Sartre never turned his hand to poetry, his sense of and sensitivity to language is poetic. As evidenced by Orestes's use of the Hive, Sartre knows that such poetic forms have their own agency and purposes. To him they are an iteration of the Other, and therefore must be urgently resisted.

3 Zygmunt Bauman, *Postmodern Ethics*, 77.

4 *HE*, 53. Because its implications contribute little to this argument and might turn me from my desire to recognize Sartre for his philosophical and aesthetic contribu-tions, I shall not attend to what this passage reveals about its author's view of the

Other, beyond its utility as an opposite that forces the self into existence. I am referring to what I take to be the intentionally provocative classification of "the Chinese,
the Indian, or the African" as members of an inferior set: "the idiot, the child, the
savage, the foreigner." The assumption of European superiority that informs this
parallelism suggests that Sartre is by no means standing beyond either his moment
or his culture. This contradiction's Eurocentric tenor cannot but color one's opinion
of Sartre and his project.

5 These limits were recognized and explored by other existentialist philosophers. For
example, Maurice Merleau-Ponty developed an interpersonal model of being and
psychological development that is well worth comparing with Sartre's. Yet, as influential as such alternative existentialisms certainly were during this movement's
heyday, it is Sartre's paradigm that dominates and still heavily influences the Euro-
American imagination. It would be difficult to imagine, for instance, a Merleau-
Pontian James Dean. While the interpersonal model seems now to make more sense
than Sartre's, the latter retains its singularly dramatic appeal. See Merleau-Ponty,
Phenomenology of Perception. I particularly recommend the chapter titled "Other
Selves and the Human World," 346–65, which concisely describes his ideas about
the human body's connective implications.

6 In *A History of God: The 4000-Year Quest of Judaism, Christianity, and Islam*, 378–80,
Mary Armstrong briefly but lucidly marks out the relationship between certain fundamental principles of existentialism and the logical positivists' elimination of even
the question of God's existence. Their common method: first accuse the Divine of
being unscientific (i.e., beyond human ken and control — He is, therefore, irrelevant); then compare His irrelevance with a picture of science as an entirely rational
worldview that guarantees happiness via material improvement.

7 Thomas, "Social Talk," 108.

8 George Eliot, *The Mill on the Floss*, 181.

9 See Huyssen, "Mapping the Postmodern," 271, and Elspeth Probyn, "Travels in the
Postmodern: Making Sense of the Local," 176–89.

10 James Cahill, *Treasures of Asia: Chinese Painting*, 32.

11 Because I am speaking about the tendencies of a civilizational nexus, my connections
must be broad and my reasoning speculative. (For the sake of connections we must
sometimes risk scholarly security and certainty.) I feel secure, however, in holding
that this narrative of a wandering sophisticate who discovers in the country a spiritual rebirth has twin religious sources: Confucian and Buddhist. This narrative also
has its secular expression, as in the poetry of T'ao Ch'ien. But T'ao Ch'ien's idealiza-
tion of country life does not entirely anticipate Jumpei's complex psychological evolution, which does not culminate in his absolute integration into the human/nature
mosaic. Perhaps, then, we should take into account the ground established for such
an "approximate" quest by the uniquely Japanese narrative, *The Tale of Genji*. According to the introduction to the portions of *Genji* that are excerpted in *The Norton
Anthology of World Masterpieces*, the novel expresses themes that we may profitably
compare with *Woman*'s. For instance, we may compare the life of Jumpei's nameless
companion with that of the typical woman in *Genji*. This novel's world is one in
which "men moved about with a great degree of sexual freedom. Women did not;
they waited. It was not only attention and affection they sat waiting for behind their

screens but a definition of themselves. . . . The whole process was fraught with uncertainty. If a man came, would he come again? A woman's position depended more on the frequency of the man's visits than on any formal arrangements" (2089). But even more resonant with *Woman* is what the writers of the Norton introduction claim as *Genji*'s point: namely, that maturation involves "the realization that all human bonds are by nature defective" (2090). Although I would not go so far as to say that *Genji* is more important to *Woman* than Kafka and Sartre, it may be worth considering that the ultimate source of Jumpei's *approximate* and *ambivalent* existentialism is grounded in Japanese rather than Western prototypes. For introductory material, bibliography, and translated selections from T'ao Ch'ien's oeuvre and Murasaki Shikibu's *The Tale of Genji*, see *The Norton Anthology of World Masterpieces*, expanded edition, vol. 1, edited by Maynard Mack et al. For the first, pp. 1288–300, esp. "Returning to the Farm to Dwell," p. 1995, 1.18–20; and for the second, pp. 2087–188.

12 We should not think that Byatt "imports" Greek mythology into the narrative. From this American's perspective, the English literary imagination tends to accommodate and even naturalize classical patterns. If this perception is accurate, then I would speculate that Byatt means all of her counter-armature to feel native. Certainly this myth and the marriage plot here seem to work well together.

13 J. M. Coetzee, "En Route to the Catastrophe," 17.

14 As part of this project I had the advantage of interviewing Byatt. When asked, in essence, if she is a postmodern writer, Byatt had this to say: "I have had to think a lot about the word postmodern because people keep asking, especially people writing theses. The fact that I have such difficulty thinking about it (or indeed "modern") in relation to my works must be significant, but whether of rejection, or of acceptance without wanting to be docketed and buttonholed I'm not sure. . . . In so far as postmodernism is fragmented, eclectic as to how it proceeds and what it quotes, I guess I am part of it. I have no modernist aspiration to wholeness. But a lot of postmodernism goes hand in hand with a kind of solipsism — nothing is real, out there, etc., etc. — it's all just allusive, all in the head. And I'm not temperamentally like that. I prefer Proust to Joyce — as Franco Moretti does not — and I think that if you read Proust line by line his world is just as eclectically fragmented as Joyce's — which is still haunted by the universalizing tendencies of Catholicism and classicism — as Proust's, for all its aspirations to aesthetic completeness (doomed to failure as he knows them to be) is not. If Proust is a modernist and Joyce is the beginning of postmodernism, then I'm an unreconstructed modernist."

15 Referring again to my interview with Byatt, I asked her whether Maeterlinck was an influence. He was indeed — along with Swift, Fabre, Michelet, and Swammerdam.

BIBLIOGRAPHY

Abe, Kobo. *The Woman in the Dunes*. Translated by E. Dale Saunders. New York: Random House, Vintage, 1964.

Addison, Joseph. *"Spectator* No. 1." In *The Longman Anthology of British Literature*, vol. 1C, *The Restoration and the Eighteenth Century*, edited by David Damrosch and Stuart Sherman. New York: Longman, 1999.

Adrados, Francisco Rodríguez. *History of the Graeco-Latin Fable*, vol. 1, rev. Translated by Leslie A. Ray. Amsterdam: Brill, 1999.

Aesop. *Aesop: The Complete Fables*. Translated and edited by Olivia Temple and Robert Temple. New York: Penguin Classics, 1998.

Aristotle. *History of Animals*. Translated by D'Arcy Wentworth Thompson. In *Great Books of the Western World*, vol. 9. Chicago: Encyclopaedia Brittanica, 1952.

——. *The Rhetoric of Aristotle*. Translated by Lane Cooper. Engelwood Cliffs, N.J.: Prentice Hall, 1960.

Armstrong, Mary. *A History of God: The 4000-Year Quest of Judaism, Christianity, and Islam*. New York: Ballantine Books, 1994.

Augustine. *On Christian Teaching*. Translated by R. P. H. Green. New York: Oxford–World's Classics, 1997.

Bachelard, Gaston. *The Poetics of Space*. Translated by Maria Jolas. Boston: Beacon Press, 1969.

——. *The Psychoanalysis of Fire*. Translated by Alan C. M. Ross. Boston: Beacon Press, 1968.

Bacon, Francis. *Novum Organum*. In *Great Books of the Western World*, vol. 30. Chicago: William Benton–Encyclopaedia Britannica, 1952.

Balzac, Honoré de. *Père Goriot*. Translated by A. J. Krailsheimer. New York: Oxford–World's Classics, 1991.

Bate, Walter Jackson. "Negative Capability." In *Romanticism and Consciousness: Essays in Criticism*, edited by Harold Bloom. New York: W. W. Norton, 1970.

Bauman, Zygmunt. *Postmodern Ethics*. Cambridge, Mass.: Blackwell, 1996.

Becker, Elizabeth. *When the War Was Over: Cambodia's Revolution and the Voices of Its People*. New York: Simon and Schuster–Touchstone, 1986.

Beehive Productions. http://www.beehivepro.com [30 August 1998].

Beehive Technologies, Inc. http://www.bzzzzzz.com [30 August 1998].

Beehive Telephone Companies. http://beehive.net [30 August 1998].

Beevor, Antony. *Stalingrad, the Fateful Siege: 1942–1943*. New York: Viking, 1998.

Birkerts, Sven. "Refuse It." In "The Electronic Hive: Two Views." *Harper's*, May 1994, 17–20. Adapted from *The Gutenberg Elegies: The Fate of Reading in an Electronic Age*.

Blackham, H. J. *The Fable as Literature*. Dover, N.H.: Athlone Press, 1985.

Bloch, Ernst. "The Fairy Tale Moves on Its Own Time." In *The Utopian Function of Art and Literature*, translated by Jack Zipes and Frank Mecklenburg. Cambridge, Mass.: MIT Press, 1993.

Bloom, Harold. *The Anxiety of Influence: A Theory of Poetry*. 2d ed. New York: Oxford University Press, 1997.

——. Introduction to *Modern Critical Views: Jonathan Swift*, edited by Harold Bloom. New York: Chelsea House, 1986.

———, ed. *Romanticism and Consciousness: Essays in Criticism*. Edited by Harold Bloom. New York: W. W. Norton, 1970.

Blumenberg, Hans. *Shipwreck with Spectator: Paradigm of a Metaphor for Existence.* Translated by Steven Rendall. Cambridge, Mass.: MIT Press, 1997.

Borges, Jorge Luis. "The Library of Babel." Translated by James E. Irby. In *Labyrinths: Selected Stories and Other Writing*. New York: New Directions, 1964.

Bowra, C. M. *From Virgil to Milton*. New York: St. Martin's, 1962.

Burke, Kenneth. *A Grammar of Motives*. Berkeley: University of California Press, 1962.

———. *A Rhetoric of Motives*. Berkeley: University of California Press, 1969.

———. *Counter-Statement*. 2d ed. Chicago: University of Chicago Press, Phoenix Books, 1953.

Byatt, A. S. Interview by author. 2 June 1999. Unpublished.

———. Interview. *Salon*. http://www.salon1999.com/08/departments/litchat.html [23 October 1998].

———. *Morpho Eugenia*. In *Angels and Insects*. New York: Random House, Vintage International, 1992.

Cahill, James. *Treasures of Asia: Chinese Painting*. New York: Rizzoli International, 1977.

Čapek, Karl, and Josef Čapek. *The Insect Play*. In *R.U.R and The Insect Play*, translated by P. Selver. New York: Oxford University Press, 1961.

Cicero. *De Oratore*. In *Cicero*, vol. 4, translated by H. Rackham. Cambridge, Mass.: Harvard University Press, Loeb Classics Library, 1992.

Clemens, Samuel [Mark Twain]. *Letters from the Earth*. In *Letters from the Earth*, edited by Bernard DeVoto. Greenwich, Conn.: Fawcett Crest, 1964.

Coetzee, J. M. "En Route to the Catastrophe." Review of *Babel Tower*, by A. S. Byatt. *New York Review of Books* 43, no. 10 (6 June 1996): 17–19.

Connor, Stephen. *Postmodernist Culture: An Introduction to Theories of the Contemporary*. Oxford: Basil Blackwell, 1989.

Conrad, Joseph. *Heart of Darkness*. 3d ed. Edited by Robert Kimbrough. New York: W. W. Norton, 1988.

Corbett, Edward P. J. *Classical Rhetoric for the Modern Student*. 3d ed. New York: Oxford University Press, 1990.

Corngold, Stanley. Introduction to *The Metamorphosis*, by Franz Kafka. Translated by Stanley Corngold. New York: Bantam Classics, 1981.

Corbusier, Le [Charles Edouard Jeanneret-Gris]. *When the Cathedrals Were White: A Journey to the Country of Timid People*. Translated by Francis E. Hyslop, Jr. New York: Reynal and Hitchcock, 1947.

Crichton, Michael. *Jurassic Park*. New York: Ballantine, 1991.

Curtius, Ernst Robert. *European Literature and the Latin Middle Ages*. Translated by Willard R. Trask. Princeton, N.J.: Princeton University Press, 1990.

Daley, Suzanne. "Foes in Angola Still at Odds over Diamonds." *New York Times*, 15 September 1995, A1, A10.

Dalley, Stephanie, trans. *Atrahasis* and *The Epic of Gilgamesh*. In *Myths from Mesopotamia*. New York: Oxford University Press, 1990.

Dante Alighieri. *Inferno*. Translated by Allen Mandelbaum. New York: Bantam, 1982.

———. *Paradiso*. Translated by Allen Mandelbaum. New York: Bantam, 1986.

———. *Purgatorio*. Translated by Allen Mandelbaum. New York: Bantam, 1984.

DeLillo, Don. *White Noise*. New York: Penguin, 1986.

De Quincey, Thomas. "A Brief Appraisal of the Greek Literature." In *The Collected Writings of Thomas De Quincey*, vol. 10. Edinburgh: Adam and Charles Black, 1890.

——. *Confessions of an English Opium-Eater*. In *Confessions of an English Opium-Eater and Other Writings*, edited by Grevel Lindop. New York: Oxford World's Classics, 1990.

Dickinson, Emily. "Awake ye muses nine, sing me a strain divine." In *The Complete Poems of Emily Dickinson*, edited by Thomas H. Johnson. Boston: Little, Brown, 1960.

Dobrée, Bonamy. *English Literature in the Early Eighteenth Century*. New York: Oxford University Press, 1959.

Earle, John. *Microcosmography*. In *Three Elizabethan Pamphlets*, edited by G. R. Hubbard. London: George G. Harrap, 1951.

Eisenstein, Elizabeth L. *The Printing Revolution in Early Modern Europe*. Cambridge: Cambridge University Press, 1990.

Eliot, George. *The Mill on the Floss*. Edited by A. S. Byatt. New York: Viking Penguin, 1987.

Emerson, Ralph Waldo. "The Poet." In *Emerson: Essays and Lectures*, edited by Joel Porte. New York: Library of America, 1983.

Eurich, Nell. *Science in Utopia: A Mighty Design*. Cambridge, Mass.: Harvard University Press, 1967.

Fabre, J. Henri. *The Life of the Caterpillar*. Translated by Alexander Teixeria De Mattos. New York: Modern Library, 1916.

Fan K'uan. *Traveling among Streams and Mountains*. Hanging scroll, early eleventh century. Ink and light color on silk. Reproduced in *Treasures of Asia: Chinese Painting*, edited by James Cahill. New York: Rizzoli International Publications, 1977.

Farrell, Joseph. *Vergil's Georgics and the Traditions of Ancient Epic*. New York: Oxford University Press, 1991.

Fatbeehive, Inc. http://www.fatbeehive.com [cited 30 August 1998].

Febvre, Lucien, and Henri-Jean Martin. *The Coming of the Book: The Impact of Printing, 1450–1800*. Translated by David Gerard. New York: Verso, 1976.

Fergusson, Francis. Introduction to *Aristotle's Poetics*, translated by S. H. Butcher. New York: Hill and Wang, 1961.

Foucault, Michel. *The Order of Things*. New York: Vintage, 1973.

Fouts, Roger, and Stephen Tukel Mills. *Next of Kin: What Chimpanzees Have Taught Me about Who We Are*. New York: William Morrow, 1997.

Freud, Sigmund. "The Uncanny." In *Writings on Art and Literature*, edited by Werner Hamacher and David E. Wellbery. Stanford, Calif.: Stanford University Press, Meridian, 1997.

Friedman, Maurice. Introduction to *The Worlds of Existentialism*. Edited by Maurice Friedman. Chicago: University of Chicago Press, 1964.

Frye, Northrop. *Anatomy of Criticism: Four Essays*. Princeton, N.J.: Princeton University Press, 1971.

Goethe, Johann Wolfgang von. "Significant Help Given by an Ingenious Turn of Phrase." In *Scientific Studies*, vol. 12 of *Goethe, the Collected Works*, edited and translated by Douglas Miller. Princeton, N.J.: Princeton University Press, 1995.

Gompers, Samuel, and Herman Guttstadt [attributed]. "AFL, Some Reasons for

Chinese Exclusion. Meat vs. Rice. American Manhood Against Asiatic Coolieism. Which Shall Survive?" U.S. Senate Document no. 137. Washington, D.C., 1902.

Gray, Alasdair. "Time Travel." In *Ten Tales Tall and True*. New York: Harcourt Brace, 1993.

Greene, Graham. *The Third Man*. In *The Portable Graham Greene*, edited by Philip Stratford. New York: Penguin, 1994.

al-Hakim, Tewfik. *The Fate of a Cockroach*. In *The Fate of a Cockroach and Other Plays*, translated by Denys Johnson-Davies. London: Heineman, 1973.

Hakluyt, Richard. "Preface to *Divers Voyages*." Reprinted in *The Original Writings and Correspondence of the Two Richard Hakluyts*. 2d ser., no. 76. London: Hakluyt Society, 1935.

Hall, Edward T. *The Hidden Dimension*. New York: Doubleday, Anchor Books, 1982.

Hardie, Philip K. *The Epic Successors of Virgil*. New York: Cambridge University Press, 1993.

———. *Virgil's Aeneid: Cosmos and Imperium*. New York: Oxford University Press, 1986.

Harding, Davis P. *The Club of Hercules: Studies in the Classical Background of Paradise Lost*. Urbana: University of Illinois Press, 1962.

Hardy, Thomas. *The Return of the Native*. Edited by A. Walton Litz. Boston: Houghton Mifflin, 1967.

———. *Tess of the D'Urbervilles*. New York: Bantam, 1971.

Harth, Phillip. Introduction to *The Fable of the Bees*, by Bernard Mandeville. Edited by Phillip Harth. New York: Penguin Classics, 1989.

Havelock, Eric A. *Preface to Plato*. Cambridge, Mass.: Harvard University Press, 1963.

Heidegger, Martin. *Early Greek Thinking*. Translated by David Farrell Krell and Frank A. Capuzzi. San Francisco: Harper and Row, 1984.

Heinlein, Robert A. *Starship Troopers*. New York: Ace Books, 1987.

Hesiod. *Works and Days*. In *Hesiod and Theognis*, translated by Dorothea Wender. New York: Penguin, 1982.

Hobbes, Thomas. *Leviathan*. New York: Penguin Classics, 1985.

Homer. *The Iliad of Homer*. Translated by Richmond Lattimore. Chicago: University of Chicago Press, 1961.

———. *The Iliad*. Translated by A. T. Murray. 2 vols. Cambridge, Mass.: Harvard University Press, Loeb Classics Library, 1988.

———. *The Odyssey*. Translated by A. T. Murray. 2 vols. Cambridge, Mass.: Harvard University Press, Loeb Classics Library, 1984.

Huxley, Aldous. *Brave New World*. New York: Harper and Row, 1946.

Huyssen, Andreas. "Mapping the Postmodern." In *Feminism/Postmodernism*, edited by Linda J. Nicholson. New York: Routledge, 1990.

Jameson, Fredric. *The Political Unconscious: Narrative as a Socially Symbolic Act*. Ithaca, N.Y.: Cornell University Press, 1988.

Jenkyns, Richard. "But Is It True?" Review of *Schliemann of Troy: Treasure and Deceit*, by David A. Traill; *Lost and Found: The 9,000 Treasures of Troy: Heinrich Schliemann and the Gold That Got Away*, by Caroline Moorhead; and *The Gold of Troy: Searching for Homer's Fabled City. New York Review of Books* (19 December 1996): 15–18.

Jones, Richard Foster. *Ancients and Moderns: A Study of the Background of the Battle of the Books*. Washington University Language and Literature, n.s., no. 6. St. Louis: Washington University Press, 1936.

Kafka, Franz. *The Metamorphosis*. Translated by Stanley Corngold. New York: Bantam Classics, 1981.

Keats, John. Letters: "To Benjamin Bailey, November 22, 1817," "To George and Tom Keats, December 21–27, 1817," and "To J. H. Reynolds, February 19, 1818." In *English Romantic Writers*, edited by David Perkins. New York: Harcourt Brace Jovanovich, 1967.

———. "What the Thrush Said." In *English Romantic Writers*, edited by David Perkins. New York: Harcourt Brace Jovanovich, 1967.

Keegan, John. *A History of Warfare*. New York: Random House, 1993.

Kelly, Kevin. "Embrace It." In "The Electronic Hive: Two Views." *Harper's*, May 1994, 20–25. Adapted from *Out of Control: The Rise of Neo-Biological Civilization*.

Kennedy, George A. *Comparative Rhetoric: An Historical and Cross-Cultural Introduction*. New York: Oxford University Press, 1998.

Knight, W. F. Jackson. *Roman Vergil*. London: Faber and Faber, 1954.

Koestler, Arthur. *The Sleepwalkers: A History of Man's Changing Vision of the Universe*. New York: Macmillan, 1959.

Kohler, Wolfgang. *Gestalt Psychology*. New York: Mentor, New American Library, 1961.

Lakoff, George, and Mark Johnson. *Philosophy in the Flesh: The Embodied Mind and Its Challenge to Western Thought*. New York: Basic Books, 1999.

Lanham, Richard A. *A Handlist of Rhetorical Terms*. 2d ed. Berkeley: University of California Press, 1991.

Lawler, Justice George. *Celestial Pantomime*. 2d ed. New York: Continuum, 1994.

Leach, Eleanor Winsor. *Vergil's Eclogues: Landscapes of Experience*. Ithaca, N.Y.: Cornell University Press, 1974.

Levi, Primo. "Novels Dictated by Crickets." In *Other People's Trades*, translated by Raymond Rosenthal. New York: Summit Books, 1989.

Lovejoy, Arthur O. *The Great Chain Of Being: A Study of the History of an Idea*. Cambridge, Mass.: Harvard University Press, 1964.

Loveridge, Mark. *A History of the Augustan Fable*. Cambridge: Cambridge University Press, 1998.

Mack, Maynard, et al. Introduction to *The Tale of Genji*, by Murasaki Shikibu. In *The Norton Anthology of World Masterpieces*, exp. ed., vol. 1. New York: W. W. Norton, 1995.

Maeterlinck, Maurice. *The Life of the Bee*. Translated by Alfred Sutro. New York: Blue Ribbon Books, 1901.

Mandelstam, Osip. *Stone*. Translated by Robert Tracy. London: Harvill, 1981.

Mandeville, Bernard. *The Fable of the Bees*. Edited by Phillip Harth. New York: Penguin Classics, 1989.

Marx, Karl. *Capital*. Translated by Samuel Moore and Edward Aveling. Rev., with additional translation, by Marie Sachey and Herbert Lamm. In *Great Books of the Western World*, vol. 50. Chicago: Encyclopaedia Brittanica, 1955.

Massachusetts Historical Society. Emblem of the Massachusetts Historical Society. *Collections of the Massachusetts Historical Society*. Ser. 4, vol. 7 (recatalogued as vol. 37), frontispiece.

Mayr, Ernst. *Toward a New Philosophy of Biology*. Cambridge, Mass.: Harvard University Press, 1988.

McGann, Jerome J. *The Romantic Ideology: A Critical Investigation*. Chicago: University of Chicago Press, 1983.

McKendry, John J. *Aesop: Five Centuries of Illustrated Fables*. New York: Metropolitan Museum of Art, New York Graphic Society, 1964.

Merleau-Ponty, Maurice. *Phenomenology of Perception*. Translated by Colin Smith. New York: Routledge, 1996.

Michelet, Jules. *The Insect*. Translated by W. H. Davenport Adams. London: T. Nelson and Sons, 1883.

Milton, John. *Areopagitica*. In *Complete Poems and Major Prose*, edited by Merritt Y. Hughes. New York: Odyssey, 1957.

———. *The Christian Doctrine*. In *Complete Poems and Major Prose*, edited by Merritt Y. Hughes. New York: Odyssey, 1957.

———. *Defensio Prima* [First Defense]. Vol. 7 of *The Works of John Milton*. General editor, Frank Allen Patterson. New York: Columbia University Press, 1932.

———. *Paradise Lost*. In *Complete Poems and Major Prose*, edited by Merritt Y. Hughes. New York: Odyssey, 1957.

Miner, Earl. *Comparative Poetics: An Intercultural Essay on Theories of Literature*. Princeton, N.J.: Princeton University Press, 1990.

Mueller, Martin. *The Iliad*. London: George Allen and Unwin, 1984.

Mumford, Lewis. *Technics and Civilization*. New York: Harcourt Brace Jovanovich, 1963.

Murasaki Shikibu. *The Tale of Genji*. In *The Norton Anthology of World Masterpieces*, exp. ed., vol. 1. Edited by Maynard Mack et al. New York: W. W. Norton, 1995.

Musil, Robert. "Binoculars." In *Posthumous Papers of a Living Author*, translated by Peter Wortsman. Eridanos Library, vol. 1. Hygiene, Colo.: Eridanos Press, 1987.

Nicolson, Marjorie Hope. *The Breaking of the Circle*. Evanston, Ill.: Northwestern University Press, 1950.

———. *Mountain Gloom and Mountain Glory: The Development of the Aesthetics of the Infinite*. New York: W. W. Norton, 1963.

———. *Science and Imagination*. Ithaca, N.Y.: Cornell University Press, 1956.

———. *Voyages to the Moon*. New York: Macmillan, 1960.

Nietzsche, Friedrich. *The Genealogy of Morals*. Translated by Francis Golffing. New York: Doubleday, Anchor Books, 1956.

———. *Thus Spake Zarathustra*. In *The Portable Nietzsche*, translated by Walter Kaufmann. New York: Penguin, 1986.

Nye, David. E. *American Technological Sublime*. Cambridge, Mass.: MIT Press, 1996.

Opie, Iona, and Peter Opie, eds. *The Classic Fairy Tales*. New York: Oxford University Press, 1974.

Ozick, Cynthia. "The Impossibility of Being Kafka." *New Yorker*, 11 January 1999, 80–87.

Pelevin, Victor. *The Life of Insects*. Translated by Andrew Bromfield. New York: Farrar, Straus and Giroux, 1996.

Perec, Georges. "Think/Classify." In *Species of Spaces and Other Pieces*, edited and translated by John Sturrock. New York: Penguin, 1997.

Peters, T. Michael. *Insects and Human Society*. New York: Van Nostrand Reinhold, 1988.

Plath, Sylvia. "Stings." In *Ariel*. New York: Harper and Row, 1965.

Plato. *The Republic of Plato*. 2d ed. Translated by Allan Bloom. New York: Harper Collins, Basic Books, 1991.

Polanyi, Karl. *The Great Transformation*. Boston: Beacon Press, 1957.

Probyn, Elspeth. "Travels in the Postmodern: Making Sense of the Local." In *Feminism/Postmodernism*, edited by Linda J. Nicholson. New York: Routledge, 1990.

Propp, Vladimir. *Morphology of the Folktale*. 2d ed. Edited by Louis A. Wagner, translated by Laurence Scott. Austin: University of Texas Press, 1968.

Quintilian. *Institutio Oratoria*. 4 vols. Translated by H. E. Butler. New York: G. P. Putnam Sons, Loeb Classics Library, 1921.

Ramírez, Juan Antonio. *The Beehive Metaphor from Gaudí to Le Corbusier*. Translated by Alexander R. Tulloch. London: Reaktion Books, 2000.

Redfield, J. M. *Nature and Culture in the Iliad*. Durham, N.C.: Duke University Press, 1994.

Rilke, Rainer Maria. "What birds plunge through is not the intimate space." In *The Selected Poetry of Rainer Maria Rilke*, edited and translated by Stephen Mitchell. New York: Vintage International, 1989.

Rousseau, Jean-Jacques. *Discourse on the Origin of Inequality*. Translated by Julia Conaway Bondanella. In *Rousseau's Political Writings*, edited by Alan Ritter and J. C. Bondanella. New York: W. W. Norton, 1988.

Sallis, John. *Being and Logos: The Way of Platonic Dialogue*. 2d ed. Atlantic Highlands, N.J.: Humanities Press International, 1986.

Sartre, Jean-Paul. *The Flies*. Translated by Stuart Gilbert. In *No Exit and Three Other Plays*. New York: Vintage–Random House, 1955.

——. "The Humanism of Existentialism." In *Essays in Existentialism*, edited by Wade Baskin. Secaucus, N.J.: Citadel Press, 1972.

——. *Les Mouches*. Edited by F. C. St. Aubyn and Robert G. Marshall. New York: Harper and Row, 1963.

——. *What Is Literature?* Translated by Bernard Frechtman. New York: Harper and Row, 1965.

Selimović, Meša. *Death and the Dervish*. Translated by Bogdan Rakic and Henry R. Cooper, Jr. Evanston, Ill.: Northwestern University Press, 1996.

Seneca. "On Gathering Ideas." In *Moral Letters*, vol. 3, translated by Richard M. Gummere. Cambridge, Mass.: Harvard University Press, Loeb Classics Library, 1952.

Sennett, Richard. *The Fall of Public Man*. New York: W. W. Norton, 1974.

——. *Flesh and Stone: The Body and the City in Western Civilization*. New York: W. W. Norton, 1994.

Shakespeare, William. *Henry V*. In *The Riverside Shakespeare*, edited by G. Blakemore Evans. Boston: Houghton Mifflin, 1974.

——. *King Lear*. In *The Riverside Shakespeare*, edited by G. Blakemore Evans. Boston: Houghton Mifflin, 1974.

——. *Shakespeare's Sonnets*. Edited by Stephen Booth. New Haven, Conn.: Yale University Press, 1977.

Shawcross, John T. "The Bee-Simile Once More." *Milton Quarterly* 51, no. 2 (May 1981): 44–47.

Shelley, Mary. *Frankenstein*. New York: Bantam Classics, 1991.

Swift, Jonathan. *Battle of the Books*. In *Gulliver's Travels and Other Writings*, edited by Miriam Kosh Starkman. New York: Bantam Classics, 1981.

——— . *Gulliver's Travels*. In *Gulliver's Travels and Other Writings*, edited by Miriam Kosh Starkman. New York: Bantam Classics, 1981.

T'ao Ch'ien. Poems. In *The Norton Anthology of World Masterpieces*, exp. ed., vol. 1, edited by Maynard Mack et al. New York: W. W. Norton, 1995.

Temple, William. "On Ancient and Modern Learning." In *Essays: "On Ancient and Modern Learning" and "Poetry,"* edited by J. E. Spingarn. New York: Oxford University Press, Clarendon Press, 1909.

Thomas, Lewis. "Social Talk." In *The Lives of a Cell*. New York: Bantam, 1984.

Thoreau, Henry David. *Walden*. In *The Harper Single Volume American Literature*, 3d ed., edited by Donald McQuade et al. New York: Longman, 1999.

Tolstoy, Leo. *War and Peace*. Translated by Ann Dunnigan. New York: Signet Classics, New American Library, 1968.

Townsend, Gordon F., and Eva Crane. "History of Apiculture." In *History of Entomology*, edited by Ray F. Smith et al. Palo Alto, Calif.: Annual Reviews, 1973.

Tuan, Yi-Fu. *Cosmos and Hearth: A Cosmopolite's Viewpoint*. Minneapolis: University of Minnesota Press, 1996.

Vico, Giambattista. *The New Science of Giambattista Vico*. Rev. and abr. Translated by Thomas Goddard Bergin and Max Harold Fisch. Ithaca, N.Y.: Cornell University Press, 1970.

Vidor, King, director and producer. *The Crowd*. MGM, 1928.

Virgil. *Aeneid*. In *Virgil*. 2 vols., rev. ed. Translated by H. R. Fairclough. Cambridge, Mass.: Harvard University Press, Loeb Classics Library, 1986.

——— . *Georgics*. In *Virgil*. Vol. 1, rev. ed. Translated by H. R. Fairclough. Cambridge, Mass.: Harvard University Press, Loeb Classics Library, 1986.

Vollman, William T. *You Bright and Risen Angels*. New York: Penguin, 1988.

Watt, George D. Cover of *Deseret Alphabet, 2nd Reader* (artist unknown). New York: Russel Brothers, 1868.

Weil, Simone. *The Iliad, or The Poem of Force*. 1940. Pendle Hill Pamphlet no. 91. Wallingford, Penn.: Pendle Hill, 1993.

Wells, H. G. "The Empire of the Ants." In *28 Science Fiction Stories of H. G. Wells*. New York: Dover, 1952.

——— . *The First Men in the Moon*. In *Seven Science Fiction Novels of H. G. Wells*. New York: Dover, [n.d].

——— . *The Island of Dr. Moreau*. New York: Penguin, Signet, 1988.

Wilkinson, L. P. General introduction to *The Georgics*, by Virgil. Translated by L. P. Wilkinson. London: Penguin, 1982.

——— . *The Georgics of Virgil: A Critical Survey*. London: Cambridge University Press, 1969.

Wilson, Edward O. *Sociobiology: The New Synthesis*. Cambridge, Mass.: Harvard University Press, 1975.

Zajonc, Arthur. *Catching the Light: The Entwined History of Light and Mind*. Oxford: Oxford University Press, 1993.

INDEX